Dreamer of the Ghetto

Israel Zangwill, *Courtesy, The Library of Congress.*

Judaic Studies Series

Leon J. Weinberger, *General Editor*

Dreamer of the Ghetto

The Life and Works of Israel Zangwill

Joseph H. Udelson

The University of Alabama Press
Tuscaloosa and London

The author is grateful to the following for quotations of selected material:
Shirley Zangwill
Rachela Zeitlin

The paper on which this book is printed meets the minimum requirements of American National Standard for Information Science-Permanence of Paper for Printed Library Materials, ANSI A39.48-1984.

Library of Congress Cataloging-in-Publication Data

Udelson, Joseph H., 1943–
Dreamer of the ghetto : the life and works of Israel Zangwill / Joseph H. Udelson.
p. cm. — (Judaic studies series)
Bibliography: p.
Includes index.
ISBN 0-8173-5171-X (pbk : alk. paper)
1. Zangwill, Israel, 1864–1926. 2. Authors, English—19th century—Biography. 3. Zionists—Great Britain—Biography. 4. Jews in literature. I. Title. II. Series: Judaic studies series (Unnumbered)
PR5923.U34 1990
823'.8—dc19
[B] 89-4781
CIP

British Library Cataloguing-in-Publication Data available

To
Dina, Chana and Devorah

May God make you like
Sara, Rivka, Rachel, and Leah

Contents

Preface

The beginning is wedged in the end.
Sefer Yetzirah

This book began on one of those long, languid summer afternoons when friends casually stop by the house to pass some time and cool off a bit. Over cold drinks and fruit salad we swapped stories. As a coda to his tale, one guest quoted the words of "the most renowned *schnorrer* of them all, Manasseh Bueno Barzillai Azevedo da Costa." Enjoying my quizzical look immensely, he explained, "You know, Israel Zangwill's hilarious hero in *The King of Schnorrers*."

Israel Zangwill, the Anglo-Jewish author? The same Israel Zangwill who had advocated establishing a Jewish homeland in "Uganda"! The same Israel Zangwill who had advocated assimilation into the American "melting pot"! I was suddenly struck by the notion that this man's biography rather resembles one of those strange and profound riddlic poems in the Anglo-Saxon *Exeter Book* that must be solved to be appreciated.

And he reminded me of so many conversations I have heard since my childhood—those conversations people have with friends and with strangers about what it really means to be "Jewish." Does being "Jewish" imply having a special culture (e.g., being an Anglo-Jewish author), or does it refer to a nationality (e.g., having a homeland somewhere, like everyone else), or is it a religion (e.g., in the American "melting pot")? (A fourth alternative, that Jews constitute a biological "race," has now generally been eliminated from most of these conversations.)

These conversations about Jewish identity usually conclude with the views you have been opposing being routed convincingly. Unfortunately there is small satisfaction in this victory, as this is also true for everyone taking part in the discussion: your own view, too, has just received a drubbing. With this all-inclusive checkmate comes the uneasy feeling that it would be better if we didn't talk about this subject again for a while. And so we don't, at least till the next time.

The origin of this difficulty in defining exactly what "Jewish" means lies somehow in the categories available in modern thought and speech we post-Enlightenment Westerners now employ in our conceptions about collective identities. In premodern traditions, the members of a society experienced their identity as an articulated notion of "we who are not they" (i.e., everyone who is unlike "we"). And "we" were defined by the organic sum of "our" distinctive values, beliefs, and practices, all of which marked "us" off clearly from "them."

But Western modernity has transmuted these cohesive collective qualities of identity into categorical descriptions of entirely discrete social roles—cultural, national, and religious—assumed by an autonomous self. Depending on which concern a particular individual wishes to address, he may now define his identity, for instance, as Western, Singaporese, or Methodist, three distinctive, nonintersecting categories.

By contrast, despite its almost two centuries of exposure to the processes of Westernization, "Jewish" as an identity continues to retain its premodern traditional connotations. It therefore intersects with all but coincides with none of these separable post-Enlightenment descriptions. Hence contemporary attempts to reduce it to just one of the available modern categories of identity, being arbitrary and incomplete, must necessarily founder.

How very disturbing this all is! If my neighbors can readily define their own identities and I cannot define mine, then I know—and they know—that I am somehow different. What is worse: I do not even know why I cannot accomplish what they do so effortlessly. But I really am unable to do any better; every category I seize upon can be refuted and so breaks down in the end. What commonly occurs, therefore, is that modern Jews do not often *think* analytically about the definition of their Jewish identity but *act* as if it implies all three categories. Thus, for the contemporary Jew, an unsettling indeterminacy has become a new and prominent component of his notion of Jewish identity.

An exception to this common pattern, Israel Zangwill did think and write extensively about the question of contemporary Jewish identity. He did so obsessively for over thirty-five years. And although we may employ a somewhat altered terminology, we really have neither progressed beyond his formulation, at the beginning of the twentieth century, of the problem of defining it nor gone beyond his proposed answers to this troubling enigma. But what we have learned during these several decades is that the definitions and the solutions proposed by Zangwill, to which we still adhere in one way or another, are simply not quite working, not any one of them. This pertinacious bewilderment is fascinatingly illustrated by Anita Desai in her recent (1989) novel, *Baumgartner's Bombay*. Thus in many ways the riddle of Israel Zangwill's life becomes also the riddle of contemporary Jewish identity.

But it would be a serious error to consider this question of group identity merely a "Jewish" riddle. In fact, it applies to any pre-Enlightenment tradition that, although having assimilated contemporary Western paradigmatic categories and assumptions, nonetheless also retains access to its own premodern heritage. Furthermore, even within European studies the uncritical acceptance of these categories may seriously inhibit accurate perceptions about one's own heritage. For instance, as C. S. Lewis began arguing in the 1930s and as medievalists have been insisting since the 1960s, contemporary Europeans have so thoroughly severed their world view from that outlook presupposed as a matter of fact throughout their own pre-Enlightenment past that without a conscious effort of educated imagination it is now impossible to understand and to appreciate medieval European literature, science, and philosophy.

A study of the contemporary difficulties of adequately defining Jewish identity, therefore, ought ideally to suggest to its readers that there are real, if still indeterminate, perimeters to modern Western notions of collective identity. To facilitate this purpose I have attempted throughout this work to employ Umberto Eco's semiotic notion of the "open text," of allowing multiple legitimate reader responses to the material presented. For this reason I have endeavored to allow Israel Zangwill and his contemporary admirers and critics to speak for themselves as often as possible and to do so without imposing my own interpretations upon the reader. I hope, on the other hand, that I have also not concealed from the reader my own views on several of the issues raised in these pages, although I have attempted to express these most often in the structural procedures of selection and organization of source material.

For its kind support at vital stages of preparing this study, I wish to acknowledge with gratitude the financial assistance granted to me by the Israel Zangwill Memorial Trust. The late Professor Oliver Zangwill of Cambridge University and Mrs. Shirley Zangwill provided much needed encouragement, insight, and original source material along the way. For so much patient help for many months, I wish to express my sincere appreciation to Mrs. Trude Levi of Mocatta Library, London, and to Mr. Ezra Kahn, Librarian of Jews' College, London, the finest and most devoted bibliographer I have ever encountered. I also wish to thank Dr. Rachel Elior, of the Hebrew University of Jerusalem, whose lightning opening of so many doors was so very helpful. A debt is equally owed Dr. Tali Loewenthal, who time and again talked me across London and England with fruitful ideas. To Dr. Samuel H. Shannon of Tennessee State University for his assiduous and critical reading of this manuscript, and to Alice, his wife, for staunching the blood running down my leg as we talked, I am also profoundly grateful. And beyond all measure and boundaries I am thankful to Terry, my wife, my *eishet chaiyil,* who worked our way through Britain and then back home again, taking the 253 each day and shopping for us all in Petticoat Lane, and who still has had the time necessary to read everything I write. Of course any errors of fact and interpretation are entirely my own responsibility.

Nashville, Tennessee

A Chronology of Israel Zangwill

1864 (21 January) Israel Zangwill is born in London, the eldest son of Moses and Ellen Zangwill.

1877 Israel becomes the first winner of the Rothschild scholastic honors medal and also wins the Reverend A. L. Green Prize for Hebrew at the Jews Free School, London, winning both medals also the following year.

1881 "Professor Grimmer," a satirical short story, wins literary contest and appears in *Society*, becoming Zangwill's first published work.

1888 Zangwill begins his popular weekly column, "Morour and Charouseth," in the *Jewish Standard*; his first novel, written together with Louis Cowen, *The Premier and the Painter*, is published.

1889 "English Judaism, A Criticism and a Classification," Zangwill's first significant philosophic essay, is published in the new *Jewish Quarterly Review*.

1890 Zangwill becomes editor and columnist of the satirical magazine, *Ariel, or The London Puck*.

1892 The Anglo-Jewish novel *Children of the Ghetto* makes Zangwill an international literary celebrity.

1895 Zangwill sponsors Theodore Herzl's first address on the Zionist program to an Anglophone Jewish audience, delivered to the Maccabean Club in London.

1897 Zangwill attends the World Zionist Organization's first congress, in Basle, as an observer; he tours the Land of Israel with fellow members of the Maccabean Club and concludes that Herzl's Zionism is quixotic.

1898 *Dreamers of the Ghetto,* Zangwill's most controversial Jewish novel, is published to enthusiastic reviews on both sides of the Atlantic.

1901 Zangwill meets and begins courtship of Edith Ayrton, joins the English Zionist Federation, which he represents as a delegate to the Fifth World Zionist Congress in Basle.

1902 As a member of the English Zionist Federation, Zangwill launches vociferous public attacks on the policies of the Alliance Israelite Universelle and the Jewish Colonization Association.

1903 At the Sixth Zionist Congress Zangwill enthusiastically embraces the "Uganda Scheme" for Jewish settlement in British East Africa; (23 November) Zangwill and Edith Ayrton marry in a civil ceremony in London and settle in the countryside at Far End in Sussex.

1905 Following rejection of the "Uganda Scheme" by the Seventh Zionist Congress, Zangwill organizes the Jewish Territorial Organization (I.T.O.) to continue pursuing the scheme, engaging in bitter polemics against the Zionist movement for its opposition to the establishment of an "Itoland."

1906 Zangwill's I.T.O. accepts American philanthropist Jacob Schiff's offer to participate in his "Galveston Plan" to settle East European Jewish immigrants in the Middle West, away from the east coast.

1907 Zangwill begins publicly campaigning for women's suffrage in Britain.

1908 In Washington President Theodore Roosevelt accompanies Zangwill at the premiere of his play *The Melting Pot.*

1911 Zangwill addresses the Universal Races Congress in London, at which he meets the prominent African-American leader W. E. B. Du Bois.

1915 Zangwill joins Zionist leader Vladimir Jabotinsky in urging the British government to establish the Zion Mule Corps of non-British Jewish recruits as a means of eliminating Ottoman rule in the Land of Israel.

1919 Zangwill urges the Zionist leadership, the British government, and the Paris Peace Conference to relocate the Arab population of Palestine in order to secure the future of Jewish settlement there.

1923 In a controversial lecture, "Watchman, What of the Night," delivered at Carnegie Hall in New York to a meeting sponsored by the American Jewish Congress, Zangwill attacks the Zionist leadership for failing to relocate the Arabs of the Palestine mandate and denounces American Jewry for failing to support Zionism abroad and unrestricted immigration at home; *We Moderns,* Zangwill's latest satirical drama, premieres in Washington and is panned by American critics.

1925 With his own funds, Zangwill decides to become his own producer for the London staging of *We Moderns,* which proves to be a critical failure also in Britain; declining health forces him to resign as president of the I.T.O.

1926 (1 August) Israel Zangwill dies in a nursing home in Midhurst, Sussex.

Dreamer of the Ghetto

ONE

Introduction

There was a small city and few men were in it, and there came to it a great king and surrounded it and built great siege works against it. And there was found in it a poor wise man who by his wisdom saved the city, but nobody remembered that poor man. And I said: wisdom is better than might but a poor man's wisdom is despised and his words are not heeded.

Ecclesiastes 9:14–16

Twins violently struggling within her womb, the miraculously pregnant Biblical matriarch Rebecca pleads with God to know the source of her terrible suffering, crying out, "If it be so, why do I live?" Prophetically she learns that two sons, Esau and Jacob, are wrestling within her and that from these two sons will arise two peoples, two archetypical antagonists, who throughout history will continue their bitter rivalry, each contending with the other for mastery.[1]

Centuries later the medieval Kabbalist Chaim Vital warns enigmatically that within every person there reside two contending souls, each determinedly straining toward an opposing direction from the other, thereby implying that the human personality includes necessarily an essential bipolar tension.[2] And in one of his famous allegorical stories, "The Wise Man and the Simple Man," the eighteenth-century Chassidic leader Rabbi Nachman of Breslov tells the tale of two friends from the same city, one very intelligent and keen to travel abroad throughout the world seeking knowledge, while the other contentedly remains at home and becomes a shoemaker; eventually the very wise man returns home and, after much suffering and contention, comes to learn the supremely valuable truth his simple friend had known all along. According to traditional allegorical interpretation, the simple man represents the pious qualities identified with the Biblical patriarch Jacob, while his wise friend depicts the assertive worldly knowledge attributed to his brother, Esau.[3]

The experiences of contemporary Western society confirm the description of the human personality portrayed by this ancient and enduring social-psychological archetype. The agenda of America's "rainbow coalition," the lilting cadences of Britain's defiant reggae "dub poets," and the rigorous isolationism the antimodernist *charedi* Orthodox Jews in the West impose upon themselves all are symptomatic of the alienation and confused anguish generated by the paradigmatic contest for the spiritual and cultural loyalties of men. These social patterns reflect the impossibility of people enduring the battle of dual identities unendingly. As the original of the archetype itself promises: "And the one people shall be the stronger than the other people."[4] Eventually one must choose, either out of profound conviction or out of maddening desperation. So it is that many acculturated blacks and Jews, alienated from the common values and heritage of Western society, are now deliberately seeking out alternatives in the traditions of their own peoples' historical pasts.

Widespread alienation among members of *acculturated* ethnic minorities is a recent, post–Second World War phenomenon in Western society. Prior to this time, the central focus among such minorities was to become integrated completely within the predominant culture, to "make it" as a "full-fledged Westerner." But the focus has now altered, and many perceive this earlier concern as flawed and false and, in its place, seek identity elsewhere and apart from Western traditions. Because the social phenomenon is new, its origins, its implications, and its possible consequences are rarely rationally considered. However, a few unusually prescient, and possibly most unfortunate, lonely individuals, having undergone this terrible conflict in the search for personal identity amid their own bitterly antagonistic twin inclinations, have already, almost a century ago, consciously and extensively explored the cultural disquiet our society is now witnessing.

As the nineteenth century drew to a close there appeared a new generation of young acculturated members of these ethnic minorities who experienced intensely the conflict within themselves of two contending traditions and who each chose eventually to struggle single-mindedly to resolve, or at the least to escape, the mounting tensions of the battle. Although the struggle was personal, not social, they recognized clearly that such trials of identity awaited their peoples as a whole and so sought to warn them in advance of the lurking dangers and to lead them to refuges of safety. But, relating experiences not yet felt by the majority of their peoples, the import of the message was misinterpreted or ignored altogether; this response only intensified the lonely authors' frustration and anger, convincing many of their contemporaries that they were, indeed, intentionally being perversely eccentric. Only now, from the vantage point of our own experiences, do we hear clearly these lone voices and may we learn from their sufferings.

Among acculturated Western Jews of that generation the most conscious and eloquent expression of the dilemma of identity was made by the Anglo-Jewish skeptic and enthusiast, Israel Zangwill.[5] His search and the conclusions he reached about it won him international acclaim during his own lifetime and have obscured his significance for ours. For the story of Israel Zangwill's life is a *mashal,* a parable, about the dilemma of the contemporary Jew and about the plight of modern man.

"From now on, Mr. Zangwill must be taken seriously." So William Morton Payne concluded in his 1898 review of Israel Zangwill's new book, *Dreamers of the Ghetto.*[6] With this work, Zangwill, already an international literary celebrity, became recognized as the most significant Jewish author of his day writing in English. Even those, such as Payne, who previously had had their doubts about the depth of his literary and intellectual abilities now became convinced by this latest expression of his fictional talents. Payne noted in his review, "The book is deeply significant, both as a richly sympathetic and imaginative interpretation of the Jewish ideal, and as an altogether unexpected revelation of the powers hitherto latent in its author."[7]

This great esteem for *Dreamers of the Ghetto* and its author persisted for over thirty years. Writing after Zangwill's death, S. L. Bensusan, reviewing the writer's career, remarked that "it was in 1898 that he published what is perhaps the most remarkable of all books that deal with Jewry. . . . It is an extraordinarily impressive book. . . . It marks the beginnings of the author's movement towards larger fields."[8]

The book was indeed extraordinarily ambitious. As Zangwill himself explained, "My object is mainly to exhibit what contributions to human thought and aspirations Jewish thinkers in every age have made."[9] In this work, Zangwill was not merely the talented storyteller he had always been, but he emerged as champion of Jewish intellectual integrity, humanist philosopher for mankind, and sensitive psychologist of the soul.

Weaving together the fictionalized biographies of historical figures with the histories of imaginary characters, Zangwill explores the fate of a variety of Jews spanning the course of several centuries. Neither a novel nor a collection of short stories, *Dreamers of the Ghetto* is a creative exploration into the intellectual and psychological dynamics of the Jew living in a non-Jewish world. It relates a record of conflict and persecution, rebellion and accommodation, tension in the search for peace and anguish as its reward. Underlying all else are Zangwill's unasked questions: can Jews and Christians ever live together with their integrity intact? Is peace, internal and external, possible or must there always remain the unbearable tensions? Zangwill, the satirist and clear-eyed rationalist, answered with his dreams.

But the critics and the commentators were wrong. *Dreamers of the Ghetto* was not the beginning of a new phase of creativity for Zangwill. Nor was the book to stand the test of time. Today, even among those who read Zangwill's fiction, *Dreamers* is generally forgotten. In fact, this work marks the genuine end of Zangwill's career as an author of fiction. True, he would continue writing for another twenty-eight years, but never again did he produce a work of prose that elicited great public praise and attention.

Instead, he launched himself on several new careers. He soon devoted all his literary talent to drama. He mounted the public platform to campaign for women's suffrage and world peace. But overshadowing all else was Zangwill's feverish passion to succeed in establishing a Jewish national homeland somewhere. For this goal he would sacrifice time, friendships, public popularity, and personal loyalties.

And in all these new endeavors, Israel Zangwill experienced a new, and to him incomprehensible, phenomenon of life: he failed! And these failures drove him all the harder, breaking his health and smashing his sanity. By 1926, denounced by Jews on both sides of the Atlantic, his plays failures in both London and New York, and his finances exhausted, Zangwill suffered a severe nervous breakdown from which he never recovered. On August 1, 1926, he died. He was sixty-two years old.

Nor was it merely the man who died in 1926. His literary reputation and the memory of his role as a leading Zionist died with him. The ashes of his international fame mingled with the ashes of his cremated body, interred together in the earth of his native London. Today his collected works sit dustily on the shelves of Judaica collections in various libraries around the globe, only occasionally disturbed as some curious explorer skims through his earliest Jewish literary triumphs, *Children of the Ghetto* and *The King of Schnorrers*. Zangwill's Zionist role is mentioned now only very briefly and not without whimsy by historians, and sociologists and politicians have long gone beyond the "melting pot" of his 1908 play that popularized the term and idea.

But Zangwill's obsessive destruction of his own literary career and the eclipse of his political reputation, although something to marvel at, is hardly surprising. He predicted it in *Dreamers of the Ghetto.* The book itself was the product of the creative tensions that the English-born Zangwill felt between his sense of Britishness and the awareness of his Jewishness. It was exactly this same tension that had produced his earlier highly acclaimed books and won for him an international reputation. But Zangwill, unaware of its creativity, sensed only the oppressiveness and the confusion arising from this consciousness of competing dual identities. He longed to escape and dreamed of peace.

However, this was not yet a man given over to mystification. *Dreamers* was a cautionary tale told by reason. Its message is clear: reality is brittlely unmalleable, the dreams all fail, and the dreamers end their lives in loneliness and disillusionment. The end of the dream is always unprincipled compromise, isolation, and death.

But his own warning could not save him. The ache of the tension mounted till it became maddening. Not to be wholly British nor to be wholly Jewish, nor to be able to fuse the two identities together into a coherent amalgam eventually proved unendurable for Zangwill. The onslaughts of tension were too great: reason was overwhelmed. Movement, flight toward a solution, became imperative.

Now, like one of his own tragic characters, he manufactured a strange dream in which two distinctive Israel Zangwills would accidentally inhabit the one body: one, a thoroughly assimilated British man of letters, and the other, an active Jewish nationalist. In fact, the theme of dual personalities in one body was not entirely new to Zangwill; he had playfully toyed with the notion as the plot line of his first novel, *The Premier and the Painter,* ten years earlier, in 1888. Only now he set out, despite the warning in *Dreamers of the Ghetto,* to live out this dream as reality. Yet the fiction had been prophetically true; his dream, too, would destroy Zangwill.

Yet for all its psychological insight, even the book itself was an imposture. The product of the tension between the British and the Jewish, *Dreamers of the Ghetto,* like its author, was one thing cloaked as another. Unlike Zangwill's previous Jewish books, which concentrated on descriptions of scenes of Jewish life drawn with sympathetic warmth and gentle humor, this work strove to dramatize the Jewish historical experience as expressing a universal philosophy of life equally relevant for Jews and non-Jews. The book was intended to convey an authentic religious message to all civilized humanity, a teaching rooted in the age-old wisdom of the Jewish people.[10] But the bearers of this message are Jewish apostates, the hero of the book is Jesus, and the religious philosophy it preached is Christianity.

Although the mode of presentation of this book was new, its Christianized interpretation of Judaism was not. In fact, *Dreamers of the Ghetto* opens with a poem on this theme first published on December 25, 1889, when the twenty-five-year-old Zangwill, then still only an obscure struggling author, was employed as subeditor of an Anglo-Jewish Orthodox newspaper.[11] The same attitude is explicitly expressed, also, in his first international literary success, *Children of the Ghetto*. Zangwill was being driven by the burden and tension of his British heritage in conflict with a Jewish identity that had surreptitiously ceased to be authentically Jewish but, although Christianized, would not allow him the comfort of being Christian.

That Zangwill was unable to distinguish between Christianity and the authentically Jewish is startling enough. It is particularly surprising in the light of his persistent denunciation of reformers of Judaism and of converts to Christianity. That he was universally recognized for over thirty years as *the* leading Jewish author writing in English and that his Christianized Judaism went completely unnoticed even among his large Jewish readership, which feted him at every opportunity, approaches the incredible.[12] And yet so it was: Zangwill achieved international acclaim through his books about the Jewish people and their religion and customs, became a leading Jewish nationalist figure, and was eventually destroyed by the unbearable tension between his warring twin selves, all founded upon a thoroughly distorted understanding of Judaism. In fact, Jews and non-Jews sometimes complained that his stories were "too Jewish"! Yet his misperception is clearly there, although, remarkably, even today Zangwill's confusion goes largely unnoticed.[13]

Obviously, then, Zangwill's distorted and Christianized conception of the Jewish heritage, like his international fame, was the product of a much broader social phenomenon. Israel Zangwill's biography—his successes, his misinterpretation of Judaism, his search for a comfortable identity, and his final collapse and eclipse—is really the history of his people, the post-Emancipation Western Jews who had emerged from the ghetto to seek a secure place for themselves in the wider secular Western world. It was a difficult journey, and many, like Zangwill, with his tragic vision, were choked in the passage.

What an exciting and frightening world these Jews had come to inhabit! After centuries of ostracism the gates of the ghetto had been flung open throughout Western Europe, and the Jews were invited to join their Christian neighbors as citizens of the nation. Legal impediments to full equality were also removed, though more slowly. In America, with its constitutional separation of church and state, freedom for the Jews was guaranteed. And the new freedom was offered not just to the Jews already resident in the West; by the closing decades of the nineteenth century, millions of people from the bigoted autocracies of Eastern Europe were fleeing to freedom there as well. The demographic contours of Jewry were shifting drastically, and with them the parameters of Judaism as well.

How tantalizing the new dawning horizon stretched before these newly emancipated Jews. How hypnotic in the morning's sparkling iridescence. The eye was dazzled by the glare of light, and the mind reeled with giddiness from the multiplicity of novel sensations: the sense of sudden freedom from the oppressive fear of persecution; the exhilaration at the realization that now they, too, had the liberty to choose their own future; the gratitude felt toward those who had torn down the ghetto wall and opened the nation's borders to their persecuted brethren.

But there was also the terrifying insecurity! For it was all so new. And those who tumbled down the ghetto were, after all, the proud descendants of those who had built it up. Doubts underlay the joy: how genuine was the freedom; would it last; what was wanted in return for it? Nothing seemed certain, nothing, that is, except that despite emancipation and equality the Jews remained somehow "different" from their neighbors, their non-Jewish fellow citizens.

For all citizens, despite the law, were still not quite equally German, or French, or British. Unlike their fellow citizens, Western Jewry's national identity remained a hyphenated compound: while *they* were Germans, or Frenchmen, or Englishmen, *you* were German-Jews, French-Jews, Anglo-Jews. And everyone was aware of the distinction, both *they* and *you*.

Of what did the essence of this difference consist? It was not a mere question of religious belief. Germans, Britons, and Americans were already deeply divided by religious differences; in fact, in these countries this division had become a source of national pride: toleration and decency had been made to prevail, and they worked. And, after all, most of the people, Jews and Christians, were already secularized in their primary values. No, the heart of the distinction lay elsewhere:

the Jews, no matter where they and their parents had been born, were all cultural immigrants to their new lands of freedom; their Christian neighbors were not. And it was here, at this point, that the joy of freedom clashed with the terror of alienation.[14]

When the Jews moved out of the ghetto and away from the Pale of Settlement, they had to leave behind much that was familiar and beloved. Just so much tradition could be packed into the departing baggage! And often it was difficult to choose what to take, which items were important and which were not. The result was that while their Christian neighbors had comprehensive traditional cultures, the newly emancipated Jews possessed only selected artifacts of theirs, and both groups naturally felt uncomfortable with this disequilibrium.

To fill the spaces, to get to feel at home again, as well as to calm the suspicions of their new neighbors, the Jews sought to borrow from the non-Jewish culture surrounding them. But to borrow also means to select, to choose what seems valuable and attractive. By the end of the nineteenth century, however, it was no longer so evident just what was of value in Western civilization.

An intellectual civil war had broken out among the bearers of Western culture. Traditional religious, social, and political values were under severe assault from the proponents of Darwinian evolution, Biblical Higher Criticism, Positivism, and socialism. Those very forces that had led to the tearing down of the ghetto walls—which had so long both trapped the Jews and allowed their traditional culture to flourish unchallenged within—were now attacking the traditional culture of the West. With normative values—both the Jewish and the Western—in such disarray, the recently emancipated Jews had immense difficulty recognizing what was valuable, what would endure, what they should borrow.

But even more significant, the Jews were certain that in such fluid circumstances they need not only borrow, they could also contribute. For if Western culture was under assault and a fluctuating displacement of values was in process, they themselves had already concluded a similar winnowing of their own culture and believed they now possessed what was valuable and endurable in it. Could they not offer these treasures to their fellow citizens, creating an atmosphere of true equality and harmonious give and take, in which both *they* and *you* would become borrowers and lenders, from which would emerge a unifying *we*?

But who, among the Jews, was to conduct this borrowing and lending? Tradition, refracted, here prevailed. As the scholars of Jewish law, the rabbis, constituted only a small elite with whom the masses rarely had any direct contact, either personally or through their erudite writings, another medium was needed to convey essential normative standards and ideals to the people. At least since the Talmudic period, fundamental Jewish values had been encoded therefore in allegorical and narrative stories for their effective transmission to the broader public. To ensure their authentic and didactic content, these works were first carefully crafted by Rabbinic scholars immersed in the Jewish religious tradition and then were widely disseminated to the common people, often orally. Collections of such ancient allegories and stories, like the ubiquitous *Ein Yaakov,* had recently been supplemented richly by the publication of popular Chassidic tales, the earliest being *Shivhei ha-Besht* (1814).[15]

To the uneducated, impoverished *shtetl* (village) residents of Central and Eastern Europe, the task of relating these didactic stories most often fell to the *maggid,* the Sabbath and Festival lay preachers. Although some *maggidim* were men of exceptional piety and wisdom, most were simple men with little learning. But literate and possessing a gift for oratory, they eked out a living by conducting daily classes for the unschooled local workmen on the weekly Bible portion and on *Ein Yaakov* and by delivering weekly homiletic sermons. The local people were accustomed to the entertainment, guidance, and occasional inspiration of the *maggid*'s talks and lessons, all rooted in the familiar Biblical allegories and the Rabbinically written tales of the lives of outstanding saints and wonder-workers.

In their knowledge of Judaism, the typical residents of the West resembled the *shtetl* Jews of Eastern Europe. Although holding the intellectual, their secular rabbi, in great esteem, they had little direct contact with him. Instead, it was to the modern *maggid,* the storyteller, that the ordinary Western Jew looked for guidance. Like the *maggid,* his secular counterpart, the storyteller, was expected not merely to entertain but also to provide edification and elucidation. A people, excited and confused in their strange new homes, sought wisdom where memories of their tradition taught them to look with confidence. And so they pressed their demands upon the storyteller.

But these were demands he was not capable of fulfilling, for, unlike the *shtetl maggid,* firmly grounded in the familiar territory of Rabbinic heritage, the secular storyteller was compelled to make his way amid the dusty potsherds of the past and the glittering facets of the present. The analogy was, in reality, a conjuror's trick of the imagination: religious *maggid* would not translate as secular storyteller.

For the author, the storyteller, who did accept and surrender to his eager public's importuning illusions, life could become an inexplicable heavy burden. For it was then his task to become the mediator between cultures, the borrower and the lender of peoples' valuables. And living as he must, lonely and in the interstices of two cultures, he could possess no home of his own, no place in which to rest and be at peace. But the tensions of this task, so unlike the *shtetl maggid*'s, could prove extraordinarily creative. Or it could destroy one!

Among English-speaking Jewry, the first author to yield to the yearning need of his public for a modern *maggid* was Israel Zangwill. With him began the tradition and the dreamer's illusion.

TWO

The Historical Setting—Sociopolitical

Why did modern secular Western Jewry need a *maggid,* and why did they turn to the weavers of fiction for their lessons? To begin to answer these questions it is necessary first to refer to the processes of historical change that metamorphosed the Jews of the ghetto into that politically unintended and philosophically embarrassing anomaly "modern secular Western Jewry."

Two fundamental transformations began to encroach upon the traditionalist Jewish communities of Europe during the final, revolutionary decades of the eighteenth century. In the course of the following century both would continue, accelerate, and spread. The first of the transformations was in the sociopolitical relationship of the Jews with their non-Jewish neighbors; the second, arising from the first, was in the personal relationship of individual Jews with their own identity as defined by traditional Judaism and its philosophic and cultural heritage.

Initiating these dramatic changes was the offer of complete sociopolitical equality gradually extended to the Jews by various Enlightenment-inspired governments in Western Europe. Discriminatory laws and communal isolation were to be replaced by full integration into the general civil community without, as formerly, requiring the Jews to convert religiously: toleration was to be granted to Judaism as it was granted to any other loyal, voluntary group within the state.

The Jews responded enthusiastically. Like Miranda imagining the wide world beyond the island home she had always known and shared with Prospero, the Jews, too, exultantly cried out, "How beauteous mankind is! O brave new world,/That has such people in't." And so at first it seemed.

However, there was an implicit, but essential, condition in the offer of equality that many Jews chose to ignore or really did not at first perceive. True, the Jews were no longer being required to alter formally their personal religious loyalties in order to achieve equality, but nonetheless they were still very much being required to undergo a conversion. This conversion, the liberal Enlightenment's price for equality, necessitated a drastic and profound transmutation in each Jew's sense of identity and in his loyalties. Required first was the abandonment of the traditional distinctive and particularist mode of serving God and second was the dissolution of the autonomous Jewish sociopolitical community. In their place Jews were expected to adopt a public loyalty pledged to the secular government and a private faith adapted to resemble the other faiths tolerated by the state. In other words, for the right to enjoy equality, the Jews were required to accept the philosophic and political assumptions of the Enlightenment, to agree freely to a process of conversion as psychologically traumatic to one's conception of personal identity as that involved in any sincere religious conversion.

And so the Jews did, enthusiastically. Not only to those living in Western Europe (and America), but also to some trapped within the borders of the reactionary, antiliberal empires of Eastern Europe, it seemed evident that the world was indeed irrevocably changing and that the Jews and Judaism, too, must change with it, as throughout their history they always had adapted to change. Despite numerous quarrels over exactly what to alter and how to refashion what was retained, the Jews in Western Europe did accept the offer of sociopolitical secular equality with the conditions it entailed. And yet, something went terribly wrong.

Both the non-Jewish liberal emancipators and the Western Jews expected that Jewish particularity would comfortably be submerged in a common secular sociopolitical citizenship. The terms of the conversion were sincerely entered into by both sides. And yet somehow, despite all expectations, the Jews continued to retain their distinctive identity, a reality becoming increasingly apparent by the second half of the nineteenth century.

For some, both Jew and non-Jew, the explanation was to be found in the failure in the very assumptions of liberalism itself. "Anti-Semitism," a deliberately innocuous term intended to mask a dangerous concept, was coined in Germany in the 1870s and reflected a loss of belief in liberal tenets by some non-Jews, while some equally disillusioned Jews turned to political radicalism as a solution to "the Jewish problem."

But many other people retained their adherence to liberalism and sought solutions compatible with its philosophic and political premises. Both Jews and non-Jews sought some explanation for the recalcitrant persistence of Jewish identity and, by so discovering its cause, sought to propose an effective liberal means to achieve the desired deracination.

Among those seeking a liberal understanding of the persistence of Jewish identity within a free, secular Western society, Israel Zangwill provided one of the most eloquent descriptions and intense analysis of the continuing sociopolitical and psychological dilemmas it posed for both the Jew and the non-Jew. Furthermore, both in his writings and in his personal and public life he actively pursued solutions he was convinced would satisfactorily resolve the issue.

Because Zangwill entered the discussion over the meaning and solution to the question of the retention of Jewish identity, as it were, in middebate, the following two chapters will briefly survey the developments before he joined the discourse. In this chapter, the sociopolitical history of the liberal emancipation of the Jews, with particular attention to Britain, will be presented. In the ensuing chapter, attention will focus primarily on the description and debate over the philosophic and psychological issues raised by a persisting Jewish identity within a secular Western context as it appeared in both non-Jewish and Jewish literary works preceding Zangwill's own literary debut.

Emancipation from the Ghetto

In some European countries, particularly in Central Europe, the ghetto had actual physical walls, with locked gates. Creature of the Western Renaissance, the walls locked the Jews in but also kept rioting Christian mobs out. Within the walls the people, crowded and physically impoverished, flourished in a milieu dominated by the teachings of the Torah as it was expounded by learned rabbis and elucidated by the oratory of *maggidim* preaching *mussar* (ethical homilies). But the ghetto walls were only as secure as the will of the government to tolerate Jews in the nation's midst—because they were of use. But sometimes expelling them from the nation was even more useful. So the gray shadow of insecurity hung constantly over the ghetto walls, even during the sunniest summer days.

Most of the ghettos of Western Europe, however, had no such walls. In the strictest sense, without physical walls there was no ghetto. But on the sociopolitical and cultural dimensions, there are other kinds of walls than those of bricks and mortar. There are also walls built from law and tradition, community solidarity and personal loyalty. These were the forces that walled in the inhabitants of the ghettos of Western Europe much more solidly than mere material barriers.

The central fact of Jewish life in Europe prior to the nineteenth century was the existence of the *kehilla,* the legally recognized autonomous Jewish communal organization. The *kehilla* exercised both religious and civil authority over the Jews living within its jurisdiction. Internal matters and disputes were adjudicated by the *dayyanim* (judges) of the *bet din,* the religious court, in accord with *halacha,* the traditional Jewish legal code. All aspects of religious observance, marriage, education, charity, and burial were regulated by the *kehilla,* as was taxation both for maintenance of its own institutions and for meeting the demands of the non-Jewish external authority. Because of the existence of the *kehilla,* only in exceptional circumstances would any individual Jew have direct contact with the non-Jewish authorities. Instead the relationship of Jews to non-Jews was communal.

Because it was formally established by the law of the land as the representative of those Jewish "aliens" resident there, membership in the *kehilla* was not voluntary. It was not a matter of conscience, but the legal prerequisite for a Jew to reside in the domain. Thus one ceased to belong to the *kehilla* only under some exceptional form of external compulsion: a move to another region, excommunication by the *bet din,* or conversion to Christianity. Until the closing decades of the eighteenth century, for a Jew to reside in Western Europe meant he fell within the immediate jurisdiction of a *kehilla,* not the non-Jewish civil authority. This was the real ghetto.

Although the tax burden imposed by the government was often onerous, the sociolegal and economic restrictions crippling, the *kehilla,* with its communal autonomy, allowed Jewish life and tradition to flourish and thrive. One did not feel oneself an isolated atom floating in a sea of isolated atoms, like Leibnitz's monads, but rather a member of a close-knit community bound together with similar communities in other places and also organically tied to the whole historical tradition of the people.

Within the externally imposed restrictions, there was freedom to explore and utilize the entire heritage of the Jewish people, at least within the boundaries fixed by *halacha* as accepted and enforced through formal and informal communal opinion. But to observe *halacha* meant then merely to be a law-abiding citizen. Thus whatever physical discomforts were imposed on the members of the *kehilla* by their non-Jewish governors, there was a psychological and spiritual assurance stemming from familiarity and the comfortable sense of belonging. One lived in a fruitful, lush oasis, surrounded by what appeared a parched and malevolent desert.

The Enlightenment-inspired emancipation of the Jews in Western Europe was directed not simply against the walled ghettos but principally against the *kehilla*.[1] The primary purpose was not religious toleration for itself but rather implementation of the doctrine of religious toleration in order to create a secular nation-state mobilizing the potential equality of all its inhabitants. To be most effective, the relationship of government to citizen therefore should be direct, without any mediating agency.[2] The goal of the emancipators was to eliminate the autonomy of the *kehilla* and to treat the individual Jew directly as citizen.

Thus emancipation of the Jews was granted conditionally, subservient to the ulterior motives of the emancipators. Legal and economic equality was granted to the Jews only provisionally, although the qualification of the offer was often not expressed explicitly. Nonetheless, the condition the Jews had to accept as the price for equality was surrender of the political and communal autonomy of the *kehilla*. The Jews were to be granted equality as individual citizens, and the *kehilla*, as repository of Jewish autonomy, was to be eliminated.

The Emancipation's purpose, then, was to strengthen the unity of the nation-state through the creation of a homogenized citizenry. It offered a sociolegal equality conditioned by the expectation of the elimination of fundamental cultural distinctions, not the recognition of their legitimacy.[3] Thus what was gained by the Jew as individual was at the cost of Jew as member of a distinctive people within the nation-state.

These were, after all, revolutionary times, not only in France itself but wherever its revolutionary armies carried the ideology of the Declaration of the Rights of Man and Citizen. A new age was dawning for non-Jew as well as Jew, and all things seemed possible. The Jews, too, caught up in the momentous changes of the times, responded to the new circumstances eagerly and with the optimism of the Age of Reason and Progress. Western Jewry, generally, reacted willingly and enthusiastically to the Emancipation. The ghetto suddenly felt squalid and constricted, and what before had appeared a desert outside now shone blossoming with opportunity and abundance. The price, its precise significance unappreciated and its consequences obscure, was deemed well worth the proffered advantages.

Not that either the Jews or their non-Jewish emancipators expected them to cease to adhere to Judaism. Such a demand would have contradicted the very spirit of this age of toleration. Rather, it was supposed that, once the Jews received sociopolitical equality as individual citizens, Judaism would become transformed into a variant religious creed comparable, except in details, to the diverse and competing Christian creeds already present in the nation—the *kehilla* metamorphosed into a voluntary association of believers.[4]

The newly liberated Jews, soon fully aware of these expectations, accepted them and strove to conform. They quickly adopted the external fashions, language, educational curriculum, and occupational goals of the general society around them. Efforts were also undertaken to reformulate traditional Judaism to approximate more closely the creeds of their neighbors. Although there was intense dissension among the reformers, violent disagreement over exactly what constituted the essentials of the Jewish heritage, all agreed that at least some modernizations and modifications were desirable.

In an era dominated by the remnants of the eighteenth-century advocates of Rationalism and by the new Romanticism, this transformation of the Jewish heritage meant the elimination of whatever could not apparently be reconciled to the standards of reason or to the positivists' interpretation of history. A people thereby became an association; an organic national heritage, a flexible creed; and a community, a voluntary collection of autonomous individuals. The national and psychological costs seemed worth the sociopolitical and economic benefits.

Yet the expectations of the emancipators and of their Jewish adherents proved generally illusory. For despite sociopolitical equality and the reformulation and reduction of the Jewish heritage to a voluntary religious creed, the distinctiveness of the Jew was not eliminated. Even among those Jews who had molded their Judaism on a Christian model or who had become thoroughly secularized and acculturated to the non-Jewish milieu, some intangible but distinctive quality of theirs remained detectable and separated them from their neighbors.[5]

This difference was extremely anxiety provoking for Jews: what were they still doing wrong? But for many of the emancipators it appeared as willful betrayal: given every opportunity and advantage of equality, Jews seemed stubbornly to continue choosing to remain apart. The good will of the tolerant liberal emancipators, frustrated by suspicion and evidence of betrayal, often fell victim to anti-Semitism. The very efforts of the Jews to combat this suspicion now only produced reinforcement for it. And even among those who did not fall prey to disillusionment and anti-Semitism, the insistence on Jewish conformity remained the fundamental condition for the ultimate recognition of their equality.[6]

Emigration from Eastern Europe

Who, exactly, were these new immigrants from Eastern Europe, and why were they emigrating? Which people these were and the reasons they had for leaving for the West determined their perceptions and behavior in their new homelands, in their Jewish affiliations there, and in their relations with the already resident Western Jewish population and also profoundly affected the attitudes of the local Jews and non-Jews toward the immigrants.

The common explanation for this sudden and relatively massive wave of migration is that it was the desperate response to the violent and bloody pogroms that were provoked by the accession of the reactionary Alexander III to the imperial Russian throne in 1881 following the assassination of his more progressive father and by the even more virulent anti-Semitism running rampant in Romania. Official persecution followed mob violence, as Jews were periodically expelled from various towns and villages, even within the restrictive Pale of Settlement to which they were already forcibly consigned. Defenseless, oppressed, threatened by raging mob violence and murder, unprotected by bigoted and hostile governments, the Jews fled for their very lives.

This is the explanation the immigrants themselves gave and believed for their flight to the West; it was accepted by their Western contemporaries, Jewish and non-Jewish, and has been repeated by historians as well.[7] And it *is* all true: the horrors—the murderous violence, the official malevolence, the appalling poverty—were all as terrible as has been claimed, dwarfed in magnitude only by the methodical and technologically sophisticated barbarism of the Nazi Holocaust.

Yet this "standard" explanation does not explain why *these specific* people came and not others. Was the opportunity to emigrate the result of random chance, or were there causative variables that led certain cohorts to choose migration and others to choose to remain? That persecution was neither the sufficient nor necessary cause for this emigration is suggested by the fact that migration from Austrian Poland, Galicia, where the Jews had been completely emancipated in 1867 and where there were now no pogroms or communal violence, was actually proportionately higher than that from Russia.[8] To discover, then, which were the decisive variables in determining who chose to migrate, a study of the social composition of the immigrants is necessary. Such analysis not only clarifies their socioeconomic characteristics but also provides significant insight into their ideological and cultural values as well.

Simon Kuznets has carried out just such a demographic analysis of Russian Jewish immigrants to the United States between 1880 and 1914.[9] His conclusions confirm those earlier suggested by Jacob Lestschinsky concerning Russian and Romanian immigrants.[10] Both studies demonstrate that the migration was neither random nor provoked by the virulence of anti-Semitism. Rather, the pogroms and anti-Jewish legislation accelerated and aggravated socioeconomic trends already in process. Because these same trends were also affecting Galicia, the migrations from its eastern neighbors served as a catalyst to intensify the out-migration from the Austro-Hungarian Empire as well.

All three areas—the Russian Pale of Settlement, Romania, and Austrian Galicia—were experiencing the dislocations of the transition from preindustrial and premodern socioeconomic structures to industrialization and urbanization. These disruptive forces affected not only the Jewish population of these regions but also the non-Jewish residents, as reflected in the intensified non-Jewish emigration from these regions plus similar developments in such countries as Scandinavia, Greece, and Italy.[11] What was unique to the Jewish situation was the additional variable of anti-Semitism, which did distinguish the Jewish pattern of migration from others: it was more family oriented, an indication that the migration was intended to be permanent.[12]

Both Kuznets and Lestschinsky agree that the operative variables in the choice of migration were age, class, and transferability of skill. Those who chose to migrate, in general, were the younger, lower middle class artisans who had no place in the reorganized and urbanized economic environment. Eager for employment, possessing skills that were portable, and living amid oppressive terror, they chose to seek new opportunities elsewhere.

But as Thomas Sowell has pointed out, this mixture of variables must also include ambition.[13] For not everyone, even among those suffering severe socioeconomic dislocation, chooses to migrate. The ones who do are primarily those driven by the belief that the chances for success are significantly better elsewhere and that no such hope remains for them in their original homeland.[14] This desire for success is essential.

The portrait of the Jewish immigrants arriving in the West after 1880, then, is of a relatively young population intending to settle permanently in new territory. These people, primarily lower middle class artisans, were economically highly motivated and possessed sufficient skills with which to realize their ambitions, especially in the economically and politically liberal nations of the West.

However, one additional variable still must be considered: the immigrants' attitude toward traditional Judaism. Of course, religiously observant Jews had migrated throughout Europe and the Near East for centuries, but were *these* particular immigrants from Eastern Europe "orthodox" in the traditional implication of accepting willingly the Jewish heritage intact? Although it is commonly assumed that they were "orthodox" in this sense, a more accurate assessment emerges by distinguishing between two anthropological phenomena: assimilation and acculturation.[15]

Assimilation is a social anthropological process referring to the adoption by one society of the values and sociointellectual standards of another society. It is primarily an intangible constellation of nonconscious attitudes and intellectual standards evidenced only in the aggregate. Acculturation, on the other hand, refers to the adoption by one society of the tangible cultural traits of another. Its expression is thus readily apparent, manifesting itself in such characteristics as language, clothing, and cuisine.

Of great importance for any analysis of these processes are the following conditions: (1) assimilation and acculturation, although related, are independent phenomena; (2) each may operate on a continuum of "more or less"; (3) although they may function simultaneously, one process may, equally, lag behind the other; and (4) not being linked, each may operate on its own, without the other.

When two societies come into intimate contact—one dominant and one subordinate—it can occur that there is almost no acculturation nor assimilation, each group maintaining a thorough distinctiveness. Alternately, the subordinate group may totally assimilate and acculturate, thus completely disappearing. However, even after great acculturation and assimilation have occurred, if each group retains identifiability, there have been limits, however unclear, to these processes.[16]

In the context of adherence to traditional Judaism, it is possible to be acculturated fully without being significantly assimilated—that is, dressing in the prevailing non-Jewish fashion and expressing oneself in the local language but thoroughly rejecting the dominant culture's values and mores for alternative standards as defined within the autonomous Jewish heritage.[17] Contrarily, it is also possible to adhere to the dominant society's values, to be assimilated, while still retaining the external appurtenances of traditional Jewish society, that is, not to be acculturated.

With regard to understanding who exactly the immigrants from Eastern Europe were, these distinctions are of the utmost importance. Clearly the immigrants were not acculturated, neither into their previous society nor immediately into their new one: they were distinctively "foreign." Their language was Yiddish; their clothing was typical of the *shtetl,* the men with beards and side curls, the married women with kerchief-covered heads; their cuisine was traditional East European kosher Jewish; and their social recreation was largely confined to various Jewish associations, including the *shuls* (the *shtetl*-like small synagogues), which functioned in the new context also as *landsmanshaftn* (social clubs of migrants from the same locale). In fact, this phenomenon of immigrants utilizing traditional religious institutions for new social purposes was not particular to the Jews but was typical of many immigrant groups: they seemed to become more "religious" after their migration as they turned to their houses of worship as refuges of familiarity in an alien land.[18] At any rate, these Jewish immigrants certainly *appeared* "orthodox." But were they really?

What of assimilation? Were their central values and attitudes derived from traditional Jewish norms or from those of the non-Jewish secularized industrial society surrounding them, both in Eastern Europe and in the West?

Except in particular instances, these were people acting in disregard of the central values advocated by traditionalist Rabbinic authority. That this was so is evident from the unanimous and unhesitating condemnation of emigration by the leading Rabbinic figures of Eastern Europe.[19] The rabbis recognized clearly the prevailing poverty and persecution there, but they were also aware that in the new lands of settlement in the West there were not available the minimum requirements for proper Jewish religious observance, such as competent Rabbinic authorities, religious schools, supervised *kashrut,* and ritual baths. Furthermore, they believed that the new communities were unstable and easily swayed into neglecting essential Jewish practices, such as Sabbath observance. Nor were the rabbis' warnings unheeded: the observant, often living amid great poverty and as subjects of hostile governments, chose to remain where the necessities of traditional Judaism were readily available, despite penury and pogroms.

The immigrants were those for whom other values prevailed. They had already assimilated the secularized ethos of their altering East European environments. What drove them westward was their ambition to succeed financially and to create a better material life for themselves and their children. What mattered most to the migrants was the opportunity to build a decent life in a peaceful land. For this choice they were willing to pay a price, although often only grudgingly and at times unconsciously. But nonetheless immigration was almost invariably an indication of assimilation and a choice against the primacy of traditionalist Judaism. Adherence to Rabbinic authority was the most powerful variable that militated against emigration.[20]

This secularization of traditional Judaism, its assimilation to the tenets of modern industrial society, may be seen in the fate of the fundamental Jewish religious value of *mesirat nefesh,* self-sacrifice for the maintenance of Jewish practice. A value adhered to by all varieties of normative Judaism throughout history, it was precisely this that the Rabbinic leadership demanded in Eastern Europe at the close of the nineteenth century. From those whose culture remained traditionally Jewish, their demand was heeded; but among those who had already assimilated to the prevailing secular norms, the demand was empty of significance. But the value of self-sacrifice still remained; however, through the transvaluation of the sacred into the secular, it now meant self-sacrifice for a brighter, more comfortable future, especially self-sacrifice for one's children's future. Thus what had previously signified sacrifice of the material present for a higher purpose came to mean sacrifice of the present for future material improvement: the immediate moment was no longer sanctified but was expendable to the secular future. With ambition-filled eyes gazing into the future, past and present paled into insignificance for the immigrants.

That precisely this hierarchy of values was so is evident from the immigrants' behavior in their new lands of settlement.[21] What always came first was adaptation to the means to material success, regardless of the cost, often unintended, to traditional values. Thus while some Catholic immigrant groups to America insisted, at great financial sacrifice, on educating their children in parochial schools, the Jewish immigrants' children flocked to the secular public schools as the surest route to future prosperity.[22] Orthodox Jewish parochial schools would only have served to exclude their pupils from many mainstream occupations, thus frustrating their parents' ambitions. Equally for this reason, little attention was devoted to creating a strong rabbinate in America or to establishing the other institutions necessary for minimal traditional observances. Priorities were clearly mirrored in the social institutions the immigrants created about them in their new homes, and they were ones in which the secular predominated.[23]

However, the East European immigrants' assimilation to secular values—already achieved in the East and only intensified in the West—did not necessarily imply for many a conscious *theoretical* rejection of traditional Jewish practices. While they were assimilated, and even often willing to acculturate once afforded the opportunity, they would not accept an acculturated Judaism. The only "true" Judaism for them remained that which they had left "back home" in Eastern Europe and now imitated in miniature in the West. The acculturated Judaisms they found already there they rejected as heterodox. Hence the immigrants rejected equally Reform Judaism and the highly acculturated but completely unassimilated orthodoxy identified with Rabbi S. R. Hirsch of Frankfurt. For the immigrants only East European orthodoxy represented Judaism: they simply nonconsciously placed other values before it. So despite both their ignoring of Rabbinic authority and their assimilation to secular culture, many immigrants continued to consider themselves—and were considered by people in the West—as "Orthodox."

But such assimilated orthodoxy—unlike Hirsch's acculturated traditionalism—was form without content. Only the reflexes of external ceremonial behavior, cuisine, and linguistic expression remained, all illuminated by the glow of nostalgia. These "Orthodox" immigrants, themselves commonly unlettered in sophisticated Jewish sources, engaged in mimetic behavior of external ceremonies they had witnessed through a child's perspective but with no intellectual or emotional commitment to the primacy of their deeper values and implications. This onionskin edifice of their Judaism cracked easily under the dual strains of acculturation and the demands of material ambition. Brittle remnants provided scant comfort to the immigrants in an alien land

and possessed no attraction to their acculturated children schooled in the virtues of the pursuit of secular success.[24]

Thus the East European Jewish immigrants and their Western brethren shared a close affinity of attitude in their perception of Judaism: all that remained of it for them were shards, although each group had chosen to treasure different collections of fragments. But, having culturally assimilated, all agreed in their fundamental judgment: traditional Judaism—its values alien even to the "Orthodox" among them—appeared quaint and outmoded amid the whirling bustle of a modern Western city. And with the past apparently so poor and eccentric, there seemed no alternative but to push forward.

Anglo-Jewry

Britain has had a Jewish presence at least since the era of the eleventh-century Norman invasion; Jewish immigrants arrived from France along with the conquerors. During the twelfth century, under the influence of the fury of the Crusades, England, too, experienced a wave of violent anti-Jewish outbursts, culminating in the riots accompanying the coronation of Richard I the Lionhearted in September 1189 and in the York Massacre of March 1190. However, Jews remained in England till the reign of Edward I, when mounting anti-Jewish sentiment led to the expulsion order of 18 July (9th of Av) 1290, which commanded the Jews to depart the kingdom by 1 November. From that date until the seventeenth century, England, at least officially, had no Jewish residents.

The rise of the Puritans during the Elizabethan and early Stuart periods aroused a sympathetic interest in the Jews. During the Republican era, over which the Puritans presided, direct contact was established by Puritan leaders and Sephardic Dutch Jewry, especially through the Marrano leader and mystic Menasseh ben Israel, who in 1654 petitioned Oliver Cromwell for official permission for the reentry of the Jews to England.

Even as Cromwell's Protectorate government debated the issue, crypto-Jews began to settle in the country. By December 1656 they were even able to espouse their Judaism openly when they rented a house in Cree Church Lane in London for a synagogue and in 1657 acquired land for a cemetery.

Finally in August 1664, following the Restoration, Charles II granted written official permission for Jews to reside again in Britain. Those who did so remained predominantly Sephardim, and their synagogue in Cree Church Lane became a sort of tourist attraction, visited, for instance, by Samuel Pepys in 1663; in 1701 they relocated to the Bevis Marks Synagogue, designed in imitation of the Amsterdam original. Still, the Jews had no political rights, as was the case for all non-Anglicans after the Glorious Revolution.

Ashkenazi Jews began to settle in England in late Stuart times and particularly after the coming of the German Hanoverian dynasty during the eighteenth century, although, as the intense controversy over the Jewish naturalization bill of 1753 shows, anti-Jewish sentiment remained potent.[25] These new settlers originated primarily from Central Europe, and by the end of the eighteenth century three large Ashkenazi synagogues existed in the City of London, the Great (or Duke's Place), the Hambro' and the New, with a few smaller congregations in London and the provinces as well.

In 1802 the Great Synagogue's rabbi, Solomon Hirschell, became generally recognized as Britain's "Chief Rabbi," and in 1844 representatives of the then five prominent London synagogues and nineteen provincial cities elected his successor, the Hanoverian-born Dr. Nathan Marcus Adler, who remained Chief Rabbi until his death in 1891, when he was succeeded by his son, Hermann.[26] During the same period a London Board of Shechita was organized, informally from 1792 and formally from 1804, to coordinate ritual slaughter for the entire London community.[27] In addition, charitable institutions, schools, and a Jewish press appeared during the course of the early decades of the nineteenth century, serving a London population numbering about 20,000 by 1850.[28] A Reform congregation was established in London in 1840.[29] The entire community structure was dominated by the "Cousinhood," an interrelated oligarchy of Cohens, Goldsmids, Mocattas, Montefiores, Montagus, and Rothschilds.[30]

The third quarter of the nineteenth century witnessed two significant achievements by Anglo-Jewry, one external and one internal. The struggle for political equality had preoccupied the Jewish community following the end of the Napoleonic wars, a struggle shared by Roman Catholics and Non-Conformists. The latter groups were granted this equality in 1828, but the exclusion of the Jews continued. Several bills to remove the disability were introduced in Parliament over the next few years, passing the Commons only to be defeated in the Lords. After 1836, Jews did begin to hold official positions in the City, despite the Parliamentary disability, which rested primarily on the requirement to swear a Christian oath to serve in the body. Only in 1858 was the Lords' resistance finally overcome and Lionel de Rothschild allowed to be sworn in as a Member of Parliament without reference to Christianity. Rothschild was soon joined by several other Jewish MPs.[31]

The most significant internal achievement of Anglo-Jewry during these years was the establishment of the United Synagogue (US) in 1870. After the middle of the nineteenth century there was a major demographic shift of the Ashkenazi population away from their traditional residences in the City to newer homes further afield. This shift meant a significant loss of membership for the three City synagogues, the Great, the Hambro' and the New, and the establishment of new congregations, often as branches of the older ones. As a result of this loss of members, the older synagogues also suffered a serious decline in income, imperiling their continued viability.

To resolve this dilemma, as well as to maintain a cohesive unity among the proliferating congregations, Lionel Louis Cohen, one of the most prominent members of the "Cousinhood," promoted the establishment of the United Synagogue, an administratively and financially centralized association of the three City synagogues, their branches, and other congregations. Its creation was officially sanctioned by act of Parliament in 1870.[32] Dominated by the oligarchy and subject to the authority of the orthodox Chief Rabbi, the US became the primary synagogal organization among Anglo-Jewry.

Yet the US, although defining itself as traditionally orthodox, was highly assimilated and acculturated; it was the very embodiment of the ideal of Anglicization promoted among the "Cousinhood."[33] The centralized organizational structure was modeled on that of the Church of England, its architectural ideal cathedral, and its "ministers" garbed in "clericals" almost indistinguishable from those of high-church Anglicans. Nor did the US display any concern for the minimum accoutrements of orthodox life, such as full-time Jewish education or ritual baths, institutions essential for normative Jewish practice and its long-term survival. Similarly the Chief Rabbi, displaying little independent initiative, ignored these matters as well, concentrating instead primarily on the issues of marriage, conversion, and synagogue decorum. Nor was the leadership of the United Synagogue required to be orthodox in personal practice. So while the US was successful as an organizational expedient, as an authority to preserve ethnic purity, and as an instrument of Anglo-Jewry cohesiveness under the tutelage of the "Cousinhood," it was Anglicized in its form and content, its orthodoxy restricted to the formalities of communal worship and kinship.[34]

Thus by the final quarter of the nineteenth century, Anglo-Jewry constituted a cohesive, well-organized, highly Anglicized community dominated by a paternalistic interrelated Ashkenazi-Sephardi oligarchy of West and Central European origin. In only its second decade of political emancipation, the precariousness of British toleration was still fresh in the minds of all: what had finally won the day for emancipation was exactly British Jewry's Anglicization, its display of mores and elite preponderance that also characterized Victorian British society.[35] As Colin Holmes observes: "toleration was not synonymous with acceptance. The liberal compromise offered emancipation in the expectation that Jews would cease to be Jewish and move closer to British society."[36] But in the 1880s the established structure of Anglo-Jewry and the arduously achieved "liberal compromise" that conditioned its acceptance by the general British community unexpectedly suffered severe strain as a new group of Jews abruptly began arriving in Britain.

The great wave of East European migration in this decade aroused the compassion and anxieties of Anglo-Jewry: they were genuinely concerned about the sufferings and aspirations of their brethren but terrified by their presence in Britain. They were willing to help the immigrants but only in allowing Britain to serve as a transit center to America or the colonial empire; those who were unable to depart overseas, Anglo-Jewish leaders encouraged, and even assisted, in returning to Russia.[37]

The immigrants posed a serious challenge to the cohesive stability within Anglo-Jewry and its public image, which had won Victorian support for Jewish emancipation. Within the Jewish community strong antagonism soon emerged between the unacculturated immigrants, numbering about 100,000, and the highly Anglicized Anglo-Jewish oligarchy.[38] The immigrants viewed the acculturated Jews of England as virtual apostates with their large, imposing synagogues whose officials wore top hats and morning-coats and whose clerically garbed ministers preached English sermons. For their part, the leaders of Anglo-Jewry feared that the "Oriental" Jews, with their alien manners, poverty, and economic ambitions, would undermine thoroughly the hard-won image of British Jewry and would unleash the latent forces of anti-Semitism still lurking in the country, a fear well justified by events.[39]

Eventually recognizing that the immigrant challenge was not temporary, the Anglo-Jewish leadership chose the tactic of Anglicizing the newcomers:

> [The liberal tradition] expected of the Jew that he would conform to "English standards," even improve the standards of his conformity. In an aura of tolerance he would inevitably define himself as the middle class gentile would have defined him. . . . And he must seek to improve others as well as improve himself, particularly the newer immigrants. . . . It was up to the Jewish rich to "remove" the anomalous behaviour of the Jewish poor. . . . Such opinions underwrote the power of the Jewish elite and its policies.[40]

To achieve their goal, the poverty and the economic ambitions of the immigrants proved to be quite useful levers. Charities, apprenticeships, workingmen's clubs, women's groups, housing facilities, and children's organizations were encouraged as vehicles both to acculturate the newcomers and to integrate them into the existing institutional structure and hierarchy of Anglo-Jewry.[41]

A particular focus for Anglicization was the young, especially through the offer of free education, the prerequisite for future success in Britain. Preeminent among the Jewish schools disseminating acculturation was the Jews' Free School, located in the predominantly immigrant London East End and with an enrollment of approximately 3,000 elementary school–age boys and girls by the end of the century.[42] The immigrant parents, with their assimilated values, eagerly acquiesced to this secular English education with a Jewish patina offered freely to their children.[43]

In one area alone were the immigrants intractable to acculturation and overt manipulation by the Anglo-Jewish "Cousinhood"—in religion. The immigrants consistently rejected the authority of the United Synagogue. To them it was *treif* (not kosher), heretical. Not that the immigrants were particularly observant Jews; all the evidence, both contemporary and scholarly, indicates that they were not.[44] It simply was that when they did choose to identify with Judaism they insisted on what they remembered from "home": small, autonomous congregations presided over without clericals, without decorum, and with the sermon in Yiddish. In other words, what the immigrants objected to was not the assimilated values of British Jewry, values that had, in fact, carried these East European Jews across the continent. Only form was the issue.

Some among the United Synagogue leadership sought to compel

the immigrants to acquiesce to this British form of Judaism. But Samuel Montagu (later Lord Swaythling) adopted the more subtle approach of co-option. Because, ultimately, no essential principles were involved, and the immigrants were not challenging the US so much as ignoring it, he felt that the most effective approach was to allow, and even assist, the immigrants to establish congregations along lines they preferred but under the financial, and ultimately political, tutelage of Anglo-Jewry.

In this fashion the Federation of (Minor) Synagogues was organized in 1887 under the nominal leadership of Lord Rothschild and actively guided by Montagu, both of whom were also leading members of the United Synagogue's governing board. The Federation accommodated the forms of the immigrants' religious preferences while integrating them into the structure of authority already dominated by the "Cousinhood": the Chief Rabbinate, the Board of Shechita, and the Board of Guardians.[45] What is extremely important to note is that the primary goal of the US leadership—whether acting directly or through Montagu's acquiescent Federation—was not the preservation of the immigrants' presumed orthodoxy but rather their Anglicization.[46] That is, the goal was social, not religious.

Despite these efforts and successes, a fierce internecine struggle did explode over a core religious principle. In 1891 a small congregation of acculturated but unassimilated orthodox German Jews, the North London Beth Hamedrash, founded in 1869, joined an equally small East European group, the Machzike Shomrei Shabbos Synagogue, established in 1890, to organize the Machzike Hadath Society, whose Lithuanian-trained spiritual leader, Aba Werner, was former Chief Rabbi of Helsinki. The central preoccupation of the Machzike Hadath and Rabbi Werner was the quality of *kashrut* of meat sold under the Board of Shechita supervision. Actually, their demands were minimal and concerned only one of three stages in the processing of kosher meats, the packing plant, while they were amenable to the Board's standards for the equally significant and problematic issues of the qualifications of the ritual slaughterers and the reliability of the retailers. Although the demands were so minimal and limited, and reflect deep concern over a basic requirement of *kasrut,* they were firmly rejected by Hermann Adler, acting as deputy for the Chief Rabbi.

The rebuff led Machzike Hadath to establish a rival communal organization to that under the jurisdiction of the Chief Rabbi, his Rabbinical court, and the Board of Shechita. For this purpose they acquired a building in Spitalfields—constructed in the eighteenth century originally as a Huguenot church and later used as a Methodist chapel—for their own new "Great Synagogue."[47] The schism became increasingly bitter as the establishment Anglo-Jewish authorities sought to enlist the support of leading East European rabbis against the secessionists.

However, in 1905 Samuel Montagu successfully mediated a settlement. In exchange for the Federation's sponsor providing funds to the debt-ridden Machzike Hadath, the latter agreed to accept the authority of the Chief Rabbi and join the Federation and the Board of Shechita, although retaining an autonomous status with regard to *kashrut*. Machzike Hadath, thus, did not compromise on its principle, and the unity of Anglo-Jewry was fully restored. Only the North London Beth Hamedrash refused to end its secession and, following the First World War, constituted the nucleus of a thoroughly independent orthodox community.[48]

In judging the level of orthodoxy of the immigrants it is significant that such a fundamental and minimal concern was advanced by only a small minority among them. Equally significant is the fact that this rival Machzike Hadath community was so feeble; not only did it lack widespread popular support among the immigrants but its very communal structure lacked credibility: there was no Rabbinical court and no full-time school for its children, who, like all others, attended the existing secular institutions. Finally, Rabbi Werner was an early supporter of the Zionist Movement, an outlook condemned by the leading Rabbinic authorities of Central and Eastern European orthodoxy.

In the final analysis, then, the schism of Machzike Hadath, although reflecting a genuine attachment to Jewish religious practice, represented more a protest against the acculturation of Anglo-Jewry than a revolt by immigrants imbued with a traditionalist religious orientation of their fundamental values.[49] Assimilated secular values—among the Anglicized and the "foreigner"—prevailed virtually unchallenged.

The East End

London's Jewish East End could not boast of a vibrant Yiddish theater, a thriving Yiddish press, or a vigorous radicalism. What it had were "sweaters" and Petticoat Lane.

Squeezing into the dank tenements lining the narrow streets of the

East End, the immigrants came to make their fortune. Living amid abysmal squalor, in a section of the capital long known as a refuge for emigrés and outcasts, harboring now the petty criminals, prostitutes, and unemployed debris of industrialized society, the hopeful migrants arrived prepared to realize their most cherished ambitions.[50]

Living on the eastern boundaries of the city, spreading out on the axes of Whitechapel and Commercial roads toward Mile End, the immigrants, after 1880, lived, toiled, and dreamed oblivious to the squalor surrounding them, a squalor, after all, not so very different from the poverty they had abandoned in Eastern Europe. Ignoring both their English neighbors and their Anglo-Jewish coreligionists, the immigrants set about establishing businesses, *chevrot* (small synagogues), and *chadarim* (after-school religious classes for young boys) for themselves. Despite the culture shocks, the congestion, the poverty, and the proximate brutality of their neighbors, the immigrant community remained generally peaceful, disciplined, and humane.[51] As the investigator Beatrice (Webb) Potter reluctantly testified at the time:

> He [the East End Jew] treats his wife with courtesy and tenderness, and they discuss constantly the future of the children. He is never to be seen at the public house. . . . [These immigrant Jews] are set down in an already over-stocked and demoralized labour market; they are surrounded by the drunkenness, immorality, and gambling of the East End streets, they are, in fact, placed in the midst of the very refuse of our civilization, and yet . . . the Jewish inhabitants of East London rise in the social scale.[52]

They rose because they were driven by ambition, prepared for hard work, and equipped with the necessary artisan skills. The most important occupations, employing both men and women, were in the new ready-to-wear clothing industry, the leather and cabinet industries, and the tobacco trade. Primarily organized into small shops, these crafts, demanding only limited skills, thrived by means of a thorough and systematic division of labor.[53]

The immigrants labored long hours for low wages in extremely unhealthy conditions not to become wealthy but in order to become masters of their own shops someday.[54] For this reason, they willingly conspired with the shop owners, the "sweaters" who worked alongside them under the same conditions, to evade the official inspections of municipal health authorities, and it was also why so little immigrant radicalism existed.[55] The only ideal was success; the only means, self-sacrificing back-breaking hard work.

Oddly enough it was just this unrestrained ambition and tireless toil that gave offense to the British. Thus after praising their general respect for the law and superiority to the morality of their neighbors, Beatrice Potter complained about the immigrants, "In short, the foreign Jew ignores all social obligations other than keeping the law of the land, the maintenance of his own family, and the charitable relief of his coreligionists."[56] *Nebech*!

It was in Petticoat Lane that all this enterprise and zeal was most evident. Centrally located in the Jewish district of the East End, lining Wentworth Street Monday through Friday, peddlers with their push-carts, hawkers from their street stalls, craftsmen in their dingy store-front shops catered to the everyday needs of the immigrants. But on Sunday, the Lane exploded outward from Wentworth, spreading onto Middlesex from Aldgate to Bishopsgate, as dense crowds of Londoners streamed in to purchase every variety of cheap goods at bargain prices.[57] As one contemporary described it: "all the shops are open; the streets are occupied by a triple line of stalls, on which are exposed for sale all kinds of things, but chiefly garments—coats and trousers. There is a mighty hubbub of those who chaffer and those who offer and those who endeavour to attract attention."[58]

And impelled by the same frenzied ambition as the Whitechapel "sweater" and the Petticoat Lane hawker, Israel Zangwill catapulted himself high above the weary toilers in the drab street of his native London and won international acclaim through his portraits of East End Jewry. But like many another immigrant's ambition, Zangwill's was insatiable, driving him on till it consumed him.

THREE

The Historical Setting—Literary

Israel Zangwill drew upon three literary traditions in composing the works that formed the basis of his international reputation. These three influences were English literature, the Western "ghetto" stories, and Anglo-Jewish fiction. Although each is a distinctive genre, they are interrelated: they all derive from the perspective of Western civilization. And in the second half of the nineteenth century this perspective meant that all three were becoming uncomfortably aware of, and sought solutions around, unforeseen obstacles that had arisen to block full realization of liberal secular societies within Western Europe.

By midcentury, English authors were coming to recognize that large segments of British society remained untouched by the political and economic reforms introduced beginning in the 1830s. In fact, it appeared as if some of these liberal reforms had actually made things worse! Realization was therefore increasing that the eighteenth-century Enlightenment's assessment of the liberal's task had, for some reason, not been fulfilled by later experience. It was by now recognized that some additional effort, some more energetic and broadened initiative, must be undertaken if all the diverse elements within society were to benefit from these reforms. A daring few authors, although not questioning the ultimate goals of the liberal heritage, did begin reformulating some of the fundamental philosophic and psychological presuppositions about the means to be employed in achieving these goals universally.

Simultaneously, on the Continent, Westernized Jewish authors of the "ghetto" stories were also displaying disappointment at the stubborn limitations that were becoming evident in the achievements of liberal reform. They, too, began tentatively reassessing some of its philosophic assumptions. For these authors, the obstacles that had arisen were particularly troubling. For despite immense efforts at acculturation, assimilation, and equal sociopolitical participation in the general society and culture, the Jews continued to be regarded as aliens, as somehow, and inexplicably, "other" than their non-Jewish fellow citizens. Especially distressing, and contrary to the confident predictions of Enlightenment philosophers, anti-Semitism, in whatever guises it now assumed, actually was increasing rather than diminishing with the actualization of liberal societies. Like their British counterparts, these authors did not despair of liberalism but rather sought new philosophic and psychological formulations that would explain what had gone wrong and how finally to eliminate effectively that still unbridgeable distance separating them from their fellow citizens.

Anglo-Jewish authors during the final decades of the nineteenth century, on the other hand, retained much greater confidence in the achievements of liberalism than their English and continental counterparts. But this is just what troubled them! Present in their works is an agitated undercurrent of regret that liberalism seems indeed to have been so very successful, that their Jewish heritage was being so irretrievably submerged in their Britishness. A sense of social and personal alienation, an aloneness, echoes through their words. They are convinced that they are thoroughly English and yet behind this confidence lurks a disturbing awareness of another self, an inner voice faintly resonating from beyond the horizon of vision and, although it is too distant to distinguish its words distinctly, clearly it is a cry of solitude and death. And these authors are conscious that, paradoxically, it is just this inner sense of another self that separates them from their fellow citizens and marks a margin to their impeccable assimilation. For although British authors occasionally may write about a mirror-image double, the Anglo-Jew knows his own other self is not a double, not a psychological negative image of his positive self, but rather a distinctive other within, a nonidentical twin with whom he cannot communicate nor even comprehend, but for whom he nevertheless longs and without whom he feels lonely and adrift.

As their heir, Israel Zangwill consciously drew upon and shared the experiences of these three literary traditions. He, too, believed that the realization of liberalism required a more energetic program if it was to affect justly all socioeconomic segments and classes of Western society, that liberalism's psychological assumptions required modification if anti-Semitism was to be combated and the Jews to share equally liberalism's benefits. And he, too, became convinced that only through a reformulation of liberalism's philosophic assumptions could the Jew's pleading twin be rescued. To grasp how

Zangwill responded to these three prior liberal literary traditions and to appreciate how he deliberately sought to remold and coalesce them into a unified philosophic, psychological, and sociopolitical program, the concerns of each must first be surveyed separately.[1]

English Literature

Much of Zangwill's literary endeavors, from his earliest fiction to his very last, were intended solely as contributions to general, non-Jewish, English literature. His earliest reputation as an author and his first published novels were all within the parameters of this genre. And certainly the British literary heritage provided the single most influential contour of his writing. While it is beyond the scope of this study to discuss English literature at any great length or depth, certain salient features of the tradition, as they were to affect Zangwill, need to be mentioned.

Toward the final third of the nineteenth century a significant bifurcation occurred in English literature. Two divergent streams now emerged. One continued to espouse the social reform of the Enlightenment tradition. The other, convinced that the eighteenth-century philosophic and psychological assumptions about human existence were in some fashion flawed, sought to discover the nature of these flaws and their remedy before embarking upon further reform. The former stressed the reality of action and the thematic plot while the latter, critical of its predecessor, demanded accuracy of psychological, and even metaphysical, portraiture.

The first literary stream followed the themes and style of Charles Dickens in its advocacy of sociopolitical relief and restructuring; for convenience, this tradition might be labeled the "social assertivist" school. The second literary tradition, influenced by the essays and fiction of George Eliot, emphasized philosophic and psychological reflection and might therefore be labeled the "solitary contemplative" school.[2]

Both outlooks deeply influenced Zangwill. As a social satirist he followed the conventions of the social assertivists, while as a philosophic belletrist, he was profoundly impressed by the works of the solitary contemplatives. That Zangwill could smoothly utilize ideas and programs derived from both these traditions was possible because they were not merely competing literary modes, each with its own special style and readership, although this is certainly also the case.

But even more so, they represented disparate intellectual and ethical responses to the apparent realities of modern human existence, each originating from legitimate but differing perspectives toward the self: the social assertivists were outwardly oriented while the solitary contemplatives were inwardly directed. This distinction is evident in reactions the two traditions provided to the collapse of the mid-Victorian ethos of confident optimism and faith.

After midcentury, the mounting effects of industrialization, Darwinian biological theory, the "higher criticism" of Scriptural texts, and Positivist philosophy combined to undermine reliance on traditional social and cultural values. Solitary contemplative English literature of this period responded by emphasizing the individual's character—one's will, responsibility, and sense of duty—in confronting the silence of the universe. Responding to the new intellectual milieu, Eliot's and Hardy's pessimism about social reality might still be cloaked as "meliorist," but in Joseph Conrad, writing at least a decade later, it is patently evident. For the solitary contemplative authors the issue was the nature of the individual's inner response to the unyielding challenges of existence. On social values, the nineteenth-century solitary contemplatives tended to be conservative, favoring preserving as much of an organic link with the past as was feasible.

The social assertivist response was more diffuse but in general continued the earlier Dickensian penchant for satire in the service of social reform. While a few authors, most notably George Gissing, expressed an embittered acquiescence to the corruption and poverty he so vividly described, and others, like Wilkie Collins, pursued the later Dickens's fascination with the mystery novel, most authors mobilized humor as a tool to unmask the fraudulent and thereby point the way to a brighter future. George Meredith's novels and George Bernard Shaw's plays are the most representative of this technique, although Jerome K. Jerome's "New Humour" movement was also an expression of this approach, albeit in a lighter vein. Their aim was not individual psychological integrity but public and social honesty and justice. Thus if the solitary contemplative writers stressed the individual's nonrational traits, such as character and will, social assertivist authors continued to employ humor in the service of reason to further social progress.

One particular and popular social assertivist approach of the period eschewed the satirical style so as to emphasize a reformist "message." In purposely didactic novels they attempted to enlighten their readers and to inspire them to undertake or support specific "noble" social endeavors. Two of these novels, widely read at the time although now long forgotten, are especially relevant for the study of Israel Zangwill, one because he so well represents the product of its philanthropic purpose, the other because he sought to emulate it.

In 1882 Walter Besant's novel, *All Sorts and Conditions of Men,* was published and became an immediate popular success. Its plot revolves around the lives of two young people, Angela Marsden Messenger and Harry Goslet, both from wealthy backgrounds although strangers to each other, who, for personal reasons, decide to live and work incognito in the East End for a time. There they meet and soon come to share a common bond of concern for the plight of the people of Whitechapel and Stepney Green.

Besant never explicitly says who these people are—no Jews are visible in the novel—but the nature of their "plight" is made abundantly clear:

> Mile upon mile of streets with houses—small, mean, and monotonous houses . . . the people living the same mean and monotonous lives, all after the same model. . . .
>
> . . . It [Whitechapel Road] was thought to be a place of reputation; it has of late years become orderly; its present condition is dull and law-abiding. . . . All day long and all year round there is a constant Fair going on in Whitechapel Road. . . . It saddens one still more to watch the current of human life in this great thoroughfare and feel that, as it is now, so it was a generation ago, and so it will be a generation hence.[3]

The problem, then, is that the people of the East End work too hard, are satisfied with their lives, and lack "culture": "They have no institutions of their own to speak of, no public buildings of any importance, no municipality, no gentry, no carriages, no soldiers, no picture-galleries, no theatres, no opera—they have nothing."[4]

Angela, the rich brewer's daughter disguised as a poor dressmaker, feels a burning responsibility to change all this: "It is, perhaps, a survival of feudal customs that in English minds a kind of proprietorship is assumed over one's dependents, those who labour for a man and are paid by him."[5]

Driven by this philanthropic impulse, Angela enlists Harry in promoting her solution to this "disastrous" state of affairs: a "Palace of Delight," which would provide the necessary facilities "so that poets and novelists should arise and the East End, hitherto a barren desert, should blossom with flowers."[6] The Palace's purpose was to sow discontent among the East Enders, to shake them out of their dull and perfectly contented lives. Angela's Palace would be a center

> for all who chose to accept it, a general and standing invitation to accept happiness and create new forms of delight; she would give them a craving for things of which as yet they knew nothing; she would place within their reach . . . absolutely free for all, the same enjoyments as are purchased by the rich. . . . They should cultivate a noble discontent; they should gradually learn to be critical; they should import into their own homes the spirit of discontent . . . , to cultivate the sense of pleasure is to civilise.[7]

Angela and Harry succeed in creating their Palace, discover each other's true identity, and marry happily. And, in fact, the East End's People's Palace was built as a direct result of Besant's novel.[8]

Although Zangwill always holds Besant's philanthropists in the greatest contempt, he demonstrates perfectly in his life the ethos they sought to instill at the "Palace of Delights." Besides borrowing the plot of the rich girl incognito among the poor for many of his plays, Zangwill continually emphasizes in his Jewish books a great discontent and restlessness with the constraints of the Jewish milieu and a powerful need to travel beyond them into the rich and delightful royal gardens of Western culture. Even when more and more these gardens appeared to him mirages, they were ones from which he desired no escape. If Angela Messenger ever had a faithful disciple it was surely Israel Zangwill.

In Besant's novel there is passing criticism of the attitude of the Salvation Army to the problems of society. The entire issue of the meaning of religion in the modern world, and its social role, was the subject of another assertivist "message" novel, Mrs. Humphrey Ward's *Robert Elsmere,* which appeared in 1888 and won immediate international acclaim. The book relates the story of the life and death of a young provincial Anglican clergyman, Robert Elsmere, who loses faith in traditional religion as a result of exposure to the advances achieved in science and in textual Scriptural criticism.

Although unable to convince completely his own wife, Catherine, Elsmere sets out for London to establish religion anew upon an enlightened basis among "the upper working class" there; his "New Brotherhood" is founded to combat both the superstitions of the old faith and the blasphemous atheism of "the Workingmen's Club." Of this endeavor, Mrs. Ward comments ecstatically: "*A new religion*! Of all words, the most tremendous!"[9]

Elsmere's "new religion" was not "Comtean" but a historical positivist faith:

> God is in everything . . . ; lean to seek God, not in any single event of past history, *but in your own soul*,—in the constant verifications of experience, in the life of Christian love. . . .
>
> . . . [He believes] in an Eternal Goodness—and an Eternal Mind—of which Nature and Man are the continuous and only revelation . . . , in the unbroken sequences of nature, in the physical, intellectual, moral—there lies the revelation of God. There is no other, my friends.[10]

Nor was Elsmere's "new religion" a break with Christianity, according to Mrs. Ward. Rather, it was to be a restoration of the true Christianity of its founder: "Jesus only superseded Judaism by absorbing and recruiting all that was best in it. . . . To reconceive the Christ!" To free the real message of Jesus from the distortions of time was the true task of the New Brotherhood.[11] Thus the very name of the new group was chosen to "show that for the members of it life rests still, as all life worth having has everywhere rested, on *trust* and *memory*!—trust in the God of experience and history; memory of that God's work in man, by which alone we know Him and can approach Him."[12]

So dedicated was Elsmere to his mission that he eventually dies from his self-sacrificing and unceasing efforts. His devoted wife, although still not completely convinced of the new creed's validity, assumes leadership of the New Brotherhood, and Mrs. Ward concludes her novel with the optimistic assurance, "The New Brotherhood still exists, and grows."[13]

Robert Elsmere and its theme were to haunt Israel Zangwill's thought and career. Not only in his censored 1912 play, *The Next Religion*, but throughout his novels and essays he explored the form and role of religion under modern circumstances. As we will see, Zangwill, like Elsmere, was convinced of the necessity that religion, including Judaism, be reformulated on a historical positivist basis; and like Elsmere also, he was obsessed by the need to restore the original Jewishly inspired message of the founder of Christianity as the foundation for this latest stage in religion's evolution. And like Mrs. Ward, Zangwill was willing to accept even a Catherine Elsmere's tentative conviction as a hopeful pointer to a more enlightened future. But perhaps most significantly, it was to write a "Jewish *Robert Elsmere*" that Zangwill was commissioned by the Jewish Publication Society of America to write his *Children of the Ghetto.*[14]

In this, his first "Jewish" novel, Zangwill sought not only to explore the future of Judaism but also consciously to combat the negative stereotypical image of the Jew in English literature. Until the final decades of the eighteenth century, the Jewish stereotype was uniformly negative. The Judas-inspired medieval red-haired satanic stage-Jew with his comical speech defects became secularized in the Elizabethan era, but, as with Shylock, the transcendent and demonic qualities were retained. As Jews came actually to reside again in England, and authors became familiar with them, the image acquired a more human quality, although still allotting the Jew only negative roles.[15]

However, in his writings from 1785 onward, playwright and essayist Richard Cumberland set about to protest against the negative stage-Jew stereotype and to portray Jews in positive roles instead.[16] By the beginning of the nineteenth century, positive treatment of the Jews became more possible among English authors, although, like Cumberland in his play, *The Jew,* the positive image was based upon his conformity to Christian values and to Enlightenment notions of a common humanity, not on toleration of the Jew as specifically Jewish.[17]

During the course of the nineteenth century, positive and negative stereotypes of the Jew contended. When an author intended a humanitarian message, the Jew was often cast heroically; when it was not the Jew's status but some other value being advocated, the Jew continued to be employed as the traditional symbol for an evil to be opposed.[18] However, while these two literary images may have contended on equal terms, dominating all others was the symbol, not of Walter Scott's Rebecca, but Charles Dickens's satanic Fagin, whom Oliver Twist first encounters beside a blazing fireplace "with a toasting-fork in his hand . . . a very old shrivelled Jew, whose villainous-looking and repulsive face was obscured by a quantity of matted red hair."[19] The image of the brutish but all too human Sykes pales into insignificance before this magnificently malevolent archetypical portrait of the Jew Fagin.

George Eliot's 1876 novel, *Daniel Deronda,* marks a truly significant departure from the Victorian pattern and a response to Dickens's manipulation of traditional stereotypes. Unlike previous philo-Semitic authors, Eliot, the solitary contemplative, portrays the Jew as Jew, as a person possessing a legitimate alternative culture to that of Christian Western Europe, with its own traditions, conflicts, and aspirations, all of which she attempts to portray sympathetically.[20]

In a key chapter, "Revelations," Eliot presents this clash of Jewish aspirations in a conversation among "The Philosophers Club" members at the *Hand and Banner* pub. There is Pash, the skeptic, Gideon, the Spinozan rationalist and assimilationist, and Mordecai, the mystic preacher of a new Jewish nationalism. The latter argues:

> the soul of Judaism is not dead. Revive the organic centre: let the unity of Israel which has made the growth and form of its religion be an outward reality. Looking towards a land and a polity, our dispersed people in all the ends of the earth may share the dignity of a national life which has a voice among the peoples of the East and the West—which will plant the wisdom and skill of our race so that it may be, as of old, a medium of transmission and understanding.[21]

Mordecai argues against superstition, disbelief, enlightened abstract reason, and assimilation. He preaches a mystical message of spiritual renaissance through national revival as the means of restoring the priestly mission of the Jews among the Gentiles and as a mechanism for Jewish self-protection and normalization.

Clearly, however, Mordecai does not envision an ingathering of all the Jewish people but rather an "organic centre, a heart and brain to watch and guide and execute; the outraged Jew shall have a defence in the court of nations, as the outraged Englishman or American."[22] Even after the founding of this national center, the Jews will remain "a nationality whose members may still stretch to the end of the earth . . . , but who still have a national hearth and a tribunal of national opinion."[23] For Mordecai the restoration of Jewish nationality signified spiritual and political health, not the elimination of the Diaspora.

In so formulating Mordecai's views, Eliot correctly perceived the parameters of Western Jewry's conception of a revived Jewish nationalism, a view diametrically opposed to the aspiration of East European Zionists.[24] And as with so many British Jews, Zangwill would identify with this message and believe himself to be the inspired Daniel Deronda chosen to realize Mordecai's dream in its most urgent formulation.

To comprehend the Jews and their aspirations properly, George

Eliot thoroughly immersed herself in the philosophic, historic, and esoteric writings of Judaism.[25] Drawing upon these established sources, her book provided an impetus for a new path in Jewish thought and also pointed to a new and controversial direction for non-Jewish perceptions of the Jews in their midst.

Among the sources that influenced the composition of *Daniel Deronda* was the short story "Die Kinder des Randar" by the Western "ghetto" author Leopold Kompert.[26] This tale provides the literary prototype for Mordecai and his message, Eliot transmuting Kompert's despairing tone into one of inspired hope. And as a result of Eliot's novel, the public's curiosity about Jewish life was aroused, and many readers turned to Kompert and his fellow "ghetto" writers for enlightenment.

Western Ghetto Stories

A result of the Western Emancipation of Jewry in the nineteenth century was the emergence of a new literary genre, Jewish fiction in the style and language of the prevailing non-Jewish society. This phenomenon was particularly strong in German-speaking lands, where several authors published stories describing Jewish life and values.

Although composed from differing perspectives, the great majority of these Western "ghetto" stories were motivated by a concern over the apparently incomplete success of the Emancipation. These authors were all keenly aware that, despite the confident predictions of Enlightenment philosophy, and despite their thorough acculturation and assimilation, some sort of a barrier, a social alienation, still separated the Jews from their non-Jewish countrymen.[27]

Remaining firm adherents of liberal philosophy, each of these men sought in his stories to provide an explanation for this unforeseen social alienation. And as reflections on how each of these authors explained the cause of this disquieting experience, their stories were intended as remedies to breach the barrier. For some, the source of error lay in a lingering ignorance, in anachronistic anti-Jewish stereotypes inherited from the "Dark Ages"; in this view, these erroneous notions could most effectively be combated educationally, through the presentation of accurate, sympathetic portraits of the Jews, both before and after Emancipation. For others, the fault lay with those groups of Jews who stubbornly still clung to the ignorance of their own unemancipated, unenlightened past, refusing to acculturate and assimilate modernity. Authors advancing this latter view, therefore, also sought the remedy in education, exposing in their stories just how it was the Jews' own archaic superstitions that inflicted the most painful injuries upon them. And for a very few the difficulty lay in both communities, each loyal to a premodern, illiberal notion of ethnicity. These authors tentatively suggested that the full realization of a liberal social order and the elimination of social alienation among peoples might necessitate a significant modification in the application of the cosmopolitan universalism of liberal philosophy; they cautiously began hinting that social equality might require just the reverse advocated in the earlier view, that is, ethnic separation, the establishment by each ethnic group of its own political entity.

Although the authors of the Western "ghetto" stories differed widely in their analyses of the post-Emancipation experiences of the Jews, all remained firmly committed to the fundamental philosophy of the Enlightenment; all were conscious that the emancipated, acculturated Jews were experiencing a disagreeable social alienation that separated them from their non-Jewish neighbors, and all agreed that the conversion to liberalism, whether by non-Jews, Jews, or both, remained incomplete. But all were also optimistically convinced that the difficulty was not intractable and that, upon proper analysis, a remedy for it would be discovered and implemented.

Typical of the new genre were Aaron Bernstein, whose novels *Vögele der Maggid* and *Mendel Gibbor* portrayed a Polish ghetto life before it was exposed to the disruptive forces of the Enlightenment; Solomon Kohn, whose *Prager Ghettobilder* and *Neue Ghettobilder* did the same for the Prague ghetto; and Nathan Samuely, whose *Kulturbilder* and *Zwischen Licht und Schatten* described the effects of the clash of ideas and generations among the people of Galician villages as the spirit of the new age challenged the traditions of the old.[28] But only two of the authors of these Western "ghetto" stories achieved widespread international audiences, Leopold Kompert and Karl Emil Franzos.

Leopold Kompert (1822–1886) was a prolific German-Jewish author, writing both Jewish and non-Jewish fiction. However, his international reputation rested on two collections of "ghetto" stories, *Aus dem Ghetto* (1848) and *Geschichten einer Gasse* (1865), both widely translated into a variety of Western European languages, the first appearing in English as *Scenes from the Ghetto: Studies of Jewish Life* (1882), and the second as *Christian & Leah & Other Ghetto Stories* (1895). Kompert's stories in these collections reflect a sentimental and tender depiction of the ghetto and its inhabitants, their affirmation of the joy of living despite the poverty and hostility of a brutish environment. He wrote for the assimilated Western children of the ghetto, recalling them to the values of their heritage.

Scenes from the Ghetto is a collection of four short stories.[29] "Schlemiel" is a humorous tale of a fellow who is luckless at everything, even at his own funeral. "Old Babele" relates the story of Hendel, an old grandmother ruined in her youth by her flirtations with a non-Jew and doomed to be the laughingstock of her children and grandchildren. "Without Authorization" tells the story of Jaekev Lederer and Rasel, who marry without official Austrian sanction, and of Jaekev's maneuvers afterward to obtain the necessary permission. The fourth story, actually a novella, "The Randar's Children," provided George Eliot with material for *Daniel Deronda* and well illustrates Kompert's attitudes.[30]

Rebb Schmul, a Jewish tavernkeeper in a non-Jewish village, is a happy, generous man, the father of two children, Moschele and Hannele. Moschele early falls under the spell of the noble and pious *schnorrer* (beggar) Mendel Wilna, who enthusiastically preaches the restoration of Jerusalem and directs him to learn Western ways so as to assist him in his mission to revive the holy city. But Mendel Wilna refuses to allow the boy to accompany him on his pilgrimage to Jerusalem. Instead, at his mother's insistence, Moschele joins the village drunk's son, Honza, in attending a Christian school in town.

Moschele, now called Moritz, faces bitter anti-Jewish discrimination at school while also witnessing the conflict between traditionalists and modernizers in the town ghetto. Although at first put off by the poverty of the ghetto, he comes slowly to appreciate its beauty and joy. At the same time, under the influence of Honza, now an anti-German Czech nationalist, he recalls Mendel Wilna's vision: "He saw in the matter [i.e., nationalism] a struggle wherein was concerned wealth, liberty, and independence; here his own personal feelings were concerned; Jerusalem and Bohemia. Did not the same gigantic spectre envelop these two gigantic corpses in the silence of the tomb?"[31]

Yet in the end Moritz decides that Mendel Wilna is a madman and his project ridiculous, founded as it was on mystical inspiration. What is needed for national revival, the youth decides, is a Jewish land built by Jewish agriculturalists: "Natural history and botany should be taught first of all in Jewish schools," not Talmud.[32] Still, despite his theorizing, Moritz finally chooses medicine to prepare for a practical career in Austria.

In the meantime, Rebb Schmul's other child, Hannele, abandoned to her own devices and left completely uneducated, is beguiled by Honza, with whom she runs off, an apostate. Her brother realizes "that it was precisely through ignorance that the girl had taken such a step."[33] Eventually he and Mendel Wilna join forces to persuade Hannele to return home repentant. At the conclusion of the story, Moritz has become a physician in a quiet Bohemian ghetto, and his sister, a lonely spinster. Mendel Wilna observes, "After all I have seen and heard it seems to me more than ever that Jerusalem ought to be built."[34] And this goal George Eliot's Daniel, unlike Moritz, set out to accomplish.

It is instructive to note that Kompert, writing in 1848, a year of revolutionary nationalist fervor, attributes, in part, Jewish aspirations to non-Jewish sources, a connection also made by Eliot.[35] But Kompert's story is generally an affirmation of the rationalist content of Jewish culture, a clarion call for education of the youth in it, and an acknowledgment of the nonrational heritage of the culture as well. As in all his stories, Kompert is here a defender of the Jew as Jew.

The title story in Kompert's other collection available in English is "Christian and Leah, A Ghetto Idyll," also really a novella.[36] Its central character, Sarah Unger, the ghetto synagogue attendant's wife, raises two children, her own daughter, Leah, and a non-Jewish orphan, Christian. She teaches them mutual toleration; each is educated according to his or her own heritage. But, several years later, when she discovers that the boy has fallen in love with her daughter, Sarah sends him away, explaining that it is necessary to avoid confirming the Jewish community's opinion that toleration breeds assimilation. The boy reluctantly obeys, and Christian and Leah are brokenhearted. Eventually, in their old age, the two do come to live together in mutual respect for each other's tradition.

Somewhat incongruously, Kompert's alter ego in the story comments in conclusion:

> At long and rare intervals this earth has produced a living example of a one-souled love. . . . In the heart of this poor woman there throbs *that* love, which will one day restore to the world its long lost universal peace and concord. For how can the wolf lie down with the lamb, and

> the viper sleep beside the innocent dove, if God provide not the world with more such women as Sarah Unger?[37]

In this story, written almost two decades after "The Randar's Children," Kompert still defends Jewish distinctiveness and values and continues to display a great distrust of the non-Jew. For Kompert, if the ghetto Jew represents the kernel of truth in the husks of superstition, the non-Jew is still the hostile brute stupefied by drink. Yet he argues that Jews must dispel the grip of superstition and accept the risks of emancipation, that through a loving toleration rooted in Jewish authenticity the Christian can also be taught toleration.

Throughout his Jewish stories Kompert remains the sentimental defender of the ghetto, seeking to reawaken his people's vitality while preserving their precious and, to him, superior heritage. Typical of his day, he was essentially a "reformer of the ghetto."

It is quite a different image of the ghetto that Karl Emil Franzos (1848–1904) conveys in his stories. Born a generation after Kompert and writing for the Western non-Jewish public, Franzos established his reputation as a "ghetto" author in 1878 with a work revealingly entitled *Aus Halb-Asien* (i.e., "Out of Semi-Asia," which, however, the 1882 non-Jewish English translator chose to replace with the more neutral title *The Jews of Barnow*). His hostility to the ghetto is explicitly expressed in the work's preface: "I have described this strange and outlandish mode of existence precisely as it appeared to me."[38] His only defense of the Podolian ghetto is that every country has the Jews it deserves and that therefore it is not the Jews' fault if Podolia (i.e., the western Ukraine) has "less civilised" Jews than England, France, and Germany.[39]

This collection of eight stories, intended as fictionalized anthropological observations, describes the ignorance and superstition Franzos believed characterized the ghetto, its petty-mindedness and materialism and its hostility to the most elementary benefits of enlightened science and education. Typical is the story "The Child of Atonement."[40]

A cholera epidemic has spread across Central Europe in 1831, and, as a consequence, among the Jews of the Podolian ghetto of Barnow a secret court has been established by "fanatics" to try suspected offenders against Jewish law. But the plague only intensifies. The people then feel the need for a "mediator" and choose the "wonder-working rabbi of Sadagora," already described by Franzos in a previous story as "the most jealous opponent of light, the most fanatical supporter of the old dark faith."[41] The rabbi decrees penitential fasting and self-mortification, which, by weakening the people's health still further, only increases the mortality rate.

Now, with his prestige at stake, the Sadagora rabbi decrees a new remedy: a couple must be chosen to be married in the communal burial ground, "as a sacrifice to the angry God," and so Nathan Goldstein, the grave digger, and Miriam Roth, a friendless orphan, are compelled to wed in the cemetery. Their first two children and Nathan die in quick succession. The son of the Sadagora rabbi, who now reigns in his father's stead, describes these deaths as "sin-offerings" and foretells of Miriam's third child: "it also will only live to be a sin-offering."[42]

The child, Lea, does fall ill, but Miriam defies the rabbi and insists that Lea will survive. But as the child approaches death, Miriam is persuaded by her neighbors to set off for Sadagora to beg a blessing from the rabbi, abandoning the child in her sickbed. However, before arriving at Sadagora, the frantic mother hurriedly returns home to nurse her daughter to recovery, employing "proper medical practice." Concludes Franzos about these "semi-Asians" of the ghetto: "The conviction that a mother's love is strong enough to conquer ill-will, and bring healing and salvation, would not have made them [the Barnow Jews] cease their rancour towards the widow and child; but this, in their eyes, was a visible miracle wrought by God, and such a miracle was of course more powerful than even a decree of the wonder-working rabbi."[43]

Franzos's most thorough treatment of Jewish-Christian relations occurs in his 1890 novel, *Judith Trachtenberg*.[44] The book's protagonist, Judith, an assimilated Jewish girl, is beguiled by Count Agenor Baranowski, who is nonetheless aware that she, a Jewess, could never be his wife. Echoing Arthur Donnithorne's dilemma in *Adam Bede*, the count, unable either to give up Judith or to marry her, decides to make her his mistress. The girl consents to the arrangement, ignorantly expecting eventually to convert and marry him, although aware that such actions would inflict great emotional suffering upon her family. In fact, when learning that his daughter has run off, Judith's father dies of a stroke, an outcome about which the unsympathetic Franzos observes, "The fanaticism of the old man is really to blame" for his death.[45]

As Count Baranowski cannot "disgrace" *his* family by actually marrying a Jewess, he decides to perpetrate a subterfuge on his mistress:

a fake priest "baptizes" Judith and "marries" the couple. Soon afterward Judith bears a child and wonders when he will be christened, although the count knows the baby is really Jewish and illegitimate. Judith eventually discovers her false position and flees.

Although recognizing that she has had no particular attachment to Judaism and was not at all averse to conversion, she nonetheless now excoriates post-Emancipation Christianity's hypocritical guise of tolerance:

> It is a creed of love, of humanity. It ordains that doors should be open to the pretty, wealthy Jewess, especially if the owner of the doors is in debt to her father. . . . But her father and brother do not count as men with them: they are only Jews—of whom the men are born to make money which Christians may borrow, and women cater to your enjoyment by their beauty.[46]

The count repents his mistreatment of his beloved and, having located her, offers to marry her legally once she converts truly. But now Judith refuses on her honor to abandon Judaism, and the couple are finally married in Weimar in a civil ceremony, a mixed marriage condemned by both Jewish and Christian communities. Judith, who has been told that she "must see that God has chosen her to demonstrate his will to poor, blind humanity, and this knowledge is a thread that will not be easily severed," cannot bear this burden.[47] She commits suicide: "She died that she might not make him [the count] miserable or herself more so. She died because, after all she had undergone, she had neither strength nor courage to live."[48] As an epitaph for Judith and the novel, Franzos writes, "She died in darkness, but the day will dawn."[49]

Franzos, like Kompert, is an advocate of toleration as the key to relations between Christians and Jews. But whereas Kompert had advocated it as a means to preserve the valuable assets of Jewish distinctiveness, Franzos, a "despiser of the ghetto," views toleration as a means of exorcising "fanaticism" from both communities and of creating a new range of mutual interactions. That Judith does not ultimately convert is not the result of any particular commitment to Judaism but rather an affirmation of her human dignity regardless of creed.[50] Franzos is Eliot's Gideon as Kompert is her Mordecai!

These "ghetto" stories were attempting to describe experience and exhort their readers as did the British didactic writers: they were hearers of a message. And whatever deep differences of perception they may have had, they shared as their overriding preoccupation the question of the future of the Jewish people in post-Emancipation Europe. Kompert and Franzos, although both advocates of Enlightenment and Emancipation, were deeply divided, a generation apart, on what this future should be: national continuity or cultural assimilation. Their clashing literary responses presage the violent identity crisis that would shake the whole people within another decade.

In Britain these Western "ghetto" authors were popular not for their messages but because of their descriptions of the "exotic." On the other hand, Anglo-Jewish authors of the period focused on other interests than the future of the people of the ghetto.

Anglo-Jewish Literature

Before Israel Zangwill began writing, Anglo-Jewry had already produced several productive literary figures.[51] Although like the authors of the Western "ghetto" stories they also experienced an irreducible distance, a social alienation, from their British neighbors, it was much less intrusive than that troubling their continental counterparts. However, particularly during the final quarter of the nineteenth century, a different sort of experience increasingly distressed Anglo-Jewish authors.

There arose an inchoate sensation that a portion of their very own self had somehow been irrevocably amputated. As they began to reflect on this troubling impression, as they became aware of this psychological alienation, Anglo-Jewish authors came to equate that lost portion of themselves with whatever it was that they identified as their "Jewishness." But having struggled so hard to divest themselves of their Jewish distinctive heritage and traditions in order to become like everyone else, like all other Englishmen, they now discovered that they had ceased to be like everyone else; for while everyone else defined themselves in relation to their past, the Anglo-Jewish authors had sacrificed their own past without being able to acquire another's. And consciousness of these chasms—from themselves, from their own past, and from their non-Jewish neighbors—intensified the Anglo-Jewish authors' awareness of being "Jewish" but without any comprehension of what that label entailed, for they had allowed themselves to float adrift of its perspective and heritage. For these authors, to know who one was had now become transformed into an anguishing conundrum from which neither escape nor relief could be discovered. And each person had to face it alone, for it was himself.

Spanning the Victorian period as this sense of psychological alienation began to stir were three significant precursors of Israel Zangwill struggling to learn who they were: Benjamin Disraeli (1804–1881), Benjamin Farjeon (1838–1903), and, most significantly for Zangwill, Amy Levy (1861–1889).

Benjamin Disraeli

Benjamin Disraeli, converted at age twelve to Christianity by his impetuous and erudite father, had no genuine connection with traditional Jewish culture nor with any sort of ghetto.[52] As novelist and politician his constituency was Christian. Yet he had a genuine fascination with his Jewish heritage, conceiving it not as religious or cultural but as genetic, as "the Hebrew race," biologically distinct, and even superior, to all others. As early as his twenty-sixth year, he made a tour of the Middle East and utilized his experiences there to color his fiction.[53]

Disraeli's earliest "Jewish" fiction was his 1833 novel, *Alroy*. Set in the twelfth century, its hero, David Alroy, sets out to restore his people, the Jews, to their rightful position among the races of mankind. In this endeavor, Alroy is advised by his teacher, a master of the mysteries of the esoteric teachings of Kabbalah, Jabaster, who inspires this man of action with the wisdom of the great principles of the past and channels his zeal into a messianic program of national redemption. Although briefly successful in his mission, Alroy betrays Jabaster's teachings by marrying the bewitching Schirene, for whom he compromises all that he had been. But in the end, Alroy returns to Jabaster's great principles and suffers a martyr's death for them.[54]

Jabaster, the mystically wise adviser, reappears in a new guise as Sidonia in the first of Disraeli's "Young England" trilogy, *Coningsby* (1844). Like the author himself, Sidonia is of Sephardi origin, tracing his ancestry to Spanish Marranos, and is now an influential international financier. Sidonia is described as an adherent of "the code of the great Legislator," as "proud of his origin, and confident of the future of his kind," and as "a great philosopher."[55]

Like Jabaster, Sidonia voices Disraeli's rejection of Liberalism's reliance on abstract rationalism: "Man is only truly great when he acts from the passions; never irresistible but when he appeals to the imagination."[56] Equally, Sidonia is a defender of Jewish ethnic pride: "You never observe a great intellectual movement in Europe in which Jews do not greatly participate."[57] Sidonia lists his proofs but then comments, "Favoured by Nature we still remain; but in exact proportion as we have been favoured by Nature we have been persecuted by Man."[58] Still, the "Hebrew genius" prevails: "But the passionate and creative genius, that is the nearest link to Divinity, and which no human tyranny can destroy . . . has found a medium for its expression, to which, inspite of your prejudices and your evil passions, you have been obliged to bow."[59]

Not through his fictional alter ego, Sidonia, but employing the authorial voice it is Disraeli himself who most eloquently eulogizes the Jews and sets the pattern for Anglo-Jewry's blurred self-image that would find powerful echoes in Zangwill's writings. In his 1849 preface to the fifth edition of *Coningsby,* Disraeli writes:

> it became necessary to ascend to the origin of the Christian Church, and to meet in a spirit worthy of a critical and comparatively enlightened age, the position of the descendants of that race who were the founders of Christianity. . . . The Jews were looked upon in the middle ages as an accursed race, the enemies of God and man, the especial foes of Christianity. No one in those days paused to reflect that Christianity was founded by Jews, that its divine Author, in his human capacity, was a descendant of King David; that his doctrines were the completion, not the change of Judaism. . . .
>
> The European nations . . . were only recently converted to a belief in Moses and in Christ; and, as it were, still ashamed of the wild deities whom they deserted, they thought they atoned for their past idolatry by wreaking vengeance on a race to whom, and to whom alone, they were indebted for the Gospel they adore.[60]

The Jews' ultimate justification, then, is that they are not only major contributors to Western civilization but also the originators and inspirers of Christianity, which is the true extension of Judaism among the non-Hebrew "races." What separates Jews from Christians, according to this view, is not creed so much as it is genetic heritage.

Sidonia reappears in the third novel of the "Young England" trilogy, *Tancred* (1847). Again he is the wise counselor, in this instance to a nineteenth-century English Alroy, a pilgrim knight to the holy land.

Here Sidonia espouses Disraeli's identification of the missions of Moses and Jesus:

> I believe that God spoke to Moses on Mount Horeb, and you [Trancred] believe that he was crucified, in the person of Jesus, on Mount Calvary. Both were, at least carnally, children of Israel: they spoke Hebrew to the Hebrews. The prophets were only Hebrews; the apostles were only Hebrews. The churches of Asia . . . were founded by a native Hebrew, and the church of Rome . . . which converted this island [Britain] to the faith of Moses and of Christ . . . was founded also by a native Hebrew.[61]

But *Tancred* also very briefly points in another direction. In an aside, the narrator describes the joyful celebration of the traditional autumn harvest festival of Sukkot in London's East End:

> Conceive a being born and bred . . . in the purlieus of our Houndsditch or Minories, born to hereditary insult, without education, apparently without a circumstance that can develop the slightest taste, or cherish the least sentiment for the beautiful amid fogs and filth, never treated with kindness, seldom with justice, occupied with the meanest, if not the vilest toil . . . ; conceive such a being, an object to you of prejudice, dislike, disgust, perhaps hatred. The season arrives, and the mind and heart of that being are filled with images and passions that have ranked in all ages among the most beautiful and the most genial of human experience. . . .
>
> He rises in the morning, goes early to some Whitechapel market, purchases some willow boughs . . . , clears out the yard of his miserable tenement, builds his bower, decks it . . . with the finest flowers and fruits that he can procure, the myrtle and the citron never forgotten, and hangs its roof with variegated lamps. After the service of his synagogue, he sups late with his wife and his children in the open air, as if he were in the pleasant villages of Galilee, beneath its sweet and starry sky.[62]

This is the Jew as Jew! And despite George Eliot's distaste for Disraeli's fiction and Zangwill's fascination with his Judaeo-Christianity, both accept in their own writing the task, hinted at here, of making British Jews sympathetically accessible on their own terms to their fellow Britons.[63] But it was the Jewish-born Christian author's coalescence of two distinctive heritages that many found most attractive in his image of the Jews. This was certainly the case for the most prolific Anglo-Jewish author of the nineteenth century.

Benjamin Farjeon

Once entering upon his literary career in London, Benjamin Leopold Farjeon's biography bears a striking similarity to Zangwill's. But even before this point, the two men, despite quite disparate circumstances, shared many common inclinations and experiences.

Farjeon was born into an observant Sephardi family in Whitechapel in 1838 and received there a rudimentary Jewish education. Even as a boy he was greatly attracted to journalism and secured a position on the *Non-Conformist* as "printer's devil" when he was but thirteen. Three years later, father and son quarreled bitterly because Benjamin had chosen to abandon Jewish religious observances. Cut off from his family and, at the same time, bitten by the elusive gold bug, in 1854 Farjeon migrated to Australia. Unsuccessful at prospecting, he moved to Dunedin, New Zealand, in 1861, where he returned to his first love, becoming a journalist for the *Otago Daily Times*.

While in Dunedin, Farjeon completed his first work of fiction, *Shadows on the Snow*, which he dedicated to his favorite author, Charles Dickens. In a brief letter in May 1866, Dickens acknowledged his appreciation. Encouraged by this note, Farjeon abandoned his career in New Zealand, rushing back to London to carry on the Dickensian literary heritage. There, in 1877, he married the non-Jewish daughter of a leading American actor of the day, Joe Jefferson, whom he had first met in New Zealand.

For several years Farjeon's stories were extremely popular, and he reveled in prosperity. But by the beginning of the twentieth century, his popularity had declined precipitously, and he had become physically ill. As his reputation, finances, and health all deteriorated, Farjeon began showing signs of mental unbalance, displaying "more and more unreasonable irritability . . . ; he was tormented, and could control less and less the electric outbursts."[64] Mentally and physically exhausted, he died in July 1903, leaving his family in financial and emotional disarray.

Although most of Farjeon's works reflect the influence of Dickens's Christmas stories and Wilkie Collins's mysteries, he did write on Jewish subjects as well. However, most of these, like *Aaron the Jew* (1894) and *Miriam Rozella* (1897), are weak and unsuccessful novels written in his declining years, inspired by a vain attempt to capitalize on the recent successes of Israel Zangwill as an Anglo-Jewish author. But Farjeon had already written one "Jewish" novel, in the 1870s, while he was at the summit of his literary career.

Solomon Isaacs: A Christmas Story reflects the influence of Dickens's last complete novel, *Our Mutual Friend.*[65] Set in Spitalfields in 1877–78, it relates the story of the rise and fall of the "old-clo' man," the mildly pious Solomon Isaacs, corrupted by sudden wealth and saved eventually by a collapse into poverty. In relating Isaacs's rise, Farjeon draws an ugly portrait of the West End nouveau riche Jews with their pretensions, vulgarity, and thoughtless squandering of money.[66]

As a poor man, Solomon Isaacs had eagerly favored the marriage of his son, Leon, to Rachel Levy, the daughter of a close and equally poor friend. But as the parvenu "Sloman Izard" he no longer considers the poor Rachel worthy of his son. Both Rachel and Leon are sorely tried by Isaacs's arguments and attempts even at bribery, but they show their moral fiber. Finally, falling again into penury, Isaacs blesses their union.

Intertwined with this plot is an unrelated subplot. One Christmas eve Rachel, out of pity, gives some money to a Christian beggar-woman. The following Christmas a messenger arrives to tell Rachel that the woman is dying, and she rushes off to comfort the doomed stranger, who entrusts her infant to Rachel's care. As the novel concludes, "the moon's rays streamed athwart a beam which stretched from floor to ceiling. The shadow of the solemn Symbol fell upon the figures in the room with Divine meaning; and, bathed in the sacred light of Humanity's Cross, the Christian died and the Jewess wept."[67] Echoing Kompert's view of Sarah Unger, Farjeon comments that his Rachel Levy symbolizes "the universal love and charity which animate the Divine Heart. The most beautiful lesson taught by civilisation is the lesson of Humanity; it stands aloof from creeds and dogmas, and far above them."[68]

But only superficially is this story like Kompert's. For Farjeon, who while not converting did intermarry, had no interest in preserving Jewish distinctiveness. Rather, his appeal is couched in the language of Richard Cumberland's enlightened universalism and Disraeli's coalescing of Jewish and Christian traditions. These attitudes, in addition to Farjeon's Dickensian description of the East End and his hostile portrayal of the nouveau riche West End Jews, signal the future themes of Anglo-Jewish literature, particularly as they crystallized in the works of Israel Zangwill. But the most powerful Anglo-Jewish literary influence upon Zangwill was neither Disraeli nor Farjeon but the tragic life and insightful writing of a talented young woman.

Amy Levy

Amy Levy remains an enigma, her life shrouded in dense mists that obscure this brilliant, tormented soul.[69] Born 10 November 1861 in Clapham, she began her schooling in Brighton. Later, she attended Newnham College, Cambridge. Here she published her first short stories. In June 1880 her "Mrs. Pierrepoint" appeared in *Temple Bar;* it relates the tale of a wealthy widow whose advances are spurned by her former lover, a Whitechapel clergyman whom she had jilted the previous year in her relentless pursuit of worldly wealth. The same year another of her stories appeared in the *Victoria Magazine,* "Euphemia, a Sketch," a story of the child of a mixed marriage, daughter of a Jewish mother and a non-Jewish father. Further short stories followed, most notably, "A Diary of a Plain Girl," in *London Society,* September 1883, and "Socrates in the Strand," in the February 1884 *Cambridge Review.*

But Amy Levy established her literary reputation primarily in poetry. Her "Xanthippe," a defense of the much-maligned wife of Socrates, appeared in the *Dublin University Magazine* when she was only sixteen; she received national attention with her first collection of verse, *Xanthippe and Other Verse,* in 1881. Her second collection, *A Minor Poet,* appeared in 1884. Her poetry displayed her talented defense of women coupled with a brooding pessimism about the nature of human existence, occasionally masked behind romantic flourishes.

This latter mood is quite evident in her novel *Miss Meredith.*[70] It is narrated by Elsie Meredith, who becomes engaged as governess to the family of the Marchessa Brogi in Pisa. There she encounters the family renegade, Andrea, who has broken with the family tradition of indolence to make his own way in life, having become a civil engineer in America. Now returning home on a visit, Andrea becomes enchanted by the young Englishwoman. The governess's sympathetic response encourages him to propose, and Elsie accepts. But the Brogi family, outraged at the "disgrace" of their aristocratic son marrying a poor common governess, pressure the girl to break off the betrothal and leave Pisa, which she agrees to do. Upon learning of this, Andrea's wrath is terrible, and his cowed family beg Elsie to remain.

Explains the family patriarch: "You must forgive us if we are slow to understand the new spirit of radicalism [i.e., love] which, it seems, is the spirit of the times."[71] Andrea and Elsie are then happily reconciled.

In her midtwenties, Amy Levy turned her attention to Jewish themes. In June 1886 her essay "The Jew in Fiction" appeared, a pioneering and trenchant commentary on the subject.[72] She observed: "It is curious, that, while the prominent position of the Jew is recognized as one of the characteristic features of English social life of the present day, so small a place should be allotted him in contemporary fiction."[73] She dismissed *Daniel Deronda* as an untrue portrait of British Jewry and continued:

> There has been no serious attempt at serious treatment of the subject; at grappling in its entirety with the complex problem of Jewish life and Jewish character. The Jew . . . , with his curious mingling of diametrically opposed qualities; his surprising virtues and no less surprising vices, leading his eager, intricate life; living, moving, and having his being both within and without tribal limits; this deeply interesting product of our civilisation has been found worthy of none but the most superficial observation.
>
> It is in the throng of aspirants to fame that must be sought a writer able and willing to do justice to the Jewish question in its social and psychological aspects.[74]

In a second article she pressed the issue further, probing its particulars and sounding a warning:

> True humour . . . has its roots in pathos; there is pathos and to spare, . . . in laughter that comes from the Paris lodging [of Heine] or which surges up to us through the barred gates of the Ghettos. . . . The old words, the old customs, are disappearing, soon to be forgotten by all save students of such matters. There is no shutting our eyes to this fact. The trappings and the suits of our [Jewish] humour must vanish with the rest; but that is not reason why what is essential of it should not remain to us a heritage of the ages too precious to be lightly lost; a defence and a weapon wrought for us long ago.[75]

Here, in 1886, is the sense of urgency, of impending loss and of the need to preserve, the awareness of the struggling twin identities "within and without tribal limits." In these two articles Amy Levy laid out the program and themes Israel Zangwill would attempt to implement six years later in *Children of the Ghetto.*

But in her very controversial 1888 novel, *Reuben Sachs,* Amy Levy herself undertook to explore these insights by means of portraying accurately a portion of Anglo-Jewry.[76] In descriptions that deliberately emphasized the shallowness and sham among West End Jewry, the empty formalism of Anglo-Jewish Orthodoxy, the unprincipled spirit of accommodation of Reform Judaism, and the narcissistic self-interest of the philanthropists, the book relates the tragic fate of the ambitious scion of a wealthy Jewish family.

Reuben Sachs is a rising lawyer, son of a well-off family ensconced in "Philistine splendours." At the wealthy Leunigers' home, he encounters the young and beautiful Judith Quixano. She has been living with the Leuniger family since she was fifteen, the daughter of one of their relations who had fallen on hard times and turned from the commercial world to that of Judaism, "one of the pure spirits of the world." Of Judith's father, the narrator comments: "He was one of this world's failures; and the Jewish people, so eager to crown success in any form, so determined in laying claim to the successful among their number, have scant love for those unfortunates who have dropped behind in the race."[77]

Judith, though intelligent and sensitive, does not share the younger Sachses' and Leunigers' desire to break out of the "tribal limits" of their elders' lives. Consoling himself, one of these young people remarks: "There is one good thing . . . and that is the inevitability—at least as regards us English Jews—of our disintegration; of our absorption by the people of the country. That is the price we are bound to pay for restored freedom and consideration." To which Reuben laments: "should I live to see it borne out, I should be very sorry. It may be a weakness on my part, but I am exceedingly fond of my people."[78]

Here is Israel Zangwill's "melting pot" of twenty years later—and his ambivalence toward it as well. Significantly, in his 1908 play, *The Melting Pot,* Zangwill conveys his message through relating the story of the Quixano family!

Reuben and Judith fall in love, but Reuben is not yet ready to marry, hoping first to satisfy his political ambitions. In the meantime, Judith is courted by the well-to-do Herbert "Bertie" Lee-Harrison, a pseudoconvert to Judaism. Although they both despise him, Judith's impoverished mother implores her to accept his proposal, and the girl wavers:

> Material advantage; things that you could touch and see and talk about, that these were the only things which really mattered, had been the unspoken gospel of her life.
>
> Now and then you allowed yourself the luxury of a fine sentiment in speech, but when it comes to the point, to take the best that you could get yourself was the only course to a person with sense. . . . But she was Joshua Quixano's daughter—was it possible that she cared for none of these things?[79]

Ultimately Judith does choose to compromise herself and accepts the despised Bertie, whose "veneer of Judaism" the Jewish community decides to regard "as the real thing, and the engagement was treated like any other."[80] And so the two are married.

Judith knows her marriage means assimilation to Bertie's world and estrangement from Reuben and from her own people, a heartrending surrender of identity:

> A sudden longing for the old faces, the old ties and associations came over her as she stood there; a strange fit of homesickness, an inrushing sense of exile.
>
> Her people—oh, her people!—to be back once more among them! When all was said, she had been so happy there.[81]

Her loneliness and agony are complete when Judith learns of Reuben's sudden death, their final separation. And comments the narrator: "This is the bitter lesson of existence; that the sacred serves only to teach the full meaning of sacrilege; the beautiful of the hideous; modesty of outrage; joy of sorrow; life of death."[82]

The novel's publication provoked a storm of protest from the Anglo-Jewish public; they complained bitterly of this "betrayal" by their talented, trusted daughter. Yet Amy Levy persisted in her views unrepentant and even took a minor character from *Reuben Sachs* as a figure in her later short story "Cohen of Trinity."[83]

In this story, Levy recounts the career of an ambitious young man from Maida Vale who had won a scholarship to Cambridge. This fellow, Cohen, falls in with a bad crowd there, although he privately holds them in contempt; by contrast, he longs for the friendship of Lord Norwood (who appears briefly in *Reuben Sachs*) and his posh set. Wonders the narrator:

> What connection there could be between these young puritans, aristocrats and scholars, the flower of the University . . . and a man of

> Cohen's way of life, it would be hard to say. In aspiring to their acquaintance I scarcely knew if to accuse the man of an insane vanity or a pathetic hankering after better things. . . .
>
> A desire to stand well in one another's eyes, to make a brave show before one another, is, I have observed, a marked characteristic of the Jewish people.[84]

Cohen's scholastic indolence leads to his dismissal from Cambridge. However, five years later he writes an extremely successful book, which is "half poem, half essay, wholly unclassifiable, with a force, a fire, a vision, a vigour and felicity of phrase that carried you through its most glaring inequalities, its most appalling lapses of taste, the book fairly took the reader by storm."[85]

But the only opinion of his work that mattered to Cohen was Norwood's. And "the book repelled him just as the man . . . had always repelled him."[86] This rejection obliterates for Cohen all his public acclaim. Comments an acquaintance, "I was struck afresh by the man's insatiable demands, which looked at times like a passionate striving after perfection, yet went side by side with the crudest vanity, the most vulgar desire for recognition."[87] Shortly thereafter, still at the height of this success, Cohen dies by his own hand.

It was almost as if the prescient author of this story was writing Zangwill's obituary still almost forty years away!

But she did not live even to comment on Zangwill's career. On 10 September 1889, Amy Levy committed suicide. She was twenty-seven years old.

FOUR

The Young Zangwill

Israel Zangwill was born 21 January 1864. Although it has often been the impression that he was himself the product of the immigrant experiences described in *Children of the Ghetto,* Zangwill was, in fact, British born, represented the generation prior to the immigrant scenes portrayed in the book, and was not reared in a tradition-oriented East End setting. Zangwill was an outsider both to Eastern European Judaism and to the Whitechapel immigrant experience as it developed after the great influx of the 1880s. Even when he did attend school in the East End, his personal situation distinguished him from that of the other children there.[1]

That Zangwill was an outsider to major currents of the immigrant ethos was often obscured even during his lifetime, the fiction of his creative writing being mistaken for the realities of the author's life. Zangwill's artistic fusion of generational sequences of experience for dramatic effect in such works as *Children of the Ghetto* and *The Melting Pot* did nothing to dispel this confusion of the observer with the observed. As will become apparent in the discussion of his mature thought, Zangwill could not dispel the public's misinterpretation of his role, for it was a confusion in which he himself became enmeshed. Fortunately, however, muddle over the historical significance and place of his own biographical experience did not damage the talented observer's ability to describe graphically the world of his fiction. But it did distort severely the philosophic interpretation of these descriptions.

To separate the artistic observer from the observed, to grasp exactly in what manner he was an outsider, and to understand how he did indeed write himself into his fiction, it is essential to examine Zangwill's youth and early literary career.

Israel Zangwill's parents: Moses, in Jerusalem, and Ellen ("Helen"), in London, ca. 1897. *Courtesy, Shirley Zangwill.*

Zangwill's Youth

Israel was the second child and eldest son of Moses and Ellen Zangwill. His father, born evidently in a small Russian Baltic town, is said to have escaped czarist conscription and arrived in Britain in 1848, at the surprising age of twelve.[2] Moses Zangwill was thus not the typical Eastern European immigrant, as the course of his entire life was to demonstrate: he was not driven from Russia by secularized assimilation and ambition but by fear of the vicious persecution and hardship suffered by all Jews in the Russian army.

After arriving in London, Moses evidently resided with a rabbi who conducted religious classes at the Great Synagogue. It was through this Rabbi Shapiro that his boarder, a hopelessly dreamy unacculturated *luftmentsch,* met his future wife, Ellen Hannah Marks. Born in a Polish town, she had arrived in Britain with a cousin, each girl staying with a relative already established in the country. These girls were much more typical of the secular upwardly mobile immigrants who would later pour into the West; to them the world was one constant alluring challenge eagerly to be met head-on and secured for the benefit of themselves, their spouses, and their children.

Although Ellen Marks did not possess a particularly strong commitment to traditional Jewish practices, including even those essential to maintaining the minimal levels of observance in the home, and although Moses Zangwill's mind ceaselessly wandered about among the traditional mysteries of the sacred mists, the couple were married in a ceremony presided over by the Chief Rabbi in the Great Synagogue on 6 February 1861.

They were from the first spiritually and psychologically completely mismatched. Moses, attached to the study and practice of a heritage ignored by society and scorned by his ambitious wife, increasingly withdrew into himself and into his dreaming, becoming isolated from his surroundings and his family, willing to make do with whatever came along. Piety, not prosperity, was his preoccupation. Here, indeed, was Amy Levy's Joshua Quixano in the flesh. And yet he did choose to marry Ellen Marks and she, him!

And her eye was always fixed enviously upon her successful relatives. Her cousin Ellen, with whom she had traveled to England, had married in Plymouth, lived a prosperous life, and her son, Joseph Cowen, a successful merchant, was to become an intimate of Theodore Herzl (who used him as the model for Joe Levy in his novel *Altneuland*) and a founder of the English Zionist Federation.[3] And her cousin Esther Solomons, with whom Ellen Marks had been raised in London, married an equally successful businessman; her son, Dr. David Eder, also a Zionist, became a leading disciple of Freud and married Edith Low, the aunt of Maxim Litvinov's wife Ivy and sister of the pioneering Freudian Barbara Low.[4]

Compared to the Cowens and the Eders, the Zangwills led a tinker's life, moving about England to scratch out a paltry living. After Moses and Ellen married, they settled in Plymouth, where their first child, Leah, and their third, Mark, the future artist, were born. In between them, Israel was born in London. After Mark's birth, the family moved to Bristol, where Louis, the minor novelist "Z. Z.," was born, and Israel began his schooling. Eventually the Zangwills settled in London, where their fifth child, Dinah, was born. There the family would remain, all except for the lonely pious old Moses who abandoned his disappointed, indifferent family to settle in Jerusalem in the early 1890s; there he lived and prayed till his death in 1908, the elderly religious father's support faithfully provided by his famous apostate son.[5]

Yet the Zangwill family in London was not destitute, neither in spiritual nor, particularly, in material circumstances. There is some evidence that a modicum of Jewish observance was maintained, at least by some of the family. For instance, in 1902 the youngest daughter, Dinah, was married in Machzike Hadath Synagogue by Rabbi Werner, and that same year Israel Zangwill invited the Sephardi religious leader Dr. Moses Gaster to visit his mother's home in St. John's Wood, describing it as "a 'Kosher' household."[6] But this was later, long after Moses had left them, despairing of the family's religious indifference, and his son, Israel, had abandoned Jewish practices altogether.

Young Zangwill's break with Jewish tradition is imaginatively portrayed in an incomplete story he wrote as a boy in his school copybook.[7] Entitled "Practical Proverbs by a disillusionised man," it humorously relates the adventures of a boy raised and educated solely by his adage-spouting impractical grandmother. Explains the boy:

> I have called myself a disillusionised man & with good reason. But in my infantile period I received with the greatest enthusiasm the potted essence served by my grandmother. It constituted in fact my intellectual breakfast, lunch, dinner, tea, supper and snacks between meals. I indeed grew *fat*, but I cannot say I thrived upon it. By no means. . . . The old lady to whom I trace all my woes drew up for my use a collection of texts, proverbs, and phrases which I learnt by heart and repeated to her on all possible occasions.[8]

In the course of time, however, "a great idea . . . stole upon my soul": the boy decides to apply these maxims in the course of his everyday life, to see if they are indeed true and also to test what they really do mean in practice. But reality, the boy quickly discovers, does not at all correspond to his grandmother's maxims and leads him into a variety of awkward adventures when he attempts to follow them literally.

The story reflects the young Zangwill's own adolescent rebellion against his father's espousal of traditional Jewish thought; it simply did not reflect reality as the son perceived it. To follow such apparently fanciful teachings would lead one in Britain to embarrassment and public humiliation; only a *schlemiel* (an awkward person) could be so foolish.

Not only does this schoolboy's tale reflect Zangwill's rejection of his father's values, but it also introduces a theme that echoes through many of his mature works: the disillusionment that results when ideals are confounded by reality.[9] Israel Zangwill's dilemma from boyhood onward was that he was never able to escape from the concatenation of his ideals, of an awareness of a reality unyielding to them, and of the haunting sense of disillusionment engendered in the clash of the ideal with the real. The impulse to escape these tensions and the awful need to believe despite them would never abate and would eventually impel him forward into disaster.

Possibly even more significant, however, is the evidence that the Zangwill family, while not nearly as prosperous as Ellen's cousins, was also not suffering the grinding poverty that came later to characterize the immigrant East End. There are two important indications of this relative affluence, despite Zangwill's own willingness to allow the matter to remain obscure.

First, although Israel was indeed born in Whitechapel, after the family's wanderings in the provinces and their return to London their fortunes improved at least sufficiently so that by 1881 their address was not in the East End at all, but the more prosperous neighborhood of South Hackney.[10] This means that at the very time the East European immigrants were beginning to settle in Whitechapel in large numbers, the Zangwills, immigrants of an earlier generation, no longer lived in the district.

A further indication that the Zangwills were not in dire poverty is the fact that the family could afford to send all three sons to the Jews' Free School. True, the school was tuition free and even provided its students with clothing, food, and medical care, but only a family with sufficient income could afford to allow its sons to continue attending past the elementary grades, when the boys would be old enough to add to their impoverished parents' meager incomes. Yet the Zangwills were not so desperate for funds that they were forced to interrupt any of their sons' secondary education.[11] In fact, the very opposite is indicated: that the Zangwills were financially secure enough to provide further opportunities for their children's future and that at least Ellen was eager to do so.

And the Zangwill brothers were no ordinary pupils; they took school honors. When Lord Rothschild, the school's primary sponsor, began awarding a medal commemorating his entry into Parliament to the most outstanding JFS student, Israel was its first winner, in 1877; he won the award the following year too. Mark later also won the medal twice and Louis, once.[12] Both years he won the Rothschild medal, Israel also won the school's Rev. A. L. Green Prize for Hebrew. These awards were presented in an assembly presided over by the leading dignitaries of Anglo-Jewry.[13] These were boys of pride and promise to their school, to their family, and to themselves.

Not surprisingly, the precocious and ambitious Israel, after completing his elementary education at JFS, continued on there as a pupil-teacher. In time, on a school scholarship, he was able to take a degree in 1884 from the University of London, where he again performed with distinction, taking honors in English, French, and Mental and Moral Science.[14]

It was really only at this time, during his adolescent years as he traveled to and taught at the Jews' Free School, that Zangwill began to observe the newly emerging immigrant world of the East End. His exposure continued as he remained a teacher until 1888, when he was twenty-four. Throughout this period he remained a commuter to Whitechapel. And by 1888 he was no longer even living with his own family, but, like Amy Levy's fictional Judith Quixano in the fashionable Leuniger home in Kensington, Israel now resided with his well-to-do relatives, the Eders, in Bloomsbury.[15]

The young Zangwill, then, was the precocious son of an immigrant family dominated by an ambitious, secular-oriented mother who overshadowed the lonely, ineffectual traditionalist father. His was a family securely established in England well before the great immigrant influx of the 1880s and with a solid, if not lofty, income. The youthful Israel's education at the Anglicizing JFS only intensified the secular orientation inculcated in his home and in the South Hackney community where he resided, an outlook further honed at the University of London. And for excelling at expressing these values, the boy won the attention and applause of his mother, his teachers, and Anglo-Jewry's leaders.

And it was only as an outsider that Israel Zangwill knew the immigrants' Whitechapel. As a student at the East End's JFS, he had completed his elementary education before the mass migration had begun and even then was singled out for special distinction. During the era of the great East European Jewish settlement in London, Zangwill knew the immigrants only as a commuter, passing through their community as he taught their children to become Englishmen and, later, as a journalist reporting on their world in a language they did not even command. He was always the observer, the outsider, looking in, gazing in wonder at his father's incomprehensible preoccupations and in fascination at the teeming, raucous streets of the immigrants' London.

These sights and wonders excited the latent literary talents of this ambitious young schoolteacher who had already begun to write successfully. In the end it was his choice of a literary career that forced a bitter rupture to his long-standing association with the Jews' Free School.

Early Literary Endeavors

Israel Zangwill's first published fiction, "Professor Grimmer," appeared in 1881, when he was seventeen.[16] It had won a literary competition, which awarded the author a £5 prize and serial publication of his story, which the editorial judges regarded as "the best and most thoroughly humorous story submitted, and we award the prize . . . to its clever author—for clever the story certainly is. The dialogue is natural and characteristic, the incidents very amusing and also probable . . . ; the leading idea is full of genuine humour, and a pleasant vein of fun permeates the composition from beginning to end."[17] Similar comments would be made about many of his later stories over the next fifteen years.

Zangwill's prize entry tells the tale of Professor Grimmer, an absent-minded, eccentric widower well known for his defense of Charles Darwin. As the story opens, we come upon the good professor placing an advertisement for a lost memento, a cuff link, the idea having been suggested to our impractical academic by his lovely daughter, Rose. The ad for "the missing link" is seen by a retired physician, Dick Stanley, whose son, Tom, is secretly in love with Rose and has actually found the lost cuff link. Dick and Tom decide to play a practical joke on this famous student of evolution by presenting him with another sort of "missing link," one dressed in a gorilla suit. But it all ends happily, with Tom and Rose becoming engaged. Professor Grimmer's pretentiously named maid, Clara Matilda Plumstock, also becomes engaged, unlike the Stanleys' maid, Mary Ann, whose name "proves *her* mother at least was a bloodless and unrebellious person, a philosopher submitting without a murmur to the decrees of FATE."[18]

That so much of the maturer Zangwill is present in this early story is remarkable. Here is his chiding at the hubris of intellectuals, his humor and satiric wit, his command of the short story form and of dialogue as a technique for advancing the narrative, even his fascination with family maids and the maid's name, Mary Ann, that later would be the subject of his most financially successful play. Here, too, is his contempt for those who lack ambition and are doltishly satisfied with their humble lot. Yet this is also a story that any bright and talented English-born lad might have composed; there is nothing noticeably Jewish about it. But most significantly—it was a success!

Two years later, however, Zangwill and his fellow pupil-teacher at JFS, Louis Cowen, joined forces to write and publish in pamphlet form a Jewish story, "Motsa Kleis," describing the frenzied, bustling activity of Petticoat Lane on the eve of Passover.[19] Although later Zangwill effectively incorporated the work into *Children of the Ghetto,* at the time it provoked the awesome wrath of Lord Rothschild, president of the JFS board; he strongly objected to the Yiddishized speech of the story's immigrant characters.[20] After all, mispronunciation of English was typical of the negative stage-Jew stereotype and touched the sensitive nerve of the Anglo-Jewish leader's attempt to "regularize" the Jews' image in Britain. The question of a "proper" image was serious business indeed for leaders of an ethnic minority still insecure with the full political equality granted less than three decades previous. Of course, in this case, the authors were merely out to portray the East End with Dickensian realism, not to defame their own people. Nevertheless, the two were sternly warned that if they were to avoid expulsion from JFS, they must either cease writing or submit to censorship.[21] And possessing no financial alternatives, the two fledgling authors had no choice but to elect silence, at least for about the next five years. Then again they collaborated, this time on a novel.

The Premier and the Painter appeared in 1888; the author was given as J. Freeman Bell, a play on the rebellious action covertly taken by the two teachers at the Jews' Free School on Bell Lane.[22] That the authors seriously intended to maintain their anonymity is clear from a letter Zangwill wrote to Moses Gaster complaining of the *Jewish Chronicle*'s "treacherous review" of a further story by "Bell" that alluded to the true identity of the authors.[23] In any event, publication of the book resulted in a row, and the two authors resigned their positions at JFS, although they insisted publicly that it was against the wishes of the school administration that they did so, a perspective evidently not shared by Lord Rothschild.[24]

The book was a failure. Overly complicated and elaborate in plot delineation, it purports to recount the adventures of "the world-weary Premier and the ambitious House-Painter [who] agreed to change places." But as Zangwill later admitted, "missing these obvious points, many readers lost themselves in the labyrinth of resultant complications."[25]

The work's difficulties may well have stemmed from its dual authorship. It appears that Cowen originally conceived the plot as a vehicle for light satire, but Zangwill, who composed the majority of the novel, insisted on employing the satire to expose the opportunism of politicians and feminist campaigners, to deride the wealthy, and to portray the domestic life of the non-Jewish poor of East London.[26]

Despite its many faults the book did attract some positive critical attention. Commented the *Athenaeum*'s reviewer:

> it is the sort of book the description of which is "very clever" is at once inevitable and inadequate. In some ways it is original enough to be a law unto itself . . . while for the most part satirical and prosaic, [it] is often touched with sentiment, and sometimes even with a fantastic kind of poetry. . . . Again, it has to be claimed for the author that . . . he is capable, when he pleases, of insight and observation of a high order, and therewith of a mastery of sobriety of tone. But he cannot be depended upon for the length of a single page; he seeks effects and his material when and where he pleases.[27]

The Premier and the Painter demonstrates the strengths and weaknesses of Zangwill as a novelist. It displays a convincing command of natural conversation as a narrative device; it is often clever and inventive, its satire being employed to convey a serious social critique; and it is particularly effective in depicting the life of poverty of Bethnal Green. But it is often tedious and extremely overwritten, frequently submerging the plot action in long bouts of didactic monologues and is especially marred by the precocious schoolboy's desire to parade his mastery of Latin.

Zangwill and Cowen collaborated on two more works.[28] *The Great Demonstration* is a one-act play employing humor to expose political fraud and folly.[29] It satirizes parlor socialists and their vapid clichés, and it mounts a sustained attack on parasitic loafers who fake socialism for the masses merely to gain some mean personal advantage. The play introduces a device Zangwill would often employ in his later dramas, an heiress disguised as a maid, the ploy already popularized by Walter Besant. As in the earlier novel, the play uses satire as a didactic device and often is heavy-handed. But this work also introduces a new theme that was to haunt most of Zangwill's later works—an abhorrence of all violence: the play concludes with its disillusioned hero rejecting revolution if, instead of a brighter future, it brings only riot and destruction. Here in this play is a resounding echo of the truth Zangwill discovered about maxims mused over tentatively in the boyish jottings of the "Practical Proverbs by a disillusionised man."

In their short story, "Under Sentence of Marriage," Zangwill and Cowen perceptively explore a Jewish theme.[30] The Reverend Raphael Simmons, a bachelor, has accepted the position of minister of a small provincial Jewish congregation on condition that he will marry within a year, a condition he must fulfill if he is to retain his post beyond this trial period. The main contenders for his hand are "the Beauty," Miss Matilda Sampson, and "the Intellect," Miss Rose Ansell. However, Raphael feels he can accept neither girl, although he has been assured by his employers that he need not be in love, but only married. Eventually he does marry his original supporter for the post, the widow Mrs. Samuels, the only person in town in whose company he feels comfortable.

This work is extremely important as an indication of basic themes that thread their way through Zangwill's writings. Beyond the obvious appearance of names he would use in *Children of the Ghetto* for its major characters, viz. Raphael and Ansell, the twin conflicts of love versus marriages of convenience and of intellect versus beauty dominate much of Zangwill's thought, as does the implication of the story's conclusion: a resolution that avoids extreme solutions and eludes unresolved underlying antinomies.

Furthermore, the story contains a succinct description of the Jewish generational conflict that dominates *Children of the Ghetto*. Explains the narrator here:

> A new generation was growing up which knew not Joseph—which was repelled by the rites and observances of the old faith, which they felt pressed upon them as hateful burdens, to be shaken off as soon as they were old enough to be independent. They had received the best education their parents could procure for them; it gave them ideas in which the old people could take no part, and hence the smattering of learning insensibly developed a species of intellectual pride, which bred a feeling almost akin to contempt for the old grooves and the old habits.[31]

This is brilliant social psychological analysis, reflecting profound insight into sensibilities of identity hardly even perceived by most others at the time. For this was Zangwill's own generation, its experience, and its grudgingly unspoken attitude. Although this is his own view too, in this description there is nonetheless clearly present also a subtle note of contempt for these young people with their "smattering of learning." For Zangwill, like Amy Levy, also writing in 1888, saw the "melting pot" looming on the horizon and was discomforted by the spectre, drawn though they both were toward it.

Zangwill follows this perceptive short story with two others, both written unequivocally by him alone, although still hidden behind a nom de plume, this time "the Baroness von S." Both powerfully evoke Jewish themes that were to stalk Zangwill throughout his life. The appearance of the first of these stories, "Satan Mekatrig," in 1889 is important for several reasons.[32] First, the story opens with a "Proem," an unusual literary conceit given contemporary prominence by George Eliot's popular 1863 novel, *Romola*.[33] This technique was not only used again by Zangwill in *Children of the Ghetto* (and also *The Master*), but the opening paragraph of the novel's "Proem" is an exact reproduction of that to this short story. However, the second paragraph of the story's "Proem" is not repeated in the novel; it reads: "Here [in the London ghetto], when the Jew who dwells outside howls down the faithful painter of his blatant self-complacency, the artist may still come to seek his material."[34] He is here referring to the bitter outcry against *Reuben Sachs*. In his own later novel, Zangwill would display the courage to combine Amy Levy's critique of West End Jewry with his own portrayal of the East End ghetto pioneered in this story.

But "Satan Mekatrig" is particularly interesting for its treatment of the nonrational element within Judaism. In this, his first attempt to describe artistically the East End, Zangwill composed a story in the style of Kompert, combining his realism with a sentimental attachment to the subject. But Zangwill went well beyond his continental predecessor. The story, the temptation and possession of the pious Moshe Grinwitz by the forces of evil, personified as a hunchback dwarf, is an allegory of truly mythic qualities, one of Zangwill's finest and most powerful pieces of writing.

As the Satan Mekatrig leads Moshe into deeper and deeper blasphemies, his victim's anguished wife, Rebecca, although recognizing that Moshe is doomed to pay for his transgressions and also that evil, like good, derives from God, is determined to save her husband and to produce a pious heir who will pray for his father's soul. Satan and Rebecca battle over Moshe's soul, the struggle reaching its climax when the faithful wife succeeds in arousing her dying husband finally to resist the evil and proclaim the Divine Unity as expressed in the fundamental Jewish prayer, the *Shema*. The dwarf dissolves, leaving the dying father grasping his infant son as the weary Rebecca gazes on. But in a powerfully mystical observation, Zangwill warns, at the story's conclusion, that evil, although temporarily subjugated, continues as a lurking threatening existence: "And the dark Vapour lifted and showed the three figures to the baleful agonised eyes of the hunchback at the open door."[35]

In this story Zangwill is at his artistic best and also closest to the heart of Jewish thought. Here deeper, more profound levels of human existence are explored than the rationalist was then willing to recognize. And exactly for this daring, the story was severely criticized, even by the Orthodox newspaper, the *Jewish Standard*. Complained the paper's reviewer: "no hint is given that the strange superstitions with which the story teems are not indigenous to Judaism, but are accretions that have gathered about it."[36] It would only be after the twentieth-century labors of Gershom Scholem that Western Jewish thought would be willing to accept the nonrational folk element as also authentically Jewish. And Zangwill, by inclination and training a rationalist, tended to concur with his critics and so chose not to write in this vein again in a serious work. Yet his great, and unwitting, fascination with the mystical and demonic elements within Jewish tradition persisted, and it does, however, occasionally appear in isolated stories and with savage force in his unfinished final novel, "The Baron of Offenbach," with Zangwill then in the throes of a struggle with his own Satan Mekatrig.[37]

The following year "Diary of a Meshumad" appeared.[38] Purporting to be the translation of the diary of a Russian Jewish apostate, a *meshumad,* it aims to expose the futility and ironic betrayal of illusion harbored in acts of religious conversion. Even the belief that it will free one's children of any onus of Judaism proves false, as the *meshumad*'s son, ignorant of his father's origins, becomes a rabid anti-Semite. As in the previous story, truth and justice must receive their due; in the end the apostate father returns to Judaism only to die in a pogrom incited by the inflammatory rhetoric of his son. Early on, Zangwill knew that repentance for faithlessness and disloyalty is necessary but that even with it one's past sins still must exact their heavy toll in this life.[39]

Journalism and the New Humour

Zangwill was able to resign his teaching post at JFS because he had secured another position. On 2 March 1888 a new Anglo-Jewish weekly newspaper, the *Jewish Standard,* appeared, proclaiming itself "The English Organ of Orthodoxy." It was owned by Aaron Vecht and edited by Harry S. Lewis until 1890, when he was succeeded by Dr. S. A. Hirsch.[40] Zangwill was the paper's feature writer, despite his nonorthodox outlook, introducing his popular column, "Morour and Charouseth," with the 11 May 1888 issue and continuing it weekly through 27 February 1891, just four months before the paper ceased publication.

Actually Zangwill not only wrote his weekly column but also served as the newspaper's subeditor.[41] In addition he contributed stories and poems to the paper bearing the initials "I. Z.," such as the poems "The London Hospital," "Reflections in a Street in Jerusalem," and serialized translation of "Antipodes" from the Western ghetto author Solomon Kohn's *Prager Ghettobilder.*[42]

But the "Morour and Charouseth" column, signed with the nom de plume "Marshallik," was his principal endeavor and the paper's chief attraction. Introducing his column, Zangwill wrote:

> No Jewish institution is complete without its fool, and some are blessed with a good many. . . . I intend shaking my bells, and cracking my feeble jokes about everybody and everything in the world of Judaea, without fear or favour . . . ! If I dole out more morour I shall deal out charouseth too; and who knows, I may even stumble into wisdom now and then, and utter an instructive word. For accidents will happen—even to the best regulated fools.[43]

Here was not only the rationale for his column in this Anglo-Jewish newspaper but Zangwill's credo of the didactic uses of humor in general.

And "Marshallik" was as good as his word. With good-humored irreverence, the feature, a blend of witty personal narrative, poems, and playlets, satirized every aspect of British Jewish life, including the writings of J. Freeman Bell. It was lively, clever, and controversial. Here was sharp-tongued satire pointing out the community's many great and small foibles, no doubt in the hope that not rancor but reform might result. Occasionally, however, the column struck a more grave note, as in its poems "Love and Death" and "The Rencontre."[44]

As subeditor Zangwill dealt with a full gamut of real-life Jewish versions of Dickensian characters. Among these was N. L. D. Zimmer, whose many letters complained continuously of incessant infringements of Jewish custom by Anglo-Jewry. But most notable of all the paper's characters was Naphtali Herz Imber, whose poems and essays appeared regularly, at least while Lewis remained editor. Imber's pompous and fanciful essays, composed in involuted Yiddishized English, purported to find Talmudic sources for almost every modern invention and a Jewish origin for almost every folkway and custom practiced in the world. "Marshallik" gently chided Zimmer and Imber in his columns, while "I. Z." translated Imber's Hebrew poetry into English, as, for instance, his "The Watch on the Jordan."[45] After Hirsch became editor, however, the paper became less tolerant of "characters" like Imber, although "Marshallik" was allowed to continue his satirical commentaries and parodies unchecked.

His three years as subeditor and columnist for the *Jewish Standard* were extremely important for the development of Zangwill's literary talent. The experience not only provided him with abundant opportunities to experiment stylistically, but it also furnished him with the model for "The Flag of Judah" in *Children of the Ghetto* and with many of the characters that people this novel. His familiarity with the East End described in his famous book equally stemmed from his days as columnist for this Jewish newspaper, a familiarity that had previously been only very limited. Perhaps, most importantly, through contacts made or significantly strengthened while working on the paper, Zangwill developed close friendships with several leading Anglo-Jewish intellectual figures, most notably Solomon Schechter and Moses Gaster, fellow Romanian academics educated at the historical positivist Jewish Theological Seminary in Breslau.[46] But one immediate consequence of his "Morour and Charouseth" was that "Marshallik" attracted the admiring attention of the "New Humour" group of writers led by Jerome K. Jerome, resulting in Zangwill's becoming editor of his own satirical weekly.

Ariel, or The London Puck first appeared as *Puck* in January 1889. In July 1890 it changed ownership, altered its name and format, and acquired a new, anonymous editor, Israel Zangwill. Transferring "Marshallik's" style to the non-Jewish British scene, Zangwill turned *Ariel* into a lively, ebullient, and irreverent publication satirizing the current fashions in art and politics. For instance, it poked fun at Mrs. Humphrey Ward's *Robert Elsmere*, commenting wryly that, "Everyone knows how the Rev. Robert Elsmere died just in time to save himself from becoming a rank atheist."[47] Continuing in a more biting tone, "Ariel" remarked: "the religion of Elsmerism has superseded Hypnotism and Spiritualism in the drawing-rooms and will be very popular this season. It is an agreeable sensation, and is much cultivated by advanced people, who regard what is called faith as nothing more than a faculty for believing what one knows to be untrue."[48] This from the man who would soon be asked to write a "Jewish *Robert Elsmere*"!

A glimpse at Zangwill's genuine anguish over the bitterly harsh fate of Russian Jewry, his impatience to alleviate their sufferings speedily, and the doubts he entertained about philanthropic attempts to aid them is apparent in an 1890 article on "Unholy Russia": "A meeting of all the religions a few days before CHRISTMAS to protest against the methods of the nation which claims to possess the only orthodox form of Christianity, is a significant sight—cheering, yet sad. It tells of the rising sun; but it tells also of the slowness of the sunrise and the weary travail of the ages."[49] This concern, the impatience, and these doubts would reemerge in Zangwill's Zionism and in his desperate Territorialist efforts over a decade later.

In September of 1891, after Zangwill stopped writing also for the *Jewish Standard, Ariel* altered its format once again, placing its editor's name openly on its masthead and eliminating all of his "Ariel" columns from its pages. In their place the paper began serializing Zangwill's *The Old Maids' Club,* the sequel to his first successful novel, *The Bachelors' Club.* However, only eleven of the novel's seventeen chapters appeared in *Ariel,* which abruptly ceased publication after its 6 February 1892 issue.

However, by then Zangwill was thoroughly involved with the "New Humour" group. He had already collaborated with Karl Marx's daughter, Eleanor Marx Aveling, on a witty, satirical essay, " 'A Doll's House' Repaired," a tongue-in-cheek rewriting of Ibsen's masterpiece to suit British Victorian attitudes, and he continued writing stories in this genre for Jerome K. Jerome's the *Idler* through 1894.[50] A final New Humour story, "The Choice of Parents," appeared in late 1895.[51]

Zangwill's first two successful books and his first successful play are in the New Humour genre. *The Bachelors' Club* appeared in 1891 and its sequel, *The Old Maids' Club,* the following year.[52] Both are really collections of short stories based on a single joke: that a club is formed by members of one of the sexes so as to avoid marriage; each story relates how one member, or prospective member, is eventually lured away into matrimony. The books are literary fluff meant for amusement. Unfortunately, as so often with Zangwill, they are overwritten, as their author strove continuously to dazzle the reader with his cleverness. The *Athenaeum*'s reviewer complained that they were "overdone" and "wearisome" and cautioned potential readers that while "recommending these stories to all classes of readers, it may be well to warn them against trying to get through too much of it at a sitting, for the book is so rich in wit that the effect of too large a dose is almost nauseating: it would be like making a meal off wedding-cake."[53]

Frivolous though these stories might appear, they indicate attitudes that do appear throughout Zangwill's later fiction. Unlike Jerome K. Jerome's New Humour fiction with its good-natured jibes at human foibles, in these stories Zangwill genuinely despises his fussy, weak-kneed characters. Fashioned to be ridiculed and to display their author's cleverness, they are mere clumsy two-dimensional cardboard figures, their creator unconcerned to provide any psychological insights into their dilemmas. The future feminist campaigner's strong suspicion of women, apparent in *The Premier and the Painter,* is also quite evident in these two works.

Possibly most significant, *The Bachelors' Club* introduces three central Zangwillian motifs: the irony of life, the fragility of idealism, and the utility of even delusive ideals. For example, in "The Original Sinner," Mandeville Brown, echoing the ideals of Besant's Angela Messenger, seeks to break out of "the web of conventionality," life's "predestined pattern," by secretly marrying while remaining a loyal member of the Bachelors' Club. Learning that even this had been done before, Brown loses his mind, a truly unconventional escape from normality. With such ironic revenge does life repay its rebels!

Idealism's fragility is the theme of "A Bolt from the Blue." In this story it is revealed that the club's founder and president, Andrew McGullicuddy, is in reality Peter Parker, a bigamist married to two sisters, the club serving as his cover to escape from his feuding wives. Repeatedly in these books, the reader is reminded that idealism is often merely a guise concealing base motives.

Yet even delusive idealism can be useful, argues Zangwill. For instance, in "The Logic of Love" he tells the story of Joseph Fogson, a physician who has created "Barbara," a feminine ideal fashioned out of the syllogisms of logic. As he explains, "Such was the maiden whom Logic brought afresh into my life, to revive my stagnant soul, perishing with blight and drought."[54] Zangwill's suspicion of intellectualism is the twin of his skepticism.

During the course of a country holiday Fogson meets a girl he mistakes for a true, flesh-and-blood incarnation of his "Barbara," even to the very name. Learning from the chiding girl later that "Barbara" is actually her infant niece and assured by her that only a baby could match his ideal, Fogson nonetheless offers to marry the aunt, Annie, provided she allow him to call her "Barbara." Even a consciously futile ideal faithfully adhered to might possess redeeming value, Zangwill argues. And it functioned as a guiding principle for many of his later political endeavors.

Although he had already written a play with Louis Cowen and had attempted to turn one of *The Old Maids' Club* stories into a drama, Zangwill's first successful play, also in the New Humour vein, was written at this time.[55] *Six Persons* was always one of his favorite pieces, a one-act farce first performed in 1893 and often revived during Zangwill's lifetime.[56] The play's theme is taken from a quotation attributed to Oliver Wendell Holmes in his *Autocrat of the Breakfast Table:* "In every conversation between two persons, Six Persons are really taking part." Zangwill interpreted this statement as implying that each person is really three: as he is, as he thinks he is, and as he thinks the other thinks he is.[57]

The play, thus, has only two characters, Eugenia Latimer, a spinster, and Charles Scott, a barrister. The two have slipped into an engagement they both have come to regret. But rather than rudely break it off, each decides to engage in a ruse so as to provoke the other into an angry dissatisfaction with their relationship that will lead him or her to sever the liaison instead. Eugenia and Charles meet, and each carries out the plan; as they do so, however, each becomes aware of the other's true love, and this discovery reawakens their own. In the end, the loving couple are happily reunited.

The play is witty, entertaining, and genuinely occupied with exploring an interesting psychological perspective with sympathy and delicacy. Unlike much of his New Humour writing, in this satirical play, Zangwill—uncharacteristically reworking the material several times—was able to restrain his penchant for authorial fireworks and for didactic dialogues so as to create appealing and believable characters. Possibly Zangwill was successful with *Six Persons* exactly because here he was not preaching the doctrines of reason nor attempting to scale the heights of literary fame but rather was modestly expressing his profound artist's insight into the quandaries inherent in human relationships and identities.

Although by 1892 Zangwill was thoroughly associated with the New Humour school, he was becoming increasingly uncomfortable at finding himself confined within the constrictive boundaries of the genre. As early as 1891, he was writing to the editor of Macmillan and Company, rejecting the designation altogether and enclosing reviews of his earliest works that, while acknowledging a humorous side to his writings, also recognized their serious intent.[58] He was alluding to *The Premier and the Painter* and the stories of the "Baroness von S."

There is no doubt that Zangwill was correct. Eager for success, he had chosen the quickest and easiest route, the light jibes of the New Humour school so suited to the surface of his talent. But although he was clever at entertaining repartee and at the bon mot, Zangwill's great strengths as a writer were as Dickensian realist and pedagogic satirist. Having slipped into literary journalism and having succeeded at it, he was now struggling to climb beyond it, to return to the interests and style of his earliest literary endeavors that would again allow for the fuller expression of his talent. Zangwill, in fact, would never be satisfied with past and present achievements; always nervously restless and impatient he constantly insisted on pushing himself, reaching ever further outward to something new. And in this case he was certainly right.

His first opportunity to shift orientation had already come, not from an appeal to the artist but rather to the intellectual. In the 1889 inaugural British-based issue of the *Jewish Quarterly Review,* Israel Zangwill's article, "English Judaism," appeared as a companion piece to those by Heinrich Graetz and Solomon Schechter.[59]

What is noteworthy here, first of all, is that an essay by the obscure youthful subeditor of the *Jewish Standard* should have been esteemed appropriate to complement those of two extremely influential and internationally renowned scholars. Neither Zangwill, the JFS medal winner and bon vivant, nor the *Quarterly*'s editors, Claude Montefiore and Israel Abrahams, nor Schechter saw any incongruity in this decision. In fact, Zangwill had never engaged in any scholarly research on Judaism, except possibly as a precocious dilettante and as a humor columnist. But the editors wanted an Anglo-Jewish contributor, and Zangwill was available, confidently willing, and had some genuinely interesting things to say. Indeed, this pattern would repeat throughout his life: English-speaking Jews seeking guidance from among one of their own turned importuningly to the autodidact Zangwill, and he would more and more assume the right to respond to these demands till, finally, established leaders would accuse him of usurpation.

Although there was more intuitive insight than scholarship in his contribution and although this awkward first attempt only hints at the brilliant belles lettres he would later learn to fashion with real

Israel Zangwill, 1895. *Courtesy, The Hampden-Booth Theatre Library at The Players.*

skill, this essay does contain some genuinely profound observations into the nature of Anglo-Jewish thought. Zangwill argues that a drastic, qualitative change had occurred within Judaism: "That, for the first time in its history, it has become necessary within the present century to say and to reiterate that Judaism is a revealed religion . . . is surely a fact of great portent and presage."[60] Exactly as had "Robert Elsmere," Zangwill maintained that the cumulative effects of Biblical criticism, "the new cosmological conceptions, the analytical spirit of the age, and the ever growing acuteness of moral perception" have undermined "supernatural Judaism" and resulted in the creation of a new, distinctive entity, "natural Judaism."[61]

What is evident about this new "natural Judaism," the varieties of which Zangwill pedantically catalogs through a microscope, is that, first, "both Biblical and Rabbinical Judaism seem to have had their day. The cloak that could not be torn off by the Tempest of Christianity and Persecution bids fair to be thrown off under the sunshine of Rationalism and Tolerance."[62] But if Orthodoxy has lost its legitimacy, Zangwill repudiates equally the validity of the Reform alternative, "an illogical creed" irrelevant to Judaism.[63]

In the contemporary condition of flux, it is important for "the few minds" capable of it to grasp the true direction of change. Zangwill interprets the process as anthropological and evolutionary: "The social organism secretes its religion, as it secretes its proportions of wisdom and folly, selfishness and altruism."[64] The principal thing to bear in mind in the social development of religion, then, is that "fossilisation is the fate of all spiritual truths expressed through material forms."[65] Rejecting adherence to a "fossilised" Orthodoxy and an artificial Reform Judaism, Zangwill optimistically conjectures:

> Yet to my mind, the real struggle of the future lies between the essence of Judaism and the essence of Christism (not of Christianity), the scientific morality of Moses and the emotional morality of Christ; and a compromise between the religious provisions for moral geniuses and those of moral dullards, will perhaps form the religion of the future [approaching] the perfection of the *Ethics* and the *Tractus Theologico-Politicus*.[66]

Here, then, in 1889 is Israel Zangwill's preoccupation with a historical positivist "religion of the future" combining the *essences* of the teachings of both Moses and Jesus, free of ceremonial and dogmatic rigidities and yet also adjusting the ideal to the mundane.[67] Zangwill never retreated from this formulation, to which he devoted much of his energies to further. But for all that, this intellectual construct repelled him emotionally.

As Harold Fisch has noted, while the argument of the entire essay is an intellectual condemnation of traditional Judaism to the dustbin of history, the essay is also an emotional paean to the past.[68] Rejecting Graetz's contempt for the traditional ghetto pattern, Zangwill wistfully eulogizes it:

> There is something touching and sublime in the common belief of a people in an apparent impossibility, in the ultimate return of its national hero, in the recovery of its olden glories, in the triumph of its national ideals after persecution and repression, something pathetic in its simple faith and credulous hope, as a mother who clasps her dead child to her breast, and will not let it go. Some such spirit, as naive and as burning, breathes through a myriad volumes of our post-exilian literature, and yet gladden the simple heart of the Russian pauper as he sings the hymns of hope and trust after his humble Friday night's meal. Some such faith still solaces the foot-sore hawker amid the jeers and blows of the drunkard and the bully, and transfigures the squalid Ghetto with celestial light. Some such hope has been the inspiration of countless sacrifices and martyrdoms, it has touched otherwise unhallowed lips with sacred fire, it has been the "blessed vision" that opened before the eyes of the dying, the sanctifying breath that preserved millions of the living from corruption.[69]

This is the passionate author of "Satan Mekatrig" exposing the smirking flippancies and shallow trivialities of "Marshallik's" satirical rationalism. This is Israel Zangwill, whose enlightened intellect admired the modern rationalist's ethereal essence of religion, lovingly caressing the palpable sacred traditions of his people's mundane lives. Were they to assimilate, as reason argued, or maintain their ethnic distinctiveness, as the heart desired?

In an essay that appeared two years later, Zangwill lamented British Jewry's assimilation and acculturation. Denouncing the decorous Anglicized formalism of the United Synagogue, he astutely warned: "The English Jew is undoubtedly on his way to assimilation, not so much in the sense of intermarriage with the heathen as of intermarriage with the heathen's ideals."[70] The New Humour editor of *Ariel* worriedly complained:

> It is impossible for the reflective Israelite, however lukewarm his personal piety, not to feel that many characteristics, pleasing, and picturesque features of the older Judaism have been gradually whittled away

> during the last half-century, while their place has been supplied by cheap imitations of Anglican "culture" and enthusiastic offering of the neck to the yoke of the British philistine.[71]

The contending alternatives Zangwill outlined sharply: "Assimilation means absorption. Without national identity more marked than that constituted by the private payment of *shool* bills instead of pew-rents, the Jew is not likely to survive his prosperity."[72] This, then, is the dilemma of identities: the melting pot or the preservation of national distinctiveness; the scientific evolutionary course blindly predetermined for the future or the inexplicable persistence of the traditions and ethos of the past. For Israel Zangwill, the dilemma was the intellectual's perception of the reality of Britain in collision with the poet's vision of the images of the age-old life of the Jews.

By 1892 Zangwill had become a successful author, journalist, and editor. Although physically frail, he was capable of prodigious literary activity, driven by a powerful ambition to excel and be esteemed. Given to wit and satire in the service of enlightened intellect, he possessed an emotional depth that evoked in him haunting images beyond the grasp of reason. Behind the fury of work and ebullient sociability lay the furious struggle for his soul, a battle he was helpless to avoid: was he the assimilated Briton or the quintessential Jew?

Unable to comprehend himself, Zangwill was called upon to explain his people to the world. Ambitious, talented, and confident as ever, he accepted the challenge and wrote a novel that won for him international fame and a prominent voice among Anglo-Jewry's leaders.

FIVE

Children of the Ghetto

Children of the Ghetto was Israel Zangwill's return to literature from the world of literary journalism. Renown, access to fashionable circles, and a certain financial security were already his. But the creative artist and nascent philosopher in him were restlessly confined within the bounds of the "New Humour" entertainer's verbal sleights of hand. What he craved was to create and to illuminate the soul's darkness with the lightning flashes of his talent and thought.[1] It was a fecund restlessness that drove him forward, despite his current easy successes, to write a book that launched a career and a new literary genre.

Not that he acted rashly. For when the offer was made to him, Zangwill did not leap at it. First, he had to be certain it was genuinely to be a return to literature, and he had also to continue simultaneously down the old path of light satire that buttered his bread, at least until the new path had proven solid enough. Later on he would not be so cautious: he would leap then even when there were no offers. But with *Children of the Ghetto* Zangwill still had to be enticed.

It was Judge Mayer Sulzberger, chairman of the publications committee of the newly established Jewish Publication Society of America, who served as midwife for the novel. Sulzberger wanted a "Jewish *Robert Elsmere*" for the JPS and, evidently having no confidence in American Jewry's literary talents, turned to Britain. In September 1890, on a visit to London, the judge decided to approach Zangwill, having been impressed by the artistic talent of the creator of "Satan Mekatrig" and by the philosophic insights of the author of "English Judaism."

Significantly, what had attracted Sulzberger's attention was not Zangwill's satiric endeavors—as coauthor of *The Premier and the Painter*, or as "Marshallik" on the *Jewish Standard*, or as editor of *Ariel*—but rather his creativity in consciously Jewish and philosophically modernist pieces. This, of course, was exactly what the JPS novel was expected to be: a didactic exposition of Jewish historical positivist religious thought. However, equally telling, Sulzberger (and also Zangwill at this point) did not perceive the profound contradictions in these two examples of their author's thought: that while he consciously and ably portrayed the contemporary Jewish scene as an artist imbued with a rationalist perspective, both pieces display a deep emotional commitment to the nonmodern traditional expression of the Jewish milieu and ethos and an equally powerful revulsion against contemporary counterfeit adaptations. And, although unperceived at the time by both author and patron, it was just these latter elements, rather than those that had attracted the judge's attention, that made the novel a success.[2]

At any rate, Judge Sulzberger approached Zangwill through Lucien Wolf, the journalist, with his offer. However, after a personal meeting, Zangwill demurred. He never allowed another's agenda, even if financially inviting, to interfere with his own.[3] He had two serious, and interrelated, reservations: (1) that his creativity as an artist would be circumscribed by the JPS's desire for an explicitly "Jewish *Robert Elsmere*" and (2) that a realist portrayal of Anglo-Jewry would lead to censorship by the wealthy sponsors of the JPS and to vituperative attacks on him, similar to what he had already experienced with his "Motsa Kleis" and as he witnessed upon the publication of Amy Levy's *Reuben Sachs*.

Zangwill was not lacking in courage or self-confidence. What concerned him were the dangers of infringement on artistic autonomy and of being limited to a Jewish, rather than universal, theme. For him, nothing—no consideration or force—should be allowed to interfere with an artist's creative integrity.[4] Naturally, a commissioned thematic novel threatened the greatest danger in this regard, especially as Zangwill intended a critical presentation of exactly the class that was commissioning the work and also a sympathetic realist portrait of the immigrants they were so anxious to acculturate. Zangwill would not compromise his artistic integrity. Rather than do so he had already turned to an alternative outlet, journalistic satires. If he was now to return to serious writing, it could only be as an artist free from all but personal and aesthetic constraints.

Nor was Zangwill, editor of *Ariel* and friend of Jerome K. Jerome and his circle, willing to restrict his efforts to the narrow confines of a limited Jewish reading public or to conveying a mere parochial message. The import of the writing need be universal, however specific the vehicle. Just as the artist must be free from censorial supervision, so he must be free from ethnic particularness and sensitivities that might limit "that cosmopolitan thing, a work of art."[5]

Fortunately, Judge Sulzberger was responsive to Zangwill's concerns and more interested in providing the JPS with a reputable Jewish-oriented novel than in producing a literary tract. After further exchanges, Israel Zangwill, reassured on the issue of artistic autonomy, agreed to write "a Jewish novel," with an advance of £200 from the JPS, which was to own its United States rights.[6] However, it is also clear that by early March 1891 Zangwill's agent, Joseph Jacobs, was attempting to interest a British publisher in the novel and that Zangwill had already completed a draft manuscript of *Children of the Ghetto*.[7] That he could have been approached in September 1890 with the idea and within seven months have completed the novel—or at least a very substantial portion of it—testifies not only to the fact that Zangwill, always an intense, energetic writer, had decided that this was indeed his vehicle back into literature, whatever the ultimate attitude of Judge Sulzberger might be, but also that he had already given much thought and effort to a Jewish-oriented novel, even before the JPS proposal had been tendered.[8]

New Wine in Old Bottles

By the time he came to write *Children of the Ghetto*, Zangwill had already successfully written for two quite distinct audiences. With "Professor Grimmer," *The Premier and the Painter*, *The Bachelors' Club*, *Ariel*, and the *Idler* stories he was appealing to the general British readership. With "Motsa Kleis," "Under Sentence of Marriage," "Satan Mekatrig," "English Judaism," and the *Jewish Standard* articles he was aiming at the insular English-speaking Anglo-Jewish community. In this new novel he would, with marvelous success, address both of these audiences.

But what is of special interest is that in writing for both Jewish and non-Jewish readers, Zangwill did not meld the particular and the universal themes into a unified whole; they remained two distinct motifs, separated even within the one novel. In fact, Zangwill did not so much as interweave the two themes through the course of the novel, as did George Eliot in *Daniel Deronda*. Instead the work is divided into two autonomous "books," the first, "Children of the Ghetto," aimed at the non-Jewish public and the second, "Grandchildren of the Ghetto," at the Jewish. And the striking and unexplained discontinuity between the two "books" of the novel disconcerted readers and reviewers even at the time.

So disparate and tangential are the two "books" that when the novel was adapted for the stage by Zangwill in 1899, "Grandchildren of the Ghetto" was not included in the dramatic version at all. This exclusion had the happy effect of freeing "Children of the Ghetto" from the novel's blatantly awkward effort at imposing an artificial interpretive unity upon the two "books" and their characters. The result is an entirely different set of interpretations of the protagonists and themes of the drama as compared with those of this section of the novel.[9]

Thus even in this novel, focused exclusively on the world of Anglo-Jewry, Zangwill could achieve no harmonious and organic bond between the British and the Jewish elements; for him, they constituted legitimate alternative perspectives requiring distinctive treatments that reflect their divergent perspectives and values. Not only is this dichotomy fundamental and unbridgeable, but the novel implies that attempts to formulate a viable convergence of the two traditions results only in a distasteful ersatz Anglo-Judaism that is authentically neither English nor Jewish. At this stage, however, Zangwill was not consciously troubled by this absence of cohesion between the English and the Jewish themes nor by the fact that they are fused in *Children of the Ghetto* only artificially by main force of the novelist's will. But later he would explore explicitly and painfully the inner agony of this dichotomy, one he was never able to resolve or to escape.

However, for both sections Zangwill utilized his previous literary endeavors and experiences. Incorporated directly into the book were "Motsa Kleis," the "Proem" to "Satan Mekatrig," and various short pieces from the *Jewish Standard*, such as his translation of Imber's "The Watch on the Jordan." Even more important for the novel was Zangwill's association with the *Jewish Standard* for providing him with direct experience of the East End and of general Anglo-Jewish society and for introducing him to several characters and settings he so skillfully weaves into the novel. His "English Judaism" provides, of course, the informing philosophy of the work. But possibly most responsible for the expeditious production of this novel was the fact that Zangwill was already working on a Jewish-oriented novel at the time Judge Sulzberger first approached him.

Among his papers is a handwritten draft of the opening chapters of a novel clearly containing material later reshaped into major portions of *Children of the Ghetto*.[10] This manuscript, so very much more overtly autobiographical than the published novel, focuses upon the life of Alfred Hyams, a young Anglo-Jew attempting to move beyond the ethnic perimeters of his own family and community and to enter, as a fully accepted member, the wider British society. It is a tale filled with disillusionment and recrimination against both communities and a haunting revelation of Israel Zangwill's inner anguish over his inability to achieve thorough and unquestionable identification with either of them.

Alfred, "young & gay & pleasure seeking," is quite a contrast to his pious father, Moses,

> old & bent with a weight beyond his years, with a face deeply lined, grave, stern, sorrowful . . . , the eyes shadowed, with Capacity for infinite suffering in their depths; the whole face that of a man who had endured much, who could endure more; a face in which he who had learnt the character might have deciphered the secret of what had produced the past of his race & its present.[11]

But, the narrator sounds the Zangwillian plaint, "he was a Jew of a fast-vanishing type."[12]

Yet despite his intense personal commitment to traditionalism, Moses has adopted a laissez-faire attitude toward his son's education: "Though somewhat stern in manner, his father had always been loving and indulgent to him; that placed no hurdle or exercise before him [for] the education which should fit him to reaching a higher social position than the parents either hoped or wished to achieve."[13] Encapsulated here is the experience of Israel Zangwill himself and of so many immigrants' children of the ghetto. And the consequences for the family and for the children are equally evident.

The Hyams household is not described as in the clutches of poverty but instead is portrayed as shabbily comfortable. The discordance in the family arises not from the stresses of material penury but rather from conflicting ethnic orientations. As father and son confront each other early in the story, Moses attempts to dissuade the determined Alfred from attending a nonkosher dinner party. But the son is adamant and, defeated, the old father retreats into the solace of the well-worn, familiar pages of his *Shulchan Aruch* (code of traditional Jewish law).[14]

For Alfred, the dinner party, hosted by a fashionable non-Jewish family, the Leiths, proves a disaster. The young man senses that "there is hardly one of Mr. Leith's guests who was not conscious of racial superiority over the intruder [Alfred]."[15] But this feeling only intensifies his determination to fit in, to win them all over.

First, however, he must win himself over. He must, for the first time in his life, eat nonkosher food: "He knew he would experience great discomfort at eating *treifa* meat, the hereditary repugnance of four thousand years which, without analyzing it, he felt was sure, make his gorge rise or give him a choking sensation."[16]

But Alfred has resolved to succeed, to make the proper impression in this company. So after choosing beef instead of pork,

> he reflected that he has been very near making a fool of himself. He had no real religious feelings of any sort; such religion as he had practised had consisted in the observance of externalities devoid of any informing spiritual life; it was really a vague superstition combined with the wrench always attendant after any sudden departure from the established & ingrained habits of years that had made him hesitate.[17]

This is trenchant psychological portraiture of the processes of generational assimilation and acculturation. Here is the child of traditionally raised parents who settled in an alien homeland and taught him a knowledge only of the empty forms of quaint ceremonies and customs but who were unable to transmit to the next generation any internalization of content, significance, or theoretic justification for their "foreign" ideas and behaviors. What the child has learned is mere attachment to old maxims and practices learned by rote and seemingly no longer to fit the realities of his everyday experience.

Nonetheless, there remains also a profound emotional attachment to the traditional that cannot be lightly rationalized away. Alfred must still construct an abstruse Talmud-like religious argument to justify his eating nonkosher meat: "After all, he thought, it was not swine flesh. That was distinctly forbidden in the Bible. But that beef was forbidden unless killed in a particular fashion was only traditional law, that it was ridiculous to imagine it binding in the nineteenth century."[18]

Accordingly, what then is to be the historical positivist criterion for Jewish observance: Biblical injunctions are binding as eternal because divinely ordained, but Rabbinic traditions need be accepted only as contemporary conditions warrant?

What is the test of what constitutes acceptability under current circumstances? Alfred's experience is paradigmatic: "By chance, he looked across at Smith; the recollection of that gentleman's sneer . . . firmly determined that he would willingly sacrifice much of his old Jewish customs in order to triumph over the men who mocked him."[19] Not principle, not reason, not faith, but pride, personal honor, and social acceptability are the ultimate tests for Alfred. And a girl.

What has actually drawn him to this dinner party is the Leiths' daughter, Belle. Rather precipitously, Alfred proposes marriage on the spot to this charming young lady who has been so kind and friendly toward him throughout the evening. But the proposal has an electrifying effect on her: "the inexplicable fascination exercised by the Semite over the English girl was shaken off by sheer force of will, as one shakes off a nightmare."[20] Her warm sociability vanishes, leaving her "like a marble statue." But Alfred persists until she finally explains: "Perhaps you could marry a Christian—but not me. I could not marry—a J—I could not marry you because you are not a Christian; because if I did my father would be unhappy."[21]

Belle's rejection traumatizes and embitters the young Jew:

> His mind was an arena of conflicting and contrastic impulses and emotions, agreeing only in bitterness. . . . Who were they [the Christians] that he should listen to them, they whose children had abused him & insulted him from infancy upwards. . . . Which of them could dress, talk, sing, better than he . . . ? No wretched set of people for whom he had made a breach with his past & even been momentarily willing to break with it altogether—for it had been revealed to him quite clearly that neither Belle nor her father could as much as conceive the thought of the change of religion coming from the female side. He loathed himself for what he had done & still more for what he had thought of doing. Now, away from the baneful spell, he could see the full enormity of the idea.[22]

Like Judith Trachtenberg, Alfred Hyams discovers that the rewards for ethnic self-abasement are haughty rejection and astringent self-loathing. He had contemplated betraying his family and faith only to discover his sacrifice scorned by the broader society that would never willingly do the same. His honor, his dignity, his conscience have been offended and his compromises, like Judith's, rejected. But he masks his angry self-disgust by throwing the blame onto Christian society. And also like Franzos's Judith, Zangwill's Alfred flees to the home he had earlier been so willing to abandon.

Entering his parents' front corridor he touches "the *mezuzah* on the front-door lightly with his finger . . . and is claimed by the re-establishment of his relations with his religion."[23] But actually Alfred's acculturated intellect remains unaffected by Belle's rejection; his response to her and this "re-establishment of relations with his religion" are both emotional and sentimental. Consequently, the conflict between his reason and his feelings has now insensibly become intensified and more complex.

Wandering into his father's study, Alfred/Israel would

> never forget the emotion that overcame him, as he stood at the open door of that familiar, peaceful room with its solid comfortable furniture, its book-case full of old Hebrew folios, its crude portraits of learned Rabbis & its ambitiously-designed Mizrach. & its ragged white haired master still studying half-aloud with the same quaint intonations which had fallen on his son's childish ears.[24]

This is also the comforting image of the ghetto so fondly and vividly evoked in "English Judaism," a solid place of peace and comfort for the restless, battle-scarred soul struggling to make its way in the scoffing outside world.

But in words that barely mask his own bitter memories, Zangwill recalls that this is the image of a mythical past, temporarily tinted by selective memory, to obscure humiliating, uncivil qualities also associated with the father's world:

> [Alfred] saw it [his childhood] through a mist of sacred fears which hallowed the past, too, & expunged the dreariness & weariness much as it had for him in reality. For once the discomforts of tedious formalism which had shadowed his infancy, the two or three unforgivable insults which his father had put upon him when a boy, when he had smacked his face in synagogue, in the sight of the congregation for not minding his prayer-book or gabbing quickly through uncouth, almost meaningless words, these were obliterated. The raw harsh air of reality, mellowed to a divine restful atmosphere.[25]

Gazing at his father, Alfred recalls "all the beautiful domestic side of Judaism, his tenderest childish thoughts & feeling surged up, charged."[26] Musing on these memories, he again looks at the old man: "The grey head & bowed form of his father agonizing there over his books stirred him to remorseful reverence. The good, simple, unassuming honourable, learned old man. . . . How generously he had dealt with his unworthy son."[27]

Reverence, remorse, resentment—these are the emotions Alfred/Israel feels for his father and for the customs he believes are no longer relevant. His parents' home is no longer his own—however comfortable, peacefully bittersweet it might be—than is the Leiths'. Alfred belongs nowhere: neither in the English nor in the Jewish world. The one will not accept him and the other he can no longer tolerate, however charming and restful is its dreamy memory. Yet when the world wounds him, it is still to his father's home that he flees.

The draft manuscript ends here, no doubt because the life upon which it was based also had not yet gone much further, either experientially or emotionally. The work lay uncompleted as Zangwill turned to his New Humour stories, and never again would he write so intensely personally and autobiographically, not even in his later unpublished attempt at autobiographical fiction, "The Baron of Offenbach."

But the draft was not forgotten and much of its material Zangwill reworked into *Children of the Ghetto.* Traces of old Moses Hyams are obvious in Moses Ansell and in Mendel Hyams in the first "book" and the generational conflict of father and son in the second, in the bitter clash of pious old Reb Shemuel and his renegade son, Levi. Most significantly, the draft's theme was not submerged but rather transformed from the personal to the communal plane.

Children of the Ghetto first appeared in 1892.[28] Book One of the novel, also entitled "Children of the Ghetto," is an extension into English of the Western "ghetto" genre. Like Franzos, Zangwill here adopted the anthropological approach for these "pen pictures of a peculiar people," intended for the general non-Jewish anglophone public.[29] However, unlike Franzos, Zangwill shares Kompert's positive evaluation of the immigrant "ghetto" world, although not to preserve or reform it but in this case to arouse the non-Jew's sympathy and understanding and to counter the traditional negative English literary stereotype.

Book Two, "Grandchildren of the Ghetto," on the other hand, is directed at a Jewish readership and fulfills the commission of composing a "Jewish *Robert Elsmere,*" albeit one much more tentative in its ideology than Mrs. Ward's work. Although there remain pleasing traces of the Western "ghetto" genre here too, Zangwill is primarily intent upon introducing a new literary category in this portion of the novel, the one implicit in his commission: he is no longer the Dickensian realist depicting memorable characters, describing social conditions, and moralizing on the need for reform; in this "book," above all he is expounding his conception of the theology and philosophic importance of a truly contemporary English Judaism. Here his aim is to provide spiritual guidance for his fellow Jews. The *maggid* of the first part assumes the guise of sage in the second. So, if the first section constitutes a continuation and culmination of the nineteenth-century Western "ghetto" literary tradition, the second is the innovation of a new genre, that of the secular storyteller as spiritual mentor of this flock.

"Proem"

Echoing the perspective on the future of the traditional Jewish milieu and the literary program proposed to describe it in Amy Levy's 1886 essay, "The Jew in Fiction," in the novel's "Proem" Zangwill explicitly states his conception of his authorial role as it relates to the immigrant world of the East End. Referring to himself, he explains: "And they who have won their way beyond its [the ghetto's] boundaries must still play their parts. . . . If they are not the Children, they are at least the Grandchildren of the Ghetto."[30]

Zangwill confirms that he is neither of the ghetto himself nor child of the ghetto. But, equally, he acknowledges his responsibility—as a "grandchild of the ghetto"—to its inhabitants to compose a truthful portrait of their lives, with all their faults and their virtues. Such is the moral mission of the artist in society.

The contemporary "London Ghetto" he conceives as possessing three distinctive characteristics. First, as Besant had already pointed out, it is a world whose perspective is narrow and constricted, whose residents' "faults are bred of its hovering miasma of persecution, their virtues straitened and intensified by the *narrowness of its horizons*."[31] And the author of this book has traveled "*beyond* its boundaries," its cramping limitations.

Second, Zangwill defines quite specifically the nature of ghetto life and traces its causes. Here, in Jewish Whitechapel, are "tragedies of spiritual struggles, comedies of material ambition—which are the aftermath of its centuries of dominance, the sequel of that long cruel night in Jewry which coincides with the Christian Era."[32] Ghetto life constitutes a tragicomedy in which religion is bathed in the tragic as the mundane is in the humorous. This evaluation, of course, clearly reflects Zangwill's own assessment of the relationship of the spiritual compared to material affairs: the former is worthy of serious treatment, the latter is meet for the comic.

And, with Disraeli, Zangwill attributes the "distortions" of ghetto life to persecution, as something imposed unnaturally upon the Jews by hostile external pressures. Implicit in this perspective is the Enlightenment assumption that emancipation leads inevitably to "normalization," a position that would increasingly loom terrifyingly in Israel Zangwill's thoughts like a "dark Vapour." But not yet.

Finally, Zangwill, like so many others, assumed that the milieu of the ghetto, as a "voluntary formation," was already quickly passing from the scene, that it was melting away. For he asks: "where are the little girls in white pinafores with pink sashes who brightened the Ghetto on high days and holidays" and where are all the others that used to throng the scene? And he replies: "The restless, bustling crowds . . . are at rest in the 'house of Life'; the pageant of their strenuous generation is vanished as a dream."[33] Still, like Alfred Hyams, we may nostalgically glance back at a past that can no longer be our present: "Perchance, here and there, some decrepit centenarian rubs his purblind eyes with the ointment of memory, and sees these pictures of the past, hallowed by the consecration of time, and finds his shrivelled cheek wet with the pathos sanctifying the joys that have been."[34]

But Israel Zangwill was no more a languishing centenarian than he was a child of the ghetto. And no matter how intellectually and culturally removed he might have been from the clamorous East End immigrants' world, no matter how convinced he felt that it constituted no more than a quaint, homely relic of a past disintegrating in the freshness of Western freedom, he was even more an emotionally complex and talented artist capable of creating a vibrant portrait of his contemporary Anglo-Jewish brethren, old and new, in the pages of this, his most enduring book.

"Children of the Ghetto"

Book One of the novel is intended to provide the outsider with a true and sympathetic introduction to life among the inhabitants of London's East End. It is this part that is most accurately described by the work's subtitle, "A Study of a Peculiar People." The tumultuous, kaleidoscopic life of Whitechapel bustles past the reader, with Israel Zangwill as witty, inspired guide. And because he willingly accepts a realist's—not an apologist's—perspective, the tour he conducts is impressive and convincing.

Because the scenery is the main object in this part of the work, plot is very subordinate. Rather, what determines the pacing of this "book" is the social topography of the community.[35] This topography is delineated both through traditional narrative techniques and through the use of extended realistic dialogues made popular in the novels of George Meredith and already employed by Zangwill as early as *The Premier and the Painter.*

The topography of the ghetto is explored primarily in serial fashion. First comes the social stratification, then the ghetto "types," and finally the immigrant institutions. But Zangwill is not rigid in this pattern and along the way he lingers here and there to point out still other interesting sites or to ride some personal hobbyhorse, as all good guides do.

The opening chapters of the book portray the classes of the immigrant community from the bottom upward. It begins with a description of the Ansells, a family headed by a pious *luftmentsch* who had been at odds with his late wife, an ambitious and practical woman frustrated by the hand-to-mouth squalor of the family. Although no doubt reflecting something of the home of Moses Zangwill transferred here to the lowest social rung, and also something of Amy Levy's Quixano family, Zangwill employs the Ansells in "Children of the Ghetto" primarily as a vehicle for social description, not as autobiography.

In fact, the Ansells are typical of many of the immigrant families. Though the parents are inescapably trapped in poverty, they are ambitious to promote the advancement of their children through an Anglicized education, a process that has the unanticipated but immediate effect of alienating parents and children culturally, linguistically, and spiritually, as already outlined in "Under Sentence of Marriage."

Concentrating on Esther Ansell, the young daughter, Zangwill not only is able to describe the immigrants' poverty, the *luftmentsch,* and the generational alienation, but he also briefly describes, with very mixed emotions, the Jews' Free School, whose bell summons

> its pupils from the reeking courts and alleys, from the garrets and the cellars, calling them to come and be Anglicized. And they come in a great straggling procession recruited from every lane and by-way, big children and little children, boys in blackening corduroy, and girls in washed-out cotton; tidy children and ragged children . . . , all hastening at the inexorable clang of the big school-bell to be ground in the same great, blind, inexorable Governmental machine.[36]

Equally effective, Zangwill expresses through Esther his immense contempt for philanthropists, the "semi-divinities" who, while the hungry await their soup-kitchen handouts, preen themselves in the sunlight of their own beneficence. Only after a plethora of mutual and self-congratulatory speeches by the lofty patricians is it that "at last the turn of the gnawing stomachs came."[37]

But what is particularly important about the Ansells is that their grinding poverty has not degraded them. They are poor only materially; in spirit, in ambition, in literacy, and in mutual consideration they remain uncorrupted. There is no drunkenness, no wife beating nor child abuse, no brutality, no hopeless surrender to the inevitability of penury. And this is the central purpose of the Ansells in this "book"—to assure the English that these Jews, even the most impoverished among them, are moral and material assets to the country, posing no threat to social order, stability, or long-term social cohesion.

Ascending the social scale next described is "The Sweater," Bear Bekovitch. By tracing his biography back through his Polish origins, his motives for migrating, and his life at home and in his shop, Zangwill is able to create a believable and generally sympathetic figure for what the general British public regarded as the archdemon of the East End. Here, although apologetic in tone, Zangwill truly reflects the ghetto's own view of its "sweaters":

> He was a tall, harsh-looking man of fifty, with grizzled hair, to whom life meant work, and work meant money, and money meant savings. In Parliamentary Blue-Books, English newspapers, and the Berner Street Socialistic Club, he was called a "sweater" and the comic papers pictured him with a protuberant paunch and a greasy smile, but he had not the remotest idea that he was other than a God-fearing, industrious, and even philanthropic citizen. The measure that had been dealt to him he did but deal to others. He saw no reason why immigrant paupers should not live on a crown a week while he taught them how to handle a press-iron or work a sewing machine. They were much better off than in Poland. He would have been glad of such an income himself in those terrible first days of English life. . . . No, no one could accuse Bear Bekovitch of fattening on the entrails of his employees.[38]

Introducing the Bekovitch family allows Zangwill not only the opportunity to describe a higher economic stratum but also to portray the complexities of their family life, as their upward economic mobility complicates and elevates the social expectations of both parents and children. Here, clearly, Zangwill gives way to the full play of his wry humor and satire, but, unlike that of his New Humour works, it is done gently, wistfully.

Finally, there is the Ansells' "rich" relation, Malka, a self-assured petit bourgeois philistine Zangwill good-naturedly satirizes. Gregarious, opinionated, and combative, Malka is ultimately good-hearted. She is the perfect vehicle to humanize the "alien" extrovert behavior of the immigrants in the eyes of reserved Englishmen. And through the ceaseless chatter of Malka and her family, the reader obtains a glimpse into the transitional nature of immigrant life—bewailing the falling away from traditional values by the younger generation while nibbling at English-style fried fish!

Turning from the social topography Zangwill then portrays sympathetically the unique, Dickensian characters typical of the immigrant world. Among these is the "pauper alien," the peddler, Moses Ansell. In a very striking passage, Moses' wanderings about Britain are movingly described:

> For the despised three-hatted scarecrow of Christian caricature, who shambled along snuffling "Old clo'," had a strenuous inner life. . . . To Moses, "travelling" meant straying forlornly in strange towns and villages, given over to the worship of an alien deity and ever ready to avenge his crucifixion; in a land of whose tongue he knew scarce more than the Saracen damsel married by legend to à Becket's father. It meant praying brazenly in crowded railway trains. . . . It meant living chiefly on dry bread and drinking black tea out of his own cup. . . . It meant carrying the red rag of an obnoxious personality through a land of bulls. It meant passing months away from wife and children, in a solitude only occasionally alleviated by a Sabbath spent in a synagogue town. It meant putting up at low public houses and common lodging houses, where rowdy disciples of the Prince of Peace often sent him bleeding to bed, or shamelessly despoiled him of his merchandise, or bullied and blustered him out of a fair price, knowing he dared not resent. It meant being chaffed and gibed at in language of which he only understood that it was cruel.[39]

It is interesting that Zangwill himself does not recognize the toughness and resiliency of character described here in a personality he considers sentimentally only a ne'er-do-well *luftmentsch.* That Zangwill the artist is capable of describing the peddler's set of values but as a Jew remains aloof from them is indicative of his conflicting cultural heritages. Like the Jews sketched in *Reuben Sachs,* Israel Zangwill was unable to appreciate the value of character not measured on the scales of public success.[40] This myopia becomes particularly apparent in the second part of *Children of the Ghetto,* as will be discussed below.

Another ghetto personality is the rabbi, in this case Reb Shemuel Jacobs. Portrayed at home with his family, "he was an official of heterogeneous duties. . . . In fine, he was a witty old fellow and everybody loved him."[41] Zangwill, at least at this point, also wants his non-Jewish reader to do likewise. Only later will a "fanatical" and overbearing side of Reb Shemuel be revealed.

If there is the ghetto's peddler and rabbi, then there must also be its intellectual, in this case "the neo-Hebrew poet," Melchitsedek Pinchas, a self-taught *shtetl* aesthete moved West. If the peddler possesses a profound inner strength and the rabbi a warm exterior, Pinchas is a brash, crackbrained bohemian termagant without scruples, and yet, for all that, in his sheer egoism and wrongheadedness there is a charm. At least Zangwill so portrays him, and he had known an original at the *Jewish Standard* where he had worked alongside Naphtali Herz Imber. Such were the "Enlightened intellectuals" of Zangwill's London ghetto.

Zangwill also introduces several other typical immigrant types. There is Sugarman, the *shadchan* (marriage-broker), a busybody mixing into everyone's affairs, Shosshi Shmendrik, whose family name means "awkward" and who is awkward, all to his immediate discomfort and eventual good fortune; there is the outcast, Dutch Debby, who had borne an illegitimate child and now lives a lonely life reading through worn old magazines; and here, too, is a Hyams family, silent among themselves, the parents alienated from the son, Daniel, the father dreaming of dying in Jerusalem, a dream eventually dissolved into disillusionment when once he visits the shabby original.

From the human topography, Zangwill turns to the institutional, where his gentle humor is particularly apparent. At times the guide leads his tour group in on tiptoe, so to speak, so as stealthily to peer in on some scene through a window or doorway; at other times, he brings them boldly into the center of events swirling frenetically about. But always he has an entertaining yarn to tell.

It is in the former way that he approaches the immigrants' religion. Two of the most typical Whitechapel religious institutions are briefly depicted, the Sabbath and a boy's bar mitzvah. More fully, but still diffidently portrayed, is one of the East End's *chevrot,* "minor synagogues," the "Sons of the Covenant." Here Zangwill has an opportunity to summarize the yearly cycle of Jewish holy days, to describe the informalities of the immigrants' synagogues and worship, and their petty politics and their poverty. But that this is not his world Zangwill makes explicit:

> Thus they lived and died, these Sons of the Covenant, half-automata, sternly disciplined by voluntary and involuntary privation, hemmed and mewed in by iron walls of form and poverty, joyfully ground under the perpetual rotary wheel of ritualism, good-humored withal and casuistic like all people whose religion stands much on ceremony; inasmuch as a ritual law comes to count one equally with a moral, and a man is not half bad who does three-fourths of his duty.
>
> The poorest life is to itself the universe and all that there is, and these humble products of a great and terrible past . . . were all the happier for not knowing that the fullness of life was not theirs.[42]

Zangwill had yet to discover that he would achieve neither: the happiness of the "Sons of the Covenant" nor "the fullness of life."

But it is into the secular institutions that he barges, leading his band of readers along. The comic ineptitude of radical labor unions and the amateurish follies of the Yiddish theater are humorously observed. And even more so the Purim ball held at the People's Palace. Here, especially, Zangwill pokes gentle fun at the Anglicized pretensions of immigrant youth; his distaste at this superficial, philistine acculturation is even stronger than his alienation from the traditional synagogue: "These young men in dress-coats were epitomes of one aspect of Jewish history. Not in every respect improvements on the 'Sons of the Covenant,' though; replacing the primitive manners and the piety of the foreign Jew by a veneer of cheap culture and a laxity of ceremonial observance."[43]

Petticoat Lane is described at length with its crush of frantic customers, the raucous clamor of its hawkers, the contrasts of rich and poor, Jew and Christian, good humor and bitter rivalry. The tourist, elbowing through it all, cannot help but feel the jostling pressure of the crowd, hear the shrill shouting of the hucksters, and smell the pungent odors of the market.

And most interestingly, Zangwill portrays the proto-Zionist members of the Chovevei Zion movement in his chapter, "The Holy Land League." A motley collection, they are convened by Guedalayah the greengrocer, who explains the group's goal:

> Let us help ourselves. Let us put our hands in our own pockets. With our *Groschen* let us rebuild Jerusalem and our Holy Temple. We will collect a fund slowly but surely—from all parts of the East End and the provinces the pious will give. With the first fruits we will send out a little party of persecuted Jews to Palestine, and then another; and another.[44]

Following this the little gathering is roused by "The Watch on the Jordan," whose words, the reader is wryly informed, have been "so nobly sung" by "the National Poet of Israel, Naphtali Herz Imber."[45]

The deprecatory portrayal of Chovevei Zion in *Children of the Ghetto*—the sense of its futile methods and its ignorant utopianism—Zangwill never saw a reason to revise. It was a movement, in whatever guise, that he would ridicule and oppose throughout his life. For him, this concept of piecemeal, practical settlement constituted nothing but a pathetic *luftmentsch*'s dream. This same attitude would later make him a "Herzlian" Zionist, then a Territorialist, and, finally, an "extremist" Zionist denouncing the moderate leadership of Chaim Weizmann.

Zangwill was not, however, a mere tourists' guide in "Children of the Ghetto." Following Kompert and Franzos, his description of the ghetto is the complement of a fictional tale, in this case the stories of two female protagonists, the young girl, Esther Ansell, and the young woman, Hannah Jacobs. Esther Ansell is often treated by commentators as the heroine of the novel, but this view is obtained only by reading the contents of "Grandchildren of the Ghetto" back into Book One. But treating this "book" on its own, or as in the stage version, Hannah clearly emerges as the more central and dramatic character of "Children of the Ghetto."

Esther's function in Book One is to provide its descriptions with a certain artistic unity. The "book" opens and concludes with her, and many of the portraits are presented in the wake of her movements and encounters through the East End. However, if in this "book" Esther's character is left rather nebulous and ill defined, two striking observations are made about her, for they are both autobiographical.

The narrator explains that:

> Esther led a double life, just as she spoke two tongues. The knowledge that she was a Jewish child, whose people had a special history, was always at the back of her consciousness. . . .

> But far more vividly did she realize that she was an English girl; far keener than her pride in Judas Maccabaeus was her pride in Nelson and Wellington. . . . Esther absorbed these ideas from the school reading books. The experience of a month overlay the hereditary bequest of a century. And yet, beneath all, the prepared plate remains most sensitive to the old impressions.[46]

This is Israel Zangwill calmly describing the turmoil wrought within between his English education and his Jewish heritage. As the final sentence indicates, at this point he still had confidence that assimilation is not inevitable and that Jewish identity may somehow be sustained. The dilemma arose when, later, Zangwill would attempt to figure out exactly how.[47]

In an equally revealing passage, Esther confesses to her brother that she enjoys reading the New Testament, which "seems just as interesting as the Old Testament," and wonders "why do I feel good when I read what Jesus said?"[48] Strange attitudes for the daughter of pious Moses Ansell! Or for the son of Moses Zangwill. But it is a true and telling admission. The inner depth and meaning of the father's piety and observance were not being transmitted to the children, and for Zangwill the spiritual vacuum lying behind the veneer of empty formal ceremony was being filled by the teaching of Jesus as expounded in the New Testament, the nondogmatic fusion of the Jewish and Christian already alluded to in "English Judaism." Mentioned here only in passing, six years later this theme will form the central motif of *Dreamers of the Ghetto.*

But in "Children of the Ghetto," the story of Reb Shemuel's daughter, Hannah, forms the primary dramatic thread interwoven through its kaleidoscope of portraits.[49] Its theme is a subtle, muted, and artistically superior version of the inner struggle of Alfred Hyams in the unpublished draft novel. It explores more deeply the observations made in "Under Sentence of Marriage" and even echoes the mood of the schoolboy's story, "Practical Proverbs by a disillusionised man." What is at issue in Hannah's story is really the fundamental preoccupation of Zangwill's entire life already alluded to by Esther Ansell: the place of traditional Judaism in modern Western society. Entailed in this issue are the conflict of generations, loyalty to family and people, even to the point of self-sacrifice, and the impediments to a "normal" life deliberately erected by the apparently outmoded and arbitrary rigidities of Jewish law.

Hannah is visiting Malka and her family; everyone is in great humor as Malka's daughter, engaged to Samuel Levine, is being given a glimpse of her wedding ring by her fiancé. Playing to the galleries for laughs, Sam suddenly grabs Hannah's right hand and forcibly puts the ring on it, declaring them married according to the traditional formula. This clowning incites general merriment among all till an old man observes that, in fact, Sam and Hannah are indeed now wed according to Jewish law. When this is confirmed by Reb Shemuel, Sam is required to grant Hannah a formal religious divorce.

In the course of time Hannah meets David Brandon, who admits to the rabbi's daughter his rejection of Jewish orthodoxy. Then she, too, confesses that if she had her own way, "I would probably go in for a change, I'm so tired—so tired of this eternal ceremony."[50] Here is a painful insight into the immigrant experience: the fathers' failure in transmitting the centrality of Jewish values to their children in the new environment; not even the rabbi succeeds. Still, Hannah cannot choose this path of rebellion: "I would never marry a man, myself, who might hurt my father's position. I should have to keep a *kosher* house or look how people would talk!"[51] Filial honor, not faith, principle, or conviction is Hannah's motive, even to the point of self-sacrifice, although in this instance not for some sacred cause but rather for the sake of her father's public image and personal self-respect.

Hannah and David eventually do decide to wed, and Reb Shemuel accepts the young man, as he has agreed to observe Jewish rituals to please the old rabbi and win his blessing. But in the course of conversation, David reveals that he is a *cohen,* a descendant of the temple priests, who by Biblical law are prohibited from marrying a divorcée, and Hannah—because of some clowning and the strictures of the law—is now ritually a divorcée. Consequently Reb Shemuel forbids the marriage.[52]

But the couple decide to elope, to run away to America, where no one will know who or what they are. Hannah is to slip out of her parents' home during the first evening of Passover in order to meet the waiting David. But when the decisive night comes, as time slowly passes and David impatiently awaits her in a London rainstorm, Hannah cannot bring herself to flee from her father's table. Finally as the end of the Passover *seder* (family ritual meal) draws near and Hannah opens the door in the traditional welcome to the Prophet Elijah, she espies her beloved and bids him good-bye. Her father's standards and her profound sense of duty to him triumph on this night of the liberation of the Jewish people from Egyptian slavery.

This Passover evening Hannah surrenders her future to her father's

Reb Shemuel forbidding the marriage of Hannah and David, from "Children of the Ghetto," performed at the Herald Square Theatre, 1899. *Courtesy, The Hampden-Booth Theatre Library at The Players.*

ancient principles and young Esther Ansell sits in her family's garret dreaming of the bright future life seems to promise her. So concludes "Children of the Ghetto," this *maggid*'s tale of the twinned destinies drawing the immigrant Jews of modern London.

"Grandchildren of the Ghetto"

The tone of Book Two, "Grandchildren of the Ghetto," is noticeably altered from that employed in the narration of Book One. Zangwill, in this portion, is aiming at a different audience and intending to accomplish an altogether different purpose. Here he is addressing Jewish readers and, rather than guiding them with entertaining stories through the immigrants' London, he is censuring their shortcomings and pleading for their reformation. This, too, is a *maggid*'s task. But even more, Israel Zangwill seeks in this "book" to elucidate the deepest philosophic truths of a modernist Judaism for his readers. This was the commissioned task from the JPS that he had accepted. In this endeavor he is no longer merely the *maggid* exhorting his flock but is aspiring to the role of sage, the expounder of the fundamental wisdom of Judaism. So Hannah Jacobs, who selflessly conforms to her father's rigid stringencies, is abandoned in this "book" to a life of sterile spinsterhood as the penalty for the nobility of character she has displayed. For this is not the choice her creator, the author, himself has made. Instead, in "Grandchildren of the Ghetto," the stories are told of Israel Zangwill and of Amy Levy.

In contrast to the closing of "Children of the Ghetto," on Passover in the East End, Book Two opens with "The Christmas Dinner" in the fashionable West End home of the Henry Goldsmiths, a prominent Anglo-Jewish family. The evening is described not in the light, tolerant tone of a knowledgeable guide displaying an interesting but foreign scene to tourists. Now there is no distance between narrator and characters; rather, a heavy hand intrudes to expose and to mock.

After all, the exasperated narrator explains, it is only so as not to offend their Irish maid, Mary, that the Goldsmiths observe Jewish rituals at all: "they hesitated to admit that they did not respect their religion . . . as much as she did hers."[53] As a result, "the dread of shocking Mary" and her "Jewish prejudices" maintain some semblance of Jewish observance in the Goldsmith household. Even their Christmas party must be disguised as a "Chanukah dinner" to avoid distressing the pious Mary. As the evening proceeds the narrator finds it increasingly difficult to restrain his wrath at these self-righteous wealthy frauds.

Although the conversation at dinner ranges over a wide variety of Anglo-Jewish topics, the central preoccupation is *Mordecai Josephs*, a novel by a certain Edward Armitage exposing the shallowness and hypocrisy of West End Anglo-Jewry and its Orthodox formalism. The Goldsmiths' guests are indignant, but the indignation of the narrator is even greater:

> Poor-rich Jews! The upper middle-classes had every excuse for being angry [at the book]. They knew they were excellent persons, well-educated and well-travelled, interested in charities (both Jewish and Christian), people's concerts, district-visiting, new novels, magazines, reading-circles, operas, symphonies, politics . . . : that they had sons

> at Rugby and Oxford, and daughters who played and painted and sang, and homes that were bright oases of optimism in a jaded society; that they were good Liberals and Tories, supplementing their duties as Englishmen with a solicitude for the best interests of Judaism.[54]

Among the guests at the Goldsmith party are two young people, Raphael Leon and Esther Ansell. Raphael has appeared briefly in "Children of the Ghetto" as a well-to-do Harrow boy attracted to Judaism and the immigrant world. He now moves to center-stage as the spokesman for an authentic Judaism, a welcome contrast for the narrator to the Goldsmiths' sham.

Raphael's view of his religious heritage mirrors the philosophy presented in Zangwill's "English Judaism":

> That there is a power outside us nobody denies; that this Power works for our good and wisely is not so hard to grant when the facts of the soul are weighed with the facts of Nature. Power, Love, Wisdom, there you have a real trinity which makes up the Jewish God. . . . That comes into collision with no modern philosophies; we appeal to experience and make no demands upon the faculty for believing. . . . History testifies that this has verily been our [Jewish] mission, that we have taught the world religion as truly as Greece has taught beauty and science.[55]

And Raphael believes this historical positivist "natural Judaism" possesses universal significance: "All practical, honorable men are Jews at heart. Judaism has never tampered with human dignity, nor perverted the moral consciousness. . . . Judaism is the true 'religion of humanity.' "[56]

But Raphael will learn the bitter lesson that his "natural Judaism" is not the hollow formalism of the Goldsmiths; it is irrelevant to the observant immigrants as well. He is taught this disillusioning truth through his experiences as the hapless editor of a new Anglo-Jewish Orthodox weekly, the *Flag of Judah*.

What saves "Grandchildren of the Ghetto" from becoming a mere series of didactic soliloquies on the themes of "English Judaism" is the merry description interwoven through it of the always perilous existence of this newspaper and its motley staff. Once again Zangwill is at his artistic best in the good-humored portrayal of this turbulent Dickensian world. At its center is the embattled Raphael struggling to bring the paper out on time amid the riotous tumult of a squabbling publishing board, a harried printer, a dearth of reporters, an overabundance of interfering community busybodies, and a gaggle of querulous contributors. Among the latter the most troublesome and amusing are *Froom* (devout) Karlkammer, the Orthodox letter-writing "zealot," and the irrepressible poet Melchitsedek Pinchas. Here, certainly, is the chaotic world of the *Jewish Standard* transformed into entertaining fiction.[57]

If Raphael echoes the author of "English Judaism," his subeditor, the irreverent "little Samson,"—"a lively young Bohemian . . . who had served an apprenticeship on the Anglo-Jewish press, and worked his way up into the larger journalistic press"—bears a striking resemblance to "Marshallik," even to his physical likeness.[58] At one point "this young gentleman, who always wore long curling locks, an eyeglass and a romantic cloak which covered a multitude of shabbiness," writes a "burlesque of the notorious *Mordecai Josephs* by comically exaggerating its exaggerations."[59] This is exactly how "Marshallik" did treat Amy Levy's *Reuben Sachs* in his parody "Dr. Reuben Green, by Amy Danby."[60] Nor is this coincidence without significance, for the true author of *Mordecai Josephs,* we learn, is Esther Ansell.

Time in *Children of the Ghetto* is a mere formal convention. Although ten years are said to elapse between its two "books," what really alters is not objective chronology but the artistic function of major characters. For purposes of "Children of the Ghetto," Esther is an East End immigrant's little girl; in "Grandchildren of the Ghetto" she is a meld of Amy Levy and her fictional protagonist Judith Quixano. The result is character discontinuity in Esther's appearance in the two parts of the novel, viz. an East End Esther and a West End Esther, a disparity also to be found in other persons Zangwill portrays in both parts of the work.

Like Judith Quixano, Esther Ansell is the daughter of a pious *luftmentsch;* also like Judith, she has been plucked from poverty to be raised in the home of a fashionable West End Anglo-Jewish family. And like Amy Levy, Esther writes a novel exposing the self-righteous arrogance, religious hypocrisy, and cultural philistinism of Anglo-Jewry. But unlike Levy's, Esther's book, a denunciation of her benefactors, appears under a nom de plume, and she continues to enjoy their hospitality while simultaneously witnessing their discomfited indignation at her novel. That she is capable of maintaining her position in the Goldsmith household after publication of *Mordecai Josephs* without any qualms of conscience is a telling commentary on the nature of the adult Esther's moral character, a discontinuity with that of the girl Esther, a discontinuity of which Zangwill himself seems unaware.[61]

What eventually provokes Esther to reveal the truth to the Goldsmiths and to break with them is not any ethical or moral consideration but a bizarre and traumatic encounter with a childhood acquaintance, Levi Jacobs, Reb Shemuel's son.

The rabbi's boy has also drastically altered. Now calling himself Leonard James, Levi has been apprenticed by his father to a lawyer but has secretly given up the apprenticeship to enter upon a career in the theater. Not surprisingly, he has also, unbeknown to this father who continues to support him, broken with all traditional Jewish observance. Shortly after meeting each other again after so many years, Levi calls on Esther at the Goldsmith home and proposes marriage. She rejects him, provoking him to mock her bitterly as "a *Schnorrer* and the daughter of a *Schnorrer*."[62] Levi stalks out and, now in a state of moral collapse, goes out on Passover eve for a night-on-the-town of eating and drinking, when he is suddenly discovered in the company of a tart by his distraught father. Levi tells the girl that Reb Shemuel is "nobody; only an old Jew who supplies me with cash," while Reb Shemuel declares his son dead.[63]

But Levi's taunts have worked their poison in Esther. Her honor, not her conscience, has been pricked. In what Zangwill presents as a heroic act, she quietly slips out of the Goldsmith home, leaving behind a letter disclosing that she is the author of *Mordecai Josephs* and explaining that she had intended no harm by the book nor felt anything but gratitude for the Goldsmiths' generosity. Esther accounts for her departure clearly in the psychological terms of Levi's sneers, not because of any ethical sensibilities: "the sphere in which you move is too high for me; I cannot assimilate with it and I return, not without gladness, to the humble sphere whence you took me."[64]

With Esther's return to Whitechapel, "Grandchildren of the Ghetto" becomes, essentially, a disquisition on the varieties of "natural Judaism." These are represented by the views of Raphael, disillusioned with the narrow Orthodoxy of the original Whitechapel proprietors of the *Flag of Judah*; of Esther, disillusioned with the fruitless piety of her father and the sham formalism of West End Orthodoxy; and of Joseph Strelitski, a scholar briefly introduced in Book One and who, in this "book" having achieved remarkable popularity as a fashionable United Synagogue minister, abandons the pulpit disillusioned.

It is Strelitski who most clearly articulates the outlook of historical positivist "natural Judaism":

> How can Judaism—and it alone—escape going through the fire of modern scepticism, from which, if religion emerges at all, it will emerge without its dross? . . .
>
> . . . We must make broad our platform, not our phylacteries. It is because I am with you in admiring the Rabbis that I would undo much of their work. Theirs was a wonderful statesmanship, and they built wiser than they knew; just as the patient labors of superstitious zealots who counted every letter of the Law preserved the text unimpaired for the benefit of modern scholarship. The Rabbis constructed a casket, if you will, which kept the jewel safe, though at the cost of concealing its lustre. But the hour has come now to wear the jewel on our breasts before all the world. The Rabbis worked for their time—we must work for ours. Judaism was before the Rabbis. Scientific criticism shows its thoughts widening with the process of the suns. . . . In every age our great men have modified and developed Judaism. Why should it not be trimmed into concordance with the culture of the time? Especially when the alternative is death? . . .
>
> . . . The world is longing for a broad simple faith that shall look on science as its friend and reason as its inspirer. . . . Now, for the first time in history, is the hour of Judaism. Only it must enlarge itself; its platform must be all-inclusive. Judaism is but a specialized form of Hebraism; even if Jews stick to their own special historical and ritual ceremonies, it is only Hebraism—pure spiritual kernel—that they can offer the world.[65]

Here is the "Jewish *Robert Elsmere*" expounding his "new religion"—a "natural Judaism." It is also Zangwill's credo, as first expounded in "English Judaism" and further developed over the years.

That Strelitski is indeed Zangwill's philosophic alter ego is evident from the contents of a speech, "Hebrew, Jew, Israelite," that Zangwill delivered in 1892, the year *Children of the Ghetto* was published. In his remarks Zangwill explains:

> The dogmas of Judaism to-day are not the dogmas of Isaiah and Hosea and the Psalmists. But the ideals to-day are precisely the ideals of the Prophets and all the great Jews that ever lived—the eternal aspiration after truth and justice—and these are the ideals of every man . . . for Hebraism has conquered the civilized world—it is in the blood of every honourable man.

. . . because we gather under the broad banner of Hebraic ideals . . . it by no means follows that we repudiate Jewish ideals. Judaism is simply a concrete expression of the Hebrew ideals—not perhaps the only possible expression but still the one which actually shaped itself in history, and has thus taken on new claims and characteristics as an historic organism; Judaism I regard as a reduction to practice of Hebrew ideals, an attempt to realise the perfect society, in accordance with a sagacious statecraft, and I by no means look on Jewish ideals as played out.

. . . I am afraid too many Jewish reformers confound Judaism with Hebraism and think that Judaism is merely Christianity minus Christ. But it is something more positive, something, which apart from its supernaturalism, is not different in essence from that which so modern a thinker as Herbert Spencer conceives the world needs to-day.

. . . If I may make a distinction I have long pondered, between our triple names—Hebrew, Jew and Israelite—the Hebrew is the ideal, the Jew the adherent of an historical system, the Israelite the Jew by birth. . . . The last, the Israelite, we cannot avoid being; it is our lowest common factor.[66]

Having served to educate the reader in the tenets of "natural Judaism," "Grandchildren of the Ghetto" concludes, significantly with Raphael remaining in Britain while Esther and Joseph sail to America. At its end we see Raphael "waving his handkerchief towards the throbbing vessel that glides with its freight of hopes and dreams across the great waters towards the New World."[67] So too Zangwill, remaining in England, looked to the United States as the land where the Hebraic ideals might yet be realized.

The Legacy, Revealed and Concealed

With publication of *Children of the Ghetto,* Israel Zangwill became the most prominent English-language Jewish novelist on both sides of the Atlantic. In it he had implemented fully Amy Levy's program of portraying the Western Jewish milieu in literature. In this effort he was following consciously in the tradition of the Western "ghetto" authors.

But enlarging upon this agenda, Zangwill sought not merely to describe but through his realistic depiction of the "private" world of the immigrants also to attack the negative literary stereotype of the Jew and to evoke a more human and sympathetic image of the Jews in Western society. In 1892 this was still a most daring venture requiring great courage, for it entailed the risks of offending "polite" British opinion and image-conscious Jewish spokesmen. That he succeeded is evident from the work's immediate reception.

Children of the Ghetto won critical acclaim among both non-Jewish and Jewish reviewers. They recognized that Israel Zangwill, with this book, had entered upon a new stage in his literary career, one to be taken much more seriously than his New Humour phase.

Typical of non-Jewish reactions was the comment of the *Athenaeum:*

> In "Children of the Ghetto" he [Zangwill] strikes out a new line . . . , the present book is a serious novel of considerable merit. . . . The chief interest of the book lies in the wonderful description of the Whitechapel Jews. . . . The picture is most sympathetically drawn. . . . But his sympathy does not blind him to their faults. . . . Moreover the vividness and force with which Mr. Zangwill brings before us the strange and uncouth characters with which he had peopled his book are truly admirable.[68]

Similarly the *Jewish Chronicle,* which had already published the "Proem" prior to the novel's release, devoted a two-page review to Zangwill's book:

> Admirable for wit and originality as Mr. Zangwill's earlier books have been, in the "Children of the Ghetto" he strikes a firmer and more ambitious note. Here he must be judged as a novelist, as a writer who seeks to portray human life, while before he was the narrator of confessedly bizarre impossibilities. And the result of a close study of Mr. Zangwill's new book is to convince the reader . . . that in Mr. Zangwill a literary star of the first magnitude has at last risen above the Jewish horizon in England.
>
> . . . That the "Children of the Ghetto" is very largely true is clear to the superficial reader, and clearer still to the careful reader. Mr. Zangwill has a mastery over Jewish custom, over Jewish life in all its crannies and ramifications, he has insight into the ideal and an eye for the mean and tawdry, a sigh for its pathos and a smile for its joy like Franzos.[69]

In private correspondence, too, Zangwill received praise for the novel. For instance, a close friend, Solomon Schechter's wife, Mathilde, wrote to him: "It is a great novel, and I confess the first book of yours which I read through in one sitting . . . and I am re-reading again with deeper emotion. The comical and the serious elements are equally attractive."[70]

Despite the general praise, reviewers also discovered certain difficulties in the work. For non-Jewish critics, these were primarily stylistic, finding the plot weak, Book Two awkward, and occasionally, especially with regard to Esther's conduct, displaying "a want of good taste."[71]

On the other hand, the *Jewish Chronicle* expressed concern that Zangwill had been too realistic: "It is realistic, and like most realistic works tells too much. . . . There is something too much of insistence on unsavoury details which do not add a jot to the vividness or truth of the picture . . . and leave an unpleasant taste in a Jewish reader's mouth." Equally disturbing to insecure Anglo-Jewry's squirming sensibilities, the review complains that "there are indeed some aspects of middle-class life of the English Jews which . . . Mr. Zangwill has not sense of humour enough to appreciate fairly."[72]

With the passage of time, however, the positive assessment of *Children of the Ghetto* prevailed, while the negative elements either faded as a result of later literary conventions or were even transmuted into merits. Best summing up the lasting achievement of the novel is the appraisal in 1926 by Stephen S. Wise, then president of the American Jewish Congress: "Zangwill's 'Children of the Ghetto' was not a book; it was an event. It was the first conscious act of self-disclosure to occur in Jewish life since the lowering of the barriers which shut the Jews out of and away from the life of the world."[73]

Children of the Ghetto thus propelled Israel Zangwill into prominence as the leading Jewish novelist among the non-Yiddish-speaking public and also considerably enhanced his reputation as an important British author. However, because of the very novelty of its immediate achievement, other elements within the novel remained unnoticed by reviewers and readers alike, although they constitute important components of the work and provide serious portents of the future course of Zangwill's career and of a new literary genre.

In the first place, for all its humor and satire, this is a profoundly pessimistic book. Both sections of the novel are pervaded by an aura of spiritual and intellectual disillusionment. Hannah Jacobs and David Brandon are the disillusioned in Book One, while Raphael Leon, Esther Ansell, Joseph Strelitski, Levi Jacobs, and Reb Shemuel all experience disillusionment in Book Two. The only genuine hope expressed in the novel is at the end, that across the sea there may exist the truly "new world" of people's dreams.

This pessimism expresses the author's own inability to identify clearly to which historical tradition he belonged. The novel reflects Zangwill's painful quandary as to whether he is ultimately an Englishman or a Jew, the two being quite distinct.[74] Equally distressing for him is a parallel dilemma: he was unable to choose between the modernist intellectual formulation of religion and the emotional attraction of the palpable heritage of traditional Judaism.

It was in order to come to terms with these quandaries that Zangwill attempts to formulate his philosophy of Judaism. As defined by it, "Israelite" refers to a biological ethnic heritage; "Hebraism," to a universal ethical teaching; and "Judaism," to a mediator between the two, to the historical expression of "Hebraism" by one particular and exemplary ethnic community.[75]

The difficulty Zangwill faced was that these three categories seemed to demand conflicting responses. "Israelite" evoked a particularist, a nationalist path; "Hebrew" required a universal, assimilationist expression; and "Judaism," caught between the two, tilted now one way, now the other. At times, expressing the "sacred sociology" of the "Israelite" people, "Judaism" pointed to a nationalist, preservationist impulse; at other times, as an expression of the "Israelite" prophets Moses and Jesus, it pointed toward a universalist direction, as "the religion of the future."

If there is any genuine consistency at all in any of the characters who appear in both "Children of the Ghetto" and "Grandchildren of the Ghetto," it is certainly Esther Ansell's persistent ambivalence toward the meaning and implication of her identity as a contemporary Jew. Every alternative offers attractions but equally holds costly disadvantages. And in the end she can discover no resolution to her quandary but instead chooses to sail away to a land of "hopes and dreams."

SIX

Literary Lion

Belying the chaotic jumble scattered about the writing desk in his bachelor's rooms at 3 Hare Court, The Temple, the impeccably attired former child of the ghetto confidently strode the streets of London. With cravat and starched collar buttressing the smooth sanguine face, pince-nez firmly clipped to the prominent nose, and fedora—helpless to constrain the masses of tousled brown curls—squashed atop his large head, Israel Zangwill appeared the epitome of the well-heeled Victorian gentleman. Meticulously courteous and with an apposite witticism always ready on his lips, his was the outward bearing of Jane Austen's Darcy, although inwardly possessing the disposition of the youthful Emma Woodhouse and the knowledge of a further half century of British history. A Puckish "Marshallik" and an "Ariel" still, but now also a world-renowned success, his ebullient company was sought after constantly to grace the tables and rostrums of the best of fashionable literary societies. And he ever eagerly bestowed it.

The triumph of *Children of the Ghetto* had propelled Israel Zangwill into the international limelight. Anglo-Jewish intellectuals and British writers' circles courted him for the pleasure of his ready wit and his keen and encyclopedic insights. And Zangwill was avid to join these, his colleagues, in voicing his thoughts and values at the debates and dinners of the cultural elites of both communities. Indeed, as he explained to one interviewer, "The chief reward [of fame] seems to me the *entrée* to the society you like best."[1] Zangwill appeared to have achieved that acceptance, and even popularity, that had so painfully eluded him during his youth. This was the decade of the apogee of his literary reputation. From 1892 through 1902 Israel Zangwill was *the* literary lion of Anglo-Jewry.[2]

Among Anglo-Jewish cultural circles, preeminent place belonged to the Maccabeans. This club, formally organized in 1891, was actually an extension of an informal group, "the Wanderers," who had pre-

Israel Zangwill, 1897. *Courtesy, The Central Zionist Archives.*

viously gathered at the London home of Solomon Schechter and included among its members Israel and Louis Zangwill, Lucien Wolf, Israel Abrahams, and Joseph Jacobs.[3] The Maccabeans' dinners, and the speeches and debates occurring at them, were always reported in detail in the *Jewish Chronicle* and indicate the intellectual and political currents preoccupying Anglo-Jewish attention at any given time during this period.

The club, comprising as it did the community's artistic, intellectual, and political elites, became the principal forum for investigating communal philosophic and cultural currents in a generally enlightened and convivial atmosphere, and Zangwill, as speaker, debater, or dinner chairman, played a prominent part in its proceedings for over fifteen years. Only after his involvement in the Zionist Movement and in the Jewish Territorial Organization did Zangwill's participation in the Maccabeans prove to be so acrimonious and divisive that he was compelled to turn to other, more complacent venues and to withdraw from an active role in the club he had helped to found.[4]

Similarly, Zangwill became active in British literary groups, particularly the Author's Club and the Vagabond's Club. In the gatherings of these circles Zangwill became personally acquainted with leading contemporary authors, such as Walter Besant, Arthur Conan Doyle, T. Hall Crane, and H. Rider Haggard.[5] It was at the Author's Club, in fact, that Zangwill sought out the acquaintance of Thomas Hardy, his efforts crowned with an invitation in 1893 to an "at home" hosted by the Hardys.[6] And although never intimate, Zangwill and Hardy maintained cordial contact for at least two decades.[7]

Among the many notables and influential members of these clubs was their secretary, Douglas Sladen, with whom Zangwill established a long, genial relationship.[8] As Sladen later reminisced:

> [Zangwill] was . . . known for his biting wit as a speaker. When the lean, arrestive figure of the Jewish ex-schoolmaster craned over an assemblage, there was always an attentive silence. . . . The curly black hair—an orator's hair—the sallow complexion of the South, the pallor of the student, the eagle nose, the assertive smile, the confident paradox—how well I recall them![9]

But if Zangwill was a social and oratorical success during this decade, his principal and sustaining influence still derived from the power of his pen. And his literary mentor remained, as it had since his days at *Ariel*, Jerome K. Jerome, "always a thorough believer in Zangwill."[10] For several years Jerome had served as a gentle prod to elicit New Humour stories from Zangwill for the *Idler* and, later, for *To-day*, a new literary journal he edited, more serious works on both Jewish and non-Jewish themes. It was equally through Jerome's efforts that Zangwill gathered his stories in the *Idler* into his collection

The King of Schnorrers and his Jewish stories, some of which appeared in *To-day*, for *Ghetto Tragedies*, and it was for Jerome's magazine that he originally wrote his novel, *The Master*. For all these, Jerome also functioned as literary agent.[11] After 1895, as his interests and self-image began to shift, Zangwill's close professional collaboration with Jerome relaxed, although their friendship continued for several more years. Certainly it is fair to say that no one contributed more to the steady ascent of Israel Zangwill's literary reputation during this decade than did Jerome K. Jerome.

Zangwill's literary output during this decade was truly prodigious. His success with *Children of the Ghetto* only provoked him to work more intently, despite the always precarious state of his health. But the twinned pattern of his writing persisted: he wrote "Jewish stories" for one set of readers and "non-Jewish literature" for another. Only occasionally did the lines blur and the two overlap.

Jewish Works

Ghetto Tragedies

In 1893 *Ghetto Tragedies*, a collection of four short stories, appeared. An expanded version, containing an additional seven stories, was published under the title *They That Walk in Darkness* in 1899. Subsequently, in 1907, these eleven stories were reissued under the original title. Written in the Western "ghetto" literary tradition, the collection evokes the fading and poignant realities of the traditional Jewish world for a generation reaching maturity amid the glaring illumination of Western culture. Less didactic than most of his other fiction, this collection contains some of Zangwill's finest writing. Here his talent for description was allowed full expression and results in portraits that are animate and true. Yet the author's gnawing pessimism is also apparent; a common theme of many of these stories is the necessity for, despite the ironic futility of, self-sacrifice and noble ideals.

The original book contained two of Zangwill's most powerful early works, "Satan Mekatrig" and "Diary of a Meshumad." Added to these were two more recent stories. "Incurables" relates the story of an East End woman confined to a hospital and ignored by her unfaithful husband. Under pressure, he finally visits his wife and demands a divorce so as to be able to solemnize the affair with his paramour.

The despairing woman agrees; her self-sacrifice is rewarded when the ex-husband's new bride begins visiting her invalid former rival.[12]

In "The Sabbath-Breaker" Zangwill tells the ironically maudlin story of a Jewish grandmother in Poland. One Sabbath eve forty years ago the woman had received a letter from her only son, who resided in a distant town; in the missive her son complained that he was feeling unwell. Distressed by this news, she decided to violate the Sabbath law to visit him, but she arrived too late, discovering that he had died that very Sabbath eve.[13] Ever since then, the woman had carried the fateful letter in her pocket, but now pulls it out and tells her departed son she is finally coming; so saying, she dies.[14]

Of the seven new stories in the later edition, three—"Transition," "The Land of Promise," and "The Keeper of Conscience"—portray the decay of traditional Judaism when exposed to the freedoms of the West.[15] But in these stories Zangwill is still able to express the hope that this very disintegration is only the prelude to the truest yet flowering of the essence of Judaism:

> If a religion that I thought all formalism is capable of producing such types of abnegation as my dear old father, then it must, too, somewhere or other, hold in solution all those ennobling ingredients, all those stimuli to self-sacrifice, which the world calls Christian. Perhaps the prosaic epoch of Judaism into which I was born is only transitional . . . for I know I felt more of its poetry in my childhood; perhaps the future will develop (or recultivate) its diviner sides and lay more stress upon a life beautiful and thus all this blind instinct of isolation may prove only the conservation of the race for its nobler future, when it may still become . . . a witness to the highest, a chosen people in whom all the families of the earth may be blessed.[16]

But this wistful, autobiographical passage equally expresses its author's subterranean sense of "isolation" from his "beautiful" childhood and his "prosaic" present and his pessimism regarding the future of his people, who twice-"perhaps" may yet recover.

Contrasting with the Jews' universalist mission is the theme of "Noah's Ark," a fictionalized account of Mordecai Noah's attempt to found a Jewish homeland, Ararat, near Buffalo, New York.[17] In this story Zangwill clearly voices his rejection of Palestine as the likely site of a new Jewish national home; incredulously he remarks: "Re-erect Solomon's Temple in Palestine! A ruined country to regenerate a ruined people! A land belonging to the Turks, centre of the fanaticism of three religions and countless sects!"[18]

In despair the narrator, Peloni, cries in the throes of a fatal pessimism: "Israel had been too bent and broken by the dispersion and the long persecution; the spring snapped, he could not recover. . . . This pious patience—this rejection of the burden on to the shoulders of Messiah and Miracle—was it more than the veil of unconscious impotence? Ah, better sweep oneself away than endure the long ignominy."[19] Witnessing Noah's failure in America, believing Palestine an impossibility, Peloni commits suicide. And shortly after writing this story Zangwill joined the Zionist Movement!

This notion—that without a solution to the awful dilemma of the meaning of continued Jewish existence in the contemporary Western world only suicide, self-immolation, remained as an acceptable response—began to haunt Zangwill at this time. Implicit in this judgment is the estimation that unlike any other ethnic group, Jewish existence as a people for themselves would not provide sufficient justification for continued Jewish survival. Without possession of a recognizable significance, life for the Jew could no longer be sustained. But although the weight of doubt was proving too unbearable, the lack of firm identity too painful, Zangwill was not yet ready to surrender: he still believed in the efficacy of "hopes and dreams."

Although Zangwill in general rejected the nonrational in his fiction after "Satan Mekatrig," two stories in this collection do explore this realm. "They That Walk in Darkness" relates the story of an East End family's only son, the prodigy Brum. On the eve of his bar mitzvah, the boy inexplicably becomes blind, and when physicians and rabbis despair of a cure, Brum's mother decides: "Science and Judaism had failed her: perhaps this unknown power, this heathen Pope, had indeed mastery over things diabolical."[20] So the distraught woman, taking her blind son, who is unaware of their destination, sets off for Rome. Along the way Brum insists on visiting the beautiful Christian sites and ponders how people could believe in pagan deities and the Pope, though neither were true. Upon arriving in Rome, the boy, still unaware, is led into the presence of the Pope: "His face was transfigured with ecstatic forevision," and he falls dead.[21] This theme—the beauty and hypnotic fatality of Christianity for the Jew—later emerges as the fundamental motif of Zangwill's *Dreamers of the Ghetto* and of his nationalist politics.

In "Bethulah," Zangwill wrote one of his most impressive and profound short stories. It relates the story of an encounter between a modern American Jew and the beautiful daughter of an East European Chassidic *rebbe.* At first attracted by the picturesque Chassidim, the American decides to remain in the town for some time. But when he learns that a girl, the *rebbe*'s only child, is being held in seclusion because of her father's "Cabalistic mystifications," the Westernized narrator is horrified, for "Bethulah was not a being to be employed as a sort of supernatural advocate, but a sad, tender creature needing love and protection. . . . And for some fantastic shadow-myth a beautiful young life was to be immolated."[22]

The narrator has learned that this group of putative Chassidim believes that the messiah will be born "of her immaculacy," to a virgin (*betulah* in Hebrew) of the *rebbe*'s family. The American Jew is now determined to save her from such a fantastic fate and secretly arranges to meet her on the eve of Chanukah, which also happens to be Christmas eve. He offers to help her flee to America, but Bethulah adamantly refuses: her duty is to remain. The narrator, confessing the author's own uncomprehending absorption with the issue of Jewish survival, admits: "My passion [to rescue Bethulah from her "mission"] seemed suddenly prosaic and selfish. I was lifted up into the higher love that worships and abnegates."[23] Even many years later and after the dispersal of the "sect" members, the American finds Bethulah faithful to her duty.

Although the story has obvious Christian roots and the distorted portrait of these Chassidim is more accurately attributable to the Sabbatean heresy that so fascinated Zangwill (and is specifically mentioned in this story), there can be no doubt that "Bethulah" expresses its author's great attraction to the nonrational and mystical realm of religion. Whatever religious emotions he experienced emanated from these sources, offensive although they may have been to his own rationalism and his intellectualized view of Judaism.[24]

More so, "Bethulah" contrasts starkly with "Noah's Ark." In the latter, Jewish existence requires rational justification in terms of some universalist "Hebraic" mission, while in the former, Jewish survival is the manifest result of a mystical fidelity to a particularist "Judaic" sense of duty. How to find peace and unity through mediating between the opposing rigors of the "prosaic" rationalism of contemporary West and the "beautiful" devotionalism of traditional Judaism was a dilemma that obsessed and, increasingly oppressed, Israel Zangwill.

Finally, in this collection of stories, of autobiographical interest is

"To Die in Jerusalem," which relates the story of a pious East European father and his alienated and contemptuous Anglicized son, so ashamed of his "grotesque parent." In lonely despair, the father departs "to die in Jerusalem." Eventually, however, remorse affects both father and son; the latter travels to Jerusalem seeking forgiveness while the former, unaware of the son's actions, returns to England to pardon his son in person. Never meeting, each dies exiled in the chosen land of the other; such is the bitter irony of travails of life.[25]

Ghetto Tragedies, the product of the antagonistic tensions within the author's psyche, displays Zangwill's artistic gifts at their finest. Skillful craftsmanship is coupled with evocative creativity to produce stories animated by the palpable realities of human experience. Here, too, is his preoccupation over continued Jewish survival, his doubts about Palestine as the site of a revived national homeland, and his belief in the universal spiritual mission of Judaism, as well as his "illicit" fascination with enigmatic mysticism. But no answers are suggested, no solutions proffered; only questions pleading for responses.

The King of Schnorrers

The King of Schnorrers; Grotesques and Fantasies is probably Israel Zangwill's most enduring and popular book after *Children of the Ghetto.* It includes the novella of the title and fourteen short stories. Most originally appeared in the *Idler* and are in the New Humour genre; several, although not all, have Jewish characters.

Among the short stories the most interesting is "Flutter-duck, A Ghetto Grotesque."[26] In the Western "ghetto," rather than "New Humour," tradition, it relates the sad biography of a flighty and impious ghetto housewife, ruined by the scruples of her observant husband, the rebelliousness of her assimilated daughter, and the general wickedness of the world. Closest to the author's experience and perceptions, it is the most truthful and effective piece in the book.

But it is the novella, "The King of Schnorrers," that attracts the greatest attention.[27] Set in eighteenth-century London, it relates the story of Manasseh Bueno Barzillai Azevedo da Costa, "the King of Schnorrers" among the Jews of the capital. In episode after episode, Manasseh, a proud man of regal bearing, exacts his due as a *schnorrer* (beggar) by manipulating the foibles and weaknesses of the wealthy members of the Sephardi community. Manasseh wreaks havoc on the little community and its institutions as he deigns to accept its charity, and he triumphs in every test of wit he encounters. Through the adventures of this disdainful king, thumbing his nose at the bloated, pretentious grandees, Zangwill satirizes the wealthy and powerful who, behind their facades, are so insecure and feckless. Manasseh wins because he is imperious, determined, and clever—and never mean-spirited.[28]

"The King of Schnorrers" is Zangwill at his wittiest and is one of the best expressions of his skill as a New Humourist. It is not profound, but it is entertaining. And it could easily have been his own proud Manasseh who, when offered congratulations on his appointment as an editor, responded: "As regards the claims of the Jewish community on my gratitude, the only thing I have to be grateful to the Jewish community for, is that I have nothing for which to be grateful to it. This may seem a poor cause for gratitude, but the recollection of it has sweetened many hours otherwise bitter."[29]

Ghetto Comedies

Ghetto Comedies is a collection of fourteen short stories, the last Jewish fiction published by Israel Zangwill.[30] Coming at the end of his career as a story writer, after his entry upon his career as dramatist, essayist, nationalist leader, and social reformer, it well demonstrates Zangwill's exhausted creativity. The book is markedly uneven in quality, containing some stories that appear to be discarded, but charming, scraps of *Children of the Ghetto,* while others extend the "ghetto" portraits to the British provinces and America. Still others continue to proclaim their author's persistent pessimism over man's fate as he discovers himself unwitting victim of life's ironic perversions of his noblest wishes and intentions. Yet, many of these stories, although lacking the power of his previous Jewish stories, are still well worth reading.

What is most striking about this book, however, is Zangwill's increasingly overt identification of the Jews with the person and teachings of Jesus, his greatly altered views on the questions of intermarriage and of Jewish nationalism, and his conclusion that without drastic spiritual adaptation to Western values the only proper response to continued Jewish existence is ethnic self-annihilation.

"The Model of Sorrows" is a tremendously bitter story of spiritual disillusionment. It relates how a painter seeking a model for his portrait of "the Man of Sorrows" discovers him in the person of a Russian

Jewish immigrant to Britain, Israel Quarriar. The painter set out "to paint not the Christ that I started out to paint, but the Christ incarnated in a race, suffering."[31] But over the course of time the artist discovers that Israel is not quite the victim he claims to be but rather a petty swindler, and so in addition to the sorrow in the portrait he adds a touch of craft and guile:

> For surely here at least was the true tragedy of the people of Christ—to have persisted sublimely, and to be as sordidly perverted; to be king and knave in one; to survive two thousand years the loss of a fatherland and the pressure of persecution, only to wear on its soul the yellow badge which had defaced its garments. . . . The true tragedy, the saddest sorrow, lay in the martyrdom of an Israel *unworthy of his suffering.*[32]

Although no doubt in part reflecting Zangwill's own bitter struggle within, and his continuing early opposition to the Zionist Movement, the story even more reflects his Disraelian identification of the Jews with the mission and image of Jesus and his condemnation of Judaism's failure to remain faithful to these truths. Again, as in "Noah's Ark," Zangwill explicitly expresses his notion that, to survive, the Jewish people must prove "worthy"; extinction of separate identity is the only just alternative.

It is important to recognize that Israel Zangwill's insistence on the necessity of a justification for continued Jewish survival is not a mere idiosyncratic fixation. Instead it reflects the very real perception that while Western national identities represent a diversity within an encompassing cultural unity, his own Jewish and Western identities are intense and equal rivals, each wooing for his exclusive love and loyalty. What Zangwill is seeking is a reconciliation of his twinned identities by the creation of a new unity for Western Jews that will be congruent with that unitary identity found among ethnic Englishmen, Frenchmen, and Germans. To achieve this unity, he is seeking to placate both combatants by compressing somehow Jewish identity within the framework of the notion of "Western": Judaism is to represent the highest, the "spiritual," component of Western culture that was previously borne among the Gentile nations in the teachings of Jesus. Without such a niche defined within Western identity, a Jewish identity has no place: it must depart, either through total cultural assimilation or through physical separation.

In this exposition, Zangwill was choosing to analyze what others found uncongenial to notice, or indeed could not even see. But at the time he wrote "The Model of Sorrow," he was still groping toward this rationalist resolution of the conflict of identities. He comes to formulate it finally only to conclude that the combatants were irremediably intractable: no theoretical "middle path" between these rival identities could ever prove genuinely viable. Only the extreme solution—departure—might work.[33]

In "The Bearer of Burdens" Zangwill displays his new positive attitude toward Jewish-Christian intermarriage, adopting a theme reminiscent of Farjeon's *Solomon Isaacs.*[34] In this story, Henry Elknan, a child of the Spitalfields "ghetto," much to his mother's horror, marries a Christian girl; his elderly mother, the narrator pointedly observes, had failed to notice "the gradual process which had sapped Henry's instinct of racial isolation, or how he had passed from admiration of British ways into entire abandonment of Jewish."[35] His mother disowns Henry, and his non-Jewish wife dies in childbirth. Henry then marries a Jewish shrew to raise his young daughter, but, unable to endure his unpleasant spouse, he eventually deserts her and the child. Meanwhile, his mother discovers that her Jewish daughter-in-law is a drunken child-beater, the very opposite of the virtuous Christian woman she had replaced and the old lady had spurned. Horrified, Henry's elderly mother rescues her Christian granddaughter from the despicable Jewish stepmother and decides to raise the young girl herself: "this child was compensation for all [the old lady] had undergone, for all the years of trudging and grubbing and patching and turning. . . . The fusion of races had indeed made her [the granddaughter] sensitive and intelligent beyond the common."[36]

In "Anglicization" Zangwill explains how a Jewish boy like Henry could have lost his "instinct of racial isolation." Repeating almost exactly the description of Esther Ansell's youth, this narrator explains how it is that Solomon Cohn's son has come to join the British army in its fight against the Boers: "Anglicization had done its work: from his school days he had felt himself a descendant, not of Judas Maccabaeus, but of Nelson and Wellington."[37] Cohn's solution to the problems of white South Africa, interesting enough, is intermarriage of Britons and Boers.

Yet this same book that extols the universalism of a New Testament Judaism and the virtues of ethnic intermarriage simultaneously also powerfully advocates Jewish nationalism.[38] "The Jewish Trinity," for instance, is the story of Leopold Barstein, a young Jewish sculptor who has joined the Zionist Movement and is courting the daughter of a wealthy Anglo-Jewish family; unfortunately for him, the girl's parents favor the "comforts" of a universalist interpretation of Judaism over the "threatening divisiveness" of Jewish nationalism. In the end Leopold's proposal of marriage is rejected by her "Podsnappian" father. Bitterly, Leopold reflects that this Anglo-Jew nabob is in reality a "Trinitarian": an Englishman, a Jew, and an anti-Semite.[39]

The story reflects Zangwill's impatience with the predominantly anti-Zionist attitude of Anglo-Jewry's leadership and sounds a new note of humorless stridency in his fictional writing hitherto absent from even his most scathing social criticisms, as, for instance, in his portrait of the Goldsmiths in "Grandchildren of the Ghetto." But Zangwill could be equally impatient with Jewish nationalists of all varieties, including his own Territorialist followers.

His urgent activist impulse pervades the final story in this collection, "Samooborona," a late work reflecting Zangwill's matured position that abstract theorizing and "middle path" compromising were not practicable resolutions to the quandary of Western Jewry's sense of multiple identities.[40] In this piece, David Ben Amram learns of plans to provoke a pogrom in the little Polish town of Milouka. Rushing there, he hopes to arouse the local Jews to organize a self-defense force ("samooborona"). But his efforts prove fruitless. Religious and irreligious, Zionists and Territorialists, assimilationists and socialists, none trusts the others, and all are caught in webs of sophistical fantasies. Bemoans an uncomfortably perceptive and despairing David:

> [All these parties] each differentiating itself with meticulous subtlety from all the other Parties, each defining with casuistic minuteness its relation to every contemporary problem, each equipped with inexhaustible polyglot orators speechifying through tumultuous nights. . . .
>
> . . . The men of to-day had merely substituted for the world of the past the world of the future and so there had arisen logically perfect structures of Zionism without Zion, Jewish Socialism without a Jewish social order, Labour Parties without votes or a Parliament. The habit of actualities had been lost; what need of them when concepts provided as much intellectual stimulus?[41]

Zangwill's impatient condemnation extends from the quietism of traditional religious Judaism to the messianism of secular Jewish politics. For him what was most pressing was *action*, immediate action undertaken to rescue desperately imperiled Jewish people. It is this impulse that had driven him, before writing "Samooborona," to champion Territorialism, that made him impatient with the Territorialists, and that later would make him such a strident opponent of the postwar Zionist leadership.

Zangwill explicitly traces the tragic immobility of all parties in the story to the Jews' confusion over their ethnic identity: "Poor bewildered Russian Jews, caught in the bewilderments both of the Russians and the Jews, and tangled up inextricably in the double confusion of interlacing coils."[42] This analysis of Westernized Jewry's malaise is incisive and ignored.

Defeated in his efforts to rescue the Jews of Milouka, David, like Alfred Hyams before him, retreats into bittersweet memories of childhood. Exhausted, he retreats into the local *beth hamedrash:*

> he would go back like a child to the familiar [religious] study-house of his youth, to the *Beth Hamedrash* where the grey beards poured over the great worm-eaten folios. . . . There lay the magic world of fantasy and legend that had been his people's true home, that had kept them sane and cheerful through eighteen centuries of tragedy—a water tight world into which no drop of outer reality could ever trickle. . . . Time and again he had raged against the artificiality of this quietist cosmos, accusing it of his people's paralysis, but to-night every fibre of him yearned for this respite from the harsh reality.[43]

But this retreat is only for a night: the present's reality will not be held at bay by the soothing fantasies of the past. The pogrom comes now inexorably to Milouka, victimizing indiscriminately members of all the squabbling parties. In despair, David commits suicide. Laments the narrator of this urgent, cautionary tale, "The same unconditional historic necessity had overtaken them all."[44]

Here, once again, is the Zangwillian twin response to the inescapable anguish of the Western Jew's conflict of identities: retreat for a time into the peaceful afterglow of dreamy childhood memories and, when implacable reality jars one awake, embrace the implacable immolation. This is the notion at the root of Zangwill's Jewish nationalism and, equally, of his intermarriage.

Non-Jewish Works

At the time that these Jewish stories were appearing, an entirely different Israel Zangwill was simultaneously at work—an English man of letters, engaged in writing serious novels, a varied assortment of short stories, and witty literary criticism. This other Zangwill was even more productive than the Jewish writer, although less artistically successful.

The Master

The Master represents Israel Zangwill's first attempt to write, completely on his own, a serious "message" novel addressing issues of general, non-Jewish preoccupation. Originally serialized during 1894 in Jerome K. Jerome's literary journal *To-day,* the revised and expanded book appeared in 1895.[45] In an interview Zangwill explained that this book reflected a deliberate effort on his part to broaden his literary perspectives: "I myself am becoming identified with the Ghetto. I wrote of the Jews at first because the subject interested me and I knew it. But my interests extend beyond the Jews, and with 'The Master' I widen my field."[46]

Written in humorless, dense prose, the novel ploddingly follows the career of Matthew Strang, a gifted Nova Scotian boy who pursues his talent for art in London, amid the often alluring pitfalls of bourgeois philistinism, artistic opportunism, social fashions, and personal temptation: "Was it for Bohemia to ape Philistia, and for Art—the last rebel against the platitudinisation of life—to bow the knee and swear allegiance to the vulgar ideals of fashion?"[47]

Seduced by these entangling webs of petty distraction from his vocation as an artist, Matt slips into marriage with an unimaginative but hardworking woman, Rosina, whom he later abandons as a grave hindrance to his career. But he then discovers himself trapped between two conflicting moral imperatives. On the one hand, if he chooses to return to the graceless Rosina and their children, it would mean abandoning society and art for marital obscurity:

> His life would be joyless, but perchance his soul would be at peace.
>
> Yes, but to give up Art! Art, which was the meaning of his life! Rosina's life stood for nothing. It was out of all proportion to give up his for hers.[48]

On the other hand, as he had previously sacrificed his wife and children to art, so now honor demanded from Matt that he sacrifice this career for his family.

Caught by the dilemmas of his complicated life, Matt dreams of his simple, blissful youth: "How happy were those times of youthful aspiration, when all things were new and all things were true, and hunger itself was but a sauce to eke out the scanty meal. . . . Oh, to be young and free again; free to be a slave to Art!"[49]

Ultimately Matt decides to return to his wife. But happily the uninspired Rosina will not accept this sacrifice of his art to his family. A studio is set aside for him at home, and her family provides the financial support for all their domestic requirements. Now, indeed, Matt is finally freed from all distortions and illusions so that he is able to pursue art unhindered by distraction:

> Solitary, silent, sorrowful, strong; not chattering about his ideas and aims, indifferent to fame or the voice of posterity, striving for self-approbation and rarely obtaining it . . . he toiled on in his humble studio, seeking the highest, with no man and no woman to inspire, encourage, or praise. He had been saved from Love and Happiness, and sent back into sympathy with all that works and suffers. . . . What he had wanted he had not got; by the time he had got it he had not wanted it; whatever he had set out to do he had not done, and whatever he had done he had not foreseen. And out of all this travail of the soul was born his Art—strong, austere, simple.[50]

Not fortuitously the English Zangwill, like the Jewish, describes an individual ensnared in a tangle of contending identities who dreams of his youth in a far-off land free of the adult's anguishing complications. Fortunately for him, the fictional Matthew is spared the consequences of selecting between alternatives, for by choosing his family he is also given an uncomplicated career as artist. Here, indeed, would seem to be a "middle path." But it is only fiction, and even in the novel it is achieved at the cost of love, happiness, and all social intercourse, a self-sacrifice and isolation so intense as to border on an act of self-immolation for the sake of art.

However, the novel was not intended as vehicle of self-revelation but rather as a serious contribution to the contemporary debate raging over the function of the artist in society. In *The Master* Zangwill is aligning himself with Max Nordau in denouncing the Pre-Raphaelite's bohemianism, Emile Zola's naturalism, and Oscar Wilde's "art for art's sake" movement.[51]

For Zangwill, agreeing with Nordau, the artist must be the bearer of a moral responsibility to society to serve as its conscience and teacher.[52] As he has Matthew Strang say: "Art had no *raison d'être* except as the expression of soul, of the upward aspiration of the Spirit towards the Good, and the Beautiful, and True, a Trinity that was mysteriously one."[53] That he took this view seriously and adhered to it for the remainder of his life is evident from his subsequent career as a playwright, extending to his very last play, *We Moderns* (1924), a parody of the Bloomsbury set.[54]

The novel met with very mixed reviews. While many admired Zangwill's arguments and his portrait of Matthew Strang, they also found the book overly ambitious, confusing in its plethora of petty detail, the plot so intricate as to be almost impossible at times to follow, and several of the characterizations most unconvincing.[55] Although not a literary success, *The Master* confirmed the general impression that Israel Zangwill was not a mere humorist but an important and intelligent author worthy of serious attention.

The Mantle of Elijah

The Mantle of Elijah, although apparently a roman à clef, in fact is Israel Zangwill's annunciation of his new role as activist social reformer. Reflecting the contemporary debate surrounding the Boer War, the novel clearly condemns Britain's role in the conflict. But this condemnation is merely the framework that provides the forum for a long series of reformist proclamations.

The novel's protagonist is Allegra, the daughter of the Radical member of Parliament Thomas Marshmont, an outspoken champion of freedom and the people against all pettiness of party and politics. As he ages, Marshmont passes on his "prophetic mantle" to his protégé, Robert Broser, whom Allegra eventually marries. But Broser, an unprincipled political opportunist, betrays his mission as he rises in the political world; he becomes a leading advocate of imperialist warfare, waving the flag in the service of the selfish mercantile interests of his unscrupulous supporters and as a means of obtaining political prominence for himself. War and death, wrapping themselves in the patriotic flag of national interest and in the cant of spreading a superior civilization, in fact, cloak unbridled greed and ambition. Laments the aging Radical: "Now that the ancient ideal of military glory is discredited and Christianity has forced hypocrisy upon the world, we pretend to conquer the world for the world's good. At bottom, it is the same lust for bigness."[56]

Allegra is horrified upon discovering her husband's betrayal of her father's mission. In her state of emotional tumult following this discovery she encounters Raphael Dominick, a Sidonia-like mysterious Jew who has withdrawn, disillusioned, from the affairs of men. But now his love for Allegra reawakens him to life's possibilities, but Allegra cannot bring herself to dishonor her marriage vows to the despicable Broser, even for her love of an otherwise doomed Raphael.

In the end Allegra realizes that she must neither surrender to Broser's treason nor to Raphael's aloofness. Instead she herself must don her father's "mantle of Elijah": "The ruin of her life had been her idea that the woman must sink her life in the man's. . . . But let men struggle for male-ideals, woman's mission was to struggle for female-ideals—ideals of love, pity, tenderness. Fate would strike the diagonal of the forces."[57] And as the book concludes, Allegra has abandoned Broser so that she may pursue a lonely life devoted to crusading for the true good of the nation and of humanity.

In the unpublished dramatic version of the novel, "The Torch-Bearer," the themes of the book emerge even more forcefully. Here, too, Allegra finds herself trapped between alternatives; Broser has abandoned the "mantle of Elijah" and Raphael refuses to accept it. Spurning Broser at his moment of imperialist victory, Allegra announces to him that she will become the new "Torchbearer":

> What Salic law forbids women to inherit such a mission! That was my mistake—to think I must find some *man* to carry on my father's work—some *man* to give my life to. . . . But a woman is a human being too. She has a life and a soul of her own. Henceforth I am no man's shadow. I am myself. . . . Yes, I tell you the hour of woman has dawned—she is the new Great Power—*she* will be the Torchbearer of civilization—she will save the world.[58]

Zangwill's belief in the unprincipled opportunism of politicians had been evident since *The Premier and the Painter.* What is important in *The Mantle of Elijah* is his proclamation of the ideals of peace and feminism, which he obviously interpreted as interrelated causes. But even more significant is Zangwill's renunciation of the artist's aloofness, idealized in *The Master* and argued for by Raphael in this book. In this novel Zangwill embraces the activist public role: where all alternatives fail, one must take upon oneself the prophet's mantle and bear to the people truth's torch.

Although in *The Master* Zangwill had somewhat reluctantly accepted the unity of art and activism as a function of one's creativity, in this work he proclaims that the pursuit of artistic truth is insufficient: one must take to the public forum. And *The Mantle of Elijah* is Zangwill's public manifesto both of his new activist vocation and of this program of social reconstruction.

Particularly interesting are the religious implications Zangwill attaches to this decision. Although the title of both the novel and the play indicate this notion of Biblical imperative, it is even more emphasized in the titles of the four acts of the drama; "(I) The Ascent of Elijah and the Bequest of the Mantle; (II) The False Disciple; (III) Twixt Prophets of Baal; (IV) Woman as Prophet."[59] The activist's role is undertaken by a "prophet" seeking to "save the world." Zangwill's is to be a prophetic mission, a religious vocation.

Like *The Master, The Mantle of Elijah* was not a critical success. Although its sentiments, especially those criticizing the Boer War, were appreciated, as was its political idealism, the novel was ajudged to be overwritten, lacking convincing characterization of several of its major figures, and containing several stylistic flaws.[60]

For a third time Zangwill had attempted to compose a nonethnic British novel and for a third time, although his flashes of brilliance were applauded, he failed to approach the widespread acclaim won by his Jewish writing. He would not publish another novel for nineteen years.

Without Prejudice

Without Prejudice, published in 1896, is a selection of essays that appeared under that title in a regular column Zangwill wrote for the *Pall Mall Magazine,* 1893–96.[61] They represent a transitional stage in Zangwill's development from the irreverent satirist Marshallik/Ariel to the serious essayist of *Italian Fantasies, The War for the World,* and *The Voice of Jerusalem.* In these belles lettres Zangwill is the clever, witty commentator, no longer on community and social foibles but on the world of art and letters.

These essays range over the whole realm of "middle brow" artistic endeavor during the 1890s in a chatty and humorous vein, with Zangwill often name dropping and straining to impress the reader with his learning and personal connections. It is exactly this schoolboy's ostentation, as well as the paucity of genuine analysis, that led to critical disparagement of the work.[62] It would be another ten years before Zangwill's talents as an insightful essayist would become fully matured. These earlier attempts may be compared to his New Humour fiction: journalistic ventures at the fringe of what Zangwill himself considered truly important; his later collections were like his later fiction and drama: works of true literature.

Nevertheless, these articles contain some revealing and interesting observations. For instance, on the moral integrity of the creative artist, Zangwill, echoing the message of *The Master,* writes:

> Only, while he is at work, the laws of art alone must be his [the artist's] masters; he must not alter or abate a jot by way of concession to the great cash question. When he has completed his work, then he may sell it in the best market. But the least preliminary paltering with the spirit of commerce is a degradation. . . . Instinctively we feel it degrading and disillusioning that inspiration shall be paid in hard cash and genius entered on the credit side of the ledger.[63]

On the relation of humor and creative genius, he observes:

> Humour is . . . the simultaneous revelation of the dual aspect of life, [its tragedy and its comedy, and] only the humorist can reproduce life. . . . Leave out humour, and you may get art and many other fine things, but you do not get the lights and shadows or the "values" of life. . . .
>
> . . . Everything rusts by use. Our moral ideas grow mouldy if preached too much; our stories stale if told too often. Conventionality is but a living death. The other side of everything must be shown, the reverse of the medal, the silver side of the shield as well as the golden. . . .
>
> . . . It [genius] is simply this: see what you do see, and not what everybody tells you to see. To think what everybody says is to be a Philistine, and to say what everybody thinks is to be a genius.[64]

In one essay, "Budapest," Zangwill explicitly refers to the confusions plaguing modern Jewish identity:

> The Jewish patriotism, which loves at once Israel and some other nation, may appear curious and contradictory; but human is nothing if not curious and contradictory, and this dual affection has been aptly compared to that of a mother for her different children.[65]

But Zangwill predicts that these dual identities will inevitably disappear under the assimilationist conditions of Western society:

> probably it is only persecution that accentuates the consciousness of Jewish brotherhood. Wherever Jews have perfect equality and have been tempted out of the Ghetto, there the beginnings of disintegration are manifest.[66]

And this prospect both attracted and repelled Israel Zangwill. He could neither surrender his dual identities nor acquiesce to this "disintegration," no matter how hard he felt compelled to try.

The Grey Wig

As if to clear his desk of all distraction so as to carry out his new political activism, in 1903 Zangwill published *The Grey Wig, Stories and Novelettes,* a collection of various non-Jewish short works that had accumulated over the years.[67]

Included in this random collection are five modest but well written short stories, all presenting a sardonic view of love. In addition to these stories are three longer pieces: "The Big Bow Mystery," a Wilkie Collins–style mystery novel originally published in 1892; "Merely May Ann," a novella that first appeared in 1893, and "The Serio-Comic Governess."[68] The latter two works Zangwill would adapt as plays; in fact, *Merely Mary Ann* made more money for its author than any of his other dramas.[69]

Of all the pieces collected together in *The Grey Wig,* "The Serio-Comic Governess" is aesthetically the most sophisticated and psychologically the most revealing. Evidently suggested by Amy Levy's *Miss Meredith,* it is the story of Eileen O'Keefe; as a schoolgirl in a French convent she had secretly felt great contempt for the pious stories related by the nuns and had surreptitiously circulated satires of them among her few friends. The girl was, in fact, enraptured by this "double life" of public piety and secret blasphemy.

Later her family's poverty compels Eileen to become a governess, her first position being at Holly Hall in the industrial north of Britain. But when the Maper family discovers that their armchair socialist son, Robert, has taken a fancy to Eileen, she is dismissed. Her next position is as governess for Mrs. Lee Carter of London. But as a lark, she agrees secretly to perform in a music hall under an assumed name, Nelly O'Neill.

From then on she leads a dual life: during the day she is the "proper" Mayfair governess Eileen O'Keefe while at night she becomes the music hall celebrity Nelly O'Neill performing before the frivolous crowd at the "Half and Half." The gulf between the rival identities progressively widens and, with it, her melancholy and despair. Eileen/Nelly begins to contemplate suicide.

In the meantime, both her childhood sweetheart and Robert Maper contact Eileen with the intention of asking her consent in marriage. But each chances upon one of Nelly's performances before meeting Eileen, and the rivals each fall in love with the music hall chanteuse. As a result Eileen eventually decides to reject the proposals of both suitors, as she feels that neither truly understands the twinned quality of her personality.

Disillusioned in the end, Eileen/Nelly abandons both governess and stage careers in order to return to the French convent of her girlhood; there she intends to repudiate study of the classical Greeks, edifying as it may be, for the service of her personal god, in the hope that her "complex corrupt soul shall be simplified and purified" and that she will be led "by the hand like a little child."[70]

In the stage version, the final point is made even more strongly; when Robert proposes he is told that both Eileen and Nelly are dead and that she who remains is returning to the convent to become a nun: "I must find my soul again. O the cool cloisters, the rows of innocent beds, the delicious gold garden . . . who knows?—I shall chance . . . upon the little white-souled girl I used to know. . . . And perhaps the wages of sin shall not be death if I pay them as my dowry to the Church."[71]

Here dual identity is no longer an interesting and even slightly amusing phenomenon upon which to contemplate and discourse. Rather, it has become a gnawing anguish shattering inner peace and paralyzing normal human intercourse. Death, beckoning as physical suicide or as spiritual withdrawal from the mundane world, becomes a constant companion. And no one else understands or even fully realizes her plight. Zangwill's protagonist experiences a profound psychological crisis: she is no longer capable of maintaining the precarious balance between her contrary identities but is equally not able to choose to be simply either all Eileen or all Nelly. Indeed, she abandons both careers as no longer tolerable.

As a "middle path" alternative—in place of her previous rationalist devotion to the classical Greeks—Eileen/Nelly decides to retreat into the mystical, airy world of childhood memories. In this fashion she yearns to recapture a lost innocence and harmony by consecrating her life to the pursuit of an ideal in which as a girl she had been unable to believe and had scornfully upheld to ridicule.

SEVEN

The Crisis

Below the surface of the glittering exterior, a canker was beginning to fester in the mind of Israel Zangwill. Throughout the course of the decade of his international literary celebrity, his public triumphs as Jewish writer and British man of letters were leading Zangwill, in private, to a hypnotic fascination with the issue of the meaning and durability of Jewish ethnicity amid the secular national identities pervading Western Jewry's consciousness.

At first the issue posed for him an exciting intellectual challenge to be explored philosophically. Following the course of his earlier essay, "English Judaism," he attempted in "The Position of Judaism" to explore the possibilities involved in a "middle path" resolution that might accommodate both contending identities. But as the decade proceeded and the intellectual's response proved emotionally vacuous, the question of continuing Jewish identity became for Zangwill a compelling and desperate obsession. The resulting creative tension sparked the artist to respond with his most unusual work of fiction, *Dreamers of the Ghetto*. But the book brought no relief; its pleas for help echoed hollowly. Finally, fully possessed by the demon of his dilemma, Zangwill was propelled into precipitant actions that repudiated his former "hopes and dreams" and thrust him into an arena of frenzied and anagogic phantasms and deeds.

"The Position of Judaism"

"The fall of the Ghettos has left Israel dazed in the sunlight of the wider world without, his gaberdine half off and half on." So Zangwill writes in the prologue of his 1895 essay, "The Position of Judaism."[1] Continuing this incisive delineation of Western Jewry's perplexity of identity, he explains: "If he throws it off, will he throw off his distinctiveness and fade into the common run of men? If he keeps it on, can he keep his place in the new brotherhood? And as he gropes, irresolute, he stumbles at every step amongst the ruins of the Ghetto wall against the *débris* of problems."[2]

Zangwill suggests in this essay that the specifics of any viable solution to the dilemma of Western Jewish identity will depend upon grasping "the common Judaism which underlies all the jarring factions and to view this essential Judaism in the light of history." According to this historical positivist formula, "All men and all ages pass through it [history] in unending procession. . . . But picturesque as the story is outwardly, it is mainly by its inner religious content that it claims consideration."[3] In other words, amid all the diversities among the Jews, Zangwill claims that a unitary and essential religious core is discoverable through an exploration of the permanent inner meaning of Jewish history that lies behind the facade of transient outward events.[4] It is as such an exploration that this essay is intended.

The essential core of Judaism, according to Zangwill, is ethical monotheism, its unique contribution to world culture:

> The religion of a race is its vision of the Good, even as its science is its vision of the True and its art, its vision of the Beautiful. Israel's vision of the Good was God; and to the unifying instinct the True and the Beautiful had no separate existence. . . . Israel first had this conception of the Creator and of his relation to a prophet-race and through it to the world. It is a unique ethical and political conception.[5]

The transmission of this religious message of Judaism to mankind was achieved by the founder of Christianity, who represents it in a most singular and pure form:

> Jesus himself drew from the nursery of Judaism those ideals which enabled him to react against their distortion in practice. . . . The loftiest sayings of Christ were familiar to the Jews in the Rabbinic lore or in their old Testament, and these dicta had never before been so fused as the expression of a personality . . . both before and after Christ. . . . To speak of the Jews rejecting Christ when it was the Jews who spread His gospel is a strange, popular blunder.[6]

Echoing views expressed earlier by Disraeli, during the final decade of the nineteenth and the early decades of the twentieth centuries several prominent Jewish religious leaders were, like Zangwill, reevaluating the relationship of Jesus to Judaism. Representative of these views is that expressed by the British founder of Liberal Judaism and Zangwill's intellectual colleague, Claude Montefiore (1858–1938). Recognizing that some of the positions espoused by Liberal Judaism might appear identical to teachings found in the New Testament, he nonetheless insisted that Jesus' expression of his Jewish heritage had been incomplete and partial: "the teaching of Jesus, great and noble though it be, was neither perfect nor complete. It may be that Jesus will be seen to take his place as a great Jewish reformer, and a great Jewish teacher, but conditioned by his age and his environment."[7]

In his own reevaluation of Jesus here, Zangwill far surpasses both Disraeli, who claims Jesus merely as a Jew, and Montefiore, who claims him as only one in an extensive tradition of great, and historically bounded, Jewish teachers. For Zangwill, on the other hand, Jesus' teachings are, in fact, the purest essence of Judaism. This centrality of Jesus' teachings for Judaism and of what he considers their content he makes clear elsewhere: "I regard Jesus as second only to Moses in the long line of Hebrew Prophets who are half revealed and half obscured in the literary masterpieces of my race which begin with Genesis and end arbitrarily with Revelations."[8] Accordingly, the essence of Judaism is to be discovered in the Bible, as comprising both Jewish and Christian Scriptures, with Moses and Jesus its most eloquent and archetypical spokesmen.

However, according to Zangwill, the Jew Jesus and his teachings should not be confused with distortions imposed upon them by later Christianity: "the mysteries of the Incarnation and Atonement were in direct opposition to the spirit of Judaism (as they seem a needless complication of the essence of Christianity)."[9] In fact, in comparison with "essential Judaism," Christianity is obviously inferior:

> This sanctified sociology [of Jewish ritual] made the sensuous sacred equally with the spiritual. Judaism sanctified the sensuous, Christianity was an abolition of the sensuous. In the result Christianity succeeded only in abolishing it from religion, not from life. . . . Judaism inspires life, Christianity inspires to negation of life. . . . Judaism aims at influencing character through conduct, Christianity at influencing conduct through emotion.[10]

Despite its inherent superiority, however, Judaism as a religion has fallen dormant as an influence upon world events. If it is to justify its own continuing survival by once again inspiring a desperately needy world, Judaism must rouse itself from its centuries of torpor and isolation:

> If I were asked to sum up in one broad generalization the intellectual tendency of Israel, I should say that it was a tendency to unification. . . . The unifying instinct of the Jew may still identify the beautiful with the good; but there is no longer need to dread the Grecian wisdom; even the infusion of the Greek scientific spirit would strengthen rather than impair. . . .
>
> Of the trinity of ideals, the Good is the most important; without it life is impossible, corrupt, distraught. Israel's mission has been the noblest, it took the largest and widest; but its only hope of influencing the future hinges of its power to absorb the culture of the day so as to bring its own particular contribution to the solution of the problems of its time, its own moral vision of the world. It must come out of the *débris* of the Ghetto and enrich humanity by its point of view.[11]

Zangwill, entangled in the skein of contradictory impulses, explains that to realize this Jewish ideal of unity even the bases of the Good might be sacrificed: "To such a creed as Judaism the verbal authenticity of its sacred book is a triviality; to such an organization as Israel even the fall of theism would not be necessarily fatal, the energy stored up in it could still be conserved to humanity's benefit."[12]

This emphasis upon harmonious unity, however vacuous, as the essential feature of Judaism leads Zangwill to the radical claim that the most fruitful contributors to world civilization are its heretics:

> But now we are confronted with the curious fact that the individuals through whom Israel has influenced the world have been for the most part divorced from the body proper. They have been heretics. . . . This is indeed a shining example of the irony of history, and almost leads to the suspicion that the function of Judaism during the last thousand years has been to conserve an environment favorable to the production of great heterodox Jews. [From] the prenatal power of the orthodox code the heterodox celebrities were indebted for their health, their head and their heart, and from the diaspora and the persecution came their assertive individuality and their cosmopolitan standpoint.[13]

This is all the more ironic because "Judaism *quâ* religion has been a waste force in the world."[14]

Not surprising in an essay that interprets the synthesizing and unifying power of Judaism as the historical product of the dialectic of orthodox and heterodox, which itself is an expression of the broader dialectic of the Jewish and the non-Jewish, Zangwill concludes his message of optimism under the shadow of a suicidal pessimism: "if [Israel's] faith and hope be a dream, it were well to abandon the search for significance in the futile and ephemeral life of man, and to look forward hopefully to the Messiah of the cosmic catastrophe."[15]

Such, then, is Israel Zangwill's intentionally heterodox message: Judaism is the religious force within human history that, through its ethical monotheism, creates a unity among the Good, the Beautiful, and the True. This triune unity is the core teaching of Moses and Jesus. Furthermore, while in itself formal "religious Judaism" is sterile, in an open dialogue between Jewish orthodoxy and the non-Jewish world, great heterodox Jews emerge who carry this essential religious core teaching of Judaism to all mankind. Thus, according to this formula, there must be preservation of the Mosaic "sacred sociology" as well as openness to the influences of the non-Jewish world. That is, Jews must retain their distinctiveness while simultaneously remaining among others; only in this manner will the great heretics be produced. And without the hope that this Jewish mission will continue—that unity can be achieved and preserved—there is left one only the promised peacefulness of death after the cataclysm.

It is indeed a peculiar argument: Judaism is best served by its heretics, its religious mission best fostered by disbelief. But Zangwill is not bothered by possible inconsistencies, for what is significant about Judaism, according to him, is its teaching of unity; its religious forms are merely the transitory expression of this core ideal. So heterodoxy is but the means by which the shells of the transitory are broken in order to allow the essential core to emerge, once again, under new circumstances.

In answer to his original question—having left the ghetto, should the Western Jew throw off his "gaberdine" and assimilate or should he instead attempt to recollect and refashion the ghetto's "*débris*"?—Zangwill replied: the Jew must do both! But how to accomplish this "middle path" he does not know.

Dreamers of the Ghetto

In *Dreamers of the Ghetto* (1898), Zangwill pursued his analysis of the "essential Judaism" as he believed it to have been transmitted through history by great heterodox Jews. However, there is in this book a noticeable shift in emphasis and mood. While in "The Position of Judaism" Zangwill presented this process as actually having occurred historically, in this book it now becomes only "the story of a Dream that has not come true."[16] It is the record of unrealized hopes, of tragic failures, as great Jewish heretics suffer isolation and even destruction through the intransigence of institutionalized Judaism and Christianity. The need is all the greater, the hope all the more desperate, and the alternative all the bleaker.

The book, neither quite a novel nor a collection of short stories, consists of a series of fictionalized historical and historical fictional vignettes. Among the genuine historical characters, Zangwill chooses Jewish heretics who had attracted great public attention, either in Western literature or in secular history, particularly as noticed in Heinrich Graetz's *History of the Jews* and in Solomon Schechter's *Studies in Judaism*.

For instance, Uriel Acosta, the first historical character to appear, was the subject of an 1847 play by Karl Ferdinand Gutzkow, popular with German- and Yiddish-speaking audiences and translated into English in 1885.[17] Reflecting Graetz's presentation, Zangwill brackets together the rationalist philosopher Spinoza and the pseudomessiah Sabbatai Zevi, noting, "It is suggestive that Sabbatai Zevi should have been acclaimed in the very age in which Spinoza was teaching . . . the universal reign of law and the irrelevance of miracles."[18] Similarly he treats Israel Baal Shem Tov, the founder of the Chassidic movement, exclusively in the light of contemporary scholarly interpretation and again contrasts the mystic with the rationalist, in this case Solomon Maimon, whose autobiography was quite popular during the nineteenth century.[19] The choice of Ferdinand Lassalle as representative of Jewish socialists was no doubt dictated by the popularity of George Meredith's fictionalized biography of Lassalle, *The Tragic Comedians* (1880), and Heinrich Heine was very widely read during this period in the original and in translation. Finally, Zangwill gives passing attention to the prominent British author and politician, Benjamin Disraeli.[20]

However, while Zangwill may have been following popular taste in his choice of which historical characters to portray, he nonetheless also displays his own intellectual and emotional preferences among them. Spinoza most clearly represents the Zangwillian ideal of the "middle path" that emerges from the dialectic of the Jewish with the non-Jewish, the orthodox with the heterodox:

> The philosophy of Spinoza, though it has affinities both with the logic of Maimonides and the mysticism of the Cabalists, and in expression sometimes recalls the grand manner of the ancient prophets, stands nevertheless entirely on its own basis and is a Gospel for the world, in which it has worked continuously whether acknowledged or not, in influencing all the best thinking.[21]

Zangwill explains this message as representing a union of the essential spiritual teaching of Judaism and a sacred sociology:

> Those who live best by Revelation through Tradition must cling to it, but Revelation through Reason is the living testament of God's word, not so liable as the dead letter to be corrupted by human wickedness. . . .
>
> . . . The first Jew to create an original philosophy, he [Spinoza] yet remained a Jew in aiming not at abstract knowledge, but at concrete conduct; and was most of all a Jew in his proclamation of the Unity. He would teach a world distraught and divided by religious strife the higher path of spiritual blessedness; bring it the Jewish greeting—Peace.[22]

That Zangwill could not accept a pure rationalism and that he does not ascribe such a view to Spinoza is evident from his generally hostile portrait of Solomon Maimon. Dying, the Enlightenment philosopher recalls the teachings of the traditionalist reformer Moses Mendelssohn and his espousal of the "middle path":

> Mendelssohn with his ordered scheme of harmonious living, with his equal grasp of thought and life, sanely balanced betwixt philosophy and letters, learning and business, according so much to Hellenism, yet not losing hold of Hebraism, and adjusting with equal mind the claims of the Ghetto and the claims of Culture, Mendelssohn shone before Maimon's dying eyes, as indeed the Wise.[23]

But if Mendelssohn, like Spinoza before him, represented the proper union of the universal and the particular, it was a union that presaged only an ephemeral dream, a flicker of essential truth in the darkness of formalism and bigotry. Ultimately, Maimon recognizes that "the only Judaism that stood stable amid this flux [of assimilationism and German anti-Semitism was] the ancient rock of Rabbinism he [Mendelssohn] has sought to dislodge, the Amsterdam Jewry refusing even the civil rights for which he had fought."[24]

If unalloyed rationalism receives rough treatment in the book, its "twin," mysticism, emanates a sympathetic attraction. This treatment is quite apparent in the presentation of Israel Baal Shem Tov. For Zangwill, conveniently, the Baal Shem Tov (Master of the Good Name) is also a heretic, a denouncer of the orthodox rabbis:

> It is such disputants [as the Rabbis] who delay the redemption of Israel from exile. . . .
>
> . . . even the worst sinners are better than their Rabbis? So blind are they in the arrogance of their self-conceit, so darkened by their pride, that their very devotion to the law becomes a vehicle for their sin. . . .
>
> . . . Ye fools, he [the Baal Shem Tov] said roughly, ye would make me as you have made the law and the world, a place for stopping at, when all things are but on the way to God.[25]

Yet the Baal Shem Tov does not reject Jewish tradition *properly interpreted:*

> For despite his detestations of the devil's knots, he held that the Talmud represented the oral law which expressed the continuous inspiration of the leaders of Israel, and that to rely on the Bible alone was to worship the mummy of religion. . . .
>
> . . . My Master [the Baal Shem Tov] believed that the breath of God vivified the universe, renewing daily the work of creation, and that hence the world of every day was as inspired as the Torah, the one throwing light on the other. The written Law must be interpreted in every age in accordance with the ruling attribute of God.[26]

But the mystic teachings of Israel Baal Shem Tov were betrayed by his Chassidic successor: according to Zangwill, "Baer [Dov Ber, the *Maggid* of Mezhirech] made of the Master's living impulse a code and a creed which grew rigid and dead."[27] Thus the beautiful dream of the Baal Shem Tov was frozen and perverted by "the delusions and distortions" of his successors, much as had previously happened to the teachings of Jesus when codified into Church doctrine. How easy it is for the uninspired disciple to trample under clumsy foot the delicate bloom of the master's airy inspiration!

The most complex and compelling portrait in *Dreamers of the Ghetto* is neither of philosopher nor of mystic prophet but of the seventeenth-century pseudomessiah, Sabbatai Zevi. So fascinated was Zangwill with his career that it is the only vignette in the book that he set out also to dramatize.[28]

What is most interesting about Zangwill's interpretation is that he treats Sabbatai Zevi as a tragic character whose dream and mission were true, only to be betrayed by his own human weaknesses. He is portrayed as a brilliant and sincere pietist who even at an early age

> grasped the casuistical hair-splittings in which the Rabbis too often indulged, but his contempt was as quick as his comprehension. A note of revolt pierced early through his class-room replies, and very soon he threw over these barren subtleties to sink himself . . . in the spiritual mysticisms, the poetic fervors, the self-martyrdoms of the Cabalistic literature.[29]

Sabbatai becomes convinced that he has a messianic mission, a view fostered by his enigmatic disciple Nathan of Gaza, although Sabbatai is never wholly convinced himself that he is the messiah. However, under the influence of his passion for "Melisselda," his mysterious and tempestuous wife, Sabbatai is finally led to embrace the messianic role fully, to abolish the restraints of the traditional law, and to surrender his rigorous asceticism to riotous indulgence.

Only at the end of his public career, when he faces the choice of heroic martyrdom or ignoble apostasy to Islam, does Sabbatai realize what he has become. Like the guilty Adam shifting blame for his "fall" onto Eve, this putative savior bitterly excoriates his wife:

> I understand at last. 'Tis through thee that I have forfeited the divine grace. . . . Yea; thy lips have wooed mine from prayer, thine arms have drawn me down from the steeps of righteousness. Thou hast made me unfaithful to my bride the Law. . . . Woman, thou has polluted me! I have lost the divine spirit. It hath gone out from me; it will incarnate itself in another, in a nobler. Once I was Messiah, now I am man.[30]

But Sabbatai Zevi still is unable to free himself from Melisselda's spell and, rather than lose her, he chooses the ignominy of apostasy and exile rather than surrender possession of her flesh through the martyrdom of a noble death: better to experience humiliation in order to possess the alluring ephemeral than the silent dignity of death eternal.

However peculiar these views might be for an avowed feminist and philosopher, they do reflect Zangwill's interpretation of the prophetic mission. For him, it is an endeavor requiring complete ascetic self-abnegation, an uncompromising devotion to the mystic inspiration of a living spiritual mission untrammeled by friendship, family ties, or material comforts. Sabbatai Zevi was a false messiah, according to Zangwill, not because of the invalidity of his original claim but because he later betrayed his mission for the selfish delights of the flesh. Thus, in Zangwill's view, Spinoza is superior to Sabbatai Zevi not because of the intrinsic difference in their teachings but because ultimately Spinoza did not surrender to the temptations of material comfort and marriage.[31]

The story of the pseudomessiah is a cautionary tale; its message is that the prophet himself may betray his mission if he surrenders his asceticism and loneliness to the seductions of social success, popularity, or the ordinary attractions of matrimony. For it is just this surrender of selfless austerity to the importunities of self that transforms the authentic into the spurious prophet. But it is a warning its own author was unable to heed.

Although over half of *Dreamers of the Ghetto* is devoted to these fictionalized historical biographies, it is the completely fictional portions that carry the main thrust of the book's message, the central dream of the author. Here, working beyond the constraining factual limitations of historical biography, Zangwill is able to teach his audience new wisdom through the medium of creative story telling.

"The Rencontre"

Israel Zangwill's dream is encapsulated in the "Prelude" to the book, a poem entitled "Moses and Jesus." It relates the kinship, the parallelism, and the agonizing estrangement of these two Jewish teachers. The poem, originally published as "The Rencontre" in the orthodox newspaper, the *Jewish Standard*, on 25 December 1889, summarizes the theme of *Dreamers of the Ghetto* and its author's lifelong "prophetic mission": his dream of harmonizing and unifying the teachings and the followers of the Jew Moses and the Jew Jesus.[32] This common motif—the Zangwillian heresy—runs through all the fictionalized biographies.

As we have seen, the message of these two prophets, as Zangwill understands it, is triune: both exemplify the Divine Unity. Moses teaches this lesson through instruction in the Good, the life-affirming

Hebraic "sacred sociology," and Jesus, through sanctification of the True and the Beautiful, the Hellenic triumphs in the sciences and in the arts. It is now Zangwill's self-assumed "mantle" to teach all mankind that this "Jewish Trinity" is "mysteriously one." So, paradoxically, these are stories of brittle formalism, inspired heresy, loneliness, and death.

The opening story, "A Child of the Ghetto," is set in the sixteenth-century Venetian ghetto and relates the story of a young Jewish boy who slips out of the Jewish quarter into the city's piazza and visits the church. Returning to the ghetto, he expresses sentiments that would have delighted Walter Besant's East End reformer, Angela, with her "civilizing" "Palace of Delights": "for something larger had come into his [the boy's] life, a sense of a vaster universe without [the ghetto's walls], and its spaciousness and strangeness and a vague unrest. He was no longer a child of the Ghetto."[33]

In "Joseph the Dreamer," Zangwill most fully expounds his dream and its futility. It relates the story of a Roman ghetto lad, Joseph, who also wanders into the Christian areas of the city and there, inspired by the beauty of the art and mass at St. Peter's: "suddenly I knew what my soul was pining for. I knew the meaning of that restless craving that has always devoured me. . . . In a flash I understood the secret of peace. [It is] sacrifice . . . to suffer, to give oneself freely to the world; to die to myself in delicious pain."[34]

For Joseph this ideal is symbolized by the life of Jesus and his apostles, and it becomes his intention to emulate them. By this means, by making the Jews Christians in the true sense, he intends to liberate them from the constrictions, distortions, and humiliations of the ghetto.

Ignoring the warnings of his loving Jewish admirer, Miriam, and of his Christian friend, Helena, Joseph implements his ideal by converting and becoming a priest, with the special mission to evangelize to the Jews. Shunned by his own people, he soon discovers that the Church has betrayed the teachings of its founder. Joseph, who previously had explained that it is "in simplicity that our Lord is revealed," now furiously harangues the Roman populace:

> Away with your beads and mummeries, your paternosters and genuflections! Away with your Carnivals, your godless farewells to meat! Ye are all foul. This is no city of God, it is a city of hired bravos and adulterous abominations and gluttonous feasts, and the lust of the eye,

and the pride of flesh. . . . He [the Pope] the representative of the meek Christ who rode upon an ass . . . ! Nay, . . . I proclaim here that he is a lie, a snare, a whited sepulchre, no protector of the poor, no loving father to the fatherless, no spiritual Emperor, no Vicar of Christ, but Anti-Christ himself.[35]

Heretical incitement to rebellion is not to be tolerated in Renaissance Rome, and the inspired renegade is arrested and condemned. Joseph the Dreamer, rejected by the bigoted hostilities of both communities in his selfless efforts to teach them true divine piety and reconciliation, suffers a martyr's death at the hand of the Inquisition. But his two chaste ladies, the Jewess Miriam and the Christian Helena, join in mourning his sad and painful defeat.

Joseph's dream, then, is of unity, the message of Moses and Jesus: that Jew and Christian, Hebrew and Englishman are truly one. But this mystic truth taught by an inspired heretic is spurned by the intransigent and corrupt of both communities, and its lonely prophet is silenced and destroyed. Joseph's dream contains also a portentous warning: that the attempt to reconcile the contending twins leads one to destruction!

"The Conciliator of Christendom" appears to be a deleted fragment from *Children of the Ghetto*, involving as it does Little Sampson and the *Flag of Judah*. Set in the East End, it tells of Zussmann Herz's dream of human brotherhood replacing the rivalries of religion and nationality. The key to reconciliation he provides in his book, *The Brotherhood of Peoples*, in which he argues: "They [the Jews] have denied their greatest son [Jesus]. Did not all the Prophets, His predecessors, cry out likewise against mere form and sacrifice? Did not the teachers of Israel who followed Him likewise insist on a pure heart and a sinless soul? Jesus must be restored to His true place in the glorious chain of Hebrew Prophets."[36]

But in the end his book is ignored by pious Jews, his humble wife dies, and Herz is left dreamily "looking up at the stars."[37]

The Christological orientation of Zangwill's interpretation of Judaism is most evident in "The Joyous Comrade." In it an American Jewish artist visiting the Tyrol witnesses a passion play performed by local villagers and afterward experiences a mystic vision:

all the divine joy of existence thrilled me to a religious rapture. And with the lifting of the mists all that ghastly mediaeval nightmare [of the play] was lifted from my soul; in that sacred moment all the lurid tragedy of the crucified Christ vanished, and only Christ was left, the simple fellowship with man and beasts and nature, the love of life, the love of love, the love of God. All in that yearning ecstasy my picture came to me—The Joyous Comrade. Christ—not the tortured God, but the joyous comrade, the friend of all simple souls . . . ; not the theologian spinning barren subtleties, but the man of genius protesting against all forms and dogmas that would replace the direct vision and the living ecstasy. . . .

. . . without the hope and the dream, who would work at all? And so, not without hope, yet with no expectation of a miracle, I give the Jews a Christ they can now accept, the Christians a Christ they have forgotten.[38]

"Chad Gadya"

It is in the final story of the book, named for the popular recursive Passover song, "Chad Gadya," that Zangwill explores most directly and openly his own inner crisis and exposes explicitly his mounting despair. It cries out from the depths of his heart of the confusion of the acculturated Jew in Western society, of the believer's soul trapped in the materialist's mind. Here there are no "hopes and dreams," only nightmares and death.

On the eve of Passover a contemporary child of the Venetian ghetto returns to the city from his wanderings abroad. Walking about, the young man envies the assurance and abiding traditional faith of his father as he commences the Passover celebrations. But this child of the ghetto can no longer return to his boyhood home even for a brief comforting visit. For him all isles of certainty amid the raging typhoons of doubt have been swamped. Science and rationalism have destroyed his ability even to participate in Jewish religious activities without providing any adequate substitute for them. Zangwill diagnoses the disease expertly: "Oh, it was a cruel tragedy, this Western culture grafted on an Eastern stock, untuning the chords of life, setting heart and brain asunder."[39]

But despite his inability to believe, what this nameless child of the ghetto craved was the transcendent, openly revealed, palpable proof against all scientific claims, philosophic speculations, and intellectual doubts:

> But for him the old craving persisted. That alone would do. God, God—he was God intoxicated, without Spinoza's calm or Spinoza's certainty. Justice, Pity, Love—something that understood. . . . His soul rejected all the solutions and self-equations of his friends. . . . But the world without God was a beautiful, heartless woman—cold, irresponsive. He needed the flesh of soul. He had experimented with Nature . . . but there was a want, a void. He had loved Nature. . . . But the passion always faded and the old hunger for God came back.[40]

Even a Jewish state would offer no genuine solution for this longing for the Divine: "He understood the fate of Christ and of all idealists, doomed to see themselves worshipped and their ideas rejected in a religion or a State founded like a national monument to perpetuate their defeat."[41]

And this tragic pessimism applied not only to Jews but to all mankind:

> And he, he foreshadowed the future of all races, as well as his own. They would all go on struggling, till they became self-conscious; then like children grown to men, the scales falling from their eyes, they would suddenly ask themselves what it is all about, and, realizing that they were being driven along by blind forces to labor and struggle and strive, they too would pass away; the gross childish races would sweep them up, Nature pouring out new energies from her inexhaustible fount. For strength was in the unconscious, and when a nation paused to ask of itself its right to Empire, its Empire was already over.[42]

This, then, is the conclusion of historical positivist religion: despair. Intellectual appreciation of nature and romantic history lead not to greater wisdom and a higher morality but rather to an anguished loneliness in a blind and deaf universe. Historical progress leads not to increased light but to the ultimate darkness.

Wandering the barren night streets of Venice, this contemporary child of the ghetto discovers the only possible solution to his crises of faith and identity: "Death, death, at any cost, death to end this long ghastly creeping about the purlieus of life. Life even for a single instant longer, life without God, seemed intolerable."[43] So despairing, Zangwill's young man throws himself into the black waters of the Grand Canal.

For the body possessed of a Westerner's mind and of a Jew's soul the only end can be suicide. The Western Jew is doomed because the very term "Western Jew" constitutes an oxymoron. Thus ultimately there can be no authentic middle path, argues "Chad Gadya."

But this is not yet Zangwill's conclusion! In the epilogue to *Dreamers of the Ghetto*, "A Modern Scribe In Jerusalem," he provides a response to the despairing child of the Venetian ghetto, even if only it allows people to "live in the beautiful illusion [of religion], so long as the ugly facts did not break through! What mattered if these sites [in Jerusalem] were true or false—the believing soul had made them true."[44] For, after all, "absolute religious truth? How could there be such a thing?"[45]

With this preamble that religion need not be authentic and true, indeed that it cannot be so, but need serve fundamentally as a veil to conceal the ugly realities of life with beautiful illusions, Zangwill presents his own religious credo of wholeness, of identity, and of peace among all peoples:

> The time had come for a new religious expression, a new language for the old everlasting emotions, in terms of the modern cosmos; a religion that should contradict no fact and check no inquiry; so that children should grow up again with no distracting divorce from their parents and their past, with no break in the sweet sanctities of childhood, which carry on to old age something of the freshness of early sensation, and are a fount of tears in the desert of life.
>
> The ever-living, darkly-laboring Hebraic spirit of love and righteous aspiration, the Holy Ghost that had inspired Judaism and Christianity, and moved equally in Mohammedanism and Protestantism, must now quicken and inform the new learning, which still lay dead and foreign, outside humanity.[46]

Here, then, is outlined Zangwill's autobiographical confession and his assumption of the prophetic "mantle of Elijah." A new spiritual "middle path" must be hewn out from the emotional shards of the past now jumbled together with the rational theorems of the present. The twinned ethnic identities wrestling in the soul must be fused and father and son reconciled. It is Peace and Beauty, not Truth and Goodness, that are the essentials of the "new religious expression," for the aim is to teach a new mystification that will comfort, ennoble, and unify humanity, at least for a time. Human survivability is the issue, and the only alternative to a new "middle path" is an unbearable soul-rending bleak suffering that can achieve release only in the blankness of death. Such is the message that concludes *Dreamer of the Ghetto*.

Writing to a correspondent in 1897 while on a pilgrimage to Palestine, Israel Zangwill referred to his preparation of *Dreamers of the Ghetto,* explaining that "I who am no Dreamer behold and declare that Jerusalem—the sacred city of the three greatest religions of the world—is by the abuses . . . in the names of all of them, the unholiest city under the sun."[47] His judgment and condemnation are particularly poignant in the light of the epilogue to his book. For who is truly the greater dreamer, one who acts upon a vision of the truth not yet actualized or one who acts upon an illusion known to be unholy and untrue?

Such had become the inner anguish of this writer who could be neither wholly Jewish nor unquestionably English, and who found this quandary no longer interesting or amusing but, on the contrary, maddeningly unendurable. This suffering would propel Zangwill to adopt a "mantle" whose mystifications would ultimately lead him to drown himself in the same black waters that suffocated his contemporary child of the ghetto.

An Unanswered Plea

Amazingly, the agonized plea for help in *Dreamers of the Ghetto,* its sanctification of heresy, and its proclamation of a "new religion" of universal Christological Hebraism has gone almost completely unnoticed. Contemporary critics, in general, praised the book for its historical portraits, its narrative quality, and its revelation of the inner world of Jewish thought.[48] In other words, the work was interpreted as a significant contribution to the world's understanding of the Jewish people and their history.

Even the critics in the *Jewish Chronicle* noticed nothing. According to these very positive reviews, Zangwill creatively explored the strength and reality of those impulses that inspired "the master figures" in Jewish religious history and he artistically expressed the historical positive truth that should guide the direction of contemporary Jewish thought.[49]

Later literary studies have equally failed to grasp the central intention and philosophy of *Dreamers of the Ghetto.* Although recognizing that the work is not a history, they continued to notice only the negative side of Zangwill's views: that the clash between ghetto and the outside world is destructive. But his teleological pessimism, his plea *for* the heretical and illusory, and his Christological Hebraism were simply not discerned.[50]

Indeed, Zangwill's belief in Jesus, proclaimed in the opening poem of the book and thematically referred to throughout it, was mentioned by only one of his contemporaries, his friend Solomon Schechter. In private correspondence, he wrote to Zangwill, rather sardonically: "Your views about a certain gentleman of Galilee are—I hardly need tell you—not quite to my taste. But there is no case arguing with Dreamers; though I thought that dreams are as a rule confined to glimpses into the future, to what will happen. What happened is a matter of history & not of dreams and prophecy."[51]

Why was Zangwill's desperate pessimism—this cry of anguish—and the very non-Jewish quality of the philosophy he took so very seriously and expounded so thoroughly in this book almost completely ignored? Of course answers to this question must be speculative and tentative, but the endeavor may nonetheless prove worthwhile and enlightening.

In the first place, we have already seen that *Children of the Ghetto* also contained both revealed and concealed themes, but, because of its literary novelty, only the revealed and obvious subjects were noticed. So, too, with *Dreamers of the Ghetto;* the novel and evident theme, Zangwill's translation of modern scholarly discussions of Jewish history into a popular format—his *maggid*'s presentation of Rabbinic wisdom, so to say—attracted the public's attention. The manifest details of the multifaceted nature of Jewish historical experience were exciting and all absorbing for both non-Jewish and Anglo-Jewish publics, the former because they had virtually no knowledge at all about this "alien world" and the latter because these stories provided a historical context—glittering shards—from which they might derive ethnic identity and self-esteem. In such a case, Zangwill's concealed theme—his anguish, his plea, his pessimism, and his theological heresy—was simply not noticed, as was the situation also with his previous Jewish novel.

Second, as a corollary to this first point, it must be recalled that English-speaking Jewry had desired a *maggid,* an ethnic storyteller. They had, in fact, recruited Israel Zangwill into fulfilling this role, and he had been extremely successful in this task. Now to have impugned the authenticity of this most prestigious and popular guide that this rudderless people possessed would have been far more painful in its social-psychological repercussions than was the overlooking of various discomforting remarks by him.

If these two observations are correct it is not at all astonishing that Solomon Schechter, an ordained rabbi and Judaica scholar of international repute, would have noticed and objected to the entire endeavor, both to its revealed and to its concealed themes. For Schechter needed no *maggid* to guide him.

Finally, Zangwill's enthusiasm for many of these historical "heretics" was no doubt shared by many in the broader Jewish community. Even his interpretation of Jesus as a Jewish prophet may not have been antithetical to many of his readers. Thus, for them, these views could also form an acceptable portion of the revealed theme of the book. Only its desperate pessimism and its appeal to the illusory as the sole route of escape remained concealed from these readers.

But for Israel Zangwill these topics were everything. He was being crushed under the weight of his isolation—social, intellectual, and spiritual—and desperately needed to escape. Like his seriocomic governess, Zangwill would flee his two previous careers—as teacher and entertainer—for a religious vocation: he would assume the "mantle of Elijah" as prophet of a new universal natural religion to all mankind. Simultaneously he would also grasp the sword of Jewish nationalism and would wield it fiercely against all foes and assimilationists. But unlike his seriocomic governess, Zangwill undertook his new vocation not by eschewing marriage but by entering into it.

Israel Zangwill's Marriage

Israel Zangwill was almost forty years old before he married. That he had romantic attachments before his marriage is evident from allusions in his fiction, particularly in the unpublished manuscript, "The Baron of Offenbach."[52] His association with actresses in his plays had even aroused suspicions.[53] But, so far documentary evidence exists for only one serious romantic episode before his marriage.

In July 1898 Mrs. Mathilde Schechter wrote an enthusiastic letter to Zangwill about his "Miss S": "You know how sincerely I often felt your lonely life—your joyless years of give and give and give, and never take and never taste of the sweet things in life."[54] Mrs. Schechter hoped that Zangwill and "Miss S" would visit her family in Cambridge.

Apparently they did, and Mrs. Schechter then changed her tune. Writing to Zangwill about his forthcoming lecture tour of America she commented: "I crave your pardon for what I am going to say—I do not think she ["Miss S"] is *the* 'zig to fit into your zigzag.' . . . The ocean once well between you, will prove to you exactly how you feel in this matter."[55]

And evidently Mathilde Schechter was right.

"Miss S" was, most probably, a young artist, Amy Stuart, with whom Zangwill publicly socialized during this period.[56]

Instead it was the young author Edith Chaplin Ayrton whom Israel Zangwill would eventually choose to marry. She was the daughter of two quite remarkable people, William E. Ayrton and his first wife, Matilda Chaplin. W. E. Ayrton was a prominent electrical engineer and physicist who in 1871 wed his cousin, a pioneering woman medical doctor in Britain; she had, in fact, been encouraged by her feminist husband to enter this profession.[57] Edith, the couple's only child, born 1 October 1875, was prematurely orphaned of her mother when the latter died in 1883.[58] Two years later Ayrton married his Jewish student, Phoebe Sarah (Hertha) Marks.

Miss Marks was a remarkable woman. Born in 1854 in Portsea, at the age of nine she was sent to live in London with her mother's sister; this aunt, Marion (Moss) Hartog, ran a school and wrote several undistinguished books of poetry and of Jewish history. During the course of her girlhood, Hertha, as Miss Marks preferred to be called, abandoned Jewish religious practices, although not the ethnic label. Through the Hartogs she became acquainted with Barbara Leigh-Smith, Madame Bodichon, a cousin of Florence Nightingale, founder of Girton College, Cambridge, a leading figure in the women's movement, and a confidante of George Eliot. In 1873 Madame Bodichon introduced Hertha to the renowned author, who took an interest in her and endeavored to further her education. This latter acquaintance later occasioned rumors that Mirah, the Jewish heroine of *Daniel Deronda,* was modeled on Hertha, an opinion no longer seriously entertained.[59]

In 1876 Hertha entered Cambridge, where she concentrated her studies on the physical sciences. During the course of these studies she became acquainted with Professor W. E. Ayrton, and in 1885 the two married, much to the consternation of Hertha's widowed mother, who disliked her daughter's intermarrying. The couple then moved to London, where Hertha began lecturing and writing on the theory of electricity. There she also became a prominent suffragette, and to this movement she eventually attracted her stepdaughter, Edith, and her own daughter, Barbara, who had married the poet and author

Gerald Gould. In the suffragette campaigns the three worked closely with Christabel Pankhurst, although only Barbara was an activist in the more militant Women's Social and Political Union founded by Pankhurst in 1906.

The Ayrtons first became acquainted with Israel Zangwill at a reception for the famous writer given by the Hartogs in 1895. Edith Ayrton, a budding author attending Bedford College, and Zangwill soon became friends.

By 1901 Hertha, having sent copies of Edith's early short stories to Zangwill, coyly wrote her stepdaughter: "it is very good of him [Zangwill] to look after them, and very nice of him to write to you every day, though I cannot say I think he displays a *large* amount of self-denial in this. I have no doubt he gets some small modicum of enjoyment out of it, too."[60]

Israel and Edith were married in a civil ceremony at the London registry office on 26 November 1903. Prior to the honeymoon in Spain, a reception for the newlyweds was hosted by the Ayrtons and attended by Zangwill's closest literary friends, Jerome K. Jerome and T. Hall Crane. Notable from the guest list is the absence of most of the groom's Jewish associates.[61]

His marriage marks a momentous watershed in Zangwill's life. Not only did it signal the activation of his commitment in his personal, as well as in his public and professional, life to his universalist and assimilationist philosophy, but it also severed him finally from his closest Jewish teachers, Solomon Schechter and Moses Gaster. Zangwill had been growing increasingly estranged from these two friends for some time, a consequence of the cumulative effects of his heterodox religious views, his violent differences with Gaster over certain Zionist policies (with Schechter, in New York from 1902, not supporting the author's vituperative attacks on his Romanian *landsman*), and, finally, his intermarriage.[62] As Zangwill ceased associating with these Jewish scholars, he turned instead to Edith's uncle, A. Chaplin, a Christian religious scholar living in Essex.[63]

Why did Israel Zangwill choose to do in 1903 what a decade earlier he would not allow Esther Ansell to contemplate and what he emphatically denounced in *Children of the Ghetto?* Why now did he intermarry? The answer lies concealed within the pages of *Dreamers of the Ghetto* and "The Serio-Comic Governess." The tensions between his incompatible identities were proving unbearable, and no "middle path" was attainable that might harmonize the combatants, even if only in a temporary truce, so as to achieve some inner respite. Movement toward escape had become imperative, no matter how desperate the attempt might be. And Zangwill knew it was desperate—and dangerous. All of *Dreamers of the Ghetto* serves as a cautionary tale against such alluring chimeras. But the psychic pressures and anguish were proving too great for balanced reason and circumspection to prevail any longer. Any action was better than remaining in the painful trap and mirky slough; he was suffocating and had to break free and gasp in some new air, however pure or polluted it might prove.

It was from this pain that Zangwill pleaded in 1900, on the eve of his engagement:

> Either let the next generation be trained to consider themselves Englishmen or let them be taught to consider themselves as noble exiles, provisionally doing their duty in the country in which their lot is cast. But let not their brains be muddled and tampered with, as mine was, by two contradictory teachings, nor their natural absorption of English ideas, ideals, and traditions checked and confused by tales of what happened two thousand miles away two thousand years before they were born.[64]

Already on the brink, Zangwill explicitly indicated his own choice between the contending identities:

> And in truth, in so far as Jews do, in the civilised communities of Europe and America, take on the characteristics of their environment and become one with it, their isolation by [refusing] inter-marriage is a mere bad habit. The more logical see this, and drift silently away; the less logical do not see this and drift along meaninglessly; the illogical publish Zionist prayer-books.[65]

Clearly Zangwill regarded himself among the "logical" and so chose—aligning his own future with that dictated by the social imperatives of Western Jewry's future—to "drift away," although not necessarily "silently." Furthermore, his scorn for the "less logical" and the "illogical" is overt and impatient. But he did not yet suspect that his "logic" was, in reality, a labyrinthian mystification.

Interestingly, Zangwill's intermarriage evoked no public comment from the Jewish community at the time. The public silence on the subject is indeed deafening. Yet among the Zionist leadership the criticism was explicit, if quite private. Thus Chaim Weizmann, already Zangwill's ideological opponent in the Zionist movement, wrote to his fellow Russian, Menachem Ussishkin, in December 1903 that "at a London Zionist meeting two weeks ago Mr. Zangwill and others disgraced themselves terribly. . . . This marriage, and the couple's appearance at a Zionist meeting, where Zangwill had been received with applause, had contributed to the decline of the prestige of Zionism in England."[66]

In another letter, Weizmann attributes to Max Nordau the view that Zangwill's marriage was "anti-national" and later quotes Nordau that "even were my private life above reproach it is nevertheless a failure from the national point of view. Zionism came one and a half years too late for me, and I cannot forgive Zangwill."[67] Still, nothing was said publicly.

Nevertheless, how could Zangwill remain a Jewish nationalist leader *after* he had deliberately chosen the opposite course in both his personal and his public life, a route explicitly dedicated to encourage Jewish assimilation? To answer this question it will be first necessary to investigate why Zangwill became a Zionist in the first place.

Zangwill and Zionism

Not coincidentally, Israel Zangwill's abandonment of an aloof but benign neutrality on the question of Jewish nationalism and his adoption of the Zionist cause occurred simultaneously with his engagement to Edith Chaplin Ayrton. Precisely at the time he decided to cast his lot in with the apparent historical destiny of Western Jewry to have its identity absorbed ineluctably into the majority population, he joined actively with those determined to rescue and preserve the Jewish people from just such absorption.

The one continuous thread that runs throughout all his life is Zangwill's consistency. His simultaneous decisions to intermarry *and* to become a Zionist activist strikingly illustrate this consistency. For both decisions constitute radical departures from previously held parallel positions and psychologically complement each other in Zangwill's furious dash for escape. They are the activist counterparts of his earlier unintegrated intellectual and emotional ruminations in his writings. To recognize this consistency, Zangwill's previous views on Zionism need to be explored. To appreciate these views, a brief summary of the origins of modern Jewish nationalism will be helpful.

The distinctly modern and political aspirations to return the Jewish people to the Land of Israel considerably antedated the founding of the Zionist movement by Theodore Herzl. We have already seen literary evidence in the writings of West European authors such as Benjamin Disraeli, Leopold Kompert, and George Eliot. Political espousal also antedated Herzl. The most notable instance in the West is *Rome and Jerusalem* (1862) by the German-Jewish political theorist Moses Hess (1812–1875).

Two things stand out among these early Western formulations of Jewish nationalism: (1) it is to be achieved by political negotiations among the leaders of peoples, and (2) it does not negate the legitimacy of the Diaspora. That the leaders of the people would initiate the rebuilding of a Jewish state is clearly what Kompert expected, as is illustrated when he portrays his Mendel Wilna on his way to Jerusalem, stopping off in Vienna to win support of the Rothschilds.[68] And this is also the crux of Hess's view as well:

> When political conditions in the Orient shape themselves so as to permit the organization of a beginning of the restoration of a Jewish state, this beginning will express itself in the founding of Jewish colonies in the land of their ancestors, to which enterprise France will undoubtedly lend a hand. France, beloved friend, is the savior who will restore our people to its place in universal history.[69]

Equally, Hess expressed the second motif, the continued legitimacy of the Jewish Diaspora: "It is well understood that when we speak of a Jewish settlement in the Orient, we do not mean to imply a total emigration of the occidental Jews to Palestine. Even after the establishment of a Jewish State the majority of the Jews who live at present in the civilized countries of the Occident will undoubtedly remain where they are."[70]

Thus the revival of Jewish national existence was viewed by Western Jews prior to Herzl as an expedient to resolve the oppression of their Eastern brethren, given the absorptive limitations of Western Jewry and the intractability of Russian autocracy, but it was not something Western Jews expected to apply to themselves.

Likewise in Eastern Europe Jewish nationalism preceded the establishment of Herzl's World Zionist Organization. Particularly significant in this regard was the Chovevei Zion (Lovers of Zion) movement that arose in Russia as a populist response to the mounting campaign of officially sponsored pogroms; its aims derived from the ideas espoused for the revival of a Jewish state by Leo Pinsker (1821–1891) in his 1882 manifesto *Auto-Emancipation*.

What characterizes East European pre-Herzlian formulations of

Jewish nationalism, such as expressed by Chovevei Zion, are: (1) it is to be achieved through direct practical action undertaken by the Jewish masses themselves: "auto-emancipation," and (2) it negates the legitimacy of a continuing Diaspora following the national revival. Thus Pinsker wrote: "We are no more justified in leaving our national future entirely in the hands of other peoples than we are in making them responsible for our national misfortune. . . . Therefore we must abandon the delusive idea that we are fulfilling by our dispersion a Providential mission."[71]

Another Russian Jewish nationalist, Moshe Leib Lilienblum (1843–1910), exhorted in 1883: "Let us only acquire positive ideals and the best of the westernized and enlightened Jews will return to us. The masses, too, will hasten to join us. . . . Work! Lay the foundation for a normal and healthy national life for the Jewish people. . . . Pay no heed to the desire for assimilation of our plutocrats . . . and to the 'enlightened' among us who follow after them."[72]

Theodore Herzl (1860–1904), a Central European, reacted to the violent outbursts of anti-Semitism in France surrounding the Dreyfus Affair by combining elements of the Jewish nationalism of his Western and Eastern precursors. Thus, like the Westerners, he insisted on an exclusively political approach to securing the new homeland:

> What is achieved by transporting a few thousand Jews to another country? Either they come to grief at once, or, if they prosper their prosperity gives rise to anti-Semitism. . . .
>
> . . . Significant experiments in colonization have been made . . . , though on the mistaken principle of gradual infiltration of Jews. Infiltration is bound to end badly. . . . Immigration, therefore, is futile unless it is based on our guaranteed autonomy.[73]

On the other hand, Herzl firmly believed, together with East European nationalists, that the new Jewish state would supplant the entire Diaspora community, and he commented contemptuously that "whoever wishes may stay behind. The opposition of *a few individuals* is quite immaterial."[74]

Where Herzl most strikingly differed from both Western and Eastern precursors was in not limiting the site of the new Jewish state to the Land of Israel. While he recognized Israel as a possibility, in his 1896 manifesto, "The Jewish State," he also willingly entertains alternative locations, particularly Argentina.[75] However, at the First

Zionist Congress in Basel, Switzerland, in 1897, while the majority endorsed Herzl's "political" Zionism (as opposed to Chovevei Zion's "practical" Zionism of "infiltration" and "colonization") and his rejection of Diaspora legitimacy, they also won from Herzl agreement to limit the site of the new homeland exclusively to Palestine.[76] This would remain the prevailing position of the Zionist movement until the commitment to the Land of Israel was challenged in 1903.

Israel Zangwill had early expressed his contempt for the Chovevei Zion movement's "practical" strategy. As we have already seen, in 1892, in *Children of the Ghetto,* he had portrayed it contemptuously as the "Holy Land League," deprecating its members as querulous and petty and its methods as trivial and utopian.

The same attitude is replicated in "The Palestine Pilgrim," a story in *Dreamers of the Ghetto.*[77] It relates the tale of the Russian immigrant living in Manchester, Aaron the Peddler, "a *schlemihl* (a ne'er-do-well), who is inspired to return to the Land of Israel by the "Society of the Lovers of Zion": "yes, the Jews must return to Palestine, there must be a great voluntary stream; great, if gradual. Slowly but surely the Jews must win back their country."[78] Eventually Aaron sets out on his voyage to Palestine. After a harrowing passage by sea he arrives at the Promised Land, only to be turned away by Ottoman officials who refuse to authorize Russian citizens to settle in their territory. So much for the idealism of such "practical" Zionists. Zangwill never doubted this evaluation.

On the other hand, his attitude toward the early endeavors of Theodore Herzl was much more ambivalent. For Zangwill was deeply concerned about the terrible oppression of Russian Jewry, a subject he had treated earnestly as early as his days as *Ariel* editor, and he interpreted Herzl's ideas in this context.[79]

In November 1895 Max Nordau (1849–1923) suggested to Herzl that he expound his Zionist program in London at the Maccabean Club and provided him with a letter of introduction to Zangwill for this purpose.[80] In London for the occasion, Herzl made Zangwill's acquaintance. His account of their first encounter is quite interesting:

> The house is rather shabby. In his book-lined study Zangwill sits before an enormous writing table with his back to the fireplace. . . . Israel Zangwill is a long-nosed Negroid type, with very woolly deep-black hair parted in the middle; his clean-shaven face displays the steely haughtiness of an honest ambitious man who had made

> his way after bitter struggles. The disorder of his room and on his desk leads me to infer that he is an internalized person. I have not read any of his writings. . . .
>
> Our conversation is laborious. We speak French, his command of which is inadequate. . . . Still, we agree on major points. He, too, is in favor of our territorial independence.
>
> However his point of view is a racial one—which I cannot accept if I so much as look at him and at myself. All I am saying is: we are an historical unit.[81]

Their areas of agreement outweighing their differences, Herzl introduced his Zionist plan at a Maccabean banquet with Zangwill in the chair that November. However, he did not persuade the English author to embrace his views on Jewish nationalism.

Zangwill reacted to Herzl's program with a mixture of confusion, ambivalence, and inconsistency. His warring impulses toward Herzl's Zionism are expressed in quite remarkable fashion in a peculiar outburst in an 1898 piece otherwise describing the East End during Passover: "[1] Who would not be a Zionist, if Zionism were not the thorniest project ever considered upon the planet! [2] For my part, I want no Embassy at Paris. [3] I would willingly start for Palestine if I could see any good in it. [4] What does it matter where one lives?"[82]

Notice that this is one continuous paragraph. In the first sentence Zangwill distances himself from Zionism, but only on account of its questionable practicality. But then, in the second, he rejects the idea outright. In the third sentence he again refers to Zionism favorably, although repeating his doubts about its feasibility. Finally, Zangwill repudiates it altogether, wondering, "What does it matter where one lives?" Obviously the parameters of his already complex Anglo-Jewish universe have been still further blurred by the intrusion of the Jewish nationalist from Vienna.

Nevertheless, that Zangwill was charmed by Herzl's person is evident in *Dreamers of the Ghetto* from his treatment of the First Zionist Congress, which he attended as an observer, in the story "Dreamers in Congress."[83] In this rather journalistic account of the congress, Zangwill appears to reject the Jewish racial bond: "Who speaks of the Jewish type? One can only say negatively that these faces are not Christian." Of Herzl he writes: "A majestic figure, the President. . . . In sooth, the beautiful sombre face of a kingly dreamer, but of a Jewish dreamer who faces the fact that flowers are grown in dung."[84]

And Herzl's "political" Zionism is clearly superior to the visions of Chovevei Zion: "Let not his movement be confounded with those petty projects for helping Jewish agriculturalists into Palestine. What! Improve the Sultan's land without any political equivalent guaranteed in advance!"[85]

Yet for all his admiration of Herzl and his ecstasy at the Zionist Congress, Zangwill remains skeptical:

> Yes, the dream still stirs at the heart of the mummied race. . . . And if our President forgets that the vast bulk of his brethren are unrepresented in his Congress, that they are content with the civic rights so painfully won, and have quite other conceptions of their creed's future, who will grudge him this moment of fine rapture?
>
> . . . The world in which prophecies are uttered cannot be the world in which prophecies are fulfilled?[86]

Ambivalence toward Zionism constitutes a continuous theme in Zangwill's writings during this period; he ponders over the "true" historical significance of Herzl's project and, simultaneously, doubts its feasibility. Thus in his special appendix to the American edition of *Dreamers of the Ghetto* Zangwill writes: "The Zionist ideal offers one possible re-baptism, but to doubt whether Palestine can support the Jews may be a higher patriotism than to rhapsodise over Zion. . . . Without an active moral Ideal . . . even a successful Zionist movement would only be a political solution to a situation which is not really pressing.[87]

Yet while his mind rejected the practicality of Zionism and counseled the well-trod path of rational skepticism, Zangwill's religious emotions were stirred by the spiritual potential of Herzl's program: "But Zionism would, at any rate, preserve the race for inspirations to come. Whereas, without either Zionism or an international spiritual ideal, Judaism must deservedly disappear."[88]

Here, then, is the Zangwillian dichotomy: the Jews are destined to assimilate into the majority populations of the West under conditions of freedom unless they are somehow able to energize the spiritual content of contemporary Judaism while remaining in the Diaspora or they must be preserved in a special autonomous territory of their own until such a spiritual revival finally does occur among them. Unfortunately both alternatives to assimilation seemed unlikely, Zangwill then believed. In other words, he was not opposed to Zionism in theory as a means to prevent assimilation or alleviate oppression, but he doubted its practicality, particularly in Ottoman Palestine.

The clearest formulation of Zangwill's original attitude toward Zionism appears in his 1899 essay, "Zionism."[89] In it he outlines four possibilities for the future of the Jewish people: (1) national regeneration, (2) religious regeneration, (3) disappearance, and (4) no solution.[90] Rejecting the last as a proper subject for serious consideration, he also subordinates the second alternative to the first: under current conditions Jewish religious regeneration is possible only as a consequence of national regeneration.[91] Hence there are really only two viable options: Jewish nationalism or total Jewish absorption.

Zangwill then assesses the feasibility of the Zionist project on his estimation of the future of Palestine. He immediately acknowledges that the Herzlian political strategy is much superior to the program of Chovevei Zion. But he believes that Palestine is so economically underdeveloped, the site of such contentious religious claims, and so insecure under the Ottomans that its possession and utility are extremely problematic for the Jews.

What is attractive to Zangwill in Herzl's Zionism is its political realism as a technique for resolving the oppressive conditions of Russian Jewry, a realism of method that does not depend, ultimately, upon the economic potential and political possession of Palestine: "the only absolute essential of the Herzl scheme lies in the phrase 'legally-secured home,' and if the two million [in money] could secure that *anywhere*, they would be well spent."[92] Again he remarks, "The case against Palestine is indeed so bleak, that one is tempted to say that Zionism would be practical but for Zion."[93] In other words, a Jewish national homeland may be politically secured not just in Palestine but anywhere; in fact, there are many more desirable locations for it than in the old Land of Israel. In this argument is the source of Zangwill's future Territorialism, a product not of the 1903 British offer of East Africa but of his own unhappy impressions of Palestine during his 1897 visit there.

Zangwill, significantly, also does not interpret Jewish nationalism as negating the legitimacy of the Diaspora: "That the Jews are to migrate *en masse* has never been suggested: a recognized centre of Jewish life is to be set up, which will be left to its own evolutionary impetus; a centre of gravity which may be trusted to attract the persecuted and the patriotic." It will become the homeland "for the orthodox and persecuted masses of semi-barbarous countries."[94] This, of course, was specifically *not* Herzl's view, but it was the traditional view of Western Jewry and would also constitute the central motif of Territorialist ideology.

Typically, Zangwill concludes his discussion of the two possibilities for the future of the Jewish people by embracing both alternatives: Diaspora assimilationism and Jewish nationalism. The former he applies to Western Jewry and the latter to Eastern Jewry. Religious revival will occur for Western Jewry in the context of a broader Hebraism while for the latter it will be a function of renewed national existence. And the revival of Judaism within an autonomous Jewish homeland, according to Zangwill, will reenforce the Hebraic religious impulses of the West. Zangwill adhered to essentially this analysis of the dual future of the Jewish people, depending upon their geographical disposition, until after the First World War, and it provided the rationale for his activist agendas and his marriage during this period.

But what is evident from this article ("Zionism") is that Israel Zangwill was not a Zionist in Herzl's sense and indeed took great pains explicitly to distance himself from identification with the Zionist movement. This attitude was dictated by his rationalist perceptions and his natural skepticism. But abruptly in 1901 Zangwill completely altered his stance on Palestine and, therefore, also on identification with Zionism.

In "The Return to Palestine," he suddenly argues that the only solution to international anti-Semitism and the sole alternative to the disappearance of the Jews is the establishment of a Jewish state *in Palestine.*[95] Notice that what is actually new in this formulation is not the analysis of the Jews' future but the evaluation of the practicality of the Zionist program, especially its feasibility with regard to politically obtaining and economically developing Palestine.

As usual Zangwill lashes out at all alternative solutions, particularly the colonization schemes of the Jewish Colonization Association, Chovevei Zion, and philanthropic endeavors in general: instead of these "futile efforts" there is only "Dr. Herzl's movement" for "the integration of the scattered forces of Israel, and the expression of this unity by a national politically guaranteed home in Palestine that may serve as a shelter for the homeless and oppressed, and a beacon for those prosperous sheltered elsewhere."[96]

Zionism, thus, must become the leitmotif of Jewish consciousness and activity:

> The problem is simply to set up a centre of Jewish life and concentrate all one's labours on it. Gradually it would become the magnet of the race.
>
> The task is difficult . . . beset with more theological and political pitfalls, unique in its problem of migration. But the very greatness should stimulate the most maligned of races to break the desolate monotony of this brutal modern world by the splendour of an antique idealism.[97]

Remarkably, all of Zangwill's doubts about Palestine—the key ingredient in this "antique idealism"—have completely and abruptly evaporated:

> Palestine is a country without a people . . . , the Jews are a people without a country. . . . There is no reason why Palestine . . . should not support even all 11,000,000 Jews. . . .
>
> . . . Only by concentrating upon one country is there a chance of achieving something. . . .
>
> . . . A brief review of the present position of Palestine will show there is nothing chimerical in the scheme of making her habitable by the Jews.[98]

His only caveat is that "it is not essential that all her [the Land of Israel's] daughters shall return to her."[99] Palestine is to serve as a "shelter" for the "homeless" and "oppressed" Eastern Jews, not the "prosperous" Jews of Western Europe, for whom a Jewish Palestine "*may*" serve as a purely "spiritual beacon." The Diaspora and its universalist mission are to continue.

Zangwill's change of attitude was not merely intellectual or rhetorical. While in 1900 he could still say, "I am not a Zionist officially," in 1901 he served as one of the official English delegates to the Fifth Zionist Congress.[100] In other words, he had converted his new-found belief into overt identification and activism.

What had changed? Why had Zangwill suddenly abandoned his skepticism and plunged into Zionism? There was nothing in Britain, in the Zionist movement, or in Palestine to account for it. But there were, indeed, two profound changes in Israel Zangwill's personal life that do account for his decision: (1) his determination to become an activist in general, and (2) his impending engagement to the non-Jew, Edith Chaplin Ayrton. As an Anglo-Jew Zangwill believed that activism dictated intermarriage and amalgamation in one's personal life and advocacy of the "Hebraic mission" in one's public profession, while as Jew qua Jew, he believed that activism dictated implementing a program designed to "save" East European Jewry from the twin damnations of Russian oppression and Western assimilation.

Zangwill thus saw the future of the Jewish people as bifurcated: "the Jew stands at the parting of the ways that no longer permits one foot on each path. Either he must consent to bring the world to Abraham's bosom, or he must at least obey the trumpet call of Isaiah [for Jewish political revival]."[101]

For himself Zangwill elected the first path: assimilation into the British people. Yet what appeared to him as a logical and inevitable step intellectually also repelled him emotionally. If he finally chose to acquiesce to his own "doom," he could not restrain himself from simultaneously acting to preserve others from a similar fate. Thus despite the fact that in 1901 one could no longer "keep one foot on each path" of ethnic identities, Zangwill—trapped in the conflicting imperatives of intellect and emotion—helplessly continued to do just that. As an English Jew he would assimilate himself; at the same time he would also fight to save those Jews not yet entangled within Western culture from facing a similar fate.

Zangwill's Zionism was thus his way of once again discovering a means of returning to his pious father's home for a peaceful respite from the anguishing complexities of the broader world. As he himself explains, Zionism represents "the splendour of an antique idealism" to counter "the desolate monotony of this brutal modern world." It is the "modern scribe's" "beautiful illusion" conjured to veil "the ugly fact."

Impelled to embark on action so as to relieve the fierce tension of conflicting identities, and no longer believing that British and Jewish could be reconciled in a middle path fusion, Zangwill deliberately decided to acquiesce to the inevitability of assimilation by intermarrying and so join what he believed to be the march of history. He opted for the future as an Englishman. From being a *maggid* to the Jews he would now assume the "mantle" of a prophet to all mankind, altering genres as he shifted his parameters.

But to counterbalance this "betrayal" of family and community—in a desperate effort to avoid the fate of the lost son of "Chad Gadya" who no longer was able to return to his father's home—Zangwill threw reason and skepticism to the wind and, simultaneously, became an activist in the Jewish nationalist cause: those not condemned to assimilation could yet be spared the dread duel of identities.

His inability to integrate his British and Jewish heritages all along was paralleled by an equal inability to choose definitely between them.

Even this effort at choosing—by intermarrying—thus was doomed to failure: he continued to insist upon living according to the values of the contemporary secular world, but he craved the comforting warmth of his traditional and childhood home. Ultimately, in 1901, Zangwill had not traveled a step beyond the conflicting attitudes expressed in his 1889 essay, "English Judaism."

To justify his dual roles as advocate of assimilationism and also as champion of Jewish nationalism, Israel Zangwill adhered to a program that bifurcated the Jewish people. For those "polluted" by the advantages of Westernism, assimilation into a universal Hebraic culture was the only intellectually acceptable fate, while for those Jews of Eastern Europe the emotionally repellent path of assimilation might yet be avoided, provided they could be protected within a politically autonomous Jewish refuge. To these dual causes—genuinely contradictory except in the diaphanous illusions of the dreamer—Zangwill devoted the following two decades of his life.

The crisis expressed in *Dreamers of the Ghetto*—how to be a Jew in a modern open British secular society—led Zangwill onto conflicting paths that could not but intensify the crisis of twinned identities until it eventually would tear his sanity asunder.

EIGHT

Jewish Nationalist

Throughout the first two decades of the twentieth century Israel Zangwill emerged as the most eloquent spokesman and energetic activist in the campaign for immediate establishment by political negotiations of an internationally sanctioned Jewish homeland. The impulse for his endeavors was precise and explicit: East European Jews living under the imminent threat of physical abuse and extinction. This contemporary fact entailed upon those Jews living securely and upon all civilized human beings the moral obligation of rescuing the endangered and providing them with a safe refuge. Zangwill's efforts during this period are thus imbued with an intense sense of urgency: lives were at stake and only concrete action undertaken immediately may avert catastrophe. Under such circumstances all obstacles must be viewed as mere temporary physical impediments to be overcome or as self-serving verbal prevarications to be exposed.

While anguish over the pressing need to rescue East European Jews from physical harm was the driving force behind Zangwill's nationalism, there was also, secondarily, a spiritual-cultural component to his activism. Beyond the issue of bodily preservation—always the fundamental objective—he was also profoundly concerned to prevent the spiritual and cultural extinction of traditional East European Judaism. Here the danger was assimilation along the lines already adopted by Western Jewry, a process, Zangwill was convinced, destined to result in the ultimate disappearance of Western Jewry as a distinctive ethnic group possessing a unique spiritual mission to mankind.

To keep alive this latent prophetic message of Judaism it was thus essential to keep alive Eastern Jewry under secure conditions. As a solution to these twin imperatives—and as a means of reactivating Judaic spirituality—Zangwill espoused the notion of a politically autonomous Jewish homeland; here was the most desirable and practical means of preserving both the lives of oppressed Jews and the spiritual-cultural elements of a still unalloyed Judaism. In such an autonomous homeland the rescued remnant of pious East European Jews would repay their Western benefactors by flourishing in a particularist state that would serve as a universal spiritual beacon for all humanity. Judaism would once again teach all mankind the Hebraic ethic.

But several ominous characteristics also accompanied Zangwill's nationalist campaign to achieve the immediate establishment of such a Jewish homeland. The original creative tensions arising from Zangwill's conflicting ethnic identities, previously so productive of works of art and social-psychological insight, now had become diverted into the aggressive practical pursuit of two distinctive and contrastive political ideals: peaceful universal harmony and militant Jewish nationalism.

And from the first, Zangwill's nationalism had assumed a bellicosity that proved brilliantly witty and entertaining but communally divisive and barren of concrete accomplishment. As a consequence, within a few years, the rational and humane ideology that had led Zangwill to advocate the immediate realization of the nationalist goal became further transmogrified into an ethereal mystification devoid of all practical content. And the fruitlessness of his nationalist activism is mirrored in Zangwill's similar unproductiveness as a Jewish storyteller during this period. An analogous pattern emerges when his universalist campaign is analyzed.[1]

During the almost twenty years of his formal nationalist activism, Zangwill's career passed through three organizational phases, although the ideology throughout remains constant. From 1901 to 1905 he was an advocate of official Herzlian Zionism; from 1905 to 1914 he was the driving force behind insurgent Territorialism; and from 1914 to 1919 he was the leading Western advocate of a Palestine-centered militant Jewish nationalism. With the conclusion of the Treaty of Versailles and the establishment of the British mandate in Palestine, an embittered and defeated Zangwill abandoned his role as nationalist activist for that of prophetic teacher and chastiser.[2]

New Enemies and Old

Zionist Conversion

When Theodore Herzl visited London in the spring of 1901, Israel Zangwill was still maintaining his diffident attitude toward Jewish nationalism. Introducing Herzl at a dinner sponsored by the Maccabean Club, he remarked: "Since the fall of the Ghetto gates the Jews have groped in the strange sunshine. Jewish life has lacked both purpose and dignity. It has come under the thumb of the practical man [Theodore Herzl]. . . . Gentlemen, Dr. Herzl may fail. But he has already written his name indelibly on the scroll of Jewish history."[3]

Yet within six months, as he was contemplating his own intermarriage, Zangwill announced his activist conversion to Herzl's Zionist Movement. In December 1901, instead of his previous attitude of attending as a journalist, he served as an official representative to the Fifth Zionist Congress.[4] All his earlier doubts seem to have been resolved, releasing Zangwill's brilliant oratory for the nationalist movement. Gleefully the *Jewish Chronicle* reported, "The only new Congress reputation was that of Mr. Zangwill."[5]

During the same month, Zangwill published an explicit exposition and defense of Zionism as an ideology and as a cause. In "The Return to Palestine," after repeating his critique of Chovevei Zion's "practical Zionism," Zangwill embraces the "political" approach of Herzl's nationalist movement:

> The task to which Israel is thus called is of an originality congruous with its unique history. Mother-lands have always created colonies. Here colonies are to create a mother-land, or rather recreate her. . . . The task is difficult . . . but the very greatness of the task should stimulate the most maligned of races to break the desolate monotony of this brutal modern world by the splendour of an antique idealism.[6]

Previous doubts over the feasibility of Jewish settlement in Palestine have evaporated with the challenge:

> Palestine is a country without a people; the Jews are a people without a country. The regeneration of the soil would bring the regeneration of the people. It is marvellous that the country should have remained comparatively empty for eighteen hundred years. . . . Thus switched into the world's markets, there is no reason why Palestine, with its 11,000 square miles (including the Lebanon district) should not support even all the 11,000,000 Jews.[7]

Thus, not only is national revival possible, but, according to Zangwill, it is essential for the very survival of the Jewish people. In a passage possessing autobiographical undertones, he argues:

> We have seen the failure of every other prescription; we have followed the largely unconscious evolution by which—even against his will—Israel's feet have been turned Zionwards at the very moment in history in which it is possible for him to reoccupy the country for the world's benefit and his own. . . . But the dullest imagination must feel what a world of romance and spiritual hope, what a ferment of religious revival and literary and artistic activity, must attend and follow the homecoming of the wandering Jew.
>
> Not to renationalise Judaism now is forever to denationalise it. . . . The crucial moment in the long life of Israel has arrived . . . and the Jew stands at the parting of the way that no longer permits one foot on each. Either he must consent to be merely a member of an international religious community welcoming the world to Abraham's bosom, or he must at last obey the trumpet call of Isaiah: "Go through, go through the gates; prepare ye the way of the people: cast up, cast up the highway, gather out the stones, light up a standard for the people."[8]

This passage encapsulates Zangwill's nationalist ideology.[9] According to it, the Emancipation created an unwilled caesura in Jewish history; survival as a distinctive ethnic group is, for the first time, now at stake.[10] How to respond to this challenge has, therefore, become *the* issue for modern Jewry. Deciding, whether deliberately or otherwise, can no longer be avoided. And only two alternatives genuinely remain available, argues Zangwill. On the one hand, Jews can elect to assimilate into the majority culture, working like a sort of Hebraic spiritual yeast upon civilization, or they can, on the other hand, resume a national existence that will generate unique contributions across the entire spectrum of culture, not merely in the religious sphere. Thus while the former alternative offers only individual talents to mankind, the latter promises that not only will Jewish lives be rescued from physical threat and oppression, but Judaism, as a vibrant stimulant to the entire range of human society, will survive and reawaken.

However, despite this ideological insistence that contemporary social and historical forces would no longer permit world Jewry to vacillate but would urgently force them to choose between these two alternatives, Zangwill did, in fact, expect the Jewish people to choose both. While allowing for individual preferences, he thought that, as a group, Western Jews would follow the assimilationist path already in process, while it would be the unacculturated, unassimilated East European Jews who would become "renationalised" to serve as a

Judaic spiritual and cultural "beacon" to the West. Thus in this same essay he writes:

> Dr. Herzl's movement is a movement for the integration of the scattered forces of Israel, and the expression of this unity by a national politically guaranteed home in Palestine that may serve as a shelter for the homeless and oppressed, and a beacon for those prosperous sheltered elsewhere. . . .
>
> . . . It is not essential that all her [Jewry's] daughters shall return to her skirts. . . . The problem is simply to set up a centre of Jewish life and concentrate all one's labours on it. Gradually it would become the magnet of the race.[11]

This is not at all Theodore Herzl's view of Zionism! For him, as for Eastern Jewry also, the nationalist movement meant an inclusive ingathering of all the Jewish people, both those facing the oppressive autocratic regimes of Eastern Europe and those imperiled by an ineradicable anti-Semitism pervading the freer societies of Central and Western Europe. Zangwill, on the other hand, is exactly following the widely held view of Western Jewry that a Jewish homeland was to serve as a refuge for those politically and physically oppressed *elsewhere* and also serve as a source of learning to the Jews and to all humanity.[12] Not surprisingly, therefore, does Zangwill, in "The Return to Palestine," echo so faithfully George Eliot's Mordecai of *Daniel Deronda:* "Revive the organic centre. . . . Looking towards a land and a polity, our dispersed people in all the ends of the earth may share the dignity of national life which has a voice among the peoples of the East and the West—which will plant the wisdom and skill of our race so that it may be, as of old, a medium of transmission and understanding."[13]

In this as yet unperceived difference in intention between the East European nationalism of the Zionists and the Westerner's perspective of Zangwill and his admirers lay the root cause of the 1905 split in the World Zionist Organization (WZO) and the creation of a rival Jewish Territorial Organization (ITO). And already in this article Zangwill indicates another of the later fundamental concerns of Territorialism: he is interested, not particularly in Palestine per se as the site of the future homeland, but rather in *any* one place on which the nationalists might concentrate all their efforts; one must not "overlook the first principle of action—concentration. . . . Only by concentrating upon one country is there a chance of achieving something. We saw this was true of political power. It is equally true of physical regeneration." Nor is this "one country" necessarily Palestine, for "there is not a little to be said for Argentina."[14]

Because he believes they dissipate nationalist efforts rather than focus them upon one site, in this, his first explicitly Zionist article, Zangwill attacks vituperatively the philanthropic endeavors at colonization undertaken by the *Alliance Israelite Universelle* and by the Jewish Colonization Association (ICA):

> Baron de Hirsch is dead, but the I.C.A. after paying over a million pounds in legacy duty to the British government goes gaily on its prodigal way—a centipede, trying to walk with every leg stepping out in different directions, and overhead flutter and fluster the benevolent busybodies, the Anglo-Jewish Association and the *Alliance Universelle.* . . .
>
> . . . Millions flow into a bottomless bucket, and the Jewish misery is greater and the Jewish honour less than when the *Alliance* started . . . and just as the *Alliance* can effect nothing politically, so can the I.C.A. with its mocking millions effect nothing practically. . . .
>
> . . . They [the philanthropic organizations] have not even warrant to speak on behalf of Israel; they are self-constituted bodies, bureaux of philanthropy, which pauperise Israel politically.[15]

The beneficiary of aristocratic charity at the JFS and the victim of its arbitrary exercise there as well, Zangwill still has not altered the harsh estimation of philanthropists he so bitterly portrayed in the opening pages of *Children of the Ghetto.* The price in personal dignity they extract from the poor, the smug self-satisfaction they receive from their munificence to the impoverished still remain too much for a child of the East End to stomach.

But his evaluation of these organizations is not primarily visceral. Zangwill knew that, along with lives, a rich living tradition was at stake. Action was urgently needed to save the lives and to preserve the culture. Tomorrow might prove too late to prevent another Jewish skull from being crushed, another Jewish child from being maimed, and it might also prove too late to halt the inroads of acculturation and assimilation. And, what was worse, by merely rescuing Jews from Eastern Europe and planting them individually or in tiny groups in the West, the philanthropists were actually accelerating acculturation, speeding up the dissolution of the Jewish people. For Zangwill, the only hope for the future survival of Jews and Judaism lay in "securing a public legally assured home in Palestine for those Jews who are unable or unwilling to assimilate."[16]

What Zangwill could not recognize throughout the remainder of his career as a Jewish nationalist activist and spokesman was the inherent contradiction between his goal and his method. Because of the urgency and the centrality of the issues involved, he rejected the gradualism of the Chovevei Zion nationalists and the meliorism of the philanthropists. But Herzl's "political Zionism," with its insistence upon official public sanction as the sine qua non for the establishment and settlement of the Jewish homeland, implied protracted diplomatic negotiations. The motive behind "political Zionism" was achievement of a "*legally guaranteed* home," that is, that its result would be lasting, not that it would be more expeditious. For Zangwill, on the other hand, the political approach always appeared the most expedient. The East Africa scheme later would only seem to confirm what was only, throughout, an illusion. It was an illusion that had led him into the Zionist movement, that would inspire him to lead the Territorialist "heresy," and that finally urged him to advocate a military solution to the "Palestine problem."

Analysis of his first article as a Zionist thus clearly displays the consistent ideology and style that were to characterize Israel Zangwill's career as a Jewish nationalist.[17] Here is his continuing belief in the inescapable twin alternatives facing contemporary Jewry: the inevitability of Western assimilation into "Hebraic" universalism and the overwhelming need to preserve the East European "Judaic" heritage. And here too is his preoccupation with the chimera of an internationally guaranteed land of refuge for East European Jews quickly achieved through diplomatic means. But what is most striking about this article is its truculent, combative style. "A Jewish national homeland" becomes Israel Zangwill's battle cry, and his first targets are the Jewish philanthropic organizations.

Homeland Against the Colonies

Israel Zangwill's endeavors during the first two years of his nationalist career focused primarily on excoriating the ICA's colonization schemes. The political and ideological controversies involved in this dispute between Zangwill and the ICA's Anglo-Jewish supporters led to the rupture of several old friendships, particularly that of Zangwill and Dr. Moses Gaster, the Sephardi Hacham.[18]

He launched his attack, not in "The Return to Palestine," but earlier, in his maiden speech as a Zionist, in Basel, on the fourth day of the WZO's Fifth Congress. Here he denounced the ICA for spoliating its funds on feeble elitist palliatives rather than in actively supporting the dynamic popular nationalist movement. Zangwill claimed that even the late Baron de Hirsch himself, had he lived, would have become a Zionist rather than have continued pursuing the by now obviously futile colonization schemes of the ICA.[19]

At an English Zionist Federation meeting on the Congress held at Shoreditch Town Hall in February 1902, he took up the cudgel against the ICA even more vigorously. In his address Zangwill claimed that the ICA was promoting pauperism among the Jews of Palestine, turning them into "*schnorrers*." Dr. Gaster, who had also been a Congress delegate, responded by strongly defending the work of the ICA and then comparing Zangwill to his own "Satan Mekatrig" for "swerving" from their common ideals to "heap up accusations against others." A bitter exchange between the two friends on the dais ensued; the resulting breach was never to be healed.[20]

His criticism of the Jewish Colonization Association and its handling of "the Hirsch millions" provoked furious counterattacks on Zangwill from establishment leaders of Anglo-Jewry. Immediately after his Shoreditch speech, Zangwill brought the dispute before the British public, writing in defense of his position:

> While Baron Hirsch had probably no intention of colonizing Palestine, since Baron Edmond de Rothschild was working that region, there is nothing in the [ICA] statutes to prevent the trustees—already spending money in Palestine—from co-operating with the Zionists in working for a charter to permit a stream of natural and healthy colonization to flow into Palestine. We know that the Sultan is not unfavourably disposed towards such a stream of immigration into this almost unpopulated province.
>
> . . . It is obvious that Russia and Rumania alone contain the necessary labour force, the necessary migratory impulse, and the necessary sentiment for the Holy Land. The labour to regenerate Palestine is ready—the capital is ready. But the labour must be diverted from its present planless, ubiquitous, and futile occupation [in ICA colonies]. The diversion of the Hirsch millions to Palestine would be absolutely legal.[21]

During the following two years the bitter public exchange of invectives over the use of ICA funds to support Zionist aims continued between Zangwill, on the one hand, and Anglo-Jewish establishment figures, particularly Claude Montefiore and Lucien Wolf, on the other.[22] Although the obvious dispute was over the allocation of funds, the deep ideological source of the argument was made explicit in 1903.

In a speech at a Zionist demonstration at the Shoreditch Town Hall in May 1903, Zangwill explained:

> You [ICA defenders] will say that Jews have managed for eighteen centuries to belong to two peoples. But this is a delusion. So long as they were kept in Ghettos, physical and moral, they belonged to one people, their own. As soon as they are let out of their protective prisons, the stronger, larger people sucks them in, and in three generations assimilates them to itself, even if they keep up the farce of marrying among themselves.[23]

For Israel Zangwill, the ICA's colonies are, ultimately, conduits to assimilation and annihilation of the Jewish people as a distinct cultural and ethnic group. Only by means of a territorial exclusivity will not only individuals of biological Jewish ancestry but a viable Jewish community survive in the contemporary world. Human identity must be singular, whether in the Christian world, in the medieval Jewish ghetto, or in a modern Jewish homeland. The historical experience of emancipated Western Jewry, which has already proven unable to sustain twinned and conflicting identities, demonstrates for Zangwill that when ghetto-nurtured Judaism is abandoned, the attractions and psychological unity of secular Westernism inevitably triumph.

And Zangwill's opponents, in a sense, completely agreed. They were Anglicized antinationalists who believed that their only homeland could be Britain, that Jews are not "dual nationals," and that their ethnic ("race") tie implies primarily philanthropic assistance to those fellow Jews suffering vicious persecution in Eastern Europe; they believed that to assist their brethren there they should seek to mobilize Western diplomatic and public pressure upon the oppressors to reform their regimes and, through organizations like the ICA, to physically resettle East European Jews in free and tolerant Western societies elsewhere (i.e., not in Britain itself).

Historically most significant is the fact that this dispute actually represents an internal conflict among Western assimilated Jews only about the future of East European Jewry. Zangwill believed it most desirable for mankind to preserve them in a distinct national homeland somewhere so that a Judaic culture might once again flourish; his ICA opponents believed it best to resettle them in any tolerant nation that would welcome them and where they might have the opportunities already enjoyed by Anglo-Jewry. Essentially what they differed on were their perceptions and evaluations of the ethnic traditional heritage as still exemplified among unacculturated, unassimilated East European Jews. But unlike Herzl and the emerging majority in the WZO, neither Zangwill nor his opponents questioned the legitimacy and humane beneficence of the Diaspora.[24] The nineteenth-century distinctions between Western and Eastern Jewish nationalists remain as potent as ever.[25]

At the Sixth Zionist Congress in Basel in August 1903, Zangwill's paper, "On Zionism and Charitable Institutions," turned out to be his final shot in his battle with the philanthropists.[26] A new issue arose at the Congress that overwhelmed all others and led to a bitterly rancorous conflict within the World Zionist movement itself.

The Uganda Scheme

In April 1903, following the infamous Kishinev pogrom, Joseph Chamberlain, England's Conservative Colonial Secretary, proposed to Theodore Herzl that a semiautonomous Jewish colony be established on the Gwas Ngishu plateau in the British East African Protectorate.[27] He was offering a sparsely settled region, about two hundred miles in length, between Nairobi and the Mau escarpment, on the Uganda Railway.[28]

The proposal, as it was officially formulated for presentation to the Sixth WZO Congress in August 1903, called for "a scheme comprising as its main features the grant of a considerable area of land, the appointment of a Jewish official as chief of the local administration and as to the management of religious and purely domestic matters, such local autonomy being conditional upon the right of His Majesty's Government to exercise a general control."[29]

Chamberlain made the offer after opposition from the British-dominated Egyptian government blocked earlier negotiations with Herzl and Leopold Greenberg (the official WZO representative in Britain) for the establishment of a Jewish settlement at El Arish in the Sinai.[30] Refugees from the Kishinev pogrom and Parliamentary consideration of an Aliens bill that would restrict immigrant entry into Britain convinced the influential Colonial Secretary to propose the

Theodore Herzl (center, with beard) flanked by his mother (right) and Israel Zangwill (left), posing with the English delegation to the Sixth World Zionist Congress, 1903. *Courtesy, The Central Zionist Archives.*

new scheme.[31] As Chamberlain himself explained in a campaign speech the following year:

> The evils of this immigration have increased during recent years. And behind those people who have already reached these shores, remember there are millions of the same kind who, under easily conceivable circumstances, might follow in their track, and might invade this country in a way and to an extent of which few people have at present any conception.
>
> . . . Now a word as to the [refugee] people themselves. . . . They have been driven from their homes by the pressure of want, by the grossest and the most brutal persecution. . . . The problem is how are they to be saved from the fate which is befalling them, how is their salvation to be accomplished without the ruin of our own people at home? While I was in office I did what I could. I had several conferences with the late Dr. Herzl, a man who made the greatest impression upon me. . . . And in principle, at any rate, I can say that we were agreed that the best solution of this question was to find some country in this world of ours, if possible under the aegis of the British flag, or under the protection if you please, of a concert of nations, in which these poor

exiles from their native land, who do not leave it out of caprice or with any desire to injure us, could dwell in safety, following their own religion and their own aspirations, and where they could find subsistence without in any way interfering with the subsistence of others.[32]

In August 1903 Herzl presented sympathetically the British East Africa offer to the Sixth World Zionist Congress in Basel.[33] Although supported by Max Nordau, the offer aroused vehement opposition, primarily among East European Zionists who insisted on a Palestine-only orientation for the nationalist movement.[34] In the end, it was agreed to establish a commission authorized only to investigate on location the feasibility of Jewish settlement in East Africa; a final decision, pending the findings of the commission, was postponed till the next congress, in 1905.

While the East European "Zionists of Zion" and others were organizing against the "Uganda scheme" within the WZO, anti-Zionist Anglo-Jewish hostility to the proposal was launched in a 28 August 1903 letter to the *Times* (London) by Lucien Wolf. Arguing from the assimilationist perspective, Wolf claimed that no Jews require "municipal autonomy" for the practice of their religion and, furthermore, that the immigrants "would be shut out from the civilizing influence to which it is one of the main objects of all Jewish emigration schemes to submit them, and to which hitherto the oppressed and sometimes degraded Oriental Jew has always magnificently responded."[35] And by October Herzl himself was questioning the political wisdom of pursuing the East Africa offer.[36]

Simultaneous with this mobilization of Jewish opposition, within the East African Protectorate itself British settlers were organizing vociferous opposition to the establishment of an autonomous Jewish settlement in their midst and were applying strong pressure on the government to reconsider the project.[37] Reflecting this widespread Jewish and non-Jewish opposition to Chamberlain's offer to the WZO, the Foreign Secretary, Lord Landsdowne, remarked in a private memorandum in mid-December 1903, "We shall probably be well out of it [the East Africa offer], but it was right to treat the [Zionist] application considerately."[38] Thus within four months after the East Africa scheme had been officially tendered to the Jewish nationalist movement, both the majority of Zionists and the British had come to regard it as a benevolently intended mistake pragmatically now best abandoned.

Israel Zangwill, on the contrary, had, from the outset, enthusiastically embraced Chamberlain's East Africa proposal as *the* solution to the dilemma of the continued survival of East European Jewry and their traditional Judaic heritage. He quickly emerged as the champion of the offer and adopted it as his cause. When Herzl had first presented the British proposal to the WZO General Action Committee on 21 August 1903, only Zangwill advocated unqualified acceptance of the offer.[39] And as Chaim Weizmann observed in October 1903, "Zangwill is the true ideologist of East Africa."[40]

In a speech on the Sixth Zionist Congress at a September 1903 meeting of the English Zionist Federation at Great Assembly Hall on the Mile End Road, Zangwill vigorously advocated the advantages of considering the East Africa scheme and denounced its opponents. In the first place, Chamberlain's plan, just the proposal from the British government in itself, represented a significant achievement for the Jewish nationalist movement:

> if they [the Zionists] consider the offer now made us to choose a tract of the most beautiful and valuable land in East Africa and there form a British settlement with Jewish Home Rule, Jewish national customs and a Jewish Governor, then even those most bitterly opposed to the new project will surely admit that merely to have obtained such an offer is a triumph for our organization. And even more than a triumph for Zionism is it a moral triumph for England, a victory for humanity.[41]

Second, he stressed the urgency of the situation and explained that the Kishinev pogrom had made the issue of Russian Jewry's safety even more pressing than it had been previously and that negotiations with the Ottoman Sultan for Palestine were not at all progressing smoothly, that Palestine may well remain closed to widespread Jewish settlement for "centuries." In recognition of these factors, Herzl had accepted the East Africa proposal in order to provide a "temporary refuge" and "thinking that if we *must* wait for Palestine, any place was better for waiting in than Russia, and reflecting also that if we could get Jewish rights in *any* part of the world, this recognition of Jewish nationality carried us already half-way to Palestine."[42]

But what was most important in the scheme was that it was not fundamentally a matter of humanitarian philanthropy directed at oppressed Jewish refugees but rather an endeavor to create the proper conditions for the revival of a flourishing Judaic culture:

> Mere refuges without Jewish rights is not our business. Let the Jewish Colonization Association or the *Alliance Israélite* attend to such charitable affairs. Ours is not a charitable movement, but a political movement. . . . Without specifically Jewish rights we will not accept any territory. We are not going to play another act of the weary comedy of the ages, with the scene simply shifted. . . .
>
> . . . With all Judea [i.e., Jews] helping us, with an able modern Jewish Governor . . . , we could create a colony that would be a source of strength, not only to Israel but to the British Empire, a colony second to none in loyalty to the British flag.[43]

Finally, in the speech Zangwill not only condemned the philanthropic organizations for rejecting the scheme, and strongly criticized its East European Zionist opponents, but he particularly attacked its British opponents. Specific targets of Zangwill's ire were the assimilationist Lucien Wolf and the Zionist Moses Gaster; Wolf had condemned the East African project in his letter to the *Times,* while Gaster had repudiated it in an open letter published on 25 August 1903 in the *Jewish Chronicle* and the *Jewish World.*[44]

Zangwill's most complete defense of the East Africa scheme appeared in a 1904 pamphlet, *The East Africa Question; Zionism And England's Offer.* In it he chastises contemporary Jews for their ambivalence: "We [Jews] have either to reconcile ourselves to our loss [of a national homeland] or set about recovering it. But to choose clearly between one alternative or the other is a faculty the Jew had lost."[45]

This ambivalence Zangwill links with the confusion of identities experienced by modern Western Jews, a contemporary version of the "Marrano mentality"—"The double life [of the Iberian Marranos] meant a life of terror, of endless bribes; and discovery—which was frequent—meant the stake and the sword."[46] Even with the Emancipation,

> the hunted creature still could not shake off this feeling that his own life was something that must be hidden. His whole public life became ostentatiously identical with that of his neighbors. Very often his modern Marranoism was completed by the Jew changing his name, and even his faith. . . .
>
> . . . The medieval Marranos at least retained their self-respect by despising the people they imitated; we admire our neighbors, and despise only ourselves.[47]

Israel Zangwill, whose inability to choose between his own warring identities was driving him to the extremes of ethnic intermarriage and particularist nationalism, prescribed Zionism as the remedy for contemporary "Marranoism": "Zionism means the end of the Marrano period and the revival of the Maccabean." But it is still the Western version of Jewish nationalism, meant to rescue only persecuted East European Jewry: "Zionism may have little to offer the prosperous American Jews, except moral dignity . . . but to the vast majority of our race—and half of the Jews of the world live in Russia—it is a gospel not only of self-respect but of salvation."[48]

That the Christological terminology is intentional and reflects explicitly Zangwill's ideology that the Jewish people require a universalist Hebraic "mission," "moral dignity," to justify their continued survival is apparent from his discussion of the unique nature of the projected Zionist state:

> Let the Jews, with their genius for righteousness, establish a Jewish State, in which morality stands higher and crime lower, in which social problems are better solved, in which women's rights are equal to men's, in which poverty and wealth are not so terribly divided, in which simple life is the universal ideal; let them light a beacon fire of theirs upon Zion's hill, or East Africa's plateau, and they will do more for the Jewish mission than twenty cents of pulpit talking.[49]

But there is a major distinction between "Zion's hill" and "East Africa's plateau," a distinction that Israel Zangwill is the first to consider seriously as a fundamental obstacle to the achievement of Jewish possession of Palestine: "There is . . . a difficulty from which the Zionist dares not avert his eyes, though he rarely faces it. Palestine proper has already its inhabitants [viz., Arabs]."[50] Therefore, "better Zionism without Zion than Zion without Zionism."[51] And, given this reality and the urgency of the problem, "East Africa, or any similar territory, if it be not Palestine, has at least the advantage of starting clear of the enormous theological and political problems that would beset us in Palestine."[52]

Faithful to this analysis and conclusion, Zangwill spoke and wrote vigorously between 1903 and 1905 to win acceptance of the East Africa scheme, and in the course of this campaign he gladly crossed swords in debates with leading British Zionist and anti-Zionist opponents.[53] The endeavor reached its climax in July 1905 at the Seventh Zionist

Congress in Basel when, despite an impassioned plea from Zangwill, a large majority, primarily of East European origin, voted to reject the East Africa scheme.[54]

Israel Zangwill's effort to rescue Russian Jewry and Judaism had been defeated by the very people he sought to save!

Territorialism

On 8 August 1905, Leopold Greenberg officially notified the British Colonial Office that the WZO Congress had decided to reject the East Africa offer and expressed the hope for continued British-Zionist co-operation in the future.[55] The entire episode appeared over. But, in fact, it was merely acquiring a new advocate, and the WZO, a new rival: the Jewish Territorial Organization.

The insurgent ITO was, from the start, Janus-faced. This duality of purpose is evident in the earliest discussions out of which the movement emerged. The initiative was Zangwill's. Still in Switzerland after the Seventh Zionist Congress, he contacted his Anglo-Jewish opponent Lucien Wolf and invited him to a friendly meeting on 23 August in which they might go about "thrashing out those questions on which we particularly disagree, largely I believe through your misunderstanding of my exact point of view."[56] After the meeting, on 1 September, Wolf wrote to Zangwill agreeing to work with the ITO and commenting:

> As a matter of fact, I have always been in favour of acceptance of the [East Africa] offer and I have thought it most unfortunate that the Zionists should have coupled their proposed acceptance of it with conditions which divided our community in regard to it. So long as those conditions were calculated to make a sort of Ghetto or "native reserve" out of the proposed Colony; so long as they aimed at reviving an obsolete polity and at crystallisation of so called national customs and modes of life which are not essentially Jewish . . . and so long as the result was likely to be to perpetuate the alien condition of the colonists in the land of their adoption, I could not but oppose it. You have now reassured me as to the view you take of these conditions; and although I am not so sanguine of success as you are, I am bound to confess that differences in principle no longer exist between us. . . . You want to utilise some of the streams of Jewish emigration which are perpetually flowing out of Russia in order to found a new Self-governing Colony in the vast waste lands of the British Empire. . . . Such a colony would

Israel Zangwill addressing the Seventh World Zionist Congress, 1905, urging adoption of the Uganda Scheme. *Courtesy, The Central Zionist Archives.*

be politically Jewish through the preponderance of its Jewish population.[57]

Zangwill, in his response on 8 September, appeared to agree with Wolf's views but without actually adopting his assimilationist conclusions:

> Your admission of the principle of self-government is all that is necessary and I am glad to have convinced you of this at least—that if we are to build up a large self-sustaining colony, a measure of autonomy is not a luxury but a necessity. . . . [But] let us hope, the spiritual genius of our race, which once found expression in Mosaic legislation and prophetic aspiration, will again be inspired to contribute to civilization's sociological improvements suited to these latter days.[58]

Thus was born Territorialism, a movement expressing the contending twinned identities attracting Jewish people. In its twenty-

Israel and Edith Zangwill in Basel for the Seventh World Zionist Congress, 1905. *Courtesy, The Central Zionist Archives.*

year history, Zangwill's movement would strive to achieve a separate and autonomous homeland for East European Jewish refugees and their Judaic heritage and, simultaneously, would endeavor to promote the successful cultural assimilation of exactly the same emigrants into the American heartland.

The ITO

The Jewish Territorial Association was originally formed to implement the British offer of land for a self-governing Jewish settlement in East Africa after the offer was rejected by the WZO. In announcing formation of the ITO, Israel Zangwill claimed that his movement was not so much a rival to the Zionists, who had in any case sacrificed their immediate responsibility for an anachronistic dream, but rather a pragmatic response to an urgent necessity, the rescue of persecuted

Russian Jewry: "If the [British] Government is in earnest in its proposal to solve the emigration question by the provision of a territory large and fertile enough to serve as a permanent home for our wanderers . . . an organization is now in existence competent to go on with the scheme."[59]

To this end, Zangwill sought to convince the Colonial Office that his organization possessed the means and the will to effectuate this project immediately. Initially, in response, the Colonial Office expressed serious doubt as to whether Zangwill and the ITO did enjoy the means to carry out the scheme.[60] But, undaunted, Zangwill energetically persisted in making his case to the government and in winning influential international sponsors for his movement.[61] And, finally, a meeting between Zangwill and the Colonial Secretary was arranged for the afternoon of 4 December 1905.[62]

But Zangwill's case had been rejected even before he had his opportunity to argue in person for it. In his preparatory notes for the meeting, Alfred Lyttleton, the Colonial Secretary, remarked:

> The [East Africa] project—if desirable—is not a human possibility. No British Minister or government could carry it through. Nor is it desirable. It is contrary to our traditions and policy to hand over the control of a particular area to the control of a particular race. . . . I would not hold out any hope to M. Zangwill of entertaining such a scheme, and I would argue that it is not to the advantage of the Jews themselves. . . . [We] should refuse to grant a great Jewish Reserve to be from the beginning a source of difficulty and possibly of danger.[63]

The meeting's failure convinced Zangwill that it was necessary to arouse public sympathy and pressure to win for the ITO a more favorable hearing from the government. In April 1906 he published "Letters And The ITO," in the *Fortnightly Review,* in which he attempted to provide evidence of widespread support for the Territorialist scheme, which "in a nutshell is to build up an autonomous Jewish State out of the refugees from Russian persecution—a State which will likewise attract a number of prosperous and idealistic Jews. In our quest for a territory we wish, if possible, to take advantage of England's offer of a virgin soil under British suzerainty."[64]

The new Liberal Colonial Secretary, Lord Elgin, remained unconvinced and refused to grant Zangwill an interview until the ITO proved capable of demonstrating to the government that its proposal had met three conditions: "(1) that it came from responsible people,

(2) that there was introduced at any rate the outline of a definite plan, (3) that there was evidence of adequate financial backing."[65] In response, Zangwill assured the Colonial Office in May that "we [the British Federation of the ITO] have no doubt that we shall be in a position to meet the reasonable demands contained in Lord Elgin's kind reply of May 8th."[66]

Desultory negotiations between Zangwill and the Colonial Office continued through the summer. No substantial change in the government's position was achieved, and Lucien Wolf, who ran the ITO London office together with its founder, had already lost confidence in the organization's prospects.[67] But Zangwill tenaciously persisted.

In the *Fortnightly Review* article he had indicated that while the ITO wished to take advantage of the already-existing East Africa proposal, the Territorialist goal, unlike the Zionist, was not limited to any one specific piece of land. He therefore now set about creating a credible international organization, at least on paper, and locating some uninhabited territory on which to establish an autonomous Jewish "land of refuge."

To acquire the necessary international popular support for the ITO, Zangwill began providing the movement's original activist impulse with an ideological rationale, an elaboration of long-standing themes from his own Jewish philosophy. In the first place, and primarily, Territorialism meant providing refuge for Jews emigrating from Eastern Europe: the ITO's aim is "to procure a territory upon an autonomous basis for those Jews who cannot or will not remain in the lands in which they at present live."[68] But such a land will not, and cannot, eliminate the Diaspora:

> Even were a new Judea successfully established, the great mass [of Jews] would long remain scattered as to-day. In so far as the Jewish problem embraces the fate of all Jews, an Itoland [i.e., the projected ITO settlement] could not solve it. The re-gathering of the Jews in any one country is, humanly speaking, impossible, least possible in Palestine.[69]

For, as before, Zangwill continued to believe that the fate of the Diaspora was assimilation: "The dispersion of the Jews can only be remedied by dissolution."[70] This observation is determined by sociological principle:

> There is nothing, indeed, in race that can long counteract the pressure or attraction of universally differing environments and mutually alien

> patriotism, unless, indeed, the race be exposed to a contemptuous isolation. . . . Without a common religion or territory the Jews could not form a nationality, not even though they had a common language and a common culture.[71]

However, for those Jews who do choose to settle in "Itoland" a psychological unity of identity will exist that might well serve as a universal inspiration for all humanity:

> Territorialism claims that it would provide the Jew with a higher status of citizenship than in any other country whatever . . . ; that there would be a new hope on the Jewish horizon, a centre to which every self-respecting Jew would tend to gravitate, or at least to send his son, in which a new and natural breed of Jews would grow up at harmony with themselves, and making a new and proud history. . . .
>
> . . . Only in Itoland could the Jew be at one with himself, for Itoland would naturally be established upon as orthodox a basis as possible, leaving the religious development of the new Judea to the natural progress of time and the lessons of the new environment.[72]

Zangwill's propaganda activities on behalf of the ITO and his attacks on Zionism as a wasteful folly served not so much to win over new converts as to arouse bitter controversy within the Anglo-Jewish community. So vituperative and disruptive was the contention within the Maccabeans that in 1906 Zangwill resigned from the club he helped found and, though he rejoined the same year, he felt compelled to resign for good in 1907.[73] And the *Jewish Chronicle,* the most influential Anglo-Jewish weekly, which had previously been non-Zionist although hostile to the East Africa scheme, was acquired by Leopold Greenberg in 1907 and now advocated the Zionist program and provided continuous criticism of Territorialist endeavors.[74] However, defiantly, these continued and even expanded.

After 1906, the ITO seriously investigated three alternative territories after failing to progress in its negotiations with the British government. In 1908 an ITO commission surveyed Cyrenaica, in North Africa, as a possible site for a Jewish "land of refuge" but was discouraged by grave irrigation difficulties.[75] The following year Zangwill began investigating Jewish settlement in Mesopotamia but was again soon discouraged by local conditions.[76] Finally, in June 1912, the Portuguese government, acting on a bill already approved by the parliament, offered to encourage Jewish settlement through the ITO on the Benguela plateau in Angola. Although Zangwill was quite excited by the offer, the international conference of the ITO was compelled to reject it because the Portuguese refused to grant political autonomy for the Jewish colonists.[77]

However, already by the beginning of 1912 Zangwill himself had experienced increasing despair over the feasibility of establishing a Territorialist land of refuge. As he confessed privately to his longstanding American admirer Mayer Sulzberger: "Alas, the chances of a territory get less and less. . . . We have struck such a materialistic world and the Jew is so hated that I fear that the ITO will have to end or transform itself."[78] In fact it was already thoroughly transformed from a quest for a territorial reserve for East European Jewish ethnicity into a funnel for assimilation in America.

The Galveston Plan

Just at the time Zangwill and Wolf were coming to recognize that the negotiations with the British Colonial Office over East Africa had stalled, a radically new proposal was offered to the ITO. In August 1906, Jacob Schiff, the American financier and philanthropist, proposed that the Jewish Territorial Organization participate in an innovative scheme to recruit and settle increased numbers of Russian-Jewish immigrants in the United States. Unlike previous generations of East European immigrants, these would disembark and be relocated in the interior of America, away from the usual East Coast sites, thus facilitating the channeling of additional immigrants into the country.[79]

Wolf urged his Territorialist partner to accept the offer as a means of providing Russian Jewry with immediate relief but to do so only in a manner that would also redound to the benefit of the ITO.[80] Zangwill himself felt compelled to accept the offer, writing Oscar Straus that "My opinion is that Schiff forces us to accept this work, for if another body undertakes it, public attention will be directed to this work and we shall be comparatively crushed."[81] However, Zangwill did attempt to modify Schiff's plan on three major points.

In the first place, he argued that the increased flow of emigrants should be settled according to the Territorialist "Itoland" model, in some place other than the United States but now benefiting from Schiff's financial contributions. Furthermore, Zangwill insisted that the ITO should be the sole official authorized agent at both ends of the resettlement operation, that is, in Russia and in the land of relocation (although transit from Bremen could be arranged through the German-Jewish philanthropic organization *Hilfsverein der Deutschen Juden*). On this point, Zangwill was seeking to eliminate ICA participation in recruitment work in Russia and Industrial Removal Office (IRO) control of the settlement arrangements in America. Finally, he argued that the immigrants should not be required to agree in advance to accept employment in America that would necessitate violating the traditional Sabbath observance.

Although Schiff refused to consider a Territorialist "Itoland," after months of negotiations he did compromise on the other two points. The ITO would become the sole official Galveston Plan agent in Russia, although the IRO would handle the American resettlement program. And potential immigrants would not be required to agree to work on the Sabbath in order to be considered for participation in the relocation program.[82]

The Galveston Plan was exactly consistent with Zangwill's well-established ethnic sociology that, for the Jews, the future offered but two positive alternatives in the West: either total assimilation *or* territorial separation, and *either* of these alternatives was preferable to the continuation of East European oppression and superstition. And the increased anti-Semitic persecution in Russia following the 1905 revolution there intensified considerably the sense of urgency. Nevertheless, an American assimilationist solution to Russian-Jewish emigration implemented under ITO sponsorship did appear to many others to contradict Territorialist ideology, and Zangwill felt the necessity of engaging in a certain amount of apologetics for his activist participation in the scheme.

For instance, in 1907 he cogently reasoned:

> This is the dilemma of the Jewish position. No undeveloped land could receive our [Russian] emigrants. No developed land would afford us autonomy. If we grasp at an immediate solution we shall never get a final [Territorialist] solution. If, on the other hand, we try for a final solution, we are left with the immediate problem. What is the escape from this dilemma? Why, the way the ITO has found: to try both for the temporary solution and the final solution. . . .
>
> . . . I freely admit that after Territorialism (which includes Zionism) America is the best solution of the Jewish question, and if the ITO should do no more than safeguard that solution it will have amply justified its brief existence.[83]

And so it did. On 1 July 1907 the first immigrants chosen by the ITO's representatives in Russia arrived at Galveston, Texas. From this port of entry they, and those who followed, were quickly "dispersed" by the IRO to communities in Colorado, Iowa, Nebraska, Minnesota, Missouri, Illinois, Oklahoma, Texas, and Wisconsin. Between 1907 and 30 September 1914, when the program was discontinued, about 10,000 Russian-Jewish immigrants were thus enabled to enter and settle in the United States under the auspices of these representatives of the Galveston Plan.[84] And although most observers, including Jacob Schiff, considered the project a disappointment in the long run, it was the one concrete positive achievement of Israel Zangwill's ITO.[85]

But with the outbreak of war in 1914 the pacifist Israel Zangwill began to perceive a new opportunity to resolve at long last the modern "Jewish question"—by the use of force, in Palestine!

Militant Zionism

Israel Zangwill had always believed that there were at least two serious obstacles to fruitful Jewish settlement in Palestine. The first was the attitude of the current Ottoman rulers of the region; not very surprisingly, the Ottomans were reluctant to settle in their own territory large numbers of subjects emigrating from their traditionally hostile northern neighbor, Russia.[86] The second obstacle was that Palestine already was populated, by Arabs.[87]

It was the apparently insurmountable persistence of these two obstacles that convinced Zangwill in 1905 that a Zionism exclusively focused upon Palestine was merely the impractical dream of *luftmentschen* and that he should himself negotiate for an "empty territory" with a "friendly nation" (e.g., British East Africa). However, even in 1905 Zangwill recognized, but did not then think feasible, that the second obstacle could be eliminated through the forcible expulsion of the Arab inhabitants of Palestine. As he explained to a Manchester audience on the eve of the Seventh Zionist Congress: "Palestine already has its inhabitants . . . so we must be prepared either to drive out by the sword the tribes in possession as our forefathers did, or to grapple with the problem of a large alien population, most Mohammedan and accustomed for centuries to despise us."[88] As neither this armed removal of the second obstacle nor any modification of Ottoman rule was practical for the Jews and their sympathizers in 1905, Zangwill adopted "Itoland" and the Galveston Plan as a means of relieving the urgent suffering of East European Jewry.

World War I, which found the British and Ottomans fighting on opposing sides, significantly altered Zangwill's estimation of the practical possibilities for Jewish settlement in Palestine. New hopes and plans soon replaced the awful despair arising from the failure to discover an "Itoland" and from the discontinuation of the Galveston Plan. British interests and Jewish needs, Zionist dreams and Territorialist plans could now all be made to converge and unite in the establishment of a new British-sponsored "Itoland" in Palestine. War could remove both obstacles to Jewish settlement there, and Zangwill, while generally an advocate of pacifism and the futility of war, set about to see that the opportunity would not be lost.[89]

Already in the spring of 1915, Zangwill was enthusiastically cooperating with Vladimir Jabotinsky (1880–1940), the father of the militantly nationalist Zionist Revisionist movement, in encouraging the establishment of the Zion Mule Corps.

Originally formed in 1915 as a transport unit in the British forces stationed in Egypt, the Zion Mule Corps was composed of non-British Jewish recruits. Jabotinsky wanted the British to transform the corps into a genuine fighting force and to employ them in the Allied conquest of Palestine from the Ottomans.

From the beginning, Zangwill wholeheartedly supported this goal and contacted his influential ITO political connections in the War Office to assist in the effort.[90] For Zangwill, as for Jabotinsky and the Zionists, the goal now was removal of the Ottoman obstacle to Jewish settlement in Palestine through the intervention of British military force. As he told a Jewish gathering in Whitechapel in March 1916: "if Palestine came their way, by falling under the power of England, all Jews in this country must stand united to take the country over and develop it as a Jewish State. . . . The Empire needed the Jews."[91] And a "Jewish Legion" fighting the battle alongside British forces would demonstrate this Imperial "need" to everyone!

On 23 August 1917 the British government officially announced formation of a battalion of Royal Fusiliers, "the Jewish Legion," recruited from non-British Jewish volunteers to fight in the conquest of Palestine from the Turks. Later a grateful Jabotinsky was to write fondly to his friend Zangwill, "I shall never forget that you were one of the first to realize the importance of the [Jewish] Legion scheme and helped me at a time when I was quite alone."[92]

On 2 November 1917 the British Foreign Secretary, Arthur Balfour, sent a letter to Lord [Lionel Walter] Rothschild stating that the British government would support the establishment in Palestine of a Jewish national home. Zangwill was ecstatic—a first major obstacle to Jewish possession of Palestine, Ottoman opposition, was gone! As he told a "Thanksgiving Meeting," chaired by Lord Rothschild, in the London Opera House in December 1917: "I have often criticized your [Zionist] leaders. But to-day I am here not for criticism, but for congratulations and co-operation. A national home in Palestine and freedom and equal rights [for Diaspora Jews] everywhere else: here, surely, is a platform that can unite all Israel."[93]

But the second obstacle, the current non-Jewish residents of Palestine, remained to be resolved. In fact, the Balfour Declaration had focused attention on this issue with its proviso that in working toward a Jewish nation home in Palestine it be "clearly understood that nothing shall be done which may prejudice the civil and religious rights of existing non-Jewish communities in Palestine."[94] And Zangwill recognized the centrality of this issue immediately. Already in November 1917, responding to a reporter's question for his reaction to the Declaration, he said, "My personal opinion is that we [Zionists and Territorialists] should work together to get Great Britain to make arrangements regarding the question of the Arabian population in Palestine."[95]

What "arrangements" exactly he had in mind he made clear during the 1919 negotiations of the Paris Peace Conference. He warned that if the Arab population were allowed to remain in Palestine there would never be a Jewish majority in the land and the Balfour Declaration would prove a sham, for "such a Palestine has neither the glamour of poetry nor the practicality of prose. It is neither Jewish nor National nor a Home. If this is what the Declaration meant, then it was an illusion and an insult."[96]

To ensure the success of the scheme for a national home in Palestine a Jewish majority must be created:

> those amicable measures of race redistribution which we have already seen to be an unavoidable part of a final world settlement will be carried out in Palestine as elsewhere. Thus the Arabs would gradually be settled in the new and vast Arabian kingdom . . . with which the Jewish Commonwealth would cultivate the closest friendship and co-operation. Only thus can Palestine become a "Jewish National Home." Only thus can Israel be told that Palestine is his country. Only thus can a final peaceful refuge be prepared. . . . And it is now or never.[97]

And it was to be never! Neither the Great Powers nor the World Zionist Organization would support Zangwill's insistence on the forcible resettlement of the existing Arab residents of Palestine. In January 1920 a bitterly disappointed Zangwill wrote:

> This is the world's share in the Jewish problem. It was thought the Allies had offered a solution to it by the restoration of Palestine to my unhappy race—Palestine, where the year's statistics fail to record a single crime among the Jewish inhabitants. Alas! the much-trumpeted prospect turns out a mirage. What is now being concocted in Paris [i.e., a League of Nations mandate] is a scheme without attraction save for mere refugees, a scheme under which a free-born Jew returning to Palestine would find himself under British military rule, aggravated by an Arab majority in civic affairs.[98]

So it was that the two decades of Israel Zangwill's energetic nationalist activism, as a Zionist, a Territorialist, and a Militant Zionist, all collapsed into an exhausted and despairing defeatism. The postwar arrangements for the Palestine mandate left him with a feeling of maddening frustration and futility. Assuming the prophetic "mantle of Elijah," Zangwill would now preach vengeance and doom against all those who he was sure had betrayed his hopes for the future of the Jewish people and for the survival of their culture. He would never forgive them.

NINE

The Melting Pot

Drama and the essay became Israel Zangwill's vehicles for instructing modern mankind in the contemporary applications of ancient Hebraic wisdom. Disseminating this wisdom universally through teaching, exemplary behavior, and genetic fusion was the mission that he now assumed for himself and that he believed Diaspora Western Jewry was inexorably destined to fulfill. For the first two decades of the twentieth century, he therefore devoted great efforts to teach non-Jewish humanity the profound universal lessons of Hebraism; he simultaneously endeavored to convince Western Jews to accept upon themselves the responsibilities entailed by their historical mission to their fellow citizens.

Zangwill's Hebraism provided a program of reform for the political activist. Among its content's most prominent planks were world peace, representative democracy, women's suffrage, and ethnic equality. In Britain and on the Continent Zangwill eagerly campaigned on the podium and in his writings to convince his fellow Europeans of the justice and necessity of adopting these universal moral imperatives. But the greatest promise for a bright future for mankind could be found, he believed, in the people and policies of the United States.

Ethnic assimilation in the great cauldron of the American "melting pot" became the cornerstone on which Zangwill constructed his vision of humanity's civilized future. From the New World would emerge the multiethnic, multiracial "new Hebraic man," a biological and cultural synthesis of the Judaic with the Gentile. For him, America remained mankind's only true land of "hopes and dreams." And it was to the American people that he so earnestly sought to teach the universal truths of Hebraism.

But the inward struggle of the twins of identity had not at all slackened. For precisely at the same time that Zangwill was devotedly propagating the doctrines of the melting pot and a universal Hebraism, he was also frantically searching for an "Itoland" in order to rescue East European Jewry from being condemned to immigrant assimilationism and the constricting limitations of the Hebraic mission.

But all of Zangwill's hopes and efforts were to no avail. Reality proved unyielding to his dreamer's vision. The didactic dramas written to win converts to the contemporary ethnic and political lessons of Hebraism were all critical and financial failures. On the other hand, while many of his essays were indeed critically praised for their insight, idealism, and style, they were eventually betrayed by the course of events arising from the conclusion of the First World War. Even America, as reflected in President Woodrow Wilson's uncompromising support for the Treaty of Versailles, appeared to belie its earlier moral promise toward mankind.

By 1920, an embittered Zangwill, already bereft of his "Itoland" in Africa and in Palestine, was denied equally the promised triumph of the Hebraic spirit over Western civilization's penchant for pagan materialism. In its stead he became convinced that rather than hope for mankind's promising future he must now devote himself to preaching a warning of the menacing doom hovering over humanity.

Assimilationism

Advocacy of Western Jewry's assimilation into the predominant culture was a powerful affirmation of social and religious views Israel Zangwill had long advanced. At considerable length, and from the beginning of his literary career, he had vigorously articulated, and after 1901 acted on, these views, while his admirers had consistently ignored their appearance in his works just as sedulously. The play *The Melting Pot* reflects Zangwill's continuing preoccupation with the literary themes and characters of the Anglo-Jewish author Amy Levy; its assimilationist ideology reflects his continuing intellectual debt to the thought of the Dutch-Jewish Enlightenment philosopher, Benedict de Spinoza (1632–1677).

It was from Spinoza, the child of Marranos, that Zangwill learned that ethnic groups are distinguished primarily by social variables, such as those of Judaism's "sacred sociology." As Spinoza wrote in his *Theologico-Political Treatise*, which Zangwill had so admired in *Dreamers of the Ghetto* and in his essay "The Position of Judaism": "Nations, then, are distinguished from one another in respect to the social organization and the laws under which they live and are governed; the Hebrew nation was not chosen by God in respect to its wisdom nor its tranquillity of mind, but in respect to its social organization and the good fortune with which it obtained supremacy and kept it so many years."[1] But should the communal environment somehow disappear, "we [Spinoza] conclude . . . that the individual Jew, taken apart from his social organization and government, possessed no gift of God above other men, and that there was no difference between Jew and Gentile."[2]

That the Jewish people survived after the political and social destruction of the Second Commonwealth, Spinoza explained by their continued communal isolation and the anti-Semitism consequent upon it: "As to their [the Jewish people's] continuance so long after dispersion and the loss of empire, there is nothing marvellous in it, for they so separated themselves from every other nation as to draw down upon themselves universal hate. . . . That they have been preserved in great measure by Gentile hatred, experience demonstrates."[3]

Jewish ceremonial law, Spinoza argues, is historically and sociologically limited, while the teachings of Jesus are not: "Christ was not so much a prophet as the mouthpiece of God. For God made revelations to mankind through Christ as He had before done through angels."[4] Spinoza's conclusion, however, was not that all people should become Christians, inasmuch as Christianity had itself become victim to error, but that Jesus' teaching pointed to a genuine "universal natural religion" for all mankind:

> To the universal religion, then, belong only such dogmas as are absolutely required in order to attain obedience to God, and without which such obedience would be impossible; as for the rest, each man—seeing that he is the best judge of his own character—should adopt whatever he thinks best adapted to strengthen his love of justice. If this were so, I think there would be no occasion for controversies in the church.[5]

In the *Theologico-Political Treatise* Spinoza lists seven tenets of the universal natural religion: (1) that the Supreme Being exists; (2) that He is one; (3) that He is omnipotent; (4) that He has supreme right and dominance over all things; (5) that the worship of God consists only in justice and charity, or love of one's neighbors; (6) that all those who obey God by their manner of life are saved and all others are lost; and (7) that God forgives the sins of those who repent.[6]

This Spinozan perspective formed the foundation of Israel Zangwill's Hebraism, with its emphasis upon the universal applications of its Christological Judaism. Already in his 1888 essay, "English Judaism," the young Zangwill had called for a new "natural Judaism," a universal "Christism" founded upon the teachings of Moses and Jesus, which might become "the religion of the future [approaching] the perfection of the *Ethics* and the *Tractus Theologico-Politicus* [of Spinoza]."[7] It was to the mission of evangelizing this universal natural religion to all mankind that he wished Western Jewry to dedicate itself and that he advocated Jewish assimilation into the American "melting pot."

Once his rationalist Spinozan assumptions are recognized, apparent logical inconsistencies in Zangwill's philosophy of Judaism are readily resolved; then only the contradictions arising from his anguished emotional ambivalence remain to disturb the stage portrait of the crucible of humanity's future tranquillity. This ambivalence, of course, had already appeared very early in his literary career, as for instance in his elegiac celebration of the traditional Jewish heritage accompanying the espousal of the rationalist Spinozan philosophy of a new "natural Judaism" in "English Judaism." And the inability to resolve this tension continued to appear regularly in later essays as well.

In 1903, as an example, in a perceptive and covertly autobiographical essay significantly entitled "Two Opposing Forces at Work on the Jew," Zangwill wrote:

> The Jewish clans, invited outside their high walls and admitted gradually to the civic life of Christendom, permitted to despecialize themselves from commerce, and brought into contact with modern critical thought, found themselves exposed to a double disintegration. They were undermined from within and absorbed from without. . . . The reason for their isolation seemed obsolete. A process of interfusion set in. . . .
>
> . . . But the freer the Jew is left the more he tends, if not toward Christianity, toward a broader view of it, and toward the acceptance of Christ in the apostolic chain of Hebrew prophets. . . .
>
> . . . The opposing forces are thus at work upon the Jew—the wind and the sun. The gaberdine, thrown open for a moment in the burst of heat [of acceptance], is buttoned tighter the next before the biting blast [of anti-Semitism]. . . .
>
> . . . The race which produced Moses, Isaiah, and Spinoza has still other messages to speak, and cross-fertilized as it now must be by all that Christianity has achieved in the sun, during its own centuries of

> hidden life, it will surely not flower . . . without bearing some new precious fruit for the human race, whose service is its highest ideal.[8]

Zangwill hoped to make his own Hebraic contributions to the progress of mankind's spiritual future by means of the stage. For the instruction of American Jewry in its role as the bearers of the universal "religion of the future" he wrote his famous drama, *The Melting Pot.* The play's world premiere at the Columbia Theatre in Washington, D.C., on 5 October 1908 was attended by President Theodore Roosevelt, who became an enthusiastic advocate of its overt message. This message, Zangwill had previously explained to the President, "dramatises your own idea of America as a crucible in which the races are fusing into the future America . . . combining as it does, the American and the American-Jewish problem."[9] The American public generally shared the President's enthusiasm, although the critics remained generally unimpressed by the drama's literary qualities.[10]

Like Amy Levy's *Rueben Sachs,* from which the theme and character names were borrowed, and Zangwill's own *Children of the Ghetto, The Melting Pot* is the story of generational conflict and ethnic assimilation. In the first of its four acts, the audience is introduced to the Quixanos, a Russian-Jewish family now living in New York. David Quixano, a young composer whose parents were massacred in the Kishinev pogrom, has been adopted by his uncle Mendel, a nonreligious piano teacher; Mendel's mother, on the other hand, has retained her unacculturated adherence to her traditional East European Jewish heritage and bemoans the Americanization of her son and David.

But David is in love—with America and with a Russian revolutionary, Vera Revendal. Activist and anti-Semite though she is, Vera, like Mendel, sympathetically listens to David's numerous paeans to the promise of America. To both he explains: "America is God's Crucible, the great Melting-Pot where all the races of Europe are melting and re-forming! . . . The real American has not yet arrived. He is only in the Crucible, I tell you—he will be the fusion of all races, perhaps the coming Superman."[11]

And when Mendel expresses some reservation on melting pot assimilation, David, like a mirror-image Territorialist, reminds him that if he had not desired Jewish ethnic disintegration he should never have agreed to emigrate to America. To this reasoning Mendel has no reply!

Act two opens with a scene reminiscent of "Grandchildren of the Ghetto": David and Mendel, having both forgotten that today is the traditional festival of Purim, are scolded by their Irish maid, Kathleen, "Call yourself a Jew and you forgettin' to keep *Purim!*" But a primary didactic purpose of the act is to stress the promise America offers for the future of all mankind, not to sentimentalize over the past. As David expostulates with a nativist descendant of the Puritans:

> It is you, freak-fashionables, who are undoing the work of Washington and Lincoln, vulgarising your high heritage and turning the last and noblest hope of humanity into a caricature. . . .
>
> . . . The only hope of mankind lies in the new world [in contrast to] Europe with her comic-opera coronets and her worm-eaten stage decorations, and her pomp and chivalry built on a morass of crime and misery.[12]

And American Jews must include themselves in this promise of the crucible of the melting pot! Zangwill emphasizes that the Jews must accept willingly the American melting pot and not cling to ethnic isolation. This notion is expressed through the American nurtured love, and desire for marital union, between David, the child of victims of Russian anti-Semitic violence, and Vera, the child of a vicious perpetrator of Russian anti-Semitism. As David explains the assimilationist notion to his uncle: "What immunity has our race? The pride and the prejudice, the dreams and the sacrifices, the traditions and the superstitions, the fast and the feasts, things noble and things sordid—they must all go into the Crucible."[13]

This theme is further explored in the third act, in which the Jew David and the Christian Vera defend their decision to marry. Vera, echoing Spinoza, patiently explains to her bigoted father that despite appearances to the contrary, her union with David involves neither intermarriage nor religious conversion, for "we are already at one—all homes and people are. Surely, father, all religions must serve the same God—since there is only one God to serve."[14]

Neither family is very pleased by the match, but David gently consoles Vera and defends the justice of their decision: "Those who love us *must* suffer, and we must suffer for their suffering. It is live things, not dead metals, that are being melted in the Crucible. . . . If only *my* folks were not so narrow about Holy Judea! But the ideals of the fathers shall not be foisted on the children. Each generation must live and die for its own dream."[15]

In act four the theme of David's and Vera's intention to marry is further developed while David's new composition, "Sinfonia Americana," premieres. At the opening, Vera observes the effects of the melting pot on the listeners: "I watched the faces—those faces of toil and sorrow, those faces from many lands. They were fired by your [David's] vision of their community of brotherhood, lulled by your dream of their land of rest."[16]

As the act concludes, David tells Vera: "Here [in America] shall they all unite to build the Republic of Man and the Kingdom of God. Ah, Vera, what is the glory of Rome and Jerusalem where all nations and races come to labour and look forward. . . . Peace, peace, to all ye unborn millions, fated to fill the giant continent—the God of *our children* give you Peace."[17]

However, the fourth act's happy triumph of Spinozan rationalism in the American melting pot appears almost as an anticlimax artificially imposed on the characters ex cathedra by some superior force external to the momentum of the play itself. The natural emotional climax of the play occurs rather toward the end of the third act. There David suddenly recalls that Vera's father had been a major participant in the Kishinev pogrom in which his parents had died, and he, acknowledging the fact, remains unrepentant. The horrors of his past Russian childhood prove too much for even the crucible of America to erase. Even when, quoting the words of the Biblical archetypical convert Ruth, Vera offers to adopt Judaism, David cannot bring himself to marry this daughter of his parents' murderer.

Doubtless there are genuine aesthetic and psychological contradictions between the third and fourth acts that weaken the literary quality of the play as a work of art and do reveal the ambivalences Zangwill experienced between his emotional attachments to the past and his rationalist dreams for the future.[18] However, as we have already seen, these ambivalences were nothing new in his works, nor was he unaware of them. In fact, at this time he was deliberately articulating these psychological contradictions, as it had become his "dream" and the goal of his "mission" to eliminate them for future generations.[19] Instead he vigorously defended the philosophic coherence of the vision of America and of American Jewry presented in *The Melting Pot*.

That the experiment of America represents the last hope for mankind's civilized future Zangwill explained to a reporter for the *Times* (London) in October 1908: "I do not think that America is the greatest country in the world, but the greatest potentiality. . . . The United States are the greatest idealistic experiment in government by the people that the world has ever tried. If it fails it will be the last great experiment of humanity. America is thus carrying mankind."[20]

This potentiality of America is the product of a Hegelian dialectical process that also provided Zangwill with the organizing principle for *The Melting Pot*'s plot development. In 1909, in reply to a hostile critic who had suggested that the drama should have been set in Russia, he retorted, "This is to misunderstand the whole play, the whole point of which is that in America alone can be found the *synthesis* in which the extremist *antitheses* can be reconciled."[21] Expanding elsewhere on exactly how the play was deliberately designed to illustrate the application of the Hegelian historical process to America, Zangwill wrote: "That in the crucible of love, or even co-citizenship, the most violent antitheses of the past may be fused into a higher unity is a truth of both ethics and observation, and it was in order to present historic enmities at their extremes that a persecuted Jew of Russia and the persecuting Russian race have been taken for protagonists."[22] Thus the separation of David and Vera at the end of the third act represents the irreconcilable antitheses of the past; their reconciliation and union in the fourth act represents the synthesis of the future to be produced in the American melting pot.

On the future of American Jewry Zangwill is more ambiguous. On the one hand he explained to the *Times* that the "melting pot" does not necessarily imply intermarriage, for "The American Jews are in the melting pot, if not bodily, spiritually. I am certain that nothing can prevent them from becoming enthusiastic Americans even if their religion or racial isolation is preserved."[23] On the other hand, complaining about criticism of the assimilationist views advocated in *The Melting Pot*, Zangwill rather cryptically remarked in 1909 to his friend, the American Jewish leader Stephen S. Wise (1874–1949): "it is no less than amazing that Jewish criticism should have fastened on the sole point in which I depart from current opinion. Even that departure has been entirely misunderstood, for I hold as strongly as you that only people of the same religion should intermarry, & my hero & heroine *are* of the same religion."[24]

The same ambiguity appears in a later defense of the views expressed in the play. On the one hand Zangwill denies that the assimilationism of *The Melting Pot* necessarily requires intermarriage: "The action of the crucible is thus not exclusively physical—a consideration particularly important as regards the Jews. The Jew may be Americanized and the American Judaized without any organic interaction."[25] But he then repeats the cryptic assertion he had made to Wise: "intermarriage with his fellow-crusaders in the new Land of Promise will naturally follow wherever, as with David Quixano and

Vera Revendal, no theological differences divide. There will be neither Jew nor Greek. Intermarriage, wherever there is social intimacy, will follow, even when the parties stand in opposite religious camps."[26]

Zangwill appears to be denying that he is advocating intermarriage as a component of assimilation and at the same time suggesting that the marriage of his Jewish hero and his Christian heroine is both desirable and inevitable. Oddly enough what he denies is that David's and Vera's union (and, by implication, his own with Edith Ayrton) is an instance of intermarriage. Actually, behind this reasoning is Zangwill's implicit assumption that the operation of the Hegelian dialectic in America will produce the Spinozan "universal natural religion" that will transcend the Jewish-Christian antitheses of the past: "It is only when a common outlook has been reached, transcending the old doctrinal differences, that intermarriage is denuded of those latent discords which the instinct of mankind divines."[27]

A further question concerning *The Melting Pot* arises. In its Spinozan implication is Zangwill looking forward to an assimilationist future for American Jewry only, or is it to apply on a broader canvas as well? Again the answer appears ambiguous. On the one hand he writes: "It is true that its [the play's] leading figure, David Quixano, advocates absorption in America, but even he is speaking solely of the American Jews. . . . He is not offering a panacea for the Jewish problem, universally applicable. But he urges that the conditions offered to the Jews in America are without parallel through-out the world."[28] But, on the other hand, "every country has been and is a 'Melting Pot.' "[29]

What Zangwlll intends here is that while "America is *the* Melting Pot" par excellence, other free Western nations, such as England, Argentina, and Brazil, also function as sociocultural melting pots.[30] But for those Jews living in despotic East European countries, assimilation is not possible and some alternative solution, such as Territorialism or the Galveston Plan, must be pursued.

The philosophic thought expressed in the plot and theme of *The Melting Pot* is impressive and expressed with a subtlety unusual in the more didactic works of Israel Zangwill. But it was a philosophy that went continuously unrecognized and unacknowledged by the drama's varied audiences. In fact, this very subtlety of thought conceals the powerful emotional ambivalences the playwright was then experiencing toward what he was convinced was the historically inevitable loss of identity facing the Jews living in the free societies of the West. While his British mind was applauding, his Jewish sentiments were writhing.

America may have remained for him, as for Esther Ansell, the land of "hopes and dreams," but like Raphael Leon, Israel Zangwill chose to continue residing in Britain. It was in the "Old World," mired in its long, tangled history, that he would strive to propagate the universal Hebraic message. Here he would seek to renew a past spirituality now shuttered away from the world behind mental walls of medieval superstition or else wantonly sacrificed to the tinsel of crude materialism. And in this age of George Bernard Shaw (1856–1950), the literary medium he selected to instruct Europe in the message of Moses, Jesus, and Spinoza was the drama.

Unfortunately Zangwill found that the first target of renewal was the field of drama itself. As early as 1904, in his presidential address, he was telling the Playgoers' Club that writers must not remain aloof from the debased quality of drama but rather must "get a footing in it and . . . try to gradually leaven it up," although this would also require "a wiser, a better, and a more educated public, which would demand a theatre of beauty."[31] However, after almost a decade of personal effort he still ruefully observed, "The British stage is now run on the principle of the lowest art for the largest number."[32] The didactic purpose of the drama had been forgotten in the rush to fill the producer's purse. But the nation's only hope for renewal remained the didactic Hebraic lessons that still might be taught audiences from the stage: "If England is not to die of fatty degeneration of the brain, she must wake up. Without spiritual elevation or capacity for sacrifice, the greatest army or navy will not save her. . . . And I would call not for compulsory conscription but compulsory subscription to the National Theatre."[33]

Zangwill himself certainly endeavored to elevate the quality of drama and edify the audience. In addition to *The Melting Pot*, several new Zangwill dramas premiered during the first two decades of the twentieth century. They addressed various major sociopolitical issues facing the British and European publics at the time, including alienation, women's rights, and war.[34] However, except for an entertaining farce based on an 1893 short story, "Merely Mary Ann," none of his new plays was a critical or financial success.[35]

Typical of the majority of Zangwill's satirical plays during these decades, *The Revolted Daughter* opened in 1901.[36] The play's protagonist, Christina Huntyngford, "inspired by Ruskin and Carlyle, revolted against her [wealthy] parents.—She hated the useless life of luxury they gave her, and she went out into the world to earn her own living by pen and to work among the poor."[37] In the first act we are also introduced to the fashionable and insensitive Mrs. Alma St. George and her appropriately rebellious daughter, Psyche. They serve as obvious vehicles for social satire.

More interesting is the benevolent Christina's friend, appropriately named Sophia. Unlike the heroine she is consciously an example of "the new woman," who in her aloof intellectualism despises Christina's activism and instead immerses herself in the study of logic and mathematics. Yet even before the conclusion of the second act we discover that this haughty rationalist suffers miserably from loneliness and also envies Christina her emotionally satisfying childhood; as she confesses: "I have always been alone, Christina, looking on the irony of life. . . . I'd willingly exchange them [her brains] for your parents. . . . Yes, think of the childhood they gave you. Oh, when I think of my childhood, I could cry my eyes out."[38] Here in Sophia's words are the echo of Zangwill's own loneliness and longing for the comforts of childhood.

But Christina quickly discovers, for her part, that the communal activist's life is not quite what Walter Besant's *All Sorts and Conditions of Men* had led its naively idealistic readers to believe; she confesses that the dreams of childhood are not really true and that "I went out to know life as it is—it is worse than I thought it was—but still I must face it."[39] But things only get worse until all the girl's childhood illusions are shattered, and she bitterly declares: "But she ["the great Mother"] is so cruel, so remorseless. Red in tooth and claw, she works through death and pain."[40] However, as the play concludes, Donald, Christina's beloved, consoles her by repeating the notions from the philosophy of the darkness of psychological and cosmological night expounded by the prodigal son in "Chad Gadya":

> Look—this river by day brawling, noisy, reeking with the vulgar roar of rowdy choristers—how it lies now [at night], solemn, silent, under the silent stars, every noise sweetened and softened by mystery! We jape and grin and play tricks under high Heaven, but the noises pass, the laughter passes, and we are drawn back towards the great silences, towards Love, towards God.[41]

The Revolted Daughter was a failure, and the criticism it received is typical of reactions to many of Zangwill's dramas. The *Athenaeum*, for instance, commented:

[Zangwill] is too enamoured of his own dialogue to spare us any of it, and he explains at some length what the public may be trusted to derive. His characters are, moreover, as a rule deficient in sympathy, and the thread of tenderness he has woven into a fabric of cynicism is too slight to affect the pattern. . . . Mr. Zangwill treats cleverly the object of his satire, and much of his dialogue is witty. Other portions are, however, diffuse, and there are moments when the whole is deficient in movement.[42]

Five similar Zangwill didactic satires appeared during the first two decades of the twentieth century. They are: *Jinny the Carrier* (1905), *Nurse Marjorie* (1908), *The Marriage of Tomorrow* (1912), *The Moment Before* (1916), and *Too Much Money* (1918). None of these was a financial or a critical success and only *Too Much Money* was ever published.[43] For all his persistence with it, serious dramatic satire was clearly not Zangwill's genre.

Quite a different approach to sociopolitical reform was employed in *The War God*. This 1911 play, a tragedy written entirely in blank verse, explores the problem of how best to eliminate war and achieve permanent world peace. The story involves the dialectic conflict between the Bismarckian Count Torgrim, Chancellor of Gothia, and the Tolstoyan Count Frithiof.

Torgrim, abetted by his servile assimilated Jewish secretary Karl Blum, has already engineered the conquest and unification of Hunland by Gothia and now aims to "expunge perfidious Alba from the map of Europe," for "Once Alba's vanquished, Europe's at our feet, And we have Europe, then,—Then the world is ours."[44] This, he explains, is merely the application to international relations of the Darwinian concept of natural selection: "What Heaven loves it breeds with life a-tingle, swift-gliding, flashing, darting death at rivals. . . . Thus were the Albans, now the turn is ours to be the chosen people of Jehovah. . . . And how fulfil it [Gothia's mission of peace] save we change this cockpit, this continent into a greater Gothia? One faith, one rule, one tongue, one endless Peace!"[45]

In an essay two years later, Zangwill analyzed this same sort of thinking in Germany: "Though blood and iron paralyze and demoralize Europe, let us find some other remedy than iron and blood. . . . And it is Nationality, not gold, that is the prize of war—the enhanced common consciousness of a group."[46] The English response to the German challenge of "blood and iron," according to Zangwill here, should be one of rational peaceable appeasement:

> But endless, ancient enmities seethe, endless aspirations and earth-hungers demand satisfaction, and if the world is not to be recarved by the sword it must be readjusted by Reason and Love. . . . If Germany desires of our [colonial] territory, she must have it. There is no reason other than the sword why Britain should possess nearly a quarter of the globe.[47]

In the play the position is argued by "a noble white-haired figure in a peasant's smock and leggings, leaning on his staff," who appears before Chancellor Torgrim and introduces himself as "Frithiof—maker of peace, it means you know."[48] The purpose of his sudden intrusion, this singular apparition announces, is to fulfill the sacred mission he has assumed: "But for your sake and Christ's I left my hut and tramped to this mad city [i.e., "Graaf"] and this mad house, where you, a passing shadow, dare to forge God's thunderbolts and doom a brother-nation. . . . I came in love to bring you peace, That peace of God which passeth understanding."[49]

Frithiof attempts not only to dissuade Torgrim from pursuing his aggressive wars of acquisition but also to persuade anarchist revolutionaries to eschew violence in their endeavors to alter Gothia's misguided political system and policies. But this advocate of passive resistance, the conciliator Frithiof, suffers the fate of so many such dreamers: he is murdered. However, in the end Frithian principles do succeed in winning support among leading members of both the government and the revolutionaries, and, in these new circumstances, the militarist chancellor, having refused to resign from office, is summarily dismissed.

The War God proved no more a critical success than did Zangwill's satires. Typical is this "mixed review" appearing in the *Bookman*; the reviewer believes that the issues dealt with in the play are indeed significant and praises Zangwill's challenging and fair discussion of them:

> It is just because Mr. Israel Zangwill has . . . stated in dramatic form one of the most urgent and puzzling problems of modern civilisation that his "tragedy" of "The War God" ought to provoke interest, and command admiration. . . . Both sides [of the issues] are allowed their full say, though the author's sympathies are with the party of peace and the clash of ideals and temperaments his protagonists provide makes an excellent basis for drama. . . . [Furthermore] it is impossible to overlook the exalted idealism, the eloquence, the humour, the irony

which inform his plea—for it is a plea—for international amity and concord.[50]

Unfortunately *The War God* is not a prose essay, and the reviewer finds that as a blank verse drama it is most ineffectual:

> But in point of fact he offers us declamation rather than action, and his play certainly resolves itself for the most part into a set of alternative harangues, while such incidents as he does employ are of far too violent and melodramatic a kind. . . . Fine rhetoric, you will perceive [in his blank verse], but no more than that; indeed you must not expect great poetry from Mr. Zangwill, you must be content with facility rather than inspiration.[51]

The War God closed after only three performances.[52]

The Next Religion

During the course of the second decade of the twentieth century Zangwill returned to his preoccupation with historical positivist religion, as first propounded in his 1888 essay, "English Judaism," and then more extensively explored in his 1892 "Jewish *Robert Elsmere*," the novel, *Children of the Ghetto*.[53] The philosophy of this later period had not shifted from Zangwill's original principles, although its applications now have become more broad. And as before, this religious ideology appears both in essays and in works of fiction, although the latter is no longer in novel form but rather in drama.

In the fascinating 1910 collection of lyrical essays, *Italian Fantasies*, immediately in the first essay, "Of Faith, Beauty, and Death," Zangwill turns his attention to what later would be called "semiotics" as he explores the foundations of Spinozan-inspired historical positivist religion:

> Who speaks of a religion as though it were dependent upon its theology? Dogmas are but its outward show; inwardly and subtly it lives by its beauty, its atmosphere . . . , and its creed is but a poor attempt to put into words a thought too large for syllables, too elusive for phrases. . . . For words must change, if only to counterbalance their own mutations and colourings, their declines and falls. They are no secure envelope for immortal truths. . . .

> . . . Why, indeed, quarrel over religion when all men agree; all men, that is, at the same grade of intellect! The learned busy themselves classifying religions . . . but in the crude working world religion depends less on the belief than on the believers.[54]

This collection of essays concludes with Zangwill delineating the means necessary for achieving the universal Hebraic "religion of the future":

> [Giuseppe] Mazzini [1805–1872] appears like the mighty prophet of the next phase of the spirit, the divine iconoclast whose fuller faith was to give the death blow to the old theology. . . . Why, then, did he, whose organising powers might have found supreme scope in establishing the religion of the future, throw away his life for Nationalism? Valuable instrument of world-progress as nationality within sane limits may be, alluring as is the idea of working through one's own nation, perfecting a model people, in whom all the families of the earth shall be blessed, the instruments of the new order exist insufficiently in any one people, if indeed they exist sufficiently in the whole population of the globe. More insistently even than nationalities the world needs a new Church.[55]

However, a few years later, in a 1917 speech on Woodrow Wilson's Fourteen Points, there is an explicit acknowledgment that nationalism is going to remain a prominent feature of contemporary civilization. Thus, according to Zangwill's analysis, one of the most pressing issues posed by postwar Western modernity, then, will be how exactly to reconcile the tensions that may well arise from the conflict of identities resulting from simultaneous commitments to a particularist political entity and adherence to the universalist "religion of the future." Concluding his lecture, Zangwlll explains: "For here, in a word, is the problem and the ideal—how to maintain the virtues of tribalism without losing the brotherhood of man; how to secure that, though there *shall* be both Jew and Greek, there shall yet be neither."[56]

The following year Zangwill returned to the issue of the tensions arising from conflicting political and religious identities, but this time he also elaborated more thoroughly on the bases of the historical positivist "religion of the future." Thus, as expressed in the traditional Biblical literature, it represents an original and invariable commitment to universalism as taught through historically varying expressions:

Israel and Edith Zangwill's children, November 1916: (from left to right) Oliver, 3; Aryton ("George"), 10; Margaret ("Peggy"), 6 years old. *Courtesy, Shirley Zangwill.*

> . . . the truth is . . . that it is precisely in the Old Testament that is reached the highest ethical note ever yet sounded. . . .
>
> . . . the God of Isaiah is already in Genesis, and the God of Abraham is not God of a tribe, but . . . the God of Reason and Love. . . .
>
> . . . If there were only a single God, and He is a God of justice and the world, how could He be confined to Israel?
>
> . . . Jesus but applied to himself . . . those conceptions of divine sonship and suffering service which were already assets of Judaism, and but for the theology of atonement woven by Paul under Greek influence, either of them might have carried Judaism forward on that path of universalism which its essential genius demands, and which even without them it only just missed? . . .
>
> . . . But if their [Jesus and Mohammed] achievements held faulty elements, is that any reason why the purer truth should shrink from universalization?[57]

Following the return of peace to Europe, in one of his most impressive essays, "The Voice of Jerusalem," Zangwill summarizes at length his notions of Hebraic historical positivist religion.[58] The central concern of this essay, as with so many of his earlier pieces, is the theme of reconciliation. This notion Zangwill finds to be the fundamental spiritual lesson of the Biblical literature, which, he argues, evolved in terms of the subtlety with which it expressed this teaching:

> For the Old Testament contains, though in a jumble of strata, all the traces of the evolution from the crude psychology of primitive civilisation to that form of Jewish psychology, popularly known as Christianity. It is this process of spiritualisation culminating in the soul of Jesus which is the true miracle to which the Bible testifies, and the only one as to which its testimony is convincing. . . . The soul of this "particular people" [the Jews] is best seen in the Bible, saturated from the first page of the Old Testament to the last page of the New with the aspiration for a righteous social order, and an ultimate unification of mankind. Of these ideals the race of Abraham originally conceived and still conceives itself to be the medium and missionary.[59]

Nonetheless, Zangwill's "religion of the future," like the "universal natural religion" of Spinoza, will not cling to the Biblical word nor to the dogmas of the past but rather will respond to the promptings of the human spirit. To achieve this "next religion," which has already found expression in the authentic Hebraic teachings of Jesus, there must be effected, according to Zangwill, the reconciliation of Judaism and Christianity:

> Judaism and Christianity alike need a new orientation. . . . Both, in fact, must now seek their authority, not in their scriptures, nor in their historic setting, but in the human soul. The theory of verbal inspiration must be jettisoned; it was a meaningless conception which owed its existence to the fact that nobody ever read the Bible, even though thousands knew every word by heart. . . .
>
> . . . In this still unresolved quarrel of Church and Synagogue [over the status of Jesus], both sides forget that the future will belong to the religion that first fits itself to the future. . . . And I should have thought the line of the future for theists lay rather in coming to some understanding on the divinity of Jesus. If Christians are ready to abandon the doctrines of the Incarnation and the Atonement, in their narrow individual and episodical sense, there is no way Jews should not admit it that the heroic tragedy of the great Galilean illumines the cosmic problem of suffering.[60]

This Hebraic "religion of the future" will be disseminated by assimilated Western Jews and those non-"Israelites" (such as Mrs. Edith Zangwill) who have come to accept the true Jewish teachings of Moses and Jesus. They will continue the Judeo-Christian "antagonism to atheism, polytheism, and pragmatic pluralism" and, while accepting the teachings of modern science, will also not be diverted from their activist mission of "salvation of the world by a people chosen for service and suffering."[61] This service must include pacifism in international relations, a just society in domestic affairs, and "kindliness" among individuals.

Although Zangwill explained the Hebraic "religion of the future" in his essays, it was in drama that he believed the concept could be most effectively taught. This was the purpose of two of his most controversial plays, *The Next Religion* (1912) and *Plaster Saints* (1914).

The Next Religion is intended to expose the falsity of the fashionable sterile religious reforms being bandied about as spiritual sops to the guilty consciences of materialistic philanthropists. In place of such a *Robert Elsmere*–style "next religion," Zangwill espouses in this drama the Hebraic "religion of the future."[62] In the play the spokesman for the "next religion" is the Reverend Stephen Trane, who, in the first act, is disillusioned with Christianity and physically threatened with blindness. In the second act, despite his wife Mary's clinging to the old Christianity, Stephen, aided by the millionaire philanthropist Sir Thomas McFadden, is now enthusiastically preaching a totally scientific "next religion" among the impoverished of Whitechapel, while his eyesight is continuing to fail. By the third act, Stephen, now completely blind, is preaching the "next religion," which has abandoned all simplicity and is celebrated with theatrical, symbolic ceremonies held in a huge, elaborate "St. Thomas' Temple" adorned with ostentatious decorations. Mary, on the other hand, has joined with Sir Thomas's son, Hal, in condemning her husband's "next religion," and the play concludes with her "fiercely" telling Stephen:

> Reason is only words. Can one know love without loving? No more can one know loss without losing. . . . I took your words for realities—now I see they are shadows. . . . What are your fine words but drugs to drowse people to the dreadful thing you preach! . . . You and your dried-up thinkers! I tell you that the great live world will never *take* your religion, and that even if you delude all male humanity, the *mothers* would rise up and tear it to pieces.[63]

Zangwill's spokesman for the Hebraic "religion of the future" is the young physician, Hal McFadden. As the play opens, Hal, as a man of science, advocates religious skepticism. However, by the third act he has become more wise and now espouses a devout, although heterodox, Christianity. Criticizing the temple's new ceremonies as less satisfying and historic than their traditional rivals, Hal questions the necessity for Stephen's entire "next religion": "Before we've worked out the last? What have you found more beautiful or uplifting than the words of Christ?" If Christianity now includes errors, he suggests to Stephen, "then vivify it, scour it, bring it back to the Founder . . . ; [for] perhaps Christ's own religion has never had a chance—perhaps *that's* the next religion." And as for a religion based totally on science, Hal assures Stephen, "I, a man of science, and a doctor, tell you that we know nothing."[64]

Despite the play's sincere probing of the profoundly disturbing issue of modernity and traditional religious faith, performance of *The Next Religion* was banned in Great Britain as offensive to public taste by order of the Lord Chamberlain.[65]

Zangwill was more successful with *Plaster Saints;* at least it was publicly performed. This play, too, discusses clergymen, religion, and science; however, unlike *The Next Religion* it is a satirical comedy, a form of theater that was evidently allowed greater liberties when it came to questions offending public taste. This situation is particularly ironic, as the explicit theme of this drama is the necessity for compromise and sin among ministers. As the flawed, heterodox protagonist, the Reverend Rodney Vaughn, declares:

> When I look at my old sermons, I blush at the impudence and ignorance with which I, an innocent at home, dared to speak of sin [i.e., personal moral culpability] to my superiors in sinfulness. . . .
>
> . . . I didn't know they [seminary students] might be qualifying [for the ministry] better through sin than through the whole college curriculum. . . .
>
> . . . Sweep away all this modern cant of the plaster saint! All the saints and prophets of the world were sown in sin—as lilies are reared in peat. St. Augustine, St. Francis, Tolstoy—there isn't a church in the world to-day, would have given any one of 'em a post![66]

As the play concludes, Vaughn decides to retire from the ministry in order to "make a profession of holiness . . . [for I] am no monster of sanctity. I will work as a man among men [to work for the religion of the future]."[67]

Like all his other dramas during these two decades, *Plaster Saints* was a failure with the literary critics, although it did play for an entire month before finally closing.[68]

After *Plaster Saints* and World War I, the mood changed. By 1920 Israel Zangwill found all his efforts had been betrayed: his dreams could not dominate reality. None of the things important to him had turned out right: the theater critics and audiences had been unable to appreciate properly any of his dramas; the Zionists had irretrievably missed the wartime opportunity of obtaining Palestine as an autonomous and secure Jewish homeland; and America and the Allies had betrayed the sacrifices of war by agreeing to a materialist, nationalist peace treaty with its miserable "League of Damnation."[69] Now the "mission" calling Zangwill was to courageously remind them all of their short-sighted treasons to the prophet's dreams of a beautiful, just, and peaceful world.

TEN

Satan Mekatrig

Mad in pursuit, and in possession so;
Had, having, and in quest to have, extreme;
A bliss in proof, and proved, a very woe;
Before, a joy proposed; behind, a dream.
All this the world knows; yet none knows well
To shun the heaven that leads men to this hell.
Shakespeare, from Sonnet 129

The rationalist's rejection of the very notion of demonic possession allows it to occur all the more readily. For that which cannot happen cannot be happening to him and therefore need not be guarded against! Yet it would be well to remember that even among Western skeptics and rationalists there remains "an inner world of dreams, fantastic and poetic as the mirage of the Orient where they were woven, of superstitions grotesque as the cathedral gargoyles of the Dark Ages in which they had birth."[1] Once ensnared in the skein of this seductive inner world of dark illusion it is almost impossible for one to revive his old reason and struggle back again into reality. But Israel Zangwill almost succeeded in doing so.

After twenty years of somnambulant activism Zangwill was abruptly jolted out of his dreams by the violence of the Bolshevik revolution, by the vengeful victors' Peace of Versailles, and by the establishment of a League of Nations' colonial-style British mandate in Palestine. All these events conformed neither to his vision of the West's Hebraic future nor to his projection of East European Jewry's national future. But what Zangwill found most disturbing in this post-war world was the smug self-congratulation of the presumptive "winners," of the Allies and of the Zionists, all loudly crowing over what they believed they had achieved.[2]

Zangwill now set out to teach the world the truth about the Paris Peace Conference. The public must be informed; the politicians must not be allowed to continue deluding their peoples with false explanations of the charade they had actually acted out in Paris. For what they had really done in the Treaty of Versailles (and in the 1920 San Remo Conference on the Middle East), according to Zangwill, was to commit treason to the universal Hebraic standards of mankind and to bury the future of the Judaic heritage of the Jewish people.

Unfortunately, Zangwill relied not only on his persuasive essays and skillful oratory to carry his message to the public but also persisted in turning to the stage to teach his truths. Despite his consistently unrelieved failure as a playwright, he still would not awaken and recognize that serious drama simply was not his literary forte. And to persist in this illusion, he would eventually be forced to pay the ultimate price.

The Melting Pot in the Cockpit

Even before the Treaty of Versailles was signed in June 1919, Israel Zangwill began denouncing its principles as dangerous departures from Hebraic universalism, particularly as it had become embodied in the Wilsonian Fourteen Points. Instead a new harbinger was on the horizon, amazingly from the East. As he explained in a speech in February 1919 at Albert Hall (later published by the Workers Socialist Federation), while he felt compelled to condemn the violence of Russia's Bolshevik revolutionaries, he rejected even more strenuously the Allied intervention against them. For in contrast to the elaborate colonialist machinations being conducted at Versailles, the goals of the Bolsheviks coincided with his own:

> The same study that convinces me of its [the Bolshevik revolution's] crudities and cruelties convinces me also that by its heroic attempt to make bread and education as common as air, by its aspiration for a world brotherhood, by its repudiation of the imperialism that is based on exploitation of coloured races . . . , it is the first attempt in history to create a model Commonwealth. . . . Bolshevism is only Socialism in a hurry. . . . It is a recognition that not property, but society is sacred.[3]

In a 1920 article Zangwill repeated his admiration for the Hebraic idealism of international socialism and the Bolshevik experiment, despite the latter's intolerable violence, in contrast to the *Realpolitik* fraudulence of the Versailles settlement:

> Socialism is unquestionably in harmony with the Jewish genius from the days of Moses, while internationalism is latent in Isaiah and Amos; not socialism in any narrow, schematic form of partition of property or destruction of individualism, but the conception of the national organism as one happy and righteous whole with the world as a federation of such peaceful systems. . . .
>
> . . . It is only in succumbing to the policy of violence as the short cut to the millennium that Trotsky has been faithless to the spirit of Judaism—that long tradition of Reason and Love. . . . But even the attempt to precipitate the millennium by force is better than the sullen determination of Christendom to continue the still more murderous order of Sovereign States united at best by a loveless League. . . . [Because the Jews remain the world's conscience] it is at the hands of Jewish publicists all over the world . . . that the brazen attempt to palm off the Paris ukases as the Wilsonian Peace-Programme meets with its stones and repudiation.[4]

To disseminate these ideas as widely and as convincingly as possible, Zangwill turned to the stage again. In 1921 he presented his ideas in *The Cockpit.* Although the play concerns the conflict between the Balkan peoples of "Valdania" and "Bosnovina," it is deliberately reminiscent of *The Melting Pot,* for the central thesis is: "It's the [American] Melting Pot versus the [European] Cockpit."[5] Explains Nicholas Stone, an elderly scholar in the United States and presumed father of the heroine Peggy, "America is still being born—born out of the travail of all races. God help the world if she proves an abortion—if she hardens into the same old nationalism as Europe—the same old fetish of the flag."[6]

Peggy, it turns out, is really the exiled heir-apparent to the throne of Valdania, "the very heart of the cockpit."[7] It is now a country tyrannically ruled by Nicholas's enemy, the former journalist Cazotti, abetted by the "millionaire Jew, Baron Gripstein." Cazotti and Gripstein have risen by exploiting the grievances of Greek Orthodox and Muslim citizens against Catholics. And General Roxo, a Catholic, arrives in America to persuade Peggy to return and assume her royal duties as a means of crushing Cazotti's despotism. Despite Nicholas's warnings, Peggy agrees to accompany Roxo in his mission.

Roxo succeeds in ousting the dictator but soon plans a war against Valdania's historic foe, Bosnovina. For an ally he seeks an alliance with the nation's other neighbor, Rolmenia, to be sealed by the marriage of Rolmenia's Orthodox prince and Valdania's Catholic Queen Margherita, the former Peggy Stone. But the queen has other ideas.

Peggy has come to the cockpit to teach it the principles of the melting pot. Complains Roxo, "she poured out a programme that wouldn't leave a penny for our glorious army—roads, bridges, canals, railways, irrigation, schools, colleges,—all things she found in America and can't find here."[8] Furthermore, the queen wishes to reject the Rolmenian marriage alliance because she refuses "to drag other countries into the war, to slaughter unfortunate men who have nothing to do with our quarrel."[9]

As the play concludes, Bosnovina, now defeated, is threatening revenge, Rolmenia is threatening war because of the refusal of its offer of an alliance, and mobs rioting against the Jews in the streets of Valdania are threatening revolution. Reflecting on what has happened to her dreams for Valdania's future, Peggy now realizes that Nicholas had been right after all: Europe will never adopt the Hebraic hope that America represents. And she is trapped as the "Queen in a cockpit!"[10]

The drama was not a success. Zangwill's skills as a playwright had not improved, and Europeans were not amused by its invidious comparison between themselves and Americans.[11] But at least someone had been willing to produce *The Cockpit* in the first place; no one at all would agree to stage *The Forcing House,* its sequel.

This 1922 play, a remarkably prescient analysis of the nature of revolutionary socialism, "the forcing house" of social transformation, is again set in Valdania. The country undergoes a Bolshevik-style revolution in the name of universal equality and democracy, but these revolutionary ideals are soon perverted by opportunists exploiting the clichés of extremist politics. The result is a regime of domestic dictatorship, loss of previously available political and social rights, police terrorism, and nationalist military expansionism. As Duke D'Azollo, Zangwill's alter ego, expresses it: "Yes, it is Socialism while you won't wait. Not a Paradise of blooming brotherhood, not a natural growth under God's heaven, but a Socialism ripened prematurely under the heat of compulsion and watered with blood; a Socialism under a sky of glass, unstable, sterile, without spontaneous sap, that can be perpetuated only by ever-renewed compulsion."[12]

Zangwill explicitly repudiates any notion that he has abandoned his advocacy of socialism in *The Forcing House,* but rather he interprets the Russian example as socialism gone astray through extremism.[13] As Zangwill explains elsewhere, unlike "the forcing house" of Bolshevism, "the *spontaneous* adoption of communism *would* be 'applied Christianity.' "[14] But those seeking social reconciliation and international compromise are still being defeated everywhere by the opportunists' demagogic manipulation of extremism. As *The Forcing House* concludes, the prerevolutionary fascist dictator Cazotti has just been proclaimed king of the "socialist" people's democracy of Valdania.

This melodrama, which might have made a brilliant essay on the sociology of totalitarianism, reflects Zangwill's growing despair over the possibility that the universal Hebraic principles could long prevail anywhere in the world. This despair would grow increasingly strong over the following two years, twinning itself with his anguish over the failure of the Zionist leadership to have immediately secured Palestine as an exclusively Jewish homeland.

Watchman, What of the Night?

Following the armistice in 1918, debates over the political strategy to be adopted at the forthcoming peace conference in Paris replaced the ebullience inspired by the Balfour Declaration originally experienced among all parties of Jewish nationalists.[15] Israel Zangwill was particularly worried once again by his long-standing concern over the threat to Jewish settlement in Palestine posed by Arab inhabitants already resident there, and over the possibility of British connivance in their opposition to the establishment of Jewish political rights and to continuing Jewish settlement in the land.

Already in December 1918 he was writing to WZO leader Chaim Weizmann:

> I cannot in the least agree that Jews have not the right to form a State because they are not at the moment in the majority. If so, then they have no right to go in and shove out another race. . . .
>
> . . . I am very sorry to see from private Palestine letters received this morning that racial friction [among Jews and Arabs] still continues, and that the Jews are losing ground to the Arabs under the passive connivance of the British authorities.[16]

To remedy these dangers for the future Zangwill proposed a militant program, urging that at the peace conference the Zionists advocate explicitly "that Palestine be earmarked as the territory for the establishment of a Jewish State under temporary trusteeship" and that

> considering . . . the impossibility of establishing a Jewish polity with the existing disproportion of 600,000 Arabs to 100,000 Jews, as well as the danger of racial friction, the measures necessary for the establishment of a Jewish State, and the safeguarding of the non-Jewish population, are not to exclude amicable arrangements for the nationalisation of the land (with expropriation and compensation of land-owners, both Jewish and Arab) and the gradual emigration of the mass of semi-nomadic *fellahin* . . . to the new Arab kingdom [in Arabia and Mesopotamia], with whose development and policies the Hebrew Palestine would be in cordial co-operation and friendship.[17]

But by 1920 it was clear that the British did not intend to interpret the Balfour Declaration's phrase "national home" in Palestine to include the notion of a Jewish *state* there.[18] Nor did they indicate an intention to relocate any of the mandate's Arab inhabitants. A prescient Zangwill bitterly observed:

> There is no example in history of an inhabited country being acquired except by force. . . . There is no way for a people once pushed out of its country to push in again unless at the point of the sword, and even less is this possible with a scattered people. . . .
>
> . . . In the tug of war between the Christian Powers, with the Arab pulling in a third direction, there is obviously scant chance of a real Jewish Palestine. . . . The interest of England in getting her new possession developed by Jewish capital and industry is outweighed if the Arabs are antagonised too deeply. . . .
>
> . . . Without any provision whether for Arab emigration or Jewish administration, Palestine bids fair to remain purely a British possession, whose reconstruction is thrown upon Jewish capital and energy.[19]

Again, claiming to support "my friend, Mr. Jabotinsky," Zangwill stressed, "Unless it is impressed upon the Arab mentality that the programme of 'a Jewish National Home' is irrevocable, Palestine will become a second Egypt to England, and an ancient Egypt to its unfortunate Jews."[20]

And elsewhere he wrote angrily:

> The world seems to prefer Jews scattered, to serve as scapegoats for its crimes and follies. In Palestine, the Arab hirelings of more Machiavellian Powers terrorize their fellow-Arabs into massacring the Jews as a way of getting rid of England and all her works. The Zionists, who had overlooked such an obscure feature of the Palestine landscape as 600,000 Arabs, are consoling themselves for the massacres by pointing to my

Israel and Edith Zangwill, November 1923. *Courtesy, The Bettmann Archive/BBC Hulton.*

> humble self as the cause. It seems that I have alarmed the Arabs by suggesting they must be expropriated, or, at least, submerged. How is it possible for a Jewish National Home to arise in Palestine without the one process or the other I do not pretend to understand—indeed, submergence by the gradual immigration of Jews is the public policy of Zionism. How else is the Basle Program feasible?[21]

And ever sensitive to the issue of Jewish identity, a despairing Zangwill concluded that if these processes of "expropriation" and/or "submergence" do not occur, then "the utmost that seems practicable is the rise of a Semitic Switzerland, in which the Jews would have an equal national status with the Arabs. . . . As a Jewish asset, or as the solution of the Jewish problem, it [a binational Palestine] will be comparatively worthless."[22]

On a tour of America in 1923, Zangwill's mounting despair, disappointment, and anger over the fate of the nationalist movement in Palestine finally erupted.[23] It reached its climax in a speech he delivered in New York on 14 October. Invited by his longtime friend, Rabbi Stephen S. Wise, Zangwill delivered a major address to a meeting sponsored by the American Jewish Congress held at Carnegie Hall.[24] Carefully and thoughtfully drafted, the lecture—entitled "Watchman, What of the Night?"—resounds with all the seething wrath and execration of a prophet thwarted.[25] The appalled audience of four thousand departed the hall after the harangue, horrified and furious.[26]

In his lecture, Zangwill discoursed on three topics: (1) world affairs, (2) the fate of the Diaspora, and (3) the Jewish future in Palestine. The first topic Zangwill touched on only briefly, noting "There is only one way to World Peace, and that is the absolute abolition of passports, visas, frontiers, custom houses and all other devices that make the population of our planet not a cooperating civilization but a mutual irritation society."[27]

Turning to the second subject, Zangwill began by emphasizing his well-established view that there would long persist a significant divergence in fate between Western Jews, the Diaspora, and those who come to settle in Palestine, and that it will be the Diaspora which will play the dominant role: "the Jewish problem lies now divided between Palestine and the Diaspora, and . . . under the most favorable development of Palestine, the scattered Jewries will long continue the overwhelming preponderant section as regards population."[28]

Thus, even "the utmost success of Zionism would make no change in this Diaspora tragedy."[29] For this reason every effort must be made to expose the "sullen and surreptitious attempt of our Anglo-Jewish Grand Dukes to undermine the [Balfour] Declaration which, while guaranteeing their own status, offered to other Jews a measure of salvation."[30] But the "American Archdukes" and their American Jewish Congress must likewise cease playing their double game of pretending to support Jewish nationalist goals in Palestine while continuing to reside comfortably in the Diaspora. That Zionism will heal the breach between Western and Eastern Jewry is mere illusion:

> The concerns of the Diaspora are all the more important because Zionism which came to demolish it, has strengthened its foundations. . . . Herzl's attempt to destroy the Diaspora has ended in arresting its natural dissolution [through assimilation], for nothing is so unifying as working together for the same object. The [Diaspora] Zionists will not live in Palestine, but in the subsidence of Judaism their work for Palestine will keep alive their common Jewish consciousness.[31]

Instead, it is time that the permanent split in the Jewish people existing between Diaspora Jews living willingly in the open societies of Western Europe and America and those Eastern Jews escaping persecution to live in Palestine should be explicitly acknowledged. And each of these segments of the Jewish people must now turn to its own task.

In the Diaspora, Jewry must resolutely accept the melting pot of assimilation and vigorously assume their mission as heirs and propagators of Hebraic wisdom. Zangwill reminds his listeners that Zionism is not at all the fundamental teaching of their heritage: "For what in a nutshell is Judaism? It is the Torch of Reason in the hand of Love."[32] And the Diaspora mission must extend these Hebraic values, already operating in America, to the world: "For the great American ideals are Jewish ideals, and their destruction would be more tragic for the world than even the destruction of the Jews."[33] Therefore it is essential to denounce the "Nordic nonsense" of racialism and nationalist religion spreading through Germany and, in opposition, "it is time we Jews reasserted the Universal God and the unity of civilization."[34]

Zangwill devoted a considerable portion of his lecture to his third topic, that of denouncing the "deluded" claims and actions of the Zionists. At the heart of his scathing attack on Zionist ideology is his rejection of their notion of equating Judaism with nationalism: "this neo-nationalism seems to me no nobler than the Balkan spirit which ravages Europe today. The eternal duel between Judaism and Nationalism is the drama of Jewish history. But you cannot reduce a people whose faith and literature have nourished continents to the category of a mere political nationality."[35]

But it is not only Zionist ideology, its misreading of the durability of the Diaspora, and its reductionist definition of the Jewish people that Zangwill finds objectionable. What really most troubles him is the WZO's actual policies toward the administration and future of Palestine:

> Zionism can . . . only rely upon as much of England's Might as suits the policy of England, and since the Zionist leaders are ready to accept any conditions, however humiliating and however impracticable, and since Britain is represented by a too tactful Jewish governor, it is clear that only a minimum of Might will be at the disposal of the Jewish National Home and that mainly in the British interest. . . .
>
> . . . For the "Jewish National Home" in Palestine is at this moment as little Jewish or National or a Home as any other part of the Diaspora, to which in fact Palestine has now been added.[36]

At the heart of the WZO's failure in Palestine, however, is not its accommodationism to British policy but rather its failure to take advantage of the immediate wartime conditions of 1918–19 to deal firmly with the Arab inhabitants of Palestine, by adopting Zangwill's 1918 program. For concessions to the Arabs now are useless. The Zionists' failure of nerve at the critical moment, Zangwill unflinchingly insists, is their most inexcusable crime:

> I shall always believe that at the critical moment the Zionist leadership, unconscious of the living forces behind it . . . failed in nerve and will-power. But the hour has passed. A great moment found, as Herzl foreboded, a small people. . . . An expropriation policy, tolerable in the immense tragedy of the war, would be inadvisable to-day. . . .
> . . . Political Zionism is dead.[37]

Pulling no punches, Zangwill concluded that, as a result of Arab numbers and intransigence, "With regard to propositions of colonization in mass, let me say briefly but bluntly that the idea that the Jews will go only to Palestine is a myth, which the presence of this great audience alone makes ridiculous."[38]

"Watchman, What of the Night?" unleashed a torrent of denunciation against Zangwill. Everyone was angry, and Rabbi Wise felt compelled to disassociate himself and the American Jewish Congress from his remarks.[39] For not only had he greatly offended Zionists throughout the world, but by his militancy he had done so in such a manner that Jewish anti-Zionist sentiment remained completely hostile to him. And as the tour proceeded, he became embroiled in vituperative public exchanges with, among others, American Federation of Labor President Samuel Gompers and American Jewish leaders Louis Marshall, Nathan Straus, and Samuel Untermeyer.[40]

Zangwill, who had become accustomed to being treated respectfully as an authoritative international figure, felt stunned and confused by the widespread and bitter recriminations now voiced against him everywhere on his American tour. These emotions are still evident a few months later in a wry remark he made from his home in Britain: "The humor of the situation is that at Chicago, Dr. Weizmann gave up both political Zionism and diaspora nationalism, for declaring both of which impossible, I have been so attacked."[41]

Bewildered and isolated, Zangwill began lashing out at Americans as he proceeded with his tour of the country and addressing its now hostile audiences. In a speech delivered in Brooklyn he berated (the non-Jewish) Charlie Chaplin for not admitting that he was actually a Jew, and in a ranting address delivered in New York's Town Hall he remarked that "in America there is no sense of humour."[42] Then, warming to his subject and losing complete control of his stage composure, he continued: "Everything is less efficient in America. You New Yorkers are lazy and inconsequential. In general, America thinks without acting and acts without thinking. You are also vulgar. . . . Your immigration policy is a cruel muddle; still, you are the best half-educated people in the world."[43]

He went on to claim that Americans possess no sense of shame and can readily tolerate injustices. He concluded by attacking Christianity for not ending the recent world war and described the Christian religion as "organised hypocrisy."[44] Stephen S. Wise, who served as rabbi of New York's prestigious Free Synagogue, immediately repudiated Zangwill's remarks entirely.[45]

As his American tour ended, Zangwill still could not comprehend what narrow, invisible line he had transgressed in "Watchman, What of the Night?" that could account for all the anger that lecture had aroused toward him. What had he said but what must be obvious to all except the most dazzled Zionist dreamer? Yet such an apparently reasonable interpretation of his remarks was obviously not correct, but Zangwill was never able to grasp why it was not. Therefore if he was to regain his equilibrium once more it was essential that he come to understand what had gone amiss with his conception of reality; without this knowledge, he must surely be lost.

Depressed and physically exhausted, Zangwill returned to Britain in early spring 1924. At home awaited the unfinished manuscript of the new novel he was writing. This was the obvious means the *maggid* Zangwill had already chosen in his struggle to repossess his forgotten understanding, the fictional ground where he was engaged in battle with his own dark "inner world of dreams." The book tells the story of a disillusioned disciple of Jacob Frank, the eighteenth-century Jewish mystic, "messiah," heretic, and charlatan. It was intended to be autobiographical.

The Baron of Offenbach

In 1922, after a hiatus of more than twenty years, Israel Zangwill returned to Jewish literature. His first new venture was a translation into English of the Hebrew religious poetry of the medieval Spanish

Jewish author, Solomon ibn Gabirol (ca.1020–1057). He had been recruited for this project, the first volume in the "Schiff Library of Jewish Classics," by his friends in the Jewish Publication Society of America.[46]

Zangwill gradually came to feel a great personal affinity to this author whom he interpreted as an early exemplar of one writing from within two conflicting cultures: "in the best Spanish-Hebrew period we see the poet [ibn Gabirol] . . . moving equally between the sacred and the profane. Gabirol is the first Hebrew poet to use the secular image of the Muse . . . and he is the first Hebrew poet to handle philosophy," a philosophy Zangwill found particularly attractive because of "an odor of heresy that clung to it."[47] As he stresses in the introduction to his translation:

> in Gabirol we catch sight of Hebrew poetry in its period of transition when it was passing from a purely devotional to a [non-Jewish] secular character. Even the devotional begins to root itself not in tradition but in the individual experience. There is thus a double movement by which the devotional is freeing itself from the hypnotism of the Biblical and liturgical *Anschauung* and taking on a personal quality, while at the same time the subject-matter is enlarging itself with elegies, epigrams, and Horatian epistles. . . .
>
> . . . It says much for Gabirol's genius that despite the familiarity with every nook and cranny of the Old Testament, which his quotations evince, he was yet able to add so much of his own to these second-hand thoughts, and to keep such a personal vision of the Universe.[48]

But it was not merely ibn Gabirol's modernistic twinned identities that attracted Zangwill. It was also very much the "odor of heresy that clung" to the mysticism of his philosophic thought. For it was while he was translating ibn Gabirol that he decided to return to the writing of Jewish fiction, in this case an ambitious historical novel centered around the figure of the heretical mystic and pseudomessiah, Jacob Frank (1726–1791).[49]

So very serious was this project for him that at first Zangwill categorically refused Stephen S. Wise's invitation to address the American Jewish Congress in 1923: "after a long gap of years largely wasted on public activities, more or less fruitless, my brain is seething with a big Jewish historic novel & when I have just started a new Polish secretary to study with me the material in that language. To switch off the creative current for some six weeks . . . would be disturbing."[50] And by June, when Zangwill allowed himself to be persuaded to accept Wise's offer, twelve sections of "my new romance, which is on a spacious scale," had already been completed.[51]

The new novel in progress, "The Baron of Offenbach, A Cabbalistic Romance," opens with an explanatory note by its "editor," Israel Zangwill. In it he explains that "the Matron of the Downtown Home in Philadelphia," on the advice of "the Rabbi who lives on the next street," has purportedly conveyed to him, the author of *Dreamers of the Ghetto,* a manuscript in French and German that had been the sole possession of a recently deceased patient, a 112-year-old Russian Jewess, Sarah Gratz.[52] The handwritten pages had evidently been left in her care by a guest, "A Frenchman, of melancholy and brooding habit, but with courteous ways and flowery expressions," who died in her husband's inn over a century ago.[53]

According to the "editor," Zangwill, the German portion of the manuscript appears to have been written by a Jewish convert to Christianity in the last quarter of the eighteenth century, one deeply influenced by Talmudic and "Cabbalistic" thought, while the French sections seem to have been composed by a Huguenot who had spent much time in London during the same period. The work, according to its "editor," provides an eyewitness and well-informed account of the neo-Sabbatean pseudomessianic Frankist sect that arose among Central European Jews at that time. Zangwill insists that the historical evidence he has checked confirms all the manuscript's details and is therefore an invaluable resource for students of Jewish history. In conclusion he warns, "Some of these [Frankist] follies or of the conceptions involved . . . may shock my friend the Matron. But I cannot well bowdlerize so historic a document or falsify that frank facing of life which the Cabbalah shares with the rest of old Hebrew literature."[54]

The twelve sections Zangwill completed before he began his American lecture tour consist of a "translation" into English of the first of two French portions of the manuscript, an autobiographic account of his involvement with the Frankists by the Huguenot dramatist François Alexandre Gaubert Lavaysse,

> a freethinker and freeliver [who came to] pass the last twenty-five years of my life among Jews, that all my thoughts and emotions would centre round Jews, that for the sake of Jews I should give up my name and fortune, honour, and philosophy, that I should finally grow so habituated to Jews as to be uneasy in other society, and that, torn at last from

> their bosom, and sent wandering ghostly through the world, I should never find, save in Jewish inns, a shadow of relief and repose.[55]

The account is devoted to relating how this skeptical rationalist found himself slowly transformed into a fervent disciple and spokesman for the charlatan mystic, Jacob Frank. About this metamorphosis the narrator remarks: "How strange is human nature! It would seem as if the greatest force in life is not arms but contagion. . . . Contagion is certainly the key to my own life."[56]

Woven through the narrative as it traces the "outsider" Lavaysse's odyssey from latter-day Spinozan to latter-day Sabbatean are explicit details of Israel Zangwill's own history. The autobiographical experiences are particularly prominent in the portrait of the Frenchman's prolonged stay in London. Here the exiled Huguenot's experiences mirror closely Zangwill's own youth in London's East End, just as that city's genuine eighteenth-century Huguenot church had actually become the twentieth-century home for the Jewish congregation, Machzike Hadath.[57]

About 1790, following his sojourn in England, the narrator arrives in Offenbach and there encounters the mysterious and controversial man who called himself "the Baron of Offenbach." Much earlier, in Poland, this same man, the authentically historical figure Jacob Frank, had declared himself the true heir of Sabbatai Zevi, the long-awaited Jewish messiah; then, in 1759, to win support from the Polish Church against his Rabbinic opponents, he underwent a pseudoconversion to Catholicism. But the following year, when the authorities discovered that surreptitiously, among his sect's followers, he was claiming to be the messianic living incarnation of God's Indwelling, Frank was imprisoned. Only after the first partition of Poland in 1772 did the Russians release him, and he immediately made his way to the West. When Lavaysse meets him, Frank and his followers had been enjoying for several years the precarious protection of the Austrian emperor, the religious innovator Joseph II; recently, however, they had removed westward to Offenbach, a small community near Frankfurt am Main. Here, although in public he continued to maintain the pretenses of devout Catholicism, Frank had, in fact, secretly established at his château the center for his antinomian, Kabbalistic Jewish sect that now had secret adherents throughout Central Europe.

It was while en route to Offenbach that Lavaysse first encountered the town's extraordinary Baron; he had come to pay a visit to an anti-Semitic Polish noble, Prince Lubomirski. Upon first seeing Frank then, the narrator recalls: "He was a formidable, pock-marked old gentleman, in a white robe and a tall turban. . . . At his breast flashed a great jewelled star. [The Baron's] eyes were already boring uncomfortably into mine under his great grizzled eyebrows, and he proffered a big green enamel snuff-box, with plaques of painted Bacchantes."[58]

The Baron and the Prince were clearly not on the best of terms, and the Baron soon engaged in trapping his host in what appeared to Lavaysse to be a conjuror's trick in which he twice produced a note that had only just been consumed in the flames of the fireplace before all those present. As he produced these strange effects, "the Baron's face was transformed—and [an] angel seemed to loom behind his pock-marks."[59]

After the Prince and the Baron finally concluded their business, the latter began to relax and turned his attention to the unknown guest, the Huguenot from abroad. Soon the Kabbalist Frank and the rationalist Lavaysse fell into an intense philosophic discussion. The Baron praised the Emperor Joseph II for allowing Jews to serve in the Austrian army and for considering matters of state from a philosophic perspective; the emperor, he said, was a true philosopher-king. But, the Baron vehemently insisted, Joseph II went seriously astray when he attempted to reduce all nature to an abstract philosophic system imposed upon it from without and when he overestimated the intelligence of his subjects. When the narrator quizzed what Joseph II should have done instead, the Baron retorted: he should have used his earthly powers to have "brought the Kingdom of Heaven."[60]

After the Baron departed, the Prince began threatening to denounce him as a blasphemer and reprobate. Just then "the room . . . was lapped by a swift wave of blue flame, followed by a gigantic crash and roar." Then "there came a plump through the [window] pane, shattering it, a small white object." On inspection this object turned out to be the twice-burned letter fixed around "a ferruginous elongated stone, blackish and glazed, such as are said to fall from the skies!" As Lavaysse looked at the objects "the room was filled with blinding light and again the artillery of heaven crashed right over our heads."[61]

Fascinated by Frank's exotic aura and reputation, the narrator traveled on to Offenbach and attempted to visit the royal château there but was barred at the gate from entering by the Baron's guards. However, through the fence he did manage a glimpse at its spacious grounds. There, as he peered through the greenery of the estate from afar he "espied a rich green lawn, on which, moving in graceful postures or playing on musical instruments, I beheld beautiful youths and maidens in the gayest of garments. It was like a pastoral of our Watteau or a scene out of one's vision of the Golden Age—except that all the figures were Jewish!"[62]

Returning from this idyllic scene, the narrator was suddenly jostled by a group of Frank's guards who were relentlessly pursuing a young woman who was desperately attempting to flee the château. Eventually they were able to seize her, and she was forcibly made to return. Disturbed by the incident, Lavaysse quizzes a crowd of loitering townspeople about why no one tried to intervene to help the girl. These spectators informed Lavaysse that it is well known there that no one is allowed into, or out of, the Baron's estate without his personal approval; obviously the woman had violated this rule and so it was no concern of theirs. They did not bother about what went on with the Baron's people. Later the narrator learned that the local people did not interfere in such matters thanks primarily to the Baron's largesse to their community.

The narrator was now greatly intrigued: where did all the Baron's money come from; why was the unknown girl attempting to flee the château; and, most fascinating of all, who really was the Baron? At this early moment in his history Lavaysse only noticed peripherally the one thing in Offenbach that was to prove the most fateful of all for his own life: Frank's beautiful daughter and eventual successor, Eve, the sect's promiscuous *betulah.* Instead what immediately most preoccupied him were the "cold thunderbolts" that had flashed through the Prince's windows after he had begun denouncing the Baron.

For Israel Zangwill, as for his protagonist Lavaysse, the mists that had shrouded his reason for the past twenty-five years were lifting. Light shone through his dark "inner world of dreams," and in "The Baron of Offenbach" Zangwill was attempting to break away from his deluded mystification and return to the rational skepticism of his youthful Jewish essays and novels. To do so, he had to understand how it happened that he had come to be lost.

His particular Zionism, the attempt to rescue East European Jewry and its unacculturated heritage from Eastern tyranny and Western assimilation, had become his own hypnotic pseudomessianic cause. Like the protagonist of "The Baron of Offenbach," Zangwill had become transformed and mesmerized by an entrancing mystification. The Spinozan rationalist of his early essays and novels, with his genuine concern over the persecution of the Jews trapped under the hostile rule of Russian autocracy and with his cautious exploration of historical positivist approaches to contemporary Jewish thought, had for the past twenty-five years forgotten his original judgments about reality and, instead, had become a fervent and unquestioning worker for the swift creation at any cost of a territorial reserve designed to save the oppressed Eastern Jews and preserve intact their traditional culture.

But the shocks of the immediate postwar period jolted Zangwill suddenly awake. The mist arising from decades of inner dreaming slowly dissipated, and he began realizing what had been happening to him for the past twenty years, how he had somehow become distracted from his rationalist perspective and had wandered down a false path. By 1923 he had decided to regain his original views and to do so by reviving those talents he had abandoned for so many years: his creative abilities as a Jewish novelist and his speculative insights as a historical positivist. In his new novel, "The Baron of Offenbach," he intended to describe the transformation that had occurred in him and, by means of a full exploration of these events in a fictional setting, to arrive at an understanding of how he had allowed himself to be seduced from his rational intellectual skepticism into irrational activist mystification.

From the descriptions of the Baron in the novel, it is clear that he is modeled, for Zangwill's autobiographic purposes, on the portrait of Theodore Herzl presented in *Dreamers of the Ghetto.* Such a parallel would have been obvious at the time, for Herzl, too, had been understood by many during his lifetime as a messianic figure, although as a secularist he vehemently eschewed any such interpretation of himself or his Zionist activities. But while Zangwill did not ever himself imagine that Herzl represented a messianic event, he did eventually, by 1901, come to believe that Herzlian Zionism could serve a salvific function for East European Jews and their Judaism.

However, it is also evident from suggestions in the manuscript that while the protagonist was fascinated by the Baron, he was enthralled by his daughter and successor, Eve (or Eva), and that it was she who eventually led him away from reason. But who was this Eve for Zangwill? Probably not the ITO, which he still was not ready to repudiate. More likely she represents Zangwill's Zionist dream of an immediate homeland that drove him frenetically after Herzl's death. But not enough is written about her in the fragment of "The Baron of Offenbach" to judge this supposition for sure.

At this preliminary stage of composition, however, what most concerned Zangwill was not to develop extensively his theme but to pose the question: how had he allowed himself to become so radically transformed? He asks this question explicitly in Lavaysse's memoir of his own metamorphosis. Reflecting back on the fateful events from the distance of his old age, the narrator recalls himself most intrigued by the Baron's "cold thunderbolts": "For I suddenly remembered in my finger-tips that the bolt of my Jove [the Baron] had launched through the [Prince's] window was not flaming, but stone-cold. Surely an authentic fire-bolt from the skies would at least have scorched the paper, if not melted the seal!"[63]

Reminiscing about his thoughts at the time and searching for his motives, Lavaysse writes in his memoir:

> Looking back now in cold blood, I fail to see why this matter should have taken such a grip on me. At the time it seemed to be the pressing duty of a good Voltairean to resent this supernatural galimatias—I recall I was particularly irritated by the second resurrection of the burned letter, and again it seemed a sort of knight-errantry to rescue the woman who was obviously imprisoned there. Yet perhaps at bottom, my real motive was obscurely connected with the glimpse I had had of all those beautiful girls on that sunlit lawn. They were like the chorus maidens I had seen in *Athalie* or *Esther*, I remember thinking, only this time the girls were real daughters of Judah and Levi. Perhaps, like that young Johannes [Goethe], I had a penchant for going behind the scenes. Or was it after all simply Destiny?[64]

What had been driving Zangwill into two decades of mystification? Had it been the fascination with Herzl's charismatic appeal, or the chivalrous challenge of rescuing East European Jewry, or the romantic vision of a Jewry physically renewed within their own homeland, or the ability to see the inner reality behind the appearances of events, or was it merely the prescribed fate of all ethnic heretics? The question remains ultimately unanswered.

Zangwill had arrived at a natural breaking point in his writing and decided that a pause would reinvigorate his creativity before continuing to recount his story and answer Lavaysse's question. Therefore he now saw no reason to refuse Wise's suggestion that he undertake an American lecture tour. As he explained quite reasonably to his American friend, "the back of the work will be broken [by the time of the tour], and the interruption will not be so serious now."[65] This decision was particularly sensible as Zangwill's health was always delicate. But perhaps, too, as the mist of dreams diminished, the searching glare of reason's light was becoming too painful for Zangwill to bear for long, and he craved a pleasant diversion from the burden of searching out his soul's secrets.

But standing at the podium on the stage at Carnegie Hall, the "cold thunderbolts" of Israel Zangwill's "inner dreams" abruptly crashed through the fragile panes of his consciousness and shattered the flickering light of his reason once again. The mist rushed back into its accustomed haunts and formed anew the old illusions he had been struggling so desperately to dispel.

Upon returning home he never again was able to return to his work on "The Baron of Offenbach" and its unanswered question. In fact, after 1923 the only attempt by Zangwill to write on Jewish thought was his 1925 essay, "My Religion," in which he restated his view, first expressed in 1888, that among the "Hebrew prophets," Jesus was "the latest and greatest example," and he repeated his Spinozan claim that "there is very little difference among the higher [religious] creeds of to-day."[66] This article is interesting because for the first time the views expressed in it aroused considerable indignation among Jewish readers, although Zangwill had explicitly espoused these positions for over thirty-five years: seeing what had been there all the time indicates the public's altered evaluation of Zangwill since his Carnegie Hall speech, not a change in his view.

Instead, what drove Zangwill to write was that final illusion—one not about the Jewish people and their "mission" nor about America and its Hebraic values, but about Israel Zangwill himself. This one entrenched illusion that had pursued him even into the novel, where he made his protagonist a successful international dramatist, now took complete possession of him. From this time onward, he would work feverishly to transform it from his personal dream into a public reality, even unto death.

We Moderns

Toward the end of his American tour Zangwill, complaining that he was "overstrung, overworked, overphoned and dependent upon drugs for sleep," announced that he had decided to retire into "an Ivory Tower of Silence."[67] His "Tower" was in the south of England, near the seaside.

As a bachelor, Israel Zangwill had spent most of his time at his

London rooms in Hare Court, The Temple. Although he kept his chambers there throughout the remainder of his professional career, when he married Edith Chaplin Ayrton in 1903 he also purchased a country house for his future family and began spending extended periods of time there, resting his always frail constitution and socializing with relatives and literary friends.

The house, Far End, lay in the small town of East Preston in Sussex and provided a peaceful relief to the frenzied pace of life in the capital of the British Empire. It was at Far End that the couple raised their three children: the eldest, Ayrton ("George"), who would study engineering and migrate about the North American continent; Margaret ("Peggy"), who survived both her brothers but whose entire adult life would be confined to a Swiss mental asylum; and Oliver, the youngest, who was to enjoy a distinguished career as professor of psychology at Cambridge.

It was to Far End that Zangwill retired to recuperate after his harrowing 1923 American lecture tour. Here he and Edith hosted lawn parties for their Sussex neighbors, amused the children by organizing family drama productions and picnic outings, occasioning even leisurely venturing off toward the sea on horseback, at times accompanied by their two-year-old nephew, Michael Ayrton, who was later to become well respected as an accomplished artist and sculptor. Periodically, too, Dr. Marie Stopes, Britain's indefatigable campaigner for planned parenthood, would motor down to visit Israel and Edith, acquaintances since the couples' active, if rather desultory, involvement in the suffragist struggles of the century's first decade.

But none of these placid *divertissements* succeeded in penetrating Zangwill's cumbrous gloom. Even on the most casual of occasions, he invariably presented the dour image of the Victorian gentleman, dressed formally in coat and tie, a starched collar at attention to bolster the immobile, melancholia-etched face, pince-nez perched upon its nose, and thinning white hair lying lank atop its skull. His might have been the look of Jane Austen's Edmund Bertram if, after having achieved a rational understanding of the true character of his former beloved, he had lived out the remainder of his life without a Fanny Price there to solace his suffering. For Zangwill, only a final, triumphant public recognition of his artistic mastery might achieve such a consolation. And faintly glimmering within the depths of his imagination, promise of just this vindicating consolation seemed to beckon.

Upon arriving at Far End he intended to observe scrupulously the public vow, made shortly before departing from the United States,

Israel Zangwill with his daughter Peggy, costumed to play Ophelia, August 1923. *Courtesy, Shirley Zangwill.*

that "he would never again speak on the Jewish question"; instead he had resolved to devote himself exclusively to drama.[68] Once at home in Sussex he was eagerly anticipating the forthcoming Broadway opening of his new play, a satirical comedy. Indeed, he was very much counting on the popular success of this drama to win for him the sort of acclaim that would make him the chief rival of Noel Coward, whom he greatly envied for his current theatrical triumphs.[69] And it was most certainly the promising responses to the draft of this play from friendly readers that, more than any other consideration, finally persuaded Zangwill to agree to break off writing "The Baron of Offenbach" and accept Wise's American lecture proposal.

But this latest stage effort, *We Moderns,* was instead the trigger of the most serious of all the repercussions for Zangwill arising from his American tour. That this play should have been so very consequential in Zangwill's life and motivations is at first rather surprising, inasmuch as his extensive efforts on its behalf while in America attracted virtually no public notice at the time. But this widespread ignorance of his artistic endeavors during the course of the lecture tour clearly illustrates Zangwill's deeply bifurcated identity: while popular attention was attracted by Zangwill's roiling Jewish lectures and disputes, the "other" Zangwill, the serious British dramatist, had also arrived in the country and was quietly going about arranging for production of his most recent play.

As the playwright himself explained in an interview upon arriving in New York on 6 October 1923, he had come to the United States to complete the final act of *We Moderns,* his latest satire, and hoped that the promising young American actress Helen Hayes (b. 1900, in Washington, D.C.) would accept the starring role in it, as she had already read the play's first act and had expressed great enthusiasm about the part.[70]

We Moderns is a rather prim "Post-War Comedy in Three Movements" about the conflict of values espoused by parents and children, reminiscent of themes in Zangwill's and Cowen's 1888 satire, "Under Sentence of Marriage."[71] The plot revolves around a series of amusing clashes between the modern perspective as declaimed by the charming ingenue Mary Sundale, her brother Dick, and their friends, and the Victorian perspective as expostulated by the Sundale parents. Eventually the play happily resolves itself in a dialectical synthesis of views drawn from both the Victorian thesis and the modernist antithesis. As Zangwill himself explained, "It was the object of my comedy to offer an eirenicon to the warring generations, to hold the balance between the old and the new, and to resolve the discord in the common pity and tragedy of life."[72]

The play opened on the road in Washington during the final week of December 1923, with Helen Hayes playing the part of Mary Sundale. It received mixed reviews, with one critic mentioning that "the strength [of the satire] lies mostly in the first act."[73] On 11 March 1924, *We Moderns* premiered, with Miss Hayes as Mary, in New York at the Gaity Theatre.

Although the critics generally praised the actors, they were merciless with regard to Zangwill's skills as a dramatist. One critic commented that " 'We Moderns' is dull, formless, and muddled. It is like an attic into which, soon or later, everything of the household is tossed."[74] Another critic observed:

> [Zangwill] is now and then interesting and provides considerable laughter. But most folk who have a sense of reality in the world about them of the probabilities of human conduct and of the prevailing integrity of character will find themselves troubled with a great unrest. . . .
>
> . . . The several people in both generations are not properly characters but only types. . . . But of life there is not a breath. There are only moral reflections and the . . . quantity of epigrams which comes as if from a phonograph hidden in hollow insides.
>
> . . . Mr. Zangwill does not seem to be aware how artificial this comedy is.
>
> . . . The airy, fantastic satirist which Mr. Zangwill struggles to become is submerged in the realist and humanist which he essentially is.[75]

From Far End, Zangwill lashed out angrily at the unfavorable response to the New York production of *We Moderns* and at its unexpectedly short run at the Gaity of less than a month. He claimed that his play obviously had not been judged at all on its artistic merits but had "become the scapegoat of my sin in criticizing America."[76] How else to explain its failure when one considers that the production "had every factor of success: entertainment, popular ethics, a happy ending, . . . a splendid company . . . containing at least one player of genius in the person of Miss Helen Hayes"?[77] To Zangwill, therefore, it was patently manifest that "when a play with such abounding elements of vitality . . . is found dead in New York, the verdict can only be 'Murder.' "[78] And should there be any question about this conclusion one need only consider that "generally failures are allowed to slip out quietly. But as if to put their motives beyond dispute, some of my critics even devote articles with big head-lines to the obsequies, full of indecent jubilation."[79]

Zangwill was now determined to secure at any cost international recognition that he was a talented dramatist, comparable to Noel Coward. This desired recognition had, indeed, been the primary purpose in writing his new play. So to prove wrong the "prejudiced" American critics and theater-going public he resolved to undertake any venture necessary to assure that *We Moderns* would be produced in England, where he had not recently been involved in any public controversy. For, despite the consistent failure of his previous plays with the British public and drama critics, he was convinced that at home his latest satire would certainly be acclaimed for its intrinsic artistic merits, and its author's estimation of himself as a significant dramatist would be vindicated.

At about the same time, Robert Atkins, who had achieved a considerable reputation for his productions of Shakespeare at the Old Vic, decided to establish his own theater company. When he learned of this remarkable opportunity, Zangwill contacted Atkins and urged him to produce *We Moderns* as the inaugural presentation of his new company. The famed producer agreed, and Zangwill's play premiered in Britain on the road in Southport in April 1925. Then, on 7 July 1925, Aktins's production of *We Moderns* opened in London at the New Theatre.[80]

The British critics were as harsh in their estimation of the play as had been the American critics. Noting that Zangwill is certainly no Shakespeare, the *Outlook* reviewer complained that

> the young Sundales . . . are chattering marionettes and not real people. . . . Mr. Zangwill does not add lightness of touch and firmness of purpose in the execution of his play. . . . And "We Moderns," for all its crop of epigrams, lacks that true dramatic wit which arises from situation, plot, and character, and is in its nature ephemeral and not quite worthy of the distinction we have learned to associate with the names of both author and producer.[81]

The *Spectator* and the *Times* (London) concurred in these observations and, in addition, complained that all the attitudes were so "old fashioned" that even the children's postwar "modernist" views represented attitudes much more typical of nineteenth-century bohemians than those of the contemporary generation.[82] The *Spectator* reviewer suggested that "Mr. Zangwill, one dares to say, has not met

Israel Zangwill. *Courtesy, The Mansell Collection.*

the young generation. Or, if he has, he unfortunately and unconsciously refutes his own argument that the older people really understand the young."[83]

As an experienced producer, Atkins quickly proposed some relatively minor alterations to the play in response to the critics' complaints and the impending failure of the production. But Zangwill, who had always refused any outside interference with his writer's prerogative, adamantly rejected all his suggestions. An acrimonious dispute between producer and playwright ensued, and Atkins finally concluded that he had no alternative but to close his production of *We Moderns*.[84]

Furious and desperate, Zangwill decided that he must produce the play himself. Although without any experience at all as a producer, Zangwill devoted himself and his financial resources completely to realizing his new project. Although already seriously ailing in health even before the Atkins rehearsals of *We Moderns* began, Zangwill now recklessly and enthusiastically threw himself into the show's preparations, traveling up by rail regularly from East Preston to London in order to supervise each detail of production.

Zangwill arranged to stage *We Moderns* at the Fortune Theatre, which had been built and was currently owned by Laurence Cowen, whose brother Louis had been Zangwill's early collaborator as "J. Freeman Bell." But completely without experience in handling the multifarious details involved in any theatrical production, Zangwill was soon overwhelmed by a plethora of minutia, resulting in numerous confusions, delays, unexpected expenses, and a lawsuit. But, finally, *We Moderns* reopened in London on 12 September 1925. It again failed miserably.[85]

And as the play failed so did Israel Zangwill's health. While completing its happy third act on his 1923 American tour, Zangwill was already being medicated for chronic insomnia. By December 1924 he informed a correspondent that he was in "very poor health" and had been ordered by his physician to "lie very low" when it came to public appearances.[86] By June 1925, while feverishly working on producing *We Moderns*, he had been forced by weakening health to resign as president of the ITO and "to restrict my activities to a minimum."[87] At the same time, his insomnia was worsening and even incapacitating him at times from attending rehearsals of his own production of *We Moderns*.[88]

The failure of *We Moderns* did nothing to reduce Zangwill's exhausting preoccupation with his career as a producer. In April 1926, commenting that he had "had a bad night last night," he explained that "I am still worried by the burrs of my theatrical adventure" and complained that the continuing repercussions arising from his attempt at theater management "only adds to my worry and insomnia."[89]

Zangwill's physical and mental health deteriorated seriously during the following two months as the incessant insomnia and anxiety acted upon his always fragile physical constitution. No longer capable of doing any work, he was confined to his home. And at the beginning of July, Edith Zangwill admitted to a friend who was intending to come down to Far End for a visit, "My husband has had a serious nervous breakdown, and is in a nursing home."[90] On 1 August 1926 Israel Zangwill unexpectedly died at the nursing home in Midhurst, Sussex; he was sixty-two years old. The funeral, at which the rabbi of London's Liberal Jewish Synagogue, St. John's Wood, officiated, was held on 5 August at the Golders Green Crematorium; Stephen S. Wise, visiting from the United States, delivered the eulogy.[91]

So it was that Israel Zangwill lived intensely, struggled valiantly, and died defeated, one additional *maggid*'s tale of Dreamers of the Ghetto.

ELEVEN

Epilogue: A Midrash

> To be a Jew means not being able to get away from God
> Even if one wishes to;
> Not being able to stop praying
> Even after all the prayers,
> Even after all the evens.
>
> Aaron Zeitlin[1]

After telling his *mashal,* his parable, the *maggid* would provide a *midrash,* an explanatory commentary, on it. Sometimes the *midrash* he chose was from the common stock explanations ready at hand to members of his profession; sometimes it was innovative and original with him. But even in the latter case the *midrash* always derived from, and was rooted in, the wisdom of the Sages. So, too, is our *midrash.*

For Israel Zangwill was a pioneer living and exploring the dilemma of the contemporary Jew and the plight of modern man. His life and his writings are not merely those of an individual, however interesting he may be in himself, but they also illustrate the experiences of many others. To recognize how this is so, the themes with which he struggled need to be traced explicitly. This will allow us to recognize these same themes and struggles in the works of others, Jew and non-Jew. And then, from these common elements may be sought an explanation of the source of their—and our—shared predicament.

Chad Gadya

From the very beginning of his literary career, Israel Zangwill was preoccupied with the psychological alienation and social alienation experienced by the Westernized Jew. Throughout his life he sought solutions to these twin experiences. But as all of his theoretical and artistic attempts at resolving them only confirmed the alienation, his preoccupation became transmogrified into obsession. He deliberately abandoned the interior life of writing for one in the exterior realm of politics and marriage in his continuing search for some means to escape, or at least to alleviate, his own pain and that which he perceived afflicted his fellow Jews and indeed all Western peoples.

As early as the 1888 short story, "Under Sentence of Marriage," Zangwill (and Louis Cowen) described the psychological alienation of the Western Jew, the "child," from his traditional Jewish past, "the father" within. The same alienation explicitly appears again in his 1889 essay, "English Judaism," as he wavers between his enthusiastic exploration of a Western historical positivist Judaism for contemporary Anglo-Jewry and his nostalgic retrospective on the religious life pulsating through the vanishing Judaism of the traditional ghetto of Eastern Europe.

In his early draft of *Children of the Ghetto,* Zangwill describes the psychological alienation of Anglo-Jews and their social alienation. Thus the Anglicized son, Alfred, is unable to share the perspective of his pious old father, whose home and the memories it contains provide a welcome relief from the tempests of the world; but it is a home in which he can no longer live nor even feel comfortable for very long. But, in addition, the Anglicized Alfred, in his very defiance of the practices of his home and of traditional Judaism, nevertheless encounters an implacable social alienation from his non-Jewish British acquaintances. The draft abruptly ends with Alfred alone within himself, alienated from past and present, and with no solution proffered.

Children of the Ghetto, amid all its humor and its Dickensian descriptions, also traces these twin alienations afflicting the lives and experiences of several of its major characters. Despite all the theorizing in Book Two, the only relief for psychological alienation the novel can offer is the concluding vision of its protagonists, Esther and Joseph, sailing off to a new world, to America, a land of "hopes and dreams."

The issue of social alienation is confronted more confidently, if not more directly, in *Children of the Ghetto.* For, unlike psychological alienation, this issue is not explored so much in the text of the novel itself as in the very decision about how to write it. Like the earlier authors of the Western "ghetto" stories, Zangwill, convinced of the ameliorating effects of education, intended his novel as a fictional antidote to the negative literary stereotype of the Jew. He was confident that Anglo-Jews, properly portrayed in all their humanity, would succeed in bridging the barrier between themselves and their English compatriots.

But, despite its critical and popular successes, the novel did not succeed in eliminating the social alienation any more than had the Western "ghetto" stories. And the anguish of psychological alienation intensified and appeared afterward not only in Zangwill's later Jewish stories but in non-Jewish works as well. Finally, in *Dreamers of the Ghetto,* he confronted the twin dilemmas directly.

Particularly in the story "Joseph the Dreamer," Zangwill addresses most immediately the question of how to resolve effectively the issue of the Jew's social alienation. Joseph, the protagonist, by choosing to share in both identities, seeks to enlighten both Christian and Jew through the unity of truth they each claim exclusively as their own and thereby to eliminate the artificial walls entrapping and deforming both groups. But just because of these walls and their deforming effects, the lonely Joseph finds himself bitterly denounced and defeated in his endeavor by both groups, and eventually he is executed. Only in death does Joseph bring together Jew and non-Jew.

A similar unhappy fate awaits the unnamed Westernized narrator in "Chad Gadya" as he contemplates the beauty of Passover in his father's home and contrasts it with his own spiritual impoverishment and emotional disquietude. But the distance separating father and son is too immense, the psychological alienation too great, and the narrator, unable to return home and unwilling to endure further his sterile cerebral meanderings, commits suicide. Only in death does the narrator finally find peace from the storms raging within himself.

Driven by the pessimism expressed so eloquently in *Dreamers of the Ghetto,* by the turn of the new century Zangwill had concluded that the source of these alienations afflicting the Jews lay in their twinned, hyphenated identities, that is, that terms such as "Western Jewry" and "Anglo-Jewry" were oxymorons. Psychological and social serenity lay therefore in wholeheartedly embracing a single identity, in severing "Jew" from "Western" and "Anglo."

By 1903 he had become convinced that to accomplish this separation of identities the Jews of the West must thoroughly amalgamate into the non-Jewish culture and society, as indeed liberal philosophy had been advocating since the eighteenth century. Accordingly, the finest example of this path was the great "melting pot" that was America. And for East European Jews, so far preserved from the "contamination" of twinned identities, their unitary Jewish identity must be preserved in some autonomous national land of refuge from physical persecution and from mental anguish.

Promptly acting upon his conviction of dual historical fates awaiting the Jews, Zangwill married a non-Jew and cast his own family's future exclusively with the English. Simultaneously, he abandoned his career as a storyteller to campaign relentlessly for a Territorialist future for East European Jewry.

But like the characters in *Dreamers of the Ghetto,* Zangwill failed to convince his audiences. Anglo-Jews, American Jews, East European Jews, Zionists, and non-Jewish European nationalities all angrily repudiated his message. Even Zangwill, now an apparently deracinated country gentleman at Far End, together with his English wife, immersed himself thoroughly in the causes of Jewish Territorialism, militant Zionism, and the continuing spiritual mission of Judaism.

Over two decades later Zangwill finally realized that his lovely diaphanous vision of the Jewish future was only the beguilement of a dream and that objective reality, on the other hand, is hard as sapphire. But it was an awareness that came too late, and the burden of failure was too great. Like Joseph in *Dreamers of the Ghetto* and the narrator in "Chad Gadya," Israel Zangwill finally achieved only that peace and unity that lies buried in death.

However, neither his experience of psychological and social alienations nor his responses to them are unique to Zangwill. Although he was one of the earliest and most articulate in portraying them effectively in the medium of secular literature, similar expressions of these dilemmas, together with parallel responses to them, have appeared in Jewish literature since his death. One of the most striking and eloquent examples is that found in the work of the American Yiddish poet, Jacob Glatstein (1896–1971).

The Polish-born poet emigrated to the United States when he was sixteen, on the eve of the First World War. Much of his poetry is suffused with the pangs of psychological alienation, allegorized, as in Zangwill, as the separation of the son's world from that of his father. And like Zangwill, too, this alienation, this separation, is experienced as a painful loss for the son, now irredeemably bereft of his own past and buffeted about by the blind impersonal forces of a vacuous present.

Resounding through much of Zangwill's Jewish fiction, from the early draft of *Children of the Ghetto* through *Dreamers of the Ghetto*'s "Chad Gadya," is the nostalgic portrayal of the father's joyful immersion in his traditional holy days and rituals and of his son's psychological inability to share these experiences and therefore also his inability even to participate externally in the festivals and ceremonies. That which is natural and pleasing for the father has become alien and burdensome for the son. This same theme Glatstein portrays beautifully in his 1961 poem, "Sabbath":

At times when a boy I measured
My desecrated Sabbath
As an ordinary weekday
Against my father's Sabbath—
Sanctified and meticulous.
Even then it was clear to me,
That my Sabbath was like a shortened Friday vanishing.
My father's Sabbath lived a year of mine.

His Sabbath-rest was a fully laden life.
As many profanations I plunged my Sabbath into,
So the day in its desecrations fled.
Each of my boyish pranks shortened the Sabbath.
My father in a single Sabbath beheld so much radiant delight,
Prayed, learned, sang,
Loved my mother with fresh eyes.

At times when a boy I followed like a shadow
My father's Sabbath with all its commands.
Me the singing Sabbath-Jew
With his homey calm fatigued,
With his delightsome deeds, dearly punished.

Gradually all the bewilderment claimed me.
I dropped off and fell asleep.
I dreamed
A silver trumpeter blew of his own accord.
My father immediately took off all his weekday-clothing.
The Sabbath descended upon him
Like a silken morning gown.

Far from me, under a brilliant sun,
He was seated and to him there
Was I unable to reach.
The Sabbath was long as the whole of Lublin.
The sun did not set
Until my father gave
A singing sign.[2]

Glatstein is also powerfully influenced by experiences of the Jew's harsh social alienation, experiences that Zangwill earlier had portrayed and combated with his fiction and that were among the forces that eventually converted him to Territorialism and militant Zionism. Thus for Zangwill, the Anglo-Jew, social alienation must result in the equally unpalatable but inevitable processes of an amalgamating "melting pot" for Western Jewry and of a separatist "land of refuge" for East European Jewry and their Judaism. For Glatstein, the East European immigrant, on the other hand, the "melting pot" of acculturation and assimilation is a mere chimera; the separatism of the ghetto, deforming as it must be, has become the only possible Jewish response to continuing social alienation.

In 1938, in one of his most famous poems, "Good Night World," Glatstein militantly proclaims his Jewish separatism:

Good night, wide world,
Great, stinking world.
Not you, but I slam the gate.
With my long robe,
With my fiery, yellow patch,
With my proud pace,
On my own order—
I return to the ghetto.
Obliterate, stamp out all the apostate traces.
I roll in your rubbish,
Praise, praise, praise,
Humpbacked Jewish life.
Excommunication, world, on your unkosher cultures.
Although all is ravaged,
I dust myself in your dust,
Mournful Jewish life.[3]

Fifteen years later he addresses the same theme in an extraordinarily lovely, hauntingly sad poem, "Beginning":

Shall we perhaps begin small and wobbly
With a small people?
Weary we both homeless among the peoples.
Farmers will bow to You.
You will live on our sacrifices
From burnt offerings of meal.
I will go about and tell folk wisdoms
That will stay within our borders,
But the least child will
Greet me with Good-Morning.

Shall we perhaps both go home
And begin again small from the very beginning?
. . . .
We followed You into the world,
Became sick with Your world.
Rescue Yourself and come with the immigrants
Back to a small land,
Become again the Jewish God.[4]

Zangwill and Glatstein, each from the depths of his own personal anguish and from the plight of his fellow Jews, have produced remarkable literary expressions of the modern alienation from self and from others and its manifestation in consciousness as the affliction of twinned identities. But these bitter experiences of psychological alienation and social alienation are not confined to Western Jewry. They have also profoundly penetrated the consciousness of other Western ethnic minorities.[5] This alienation is particularly evident in the case for black Americans, and their entanglement in twinned identities and alienations are signally evoked in the remarkable life and writings of a contemporary of Zangwill, W. E. B. Du Bois.

Dusk of Dawn

Remarkable parallels occur between the lives of Israel Zangwill and W. E. B. Du Bois. Both were outsiders to many of the experiences of their own people whom they earnestly wished to serve; both were men of high intelligence, sensitive insight, and notable literary talent; both emerged as controversial spokesmen for their own people by the first decade of the twentieth century and joined organizations devoted to the improvement of their people's conditions against ethnic bias and violence; both became haunted by despair at the apparent failure of accomplishing their goals immediately and slipped away from the nonmalleable hardness of objective reality into the flexible illusions of doctrinal dreams; both eventually adopted strident ethnic separatist doctrines that forced them to resign from the ethnic movements in which they had been playing a prominent role and that forced them to face denunciation and ostracism by mainstream ethnic leaders; and, finally, both were incessantly plagued by an inescapable consciousness of their twinned identities.

As Zangwill had been born into a family in which the parents displayed differing historical perspectives, so too William Edward Burghardt Du Bois's parents represented divergent traditions; his father's family descended from French Huguenots, while his mother's family was primarily African in ancestry.[6] And again mirroring Zangwill's youth, Du Bois attended Fisk and Harvard universities as a scholarship student.[7]

But what is most striking is that, like Zangwill who was an outsider to the immigrant East End where he received his schooling at the JFS and which he later sought to describe and guide, so, too, Du Bois, born 22 February 1868, in Great Barrington, Massachusetts, was equally an outsider, both to the American slave heritage and to the rural experiences of the post–Civil War Southern black masses, also encountering them first as a quite extraordinary student at Fisk University in Nashville, Tennessee.[8]

Like the precocious Zangwill in England, Du Bois in America quickly displayed a willingness to proffer unsolicited guidance to his people and an aggressive combativeness to those within his community with whom he disagreed. These characteristics became evident by 1905 when he became embroiled in a bitter, irreconcilable dispute over strategy and objectives with the most prominent American black leader of the time, Booker T. Washington. As with Zangwill these traits of independence of thought, frankness of expression, and contentious aggressiveness marked Du Bois's entire public career.

Acting on his own sociopolitical analysis and responding to the mounting racial violence and discrimination experienced by black Americans, in 1905 Du Bois, then on the faculty of Atlanta University, initiated the founding of the Niagara Movement to promote political and economic equality for all citizens; in 1910 this group merged into the newly organized National Association for the Advancement of Colored People (NAACP).

At the same time that Du Bois was actively promoting sociopolitical racial integration, he was equally concerned over the preservation of black culture and bemoaned the erosion of its rural Southern expression through the encroachments of voracious, homogenizing modernity.[9] For Du Bois, black culture was not parochial but the bearer of a universal message: "For the development of Negro genius, of Negro literature and art, of Negro spirit, only Negroes bound and welded together, Negroes inspired by one vast ideal, can work out in its fullness the great message we have for humanity."[10] And like his British counterpart, he too formulated its universal contribution in trinitarian terms: "What has this Beauty to do with the world? What has Beauty to do with Truth and Goodness . . . ? The [Negro] apostle of Beauty thus becomes the apostle of Truth and Right not by choice but by inner and outer compulsion."[11]

Du Bois's dual careers as advocate of racial integration and equality and as defender of black culture and solidarity is reflected in his growing consciousness of his twinned identities. Already in 1897, he asks:

> What, after all, am I? Am I an American or am I a Negro? Can I be both? . . .
>
> . . . We are Americans, not only by birth and by citizenship, but by our political ideals, our language, our religion. Farther than that, our Americanism does not go. At that point, we are Negroes, members of a vast historic race.[12]

In his 1903 book, *The Souls of Black Folk,* he provides a remarkable description of the painful experience of contending twin identities:

> It is a peculiar sensation, this double consciousness. . . . One ever feels his two-ness,—an American, a Negro; two souls, two unreconciled strivings; two warring ideals in one dark body. . . . This waste of double aims, this seeking to satisfy two unreconciled ideals, has wrought sad havoc with the courage and faith and deeds of ten thousand thousand people,—has sent them often wooing false gods and invoking false means of salvation, and at times has even seemed about to make them ashamed of themselves.[13]

As it happened, Du Bois was himself not immune from "wooing false gods and invoking false means of salvation." In 1919, he attended the Paris Peace Conference officially and, despite vigorous opposition from the European colonial powers, organized the first Pan-African Congress there. But, like Zangwill, he was disillusioned by the Treaty of Versailles and returned to the United States with a radically new agenda for international and domestic race relations.

He, as had the Territorialist leader Zangwill, now also came to view a territorial base as necessary to sustain a healthy sense of ethnic identity. In 1919 he wrote, "The African movement means to us what the Zionist movement must mean to the Jews, the centralization of race effort and the recognition of a racial fount."[14] And for black Americans, suffering from the imposition of segregation, "a contemptuous isolation," Du Bois, like his British counterpart, now advocated a separatist ethnic autonomy and policy of self-help, although also allowing for a possible future emigration to a land of freedom.[15]

The separatist program Du Bois advocated increasingly brought him into ideological conflict with the integrationist program of the NAACP, and, ineluctably, in 1935 he resigned from the organization he had helped found and had served for twenty-five years. But the continuing lack of any practical success for his own separatist program generated a mounting frustration that drove him ever further into the embrace of delusive political panaceas. Following the Second World War he actively identified with pro-Soviet organizations in the United States and abroad, attracting the punitive attention of the federal government, especially during the early 1950s. Finally, in 1961, despairing of the future of blacks in the United States, Du Bois accepted an invitation from Kwame Nkrumah to settle across the sea in a land of "hope and dreams," in the "old new land" of Ghana. And it was there, in self-imposed exile from the land of his birth, that in 1963 W. E. B. Du Bois died at the age of ninety-five.

But his legacy is still very much alive. The "double consciousness" he so trenchantly described now seriously afflicts many black Americans. It is that agonizing consciousness of what one author, reflecting upon his own experience, describes as being "double-bound," as possessing twin identities, and yet also being aware that "I could have one but not both."[16] And as in the case of modern Jews, this is not a unitary phenomenon but rather the expression in consciousness of both social alienation and psychological alienation.

The social alienation reflects the persistent subtle racial barrier in America still separating black from white despite the triumph of legal and civic equality. It is analogous to the social alienation that the Jews of Western Europe faced despite the triumph of the Emancipation.

The psychological alienation among black Americans would seem to differ in its external expression from that of the Jews. For the Jews, this alienation often was symbolically projected as the insurmountable generational alienation of the acculturated, assimilated children from the traditional patterns of life of their parents. For black Americans, on the other hand, as a result of differing historical experiences, psychological alienation may be projected symbolically within the black community itself in terms of the conflicting loyalties antagonizing relations between two social classes, that is, as a conflict between the black middle class (e.g., Du Bois's "talented tenth") and the black masses (e.g., for Du Bois, in 1905, clearly represented by Booker T. Washington).

In any case, the experience of twinned identities, of double consciousness, is neither idiosyncratic to Israel Zangwill nor even to Western Jewry. It has clearly been the distressing experience of other individuals and continues seriously to trouble the lives of a significant portion of contemporary humanity.[17]

The Small City

To achieve some understanding of the etiology of the phenomenon of social and psychological alienations and their conscious expression as conflicting twinned identities, it is necessary to discuss briefly the history of the philosophy of the human personality (i.e., the psyche, the soul, the self). For it is in modern perceptions of the nature of the human personality that the difficulty lies.

Classical and medieval philosophy analyzed the human personality as ontologically bipolar, consisting of two components.[18] One, the animating, vivifies the otherwise inert physical body and also includes the instinctual drives, affects, imagination, and practical wit (i.e., "common sense"); these are all characteristics that the human species shares with the animals. What distinguishes mankind from all other corporeal creatures is the second component, the intellective faculty, consisting of wisdom (*chochma, intellectus*), the initial flash of noetic insight, and understanding (*bina, ratio*), the logical cognitive expansion of insight into the totality of its implications; it is also from this intellective faculty alone that the distinctively human perception of morality derives.

Attendant to this inherent bipolarity of the human psyche is the tension between its two components. Originating in the unconscious, each faculty attempts to attract the individual's consciousness into the exclusive service of its own purposes.[19] Traditional philosophy accepted not only the ontological necessity of human bipolarity but also recognized the resulting necessary inner tension arising from it. For the two components are not autonomous and isolated from each other but, rather, are competitors. What the philosophers, rabbis, and priests, each in his own manner, sought to accomplish was to provide people with the means by which their essential human qualities, reason and morality, might prevail over and effectively utilize the qualities and energies of the animating forces of the body.

Traditional philosophy also developed a hierarchical cosmology that complemented this analysis of the bipolar personality. Thus in physics, too, a dualism existed between the laws governing the terrestrial sphere of mutability and the laws governing the immutable celestial sphere. Similarly in metaphysics, too, there were the dual realms of the corporeal and the incorporeal. Thus the microcosm, man, mirrored the macrocosm, the whole of creation.

But the elaborate structure of this millennia-old cosmology came under severe attack during the course of the sixteenth century as it became increasingly evident that no dualism existed in physics and that terrestrial physical laws applied equally to the cosmos. Because of the traditional hierarchical parallel bipolarities, this development in science therefore challenged not only Aristotelian physics and Ptolemaic astronomy but also the philosophic analyses of the human microcosm and the spiritual macrocosm. In Christian Europe, this challenge to traditional cosmology eventually ignited a bitter conflict between the defenders of religious doctrine and the disciples of scientific investigation.[20]

Finally, in the seventeenth century René Descartes (1596–1650) provided a pragmatic compromise accommodating the claims of both the religious and the scientific perspectives.[21] In accord with the postulates of the new science, he replaced the traditional hierarchical bipolarities in humanity, the world and creation, with an ontological vertical dualism of mind and matter, each defined as a substance governed by its own unitary system of laws and forever autonomous and beyond the influence of the other. The proper sphere of religious and philosophic study was now defined as "mind," while the proper sphere of science, with its quantitative and mechanistic laws, was to be limited to the study of "matter." An unbridgeable chasm must, by the very definition of created existence, forever separate the two. Hence the study of the physical environment and human body were to be circumscribed within the exclusive purview of the natural sciences, while the nonmaterial *psyche*, the "mind" and "soul," were forever to be confined to the domain of the humanities. Although a radical departure from all previous ontological formulations, Cartesianism proved a practical solution to the immediate ideological conflict between science and religion, and each eventually adopted one or another variant of this fundamental vertical dualism.

For modern Western culture, the result has been the establishment of an unassailable breach between the objective world of "matter" and the subjective world of "mind." Human consciousness has been eternally confined with the subjectivism of one's own individual mind. And "mind," already with Descartes, has become limited to the qualities of the personality's animating component; the existence of the intellective faculty has been denied or, at best, redefined as "the soul" and subsequently emptied of all cognitive content. The animating component of the psyche has thus attempted to usurp the entire domain of the individual "self" and, in addition, has sought to appropriate new realms for this "self."

Since Giambattista Vico's *New Science* appeared in 1725 and Jean-Jacques Rousseau published his Romantic *Discourse* in 1755, the subjective realm of "mind" has been steadily extended; it now claims as its own not only itself (i.e., human psychology) but also that which it avers are its products (e.g., history, society, economics, philosophy, theology, culture, and the arts). And as the physical sciences pursue mathematical truths in the material world, so the "human sciences" claim to reveal truths (or, as with Vico and Hegel, Truth) in the world of "mind" and "ideas."

But desire, passion, and imagination cannot alter objective reality, however much they may strive to disguise it. The paramountcy of the animating component over the consciousness of mankind is impotent to abolish the reality of the *psyche's* ontological bipolarity. The intellective faculty continues its struggle within the unconscious to displace its rival. In contemporary Western culture there are two complementary overt expressions of this conflict within the *psyche*. Each has a distinctive origin and is experienced *by someone* as alienation; however, in the one case it is as object of projection while in the other it is as subject/object of projection.[22]

In the first instance, the struggle of the animating component to maintain its dominance within individual consciousness is projected outward onto one or another social phenomenon, an arena already claimed as its own creation by the subjectivist "mind" of Cartesian dualism. Thus the internal struggle of the animating component against its intellective rival is experienced externally as hostility to some distinctive social "other," whether this "other" be a religious, ideological, class, racial, ethnic, or national group. The social conflict is initially actually a secondary expression of an internal psychic duel, so neither objective reality nor accommodation by the targeted group can resolve, nor even diminish, the antagonism directed against it. Such is the origin of the experience of social alienation among the innocent object of projection, the targeted group.

The second instance of projection of the rival intellective faculty is onto some distorted externalized symbol of oneself. Such a projection may be symbolized by a parent, a sibling, a child, a compatriot, or a phantom double. Although a bitter hostility emanates from the animating faculty toward this symbol as object, because the symbol is also the subject, oneself, mingled with this anger are often also inchoate feelings of separation, longing, and guilt. Such is the origin of psychological alienation. Nor is it resolvable as long as existence of a psychic rival to the animating soul is denied.

Hence, in their acculturation and assimilation (i.e., their "conversion") to Western culture as a result of sociopolitical emancipation, the Jews, like their non-Jewish counterparts, denied a voice to their intellective faculty, which became for them the ghostly echo of their forebears' traditional Jewish culture and of their own Jewish identity. It was a call they could neither avoid, answer, nor escape. And as a continuing distinctive social "other" within Western societies, the Jews also became the target group for the projection of psychic hostility from non-Jews and so also came to experience an inexplicable, ceaseless social alienation. And within the existing structure of Western Cartesian categories there can be no relief from either the psychological or the social alienations, save through death.

But, by the twentieth century it is becoming increasingly evident that Cartesian ontology is, quite simply, fallacious. Relativity theory and quantum mechanics have persuaded physicists that Cartesian dualism is erroneous; matter and the mind intrinsically interact, and valid cosmological and epistemological theories must include, and account for, this relationship. The new theories being advanced in the natural sciences, therefore, reintegrate the cognitive and conative microcosm, man, with the objective phenomena of the macrocosm, the physical universe. And this reintegration has been accomplished without returning to the antiquated hierarchical bipolarities of classical and medieval physics.

Interestingly enough, however, the "human sciences" continue to cling stubbornly to the obsolescent Cartesian notion of the dualism of "mind" and "matter," the animating faculty refusing to acquiesce to its dethronement as sole master of man and his destiny. But the objective reality of the existence of the intellective faculty within the human personality, the epistemological and cosmological implications of the natural sciences, the intensifying social pathologies affecting large segments of the population, and the incessant malaise experienced by many individuals should eventually produce new philosophic formulations that will, without returning to antiquated notions of the past, again recognize the ontological bipolarity of the human personality and rediscover procedures by which its competing components may become harmoniously reconciled.

The understanding of the composite nature of the human personality is indeed quite ancient. In the Biblical book Ecclesiastes (9:14–16) a magnificent parable describes man's bipolar *psyche* and the proper relationship that should exist between its twin components.[23] It tells of a small city besieged by a great king and saved by an unremembered poor wise man and his wisdom. The "small city" allegorically represents the physical body; the "great king," the animating faculty of the psyche; and the "poor wise man," the intellective faculty. And only by employing the wisdom of its intellect is mankind to be rescued from the insatiable ravages of its purblind passions and imaginings.

In our story, Israel Zangwill is the small city; his theological, aesthetic, and cultural aspirations and dreams, the great king; and his reason, the poor wise man, whose voice he could hear but would not heed.

Notes

1: Introduction

1. Genesis 25:22–23 and the commentary there by Rashi (acronym for Rabbeinu Shlomo ben Yitzchak [1040–1105]).

2. Chaim Vital, *Shaar ha-Kedusha* and *Etz Chaim,* Gate 50, chap. 2.

3. Rabbi Nachman of Breslov, "MeiChacham v'Tam," in *Sippurei Ma'asiot* (Jerusalem: Meshech HaNachal, 1980), pp. 78–106, and the appended commentary *Rimzei haMa'asiot,* pp. 94–96; see also the excellent annotated English translation, "The Sophisticate and the Simpleton," in *Rabbi Nachman's Stories,* trans. Aryeh Kaplan (New York: Breslov Research Institute, 1983), pp. 160–96. In Genesis 25:27, Jacob is called "simple, dwelling in tents" and Esau, "a knowledgeable hunter, a man of the field."

4. Genesis 25:23.

5. W. E. B. Du Bois (1868–1963) represents the most outstanding such individual among this generation of black Americans; for a discussion of parallels between the lives of Du Bois and Zangwill see Chapter 11.

6. *Dial,* August 1, 1898, pp. 78–79.

7. Ibid.

8. S. L. Bensusan, "Israel Zangwill," *Quarterly Review* 247 (April 1926): 288–89.

9. Isadore Harris, "Mr. Israel Zangwill Interviewed," *Bookman* (New York) 1 (February 1898): 149.

10. *Dreamers of the Ghetto* is discussed in detail in Chapter 7.

11. See "The Rencontre" in "Morour and Charouseth," *Jewish Standard,* December 25, 1889, p. 5. Zangwill's experiences on this newspaper play an important role in the creation of the story and characters of *Children of the Ghetto,* as discussed in Chapter 5.

12. The one notable exception was Zangwill's longtime friend Solomon Schechter, though he complained only in private. See Chapter 7.

13. See, for example, the studies of Elsie Bonita Adams, *Israel Zangwill* (New York: Twayne Publishers, 1971); Bernard Winehouse, "Israel Zangwill's *Children of the Ghetto:* A Literary History of the First Anglo-Jewish Best-Seller," *English Literature in Transition* 16:2 (1973): 93–117; Maurice Wohlgelernter, *Israel*

Zangwill (New York: Columbia University Press, 1964); and Linda G. Zatlin, *The Nineteenth-Century Anglo-Jewish Novel* (Boston: Twayne Publishers, 1981), pp. 114–21.

14. See Sander L. Gilman, *Jewish Self-Hatred: Anti-Semitism and the Hidden Language of the Jews* (Baltimore: Johns Hopkins University Press, 1986), for a psycholinguistic analysis of some prominent (primarily German-speaking) nineteenth-century Jewish authors and their responses to the sense of social-psychological alienation experiences by acculturating Jews.

15. *Ein Yaakov* consists of the nonlegal portions of the Talmud; *Shivhei ha-Besht* recounts the wondrous events in the life of the founder of the Chassidic movement, Israel Baal Shem Tov (1698–1760). For a discussion of Zangwill's treatment of the Baal Shem Tov in *Dreamers of the Ghetto,* see Chapter 7.

2: The Historical Setting—Sociopolitical

1. For a discussion of the *kehilla* and its dissolution see Salo W. Baron, *The Jewish Community* (Philadelphia: Jewish Publication Society of America, 1942), vol. 2; Calvin Goldscheider and Alan S. Zuckerman, *The Transformation of the Jews* (Chicago: University of Chicago Press, 1984), pp. 31–41; Raphael Mahler, *A History of Modern Jewry 1780–1815* (London: Vallentine, Mitchell, 1971); and Cecil Roth, *Short History of the Jewish People,* 2d ed. (London: East and West Library, 1943), chaps. 27–28.

2. The American Founding Fathers so feared the social and political consequences of an unmediated governmental authority that they deliberately created multiple mediators in the constitutional system.

3. See Leon Poliakov, *The History of Anti-Semitism,* trans. Miriam Kochan (London: Routledge and Kegan Paul, 1975), vol. 3, for a general survey of the aims of the emancipators; Nathan Rotenstreich's "Enlightenment: Between Mendelssohn and Kant" in *Studies in Jewish Religious and Intellectual History,* ed. Siegfried Stein and Raphael Loewe (University: University of Alabama Press, 1979), pp. 263–79, provides insight into the ideological perspective and values of the emancipators. Todd M. Endelman in *The Jews of Georgian England 1714–1830* (Philadelphia: Jewish Publication Society of America, 1979) analyzes the explicit political and economic conditions proposed by those advocating toleration of the Jews in Britain during the eighteenth century. Colin Holmes, in *Anti-Semitism in British Society, 1876–1939* (New York: Holmes and Meier, 1979), pp. 9–10, 104, thoroughly explains the conditional terms underlying liberal British toleration of the Jews. See Jacob Katz, *From Prejudice to Destruction* (Cambridge: Harvard University Press, 1980), for a thorough discussion of the subject as it applied to Germany.

4. Endelman, *Georgian England;* Katz, *From Prejudice;* and Poliakov, *Anti-Semitism.*

5. Goldscheider's and Zuckerman's "network cohesion model" provides a convincing explanation for the continued ethnicity of secularized and ac-

culturated Jews. See also Jacob Katz, "German Culture and the Jews," *Commentary* 77:2 (February 1984): 54–59.

6. Katz, *From Prejudice*, pp. 147–58, 245–59.

7. See, for instance, Roth, *Short History*, chap. 29; M. L. Margolis and A. Marx, *A History of the Jewish People* (London: Routledge and Sons, 1927); James Parkes, *A History of the Jewish People* (London: Weidenfeld and Nicolson, 1962), chap. 6; and Howard M. Sachar, *The Course of Modern Jewish History* (London: Weidenfeld and Nicolson, 1958), chap. 15.

8. This point is noted in Lloyd P. Gartner, *The Jewish Immigrant in England, 1870–1914* (London: George Allen and Unwin, 1960), p. 41; Simon Kuznets, "Immigration of Russian Jews to the United States: Background and Structure," in *Perspectives in American History* 9 (1975): 88, 120; and Eli M. Lederhendler, "Jewish Immigration to America and Revisionist Historiography: A Decade of New Perspectives," *YIVO Annual of Jewish Social Science* 18 (1983): 393.

9. Kuznets, "Immigration of Russian Jews."

10. Jacob Lestschinsky, "Jewish Migrations, 1840–1956," in *The Jews: Their History, Culture and Religion*, ed. Louis Finkelstein (London: Peter Owen, 1961), 2:1536–96.

11. Kuznets, "Immigration of Russian Jews," pp. 120–21.

12. Ibid., p. 122.

13. See this argument throughout Thomas Sowell, *The Economics and Politics of Race* (New York: William Morrow and Co., 1983).

14. Goldscheider and Zuckerman, *Transformation of Jews*, pp. 60–84, 163–64, argue persuasively that the out-migration from Eastern Europe, a "mass migration" only from the perspective of people in the West, proceeded selectively among the Jewish population and derived primarily from "structural changes" arising from "the processes of modernization" occurring in the countries involved.

15. The following discussion of "acculturation" and "assimilation" as applied to the Jewish population is derived from Celia S. Heller, *On the Edge of Destruction* (New York: Columbia University Press, 1977). Often the distinction between these phenomena is unfortunately obscured by exclusive focus on processes of "secularization" or "modernity."

16. In *Jewish Continuity and Change* (Bloomington: Indiana University Press, 1986), Calvin Goldscheider thoroughly illustrates the "network cohesion model" of continued and adapted ethnicity lying behind the facade of assimilationist "acculturation."

17. This is exactly the explanation demonstrated for the dynamics of Yiddish as an autonomous, distinctive Jewish language by Max Weinreich in *History of the Yiddish Language*, trans. Shlomo Noble (Chicago: University of Chicago Press, 1980).

18. See Thomas Sowell, *Ethnic America* (New York: Basic Books, 1981), for a comparative study of this phenomenon among a variety of immigrant groups in the United States.

19. See, for instance, *N'futzos Yisroel* (The Dispersion of Israel) by Rabbi Israel Meir Kagan, the beloved "Chaftez Chaim" of the East European orthodox masses.

20. Goldscheider and Zuckerman, *Transformation of Jews*, p. 164.

21. Thomas Kessner, "Jobs, Ghettoes and the Urban Economy 1880–1835," *American Jewish History* 71:2 (December 1982): 218–38.

22. Sowell's *Ethnic America* illustrates this comparison at length.

23. J. W. Joselit, "What Happened to New York's 'Jewish Jews'?" *American Jewish History* 73:2 (December 1983): 163–72; Abraham J. Karp, "New York Chooses A Chief Rabbi," *Publications of the American Jewish Historical Society* 44:4 (June 1955): 129–98; Aaron Rothkoff, "The American Sojourns of the Ridbaz," *Publications of the American Jewish Historical Society* 57:4 (June 1968): 557–72. Goldscheider, *Jewish Continuity*, p. 152, argues that this secularization need not negate Jewish ethnic identity, but, instead, "opportunities for new forms of expression of Jewishness have developed as alternative ways to reinforce Jewish cohesion, even as links between religion and Jewishness have weakened." Crises of identity occur during periods of transition and reconsolidation.

24. Karp, "A Chief Rabbi," and Rothkoff, "American Sojourns." Bernard Cohen, in *Sociocultural Changes in American Jewish Life as Reflected in Selected Jewish Literature* (Rutherford, N .J.: Fairleigh Dickinson University Press, 1972), pp. 90–103, 251, analyzes the values of the immigrants' children, the "second period," as reflected in the works of various American Jewish authors.

25. Endelman, *Georgian England*, pp. 13–49; Cecil Roth, *A History of the Jews in England* (Oxford: Clarendon Press, 1941).

26. Roth, *A History*, and Cecil Roth, "The Chief Rabbinate of England," in *Essays in Honour of the Very Rev. Dr. J. H. Hertz*, ed. I. Epstein, E. Levine and C. Roth (London: Edward Goldston, 1942), pp. 371–84.

27. Albert Hyamson, *The London Board of Shechita 1804–1954* (London: London Board for Shechita, 1954), pp. 11–15.

28. V. D. Lipman, *Social History of the Jews in England 1850–1950* (London: Watts and Co., 1954), pp. 9, 38–57; Laurie Magnus, *The Jewish Board of Guardians and the Men Who Made It 1859–1909* (London: Jewish Board of Guardians, 1909), pp. 9–16; *The Jewish Chronicle 1841–1941* (London: Jewish Chronicle, 1949).

29. Michael Leigh, "Reform Judaism in Britain (1840–1970)," in *Reform Judaism, Essays on Reform Judaism in Britain*, ed. Dow Marmur (London: Reform Synagogues of Great Britain, 1973), pp. 3–50. On the later establishment of Liberal Judaism in Britain, see Chapter 7.

30. Endelman, *Georgian England;* V. D. Lipman, "The Age of Emancipation," in *Three Centuries of Anglo-Jewish History*, ed. V. D. Lipman (London: Jewish Historical Society of England, 1961), pp. 69–106.

31. Michail C. N. Salbstein, *The Emancipation of the Jews in Britain* (Rutherford, N.J.: Fairleigh Dickinson University Press, 1982); see also Geoffrey

Alderman, *The Jewish Community in British Politics* (Oxford: Clarendon Press, 1983), pp. 14–30; Roth, *A History*, pp. 259–66; and Lipman, "Age of Emancipation," pp. 78–82.

32. Aubrey Newman, *The United Synagogue 1870–1970* (London: Routledge and Kegan Paul, 1976), pp. 2–17.

33. Endelman, *Georgian England*, pp. 118–65.

34. Newman, *United Synagogue*, pp. 49–56.

35. Endelman, *Georgian England*, p. 292.

36. Holmes, *Anti-Semitism*, p. 104.

37. Gartner, *Jewish Immigrant*, p. 42.

38. Ibid., pp. 50–54; Lipman, *Social History*, p. 87; Israel Finestein, "The New Community," in Lipman, *Three Centuries of Anglo-Jewish History*, p. 109.

39. See especially C. Russell, "The Jewish Question in the East End," in *The Jew In London* by C. Russell and H. S. Lewis (London: T. Fisher Unwin, 1900), pp. 24–27; also useful are Newman, *United Synagogue*, pp. 61–62, and Alderman, *Jewish Community*, pp. 66–85. Theodore Hamerow's "Cravat Jews and Caftan Jews," *Commentary* 77:5 (May 1984): 29–38, also provides interesting insights.

40. Bill Williams, "The Anti-Semitism of Tolerance: Middle Class Manchester and the Jews 1870–1900," in *City, Class and Culture*, ed. A. J. Kidd and K. W. Roberts (Manchester: Manchester University Press, 1985), p. 91.

41. Gartner, *Jewish Immigrant*, pp. 155–75; Magnus, *Jewish Board of Guardians*, pp. 28–47; Jerry White's *Rothschild Buildings* (London: Routledge and Kegan Paul, 1980) is an excellent study of many facets of this campaign.

42. Gartner, *Jewish Immigrant*, pp. 221–22.

43. Ibid., p. 231.

44. Russell, "Jewish Question," pp. 35–36; Gartner, *Jewish Immigrant*, pp. 193–97. For the American parallel—the Reform elite's subvention of the traditionalist Jewish Theological Seminary—see Moshe Davis, *The Emergence of Conservative Judaism* (New York: Burning Bush Press, 1963), pp. 321–26.

45. Gartner, *Jewish Immigrant*, pp. 200–208; Lipman, *Social History*, pp. 119–22; Newman, *United Synagogue*, pp. 62–75; Joseph E. Blank, *The Minutes of the Federation of Synagogues* (London: E. W. Rabbinowicz, 1912); Cecil Roth, *The Federation of Synagogues 1912–1937* (London: N.p., 1937).

46. Stephen Sharut, "Native Jewry and the Religious Anglicization of Immigrants in London: 1870–1905," *Jewish Journal of Sociology* 16:1 (June 1974): 39–56.

47. Zangwill would allude to the history of this building to make personal references in his veiled autobiography, "The Baron of Offenbach," discussed in Chapter 10. The building now serves as a mosque.

48. Bernard Homa, *A Fortress in Anglo-Jewry* (London: Shapiro, Vallentine and Co., 1953), pp. 6–70; Gartner, *Jewish Immigrant*, pp. 209–14; Hyamson, *Board of Shechita*, pp. 45–48, 71–73; Lipman, *Social History*, pp. 123–26.

49. Russell, "Jewish Question," pp. 104–06, takes just this position, in

1900, at the height of the controversy. He interprets the Zionism of the immigrants in the same light, which helps explain its attraction for Machzike Hadath as well.

50. See White, *Rothschild Buildings*, chap. 1, and Millicent Rose, *The East End of London* (Bath: Cedric Chivers, 1973), for discussions and descriptions of East End history and conditions. Jack London's *The People of the Abyss* (New York: Macmillan Co., 1903) provides a vivid and sympathetic, although rather Social Darwinist, portrait of the non-Jewish population of the East End.

51. For a contemporary account see Beatrice (Webb) Potter's "The Jewish Community" in *Life and Labour of the People in London*, ed. Charles Booth (London: Macmillan and Co., 1889), 1st ser. 3:169–72, 181–86. See also Harold Pollins, *Economic History of the Jews in England* (East Brunswick, N.J.: Associated University Presses, 1982), pp. 135–37.

52. Potter, "Jewish Community," p. 186.

53. Booth, *Life and Labour*, 1st ser. 1:78–79; Lipman, *Social History*, pp. 107–14; Pollins, *Economic History*, pp. 144–45.

54. Lipman, *Social History*, p. 111.

55. In "Polish Colony of Jew Tailors," *Lancet*, May 3, 1884, pp. 817–18, the medical investigators vividly describe the conditions of "sweating" and bitterly complain of the workers' complicity in it. See also Lipman, *Social History*, pp. 117–18, and Walter Besant, *East London* (London: Chatto and Windus, 1901), p. 194.

56. Potter, "Jewish Community," p. 191.

57. Booth, *Life and Labour*, 3d ser. 2:59–60; Besant, *East London*, pp. 198–200. Petticoat Lane continues to operate exactly in this same fashion today, although the ethnic composition of the shopkeepers, hawkers, and customers has significantly altered.

58. Besant, *East London*, p. 198.

3: The Historical Setting—Literary

1. "Liberalism" is employed here to denote the philosophic heritage of John Locke and René Descartes, not any particular political or economic doctrine. See Chapter 11 for discussion of some additional twentieth-century instances of these three responses to liberalism and for a suggestion as to their fundamental causes.

2. For a helpful introduction to Dickens's literary heritage see F. R. Leavis and Q. D. Leavis, *Dickens the Novelist* (London: Chatto and Windus, 1970). George Eliot's literary values appear in her essay "The Natural History of German Life," which first appeared in *Westminster Review* 66 (July 1856): 51–79 and is reprinted in *Essays of George Eliot*, ed. Thomas Pinney (London: Routledge and Kegan Paul, 1963), pp. 266–99. The labels "social assertivist" and "solitary contemplative" generally coincide with the vertically valued

terms "middle brow" and "high brow," while the labels employed here are horizontally oriented with respect to the self.

3. Walter Besant, *All Sorts and Conditions of Men,* 2d ed. (London: Chatto and Windus, 1897), pp. 20, 35–36.

4. Ibid., p. 15.

5. Ibid., pp. 27–28.

6. Ibid., p. 31.

7. Ibid., p. 70.

8. Charles Booth, ed., *Life and Labour of the People in London,* 1st ser., (London: Macmillan and Co., 1889), 1:118; Robert Sinclair, *East London* (London: Robert Hale, 1950), p. 353. Located on Mile End Road, the People's Palace has since evolved into Queen Mary College of the University of London.

9. Mrs. Humphrey Ward, *Robert Elsmere* (London: Macmillan and Co., 1888), p. 572. Emphasis in original.

10. Ibid., pp. 356, 494. Emphasis in original.

11. Ibid., pp. 495–96.

12. Ibid., p. 554. Emphasis in original.

13. Ibid., p. 602.

14. See Chapter 5.

15. Abba Rubin, *Images in Transition* (Westport, Conn.: Greenwood Press, 1984), pp. 47–93. See also Edward Coleman, *The Jew in English Drama* (New York: New York Public Library, 1970); M. J. Landa, *The Jew in Drama* (London: P. S. King and Sons, 1926); and Montagu Modder, *The Jew in the Literature of England to the End of the 19th Century* (Philadelphia: Jewish Publication Society of America, 1939), for full treatment of the history of the stereotype.

16. Rubin, *Images,* pp. 93–95, 103, 107–08.

17. Ibid., p. 107.

18. Ibid., p. 112. See also Harold Fisch, *The Dual Image* (London: World Jewish Library, 1971), pp. 59–69, and Anne A. Naman, *The Jew in the Victorian Novel* (New York: AMS Press, 1980), p. 56.

19. Charles Dickens, *Oliver Twist* (Harmondsworth: Penguin Books, 1966), p. 105.

20. As Naman notes in *Jew in the Victorian Novel,* p. 202, while the predominant view in Victorian literature advocated complete Jewish assimilation, in *Daniel Deronda* Eliot "supports the values of [Jewish] nationalism and 'separateness with communication.' "

21. George Eliot, *Daniel Deronda* (Harmondsworth: Penguin Books, 1967), p. 592.

22. Ibid., p. 595.

23. Ibid., p. 596.

24. See Chapter 8.

25. William Baker, in *George Eliot and Judaism* (Sulzburg: Institut für Englische Sprache und Literatur, 1975), documents her extensive research into Jewish sources before setting out to write *Daniel Deronda.*

26. Ibid., pp. 139–40.

27. Sander L. Gilman, in *Jewish Self-Hatred: Anti-Semitism and the Hidden Language of the Jews* (Baltimore: Johns Hopkins University Press, 1986), although he does not discuss the Western "ghetto" stories and their authors, examines the Jews' experience of social alienation and its origin and expression in the writings of several continental authors during the same period under discussion here; see particularly the summation of his psychological explanation, p. 20.

28. Meyer Waxman, *A History of Jewish Literature* (New York: Thomas Yoseloff, 1941), 4:586–87.

29. Leopold Kompert, *Scenes from the Ghetto: Studies of Jewish Life* (London: Remington and Co., 1882).

30. Ibid., pp. 79–280.

31. Ibid., p. 175.

32. Ibid., p. 245.

33. Ibid., p. 267.

34. Ibid., p. 279.

35. Eliot, *Daniel Deronda,* p. 595. The reference is to Giuseppe Mazzini.

36. Leopold Kompert, *Christian & Leah & Other Ghetto Stories* (London: J. M. Dent and Co., 1895), pp. 1–130.

37. Ibid., pp. 129–30. Emphasis in original.

38. Karl Emil Franzos, *The Jews of Barnow,* trans. M. W. MacDowall (Edinburgh: Blackwood and Sons, 1882), p. vi.

39. Ibid., p. vii.

40. Ibid., pp. 141–71.

41. Ibid., p. 57.

42. Ibid., p. 155.

43. Ibid., p. 171.

44. It appeared in English almost immediately as *Judith Trachtenberg,* trans. L. P. Lewis and C. T. Lewis (New York: Harper and Brothers, 1891).

45. Ibid., p. 89.

46. Ibid., p. 191.

47. Ibid., p. 196.

48. Ibid., pp. 220–21.

49. Ibid., p. 221.

50. Waxman, *Jewish Literature,* p. 583.

51. See Linda G. Zatlin, *The Nineteenth-Century Anglo-Jewish Novel* (Boston: Twayne Publishers, 1981), for a comprehensive survey of the authors and their works (except Benjamin Disraeli, a youthful convert to Christianity) for this period.

52. See Sarah Bradford, *Disraeli* (New York: Stein and Day, 1983), for a comprehensive biography.

53. See Robert Blake, *Disraeli's Grand Tour: Benjamin Disraeli and the Holy Land, 1830–31* (London: Weidenfeld and Nicolson, 1982), for an account of this trip.

54. Benjamin Disraeli, *Alroy* (London: M. Walter Dunne, 1904). For a discussion of this novel see Richard A. Levine, *Benjamin Disraeli* (New York: Twayne Publishers, 1968), pp. 51–57, and Muriel Masefield, *Peacocks and Primroses: A Survey of Disraeli's Novels* (London: Geoffrey Bles, 1953), pp. 75–77.

55. Benjamin Disraeli, *Coningsby* (Oxford: Oxford University Press, 1982), p. 192. Levine, *Disraeli,* pp. 47–48, suggests that the prototype for Sidonia was Peter Winter, a character in Disraeli's 1832 novel, *Contarini Fleming.*

56. Disraeli, *Coningsby,* p. 210.

57. Ibid., p. 219.

58. Ibid., p. 221.

59. Ibid., p. 222.

60. Benjamin Disraeli, *Coningsby* (London: M. Walter Dunne, 1904, reprint of 1849 5th ed.), pp. xvi–xvii. See Chapter 7 for a discussion of Zangwill's and Anglo-Jewry's attempts to reevaluate Jesus' relationship to Judaism.

61. Benjamin Disraeli, *Tancred* (Westport, Conn.: Greenwood Press, 1970, reprint of 1870 ed.), p. 122.

62. Ibid., pp. 389–90.

63. However unintended, Eliot's Mordecai has a good deal of Sidonia about his characterization.

64. Eleanor Farjeon, *A Nursery in the Nineties* (London: Victor Gollancz, 1935), p. 505. This memoir by his daughter is the only available biography of Benjamin Farjeon to date, unfortunately. Zatlin, *Anglo-Jewish Novel,* pp. 70–86, provides a useful survey of Farjeon's life and works, differing in its conclusions from those expressed here.

65. Benjamin L. Farjeon, *Solomon Isaacs: A Christmas Story* (London: Robson and Sons, n.d.).

66. Ibid., pp. 85–86.

67. Ibid., p. 96.

68. Ibid., p. 1.

69. There is no satisfactory biographical study of Amy Levy. The most comprehensive study is Beth Zion Lask's "Amy Levy," *Transactions, The Jewish Historical Society* 11 (1928): 168–89; see also Richard Garnett's article in *The Dictionary of National Biography* (London, 1922), 11:1041, and "Amy Levy," *Jewish Chronicle,* 13 September 1889, p. 6. Zatlin, *Anglo-Jewish Novel,* pp. 90–97, presents a helpful survey of Levy's life and works, although differing considerably in its conclusions from those expressed here.

70. Amy Levy, *Miss Meredith* (London: Hodder and Stoughton, 1889). The work was first serialized in *British Weekly,* beginning with the 19 April 1889 issue.

71. Ibid., p. 126.

72. "The Jew in Fiction," *Jewish Chronicle,* 4 June 1886, p. 13.

73. Ibid.

74. Ibid.

75. "Jewish Humour," *Jewish Chronicle,* 20 August 1886, pp. 9–10.

76. Amy Levy, *Reuben Sachs, A Sketch* (London: Macmillan and Co., 1888).

77. Ibid., p. 107.
78. Ibid., p. 119.
79. Ibid., pp. 232–33.
80. Ibid., pp. 234–35.
81. Ibid., p. 258.
82. Ibid., p. 266.
83. Amy Levy, "Cohen of Trinity," *Gentleman's Magazine* 266:1901 (May 1889): 417–24.
84. Ibid., pp. 419–20.
85. Ibid., pp. 421–22.
86. Ibid., p. 422.
87. Ibid., p. 423.

4: The Young Zangwill

1. For interesting parallels to the life of W. E. B. Du Bois, see Chapter 11.
2. The information on Moses Zangwill is derived from Joseph Leftwich's memoir, *Israel Zangwill* (New York: Thomas Yoseloff, 1957), pp. 75–76, and the *Times* (London), obituary, 13 August 1908, p. 9. If he was, in fact, seventy-two years old at the time of his death in 1908 and if Leftwich is correct that he arrived in Britain in 1848, then his desperate migration across Europe at such a young age is certainly a remarkable achievement; it is also highly questionable. But details about Moses Zangwill's biography are very scanty.
3. Michael Heymann, ed., *The Uganda Controversy* (Jerusalem: Institute for Zionist Research at Tel-Aviv University, 1977), 2:54, 365.
4. See John Carswell, *The Exile* (New York: Faber and Faber, 1984), for information on the Low and Eder families.
5. See Leftwich, *Zangwill,* chap. 3, for information on the Zangwill family and Central Zionist Archives, Jerusalem, file A120/72, for correspondence on Israel Zangwill's support for his father in Jerusalem.
6. Gaster Papers, 17 February 1902, Mocatta Library, London.
7. Central Zionist Archives, A120/34/6. This copybook is filed with several other works of Zangwill's youth.
8. Ibid. Emphasis in original.
9. The grandmother in *The Melting Pot* is particularly reminiscent of the character portrayed in this schoolboy's story.
10. In *Society* 2:47 (22 October 1881): 26, Israel Zangwill's address is listed as 89 New-Terrace, Morning Lane, Mare Street, Hackney E.
11. This observation I owe to Mrs. J. Wagerman, Headmistress, JFS Comprehensive School.
12. A list of all Rothschild medal winners is on display at JFS Comprehensive School.

13. *Jewish Chronicle*, 29 June 1877, p. 11, and 28 June 1878, p. 28.

14. Elsie Bonita Adams, *Israel Zangwill* (New York: Twayne Publishers, 1971), chronology.

15. Leftwich, *Zangwill*, p. 56.

16. Israel Zangwill, "Professor Grimmer," *Society* 5:133–35 (14–30 November 1881). Zangwill recounts how he came to enter the competition in his essay, "My First Book—The Premier and the Painter," in *My First Book*, ed. Jerome K. Jerome (London: Chatto and Windus, 1894), pp. 164–66. (This essay appeared originally in the *Idler*, February 1893, pp. 629–41).

17. "Humorous Story Competition," *Society* 2:47 (22 October 1881): 26.

18. Zangwill, "Professor Grimmer," no. 133, p. 12. Emphasis in original.

19. Zangwill, "My First Book," pp. 167–68. The title evidently is intended as the Yiddish for "matza balls."

20. Zangwill, "My First Book," p. 168; Leftwich, *Zangwill*, pp. 22–23. Mrs. J. Wagerman informs me that Lord Rothschild was known at JFS to have two hobbyhorses: boys who put their hands in their pants pockets, and mispronunciation of English put in the mouth of Jews. In consequence, he had the JFS issue suits without pockets to its students and attacked Zangwill and Cowen.

21. Leftwich, *Zangwill*, pp. 22–23.

22. J. Freeman Bell, *The Premier and the Painter* (London: Spencer Blackett, 1888).

23. Zangwill to Gaster, 15 October 1888; Gaster Papers. The *Jewish Chronicle*'s review appeared in the 12 October 1888 issue, p. 11.

24. Letter to the editor, "A Personal Question," from Louis Cohen (i.e., Cowen) and Israel Zangwill, *Jewish Standard*, 22 June 1888, p. 11.

25. Israel Zangwill, *The Premier and the Painter* (Chicago: Rand, McNally and Co., 1896), preface to the 3d ed.

26. Zangwill, "My First Book," pp. 172–74. Zangwill's claim to have written the majority of the book is borne out by his handwritten draft of many of its chapters, in Central Zionist Archives, A120/34/2.

27. "Novels of the Week," *Athenaeum*, 21 April 1888, p. 497. These comments on Zangwill's novel are strikingly similar to Amy Levy's fictional "review" of the book by "Cohen of Trinity," discussed in Chapter 3.

28. A third, an article, "The Idler's Club," by "J. Freeman Bell," appeared in the *Idler* in January 1895, pp. 638–40, on "the abolition of Christmas," but it appears to be a solo effort by Zangwill, employing his old pseudonym to disguise his authorship of a specifically "Christian" article.

29. Israel Zangwill and Louis Cowen, *The Great Demonstration* (London: Capper and Newton, 1892). The play was first performed at the Royalty Theatre, London, 17 September 1892.

30. J. Freeman Bell, "Under Sentence of Marriage," *The Jewish Calendar, Manual, and Diary, 5649* (London, 1888), pp. 54–79.

31. Ibid., pp. 57–58.

32. Baroness von S., "Satan Mekatrig: A Romance of the London Ghetto," *The Jewish Calendar, Manual, and Diary, 5650* (London, 1889), pp. 52–76. (The story is reprinted without the "Proem" in *Ghetto Tragedies* [London: McClure and Co., 1893], pp. 3–96.)

33. That Zangwill borrowed more than the notion of an introductory "Proem" from *Romola* will be discussed in Chapter 5.

34. Baroness von S., "Satan Mekatrig," p. 52.

35. Ibid., p. 76. Zangwill's portrayal of evil here reflects exactly traditional Jewish teaching; see, for instance, the eighteenth-century Chassidic classic by Schneur Zalman of Liadi, *Likutei Amarim*.

36. "Reviews," *Jewish Standard*, 7 February 1890, pp. 9–10.

37. See Chapter 10. However, manuscript evidence indicates that Zangwill did write another story of the esoteric at this time, "Bethulah," although it did not appear in print until 1899 in the revised collection of *Ghetto Tragedies, They That Walk in Darkness*. See Central Zionist Archives, A/120/34/3.

38. Baroness von S., "Diary of a Meshumad," *The Jewish Calendar, Manual, and Diary, 5651* (London, 1890), pp. 54–76. The story was reprinted in *Ghetto Tragedies*, pp. 99–187.

39. This is the traditional Jewish view that punishment in this life, for some, alleviates the sufferings in the World-to-Come; see, for instance, (Jerusalem Talmud tractate) *Pe'ah* I,1 and Nachmanides, *Shaar haGemul*.

40. "Death of Israel Zangwill," *Jewish Chronicle*, 6 August 1926, p. 16; *The Jewish Chronicle 1841–1941* (London: Jewish Chronicle, 1949), p. 161. Zangwill's column was evidently modeled on one entitled "Mustard and Cress" in the periodical, *Referee*.

41. That he served in both roles is clear from several letters he wrote to Dr. Moses Gaster in this capacity, now among the Gaster Papers, Mocatta Library, and also from clues he himself provides in *Children of the Ghetto*, as discussed in Chapter 5.

42. "The London Hospital," *Jewish Standard*, 15 June 1888, p. 4; "Reflections in a Street in Jerusalem," 8 May 1891, p. 9; and "Antipodes" began appearing with the 5 September 1888 issue.

43. "Morour and Charouseth," *Jewish Standard*, 11 May 1888, pp. 6–7. *Morour* refers to the bitter herbs of the Passover service; *charouseth* refers to the sweet mixture of nuts, apples, and wine into which the *morour* is dipped.

44. "Love and Death," in "Morour and Charouseth," 14 June 1889; "The Rencontre," in "Morour and Charouseth," 25 December 1889. The latter poem provides the theme for *Dreamers of the Ghetto*; see Chapter 7.

45. "The Watch on the Jordan," *Jewish Standard*, 20 July 1888, p. 5. Zangwill would use this poem in *Children of the Ghetto* in his treatment of Jewish nationalists; see Chapter 5.

46. Zangwill's acquaintance with Moses Gaster began even before the latter became Sephardi Hacham of Britain in 1887; Zangwill's letters of 1886, in the Gaster Papers, suggest he sought out Gaster's acquaintance and, through

him, Schechter's; Gaster certainly knew who "J. Freeman Bell" and "Marshallik" were. Zangwill was acquainted with the Schechter family at least since 1887, with a very warm friendship ensuing, from the evidence of correspondence in Central Zionist Archives, file A/120/58/6. By 1903, however, Zangwill's friendship with both men had ended; see Chapter 7.

47. "Ariel's Album," *Ariel*, 13 December 1890, p. 371.

48. Ibid.

49. "Ariel's Arm Chair," *Ariel*, 20 December 1890, p. 386.

50. Israel Zangwill and Eleanor Marx Aveling, " 'A Doll's House' Repaired" (London, n.d.), reprinted from *Time*, March 1891, by Zangwill and Aveling. See Central Zionist Archives, A120/41/5.

51. "The Choice of Parents," *Chapman's Magazine*, Christmas no., 1895, pp. 339–50. Most of Zangwill's contributions to *Idler* were collected in *The King of Schnorrers; Grotesques and Fantasies* (London: William Heinemann, 1894); see Chapter 6 for discussion of it.

52. *The Celibates' Club*, a combination of the two books, first appeared in 1898.

53. "Old Maids' Club," *Athenaeum*, 22 July 1892, p. 128.

54. Israel Zangwill, *The Bachelors' Club* (London: Henry and Co., 1891), p. 179.

55. Zangwill's draft play, *Threepenny Bits, A Tragic Farce*, is based on *The Old Maids' Club*; see Central Zionist Archives, A120/40/2. In A120/39/2 are several drafts of what appears to have been Zangwill's first adult attempt at drama, "Aladdin at Sea," which, however, seems never to have been publicly performed.

56. *Six Persons* was first produced by H. Beerbohm Tree at the Theatre Royal, London, 23 December 1893. A published edition was printed by Samuel French (London, 1898). A handwritten draft entitled "A Lover's Quarrel" appears to date from Zangwill's early years with the *Jewish Standard*, while a typed version reflects the later *Ariel* or *Idler* period; see Central Zionist Archives, A120/34/2 and A120/40/3.

57. Ibid.: Zangwill's hand-corrected version of the printed edition of the play.

58. I. Zangwill to F. Macmillan, 6 March 1891; British Library, Macmillan Collection, 55259/225.

59. Israel Zangwill, "English Judaism, A Criticism and a Classification," *Jewish Quarterly Review* 1 (July 1889): 376–407.

60. Ibid., pp. 384–85.

61. Ibid., p. 387.

62. Ibid., p. 399.

63. Ibid., pp. 390, 401–03.

64. Ibid., pp. 395–96.

65. Ibid.

66. Ibid., pp. 401–03.

67. The reconciliation of Moses and Jesus is equally the theme of Zangwill's 1889 poem, "The Rencontre," and forms the motif, ten years later, of his *Dreamers of the Ghetto.* See the discussion of this concept in Chapter 7.

68. Harold Fisch, "Israel Zangwill: Prophet of the Ghetto," *Judaism* 13:4 (Fall 1964): 414.

69. Zangwill, "English Judaism," pp. 406–07.

70. Israel Zangwill, "The Growth of Respectability," *Jewish Chronicle,* Jubilee supplement, 13 November 1891, pp. 19–20.

71. Ibid.

72. Ibid.

5: Children of the Ghetto

1. In the Introduction to *The Guide of the Perplexed,* trans. Shlomo Pines (Chicago: University of Chicago Press, 1963), 1:7, Maimonides writes: "You should not think that these great *secrets* are fully and completely known to any one among us. They are not. But sometimes truth flashes out to us." Emphasis in original.

2. It might, in fact, be more accurate to say that it was exactly the traditionalist portions of the novel that were most successful, while the overtly didactic and philosophic dialogues were frequently criticized or even completely ignored. See the discussion later in this chapter for details on this point.

3. In 1887 Zangwill, then an ambitious teacher at JFS, wrote the new Sephardi Hacham, Dr. Moses Gaster, with whom he was very eager to establish a friendship, to refuse his request to give him lessons to improve the Romanian-born Hacham's command of English. Justifying his decision, Zangwill explained: "Reflection has only strengthened me in the policy which I have always pursued—viz. never to give private lessons over & above my routine school-work for the sake of temporary profit. I have never broken through the rule." I. Zangwill to Moses Gaster, 2 October 1887; Gaster Papers, Mocatta Library, London.

4. See "Art in England," in his *Without Prejudice* (London: T. Fisher Unwin, 1896), pp. 31–42, for a clear exposition of Zangwill's views on the duties of the artist to creativity. He expands these ideas even further in "Of Facts with Alien Autocosms: Or the Futility of Culture," in *Italian Fantasies* (London: William Heinemann, 1910), pp. 120–36.

5. Quoted from a letter of February 1891 from Zangwill to Sulzberger, cited in Bernard Winehouse, "Israel Zangwill's *Children of the Ghetto:* A Literary History of the First Anglo-Jewish Best-Seller," *English Literature in Transition* 16:2 (1973): 194–95; the letter is also quoted in Joseph Leftwich, *Israel Zangwill* (New York: Thomas Yoseloff, 1957), p. 62. Zangwill particularly emphasized this serious artistic intent in his letter to Macmillan and Company in his attempt to convince them to become British publisher of *Children of the Ghetto.*

See I. Zangwill to F. Macmillan, 6 March 1891; British Library, Macmillan Collection, 55259/225.

6. The account of Zangwill's negotiations with Judge Sulzberger is based on Winehouse, "Zangwill's *Children,*" pp. 94–98, and Leftwich, *Zangwill,* pp. 61–64.

7. I. Zangwill to F. Macmillan, 6 March 1891, Macmillan Collection, 55259/225. This letter accompanied the manuscript. What is not clear, however, is whether this was a draft of the entire novel or of only the first half, also entitled "Children of the Ghetto." The novel, ultimately, was published in Britain by Heinemann.

8. In fact Zangwill fulfilled his commission from the JPS by imposing onto his original plan for a Jewish novel, reflected in *Children of the Ghetto*'s very successful Book One, a second plot, confined to the less successful Book Two. See further discussion later in this chapter.

9. Abraham Cahan's "Zangwill's Play, 'Children Of The Ghetto,' " *Forum* 28 (December 1899): 503–12, makes this plain. See also the review in the *Jewish Chronicle,* 15 December 1899, pp. 12–13. This disparity and its implications will be discussed at length later in this chapter.

10. Central Zionist Archives, Jerusalem, file A120/34/2. The handwritten draft, much corrected, is untitled and includes only three chapters of the novel. Zangwill's wife, Edith, has written on its cover, "Apparently the first and very early attempt at Children of the Ghetto," which is certainly correct in the sense that material in this draft was later reworked into the novel; however, the draft suggests that the focus of this work was completely different from that of the later published novel. The story line reads much like that of *The Schlemiel,* a novel serialized in the *Jewish Standard,* 18 April 1890 to 1 May 1891, that Louis Zangwill attributed to Louis Cowen and claimed was modeled on Israel Zangwill (see Leftwich, *Zangwill,* p. 28). If Cowen used Zangwill as his model, it was not for the humor of the story alone but also for the conflicts portrayed in his novel of the Jew's attempt to integrate into British society; it is on this subject that Zangwill's draft and *The Schlemiel* are so closely parallel. The draft seems to date from the period of Zangwill's association with Cowen and with the *Jewish Standard.*

11. Zangwill, draft manuscript, p. 5.

12. Ibid. The fond description and the sense of loss recalls Amy Levy's tone in *Reuben Sachs;* see Chapter 3.

13. Ibid., p. 32.

14. Ibid., pp. 7–19.

15. Ibid., pp. 23–24.

16. Ibid., p. 25. "*Treifa*" here means "nonkosher."

17. Ibid., p. 31.

18. Ibid., pp. 31–32. Alfred evidently is distinguishing between Biblical and Rabbinic commandments, a traditional legal, although not ritual, distinction.

19. Ibid., p. 32.

20. Ibid., p. 42.

21. Ibid.

22. Ibid., p. 43. This autobiographical rebuff of his proposal haunted Zangwill throughout his life and is recounted again in another context in his unfinished ms., "The Baron of Offenbach"; see Chapter 10.

23. Ibid., p. 48.

24. Ibid.

25. Ibid., pp. 49–50.

26. Ibid., p. 50.

27. Ibid.

28. The British edition was published by Heinemann in 1892; the American edition was published the same year by the Jewish Publication Society (after 1895 Macmillan became the American publisher).

29. Winehouse, "Zangwill's *Children*," p. 106, points out that this was the original subtitle of the novel, although it was later revised to "A Study of a Peculiar People."

30. Israel Zangwill, *Children of the Ghetto*, 3d. ed. (New York: Macmillan Co., 1895), p. ix.

31. Ibid. Emphasis added.

32. Ibid.

33. Ibid., pp. xviii–xix. "House of Life" is, of course, the normative Hebrew euphemism for "cemetery."

34. Ibid., p. xix.

35. For an interesting parallel in the life of W. E. B. Du Bois, see Chapter 11.

36. Zangwill, *Children*, p. 32.

37. Ibid., p. 8.

38. Ibid., pp. 17–18. Harold Fisch, in *The Dual Image* (London: World Jewish Library, 1971), pp. 75–77, argues that this contrast between how the ghetto Jews, such as the "sweater," appeared to the non-Jewish public and how they were viewed within their own community is the central theme in Zangwill's novel. It might be more accurate to claim that a primary purpose in it was not merely to illustrate such "dual images" but to reconcile the duality by means of publicizing the Jewish view of their own community.

39. Zangwill, *Children*, p. 66. The hostility the peddler experienced, as described here, is certainly a faithful rendering of lower class British antagonism toward the Jews.

40. Levi's observation to the contrary, this contrast between an individual's status defined by public approbation instead of by private inner harmony is not a particularly "Jewish" trait but rather is a product of Western post-Renaissance secularization; for some interesting observations on early literary expressions of this trait in English see I. G. Salingar, "The Elizabethan Literary Renaissance," in the *Age of Shakespeare*, ed. Boris Ford (Harmondsworth: Penguin Books, 1982), pp. 51–116.

41. Zangwill, *Children*, p. 80.

42. Ibid., p. 145.

43. Ibid., p. 128. In the dramatic version of *Children of the Ghetto* the Purim ball forms the setting for act 2, "The Spirit of Love," in which Zangwill expands this description much further.

44. Ibid., pp. 180–81.

45. Another poem of Naphtali Herz Imber (1856–1909), "Tikvateinu," later provided the words for the Zionist anthem "HaTikva"; see *Encyclopaedia Judaica* (Jerusalem, 1972), 7:1470–72.

46. Zangwill, *Children*, pp. 103–04.

47. That these observations were written in English for English-speaking Jews indicates at least tacit acquiescence to the thorough success of acculturation, although later even this acculturation would greatly trouble Zangwill.

48. Zangwill, *Children*, pp. 174–75.

49. That Hannah is the main protagonist in the stage adaptation of the book, which was also written by Zangwill (see Central Zionist Archives, A120/34/2), is evident from all the reviews of it (see references in n. 9 above).

50. Zangwill, *Children*, p. 138.

51. Ibid.

52. In his review of the stage version of this episode, the famed editor of the *Jewish Daily Forward*, Abraham Cahan ("Zangwill's Play," p. 509), praises Reb Shemuel's adherence to his principles of Jewish law in Hannah's case, recognizing that the real culprit is the frivolous Sam and his irresponsible treatment of the young woman.

53. Zangwill, *Children*, p. 321.

54. Ibid., p. 331.

55. Ibid., p. 342. Raphael's expression "real trinity" reflects Zangwill's syncretic values and categories of thought; they continue to provide a fundamental component of the Christianized Jewish philosophy he explores further in later books and essays. No version of Judaism propounds a "trinity" of principles.

56. Ibid., p. 344.

57. Zangwill, in fact, was forced to assure the original owner of the *Jewish Standard*, Aaron Vecht, that he is not in the book; see "Death of Israel Zangwill," *Jewish Chronicle*, 6 August 1926, pp. 20–21. And Naphtali Herz Imber actually initiated suit proceedings against those who identified him with Melchitsedek Pinchas; see Winehouse, "Zangwill's *Children*," p. 99. And, in actuality Zangwill has transformed and fictionalized reality; even his own role is transmuted into that of two characters on the paper.

58. Zangwill, *Children*, p. 364.

59. Ibid., pp. 364, 443. *Children*'s plot here strikingly resembles that of Thomas Hardy's popular early novel, *A Pair of Blue Eyes* (1873).

60. "Morour and Charouseth," *Jewish Standard*, 1 March 1889, pp. 9–10.

61. Unlike *Mordecai Josephs*, *Reuben Sachs* appeared under Amy Levy's own name, and she openly faced the criticisms of Anglo-Jewry while continuing to live in her parents' home.

62. Zangwill, *Children,* p. 431.

63. Ibid., p. 435. This scene in *Children of the Ghetto* exactly mirrors Tito's spurning his father as "Some madman, surely," in George Eliot's *Romola,* chap. 22, which itself echoes Shakespeare's King Harry repudiating Falstaff: "I know thee not, old man" (*2 Henry IV,* act 5, sc. 5). Israel Zangwill similarly treated his own father, spiritually at least, if not also in overt deed.

64. Zangwill, *Children,* p. 458.

65. Ibid., pp. 510, 511–12 (These desperate polar alternatives [viz., accommodate or die] increasingly characterize Zangwill's twin approaches to the issue of Jewish ethnic survival, as becomes apparent in *Dreamer of the Ghetto* and in his later nationalist activities), p. 513. Maimonides, *Guide,* 1:12, writes that a Biblical "saying uttered with a view to two meanings is like an apple of gold overlaid with silver filigree-work having very small holes. . . . When looked at from a distance or with imperfect attention, it is deemed an apple of silver; but when a keen-sighted observer looks at it with full attention, its interior becomes clear to him and he knows that it is gold." Strelitski's notion of Judaism as a species of "Hebraism" reflects the views made current by Matthew Arnold in *Culture and Anarchy* (1869).

66. Israel Zangwill, "Hebrew, Jew, Israelite," *Jewish Chronicle,* 18 November 1892, pp. 6–8.

67. Zangwill, *Children,* p. 549.

68. "Children of the Ghetto," *Athenaeum,* 5 November 1892, p. 626.

69. Israel Abrahams, "Children of the Ghetto," *Jewish Chronicle,* 14 October 1892, pp. 7–8. The "Proem" to Zangwill's novel was published in the 30 September 1892 issue of this weekly, pp. 15–16.

70. Mathilde Schechter to Israel Zangwill, 12 October 1892; Central Zionist Archives, A120/58/6. In a prior letter to Zangwill she had praised "Marshallik," 30 August 1889, and "Diary of a Meshumad," and " 'A Doll's House' Repaired," 19 March 1891.

71. *Athenaeum.* See also "Recent Novels," *Spectator,* 26 November 1892, p. 774.

72. Abrahams, "Children," p. 7.

73. Stephen S. Wise, "Address," in *In Memory of Israel Zangwill* (New York, 1926), p. 19, in Central Zionist Archives, A120/96. Similar sentiments were expressed at the time of Zangwill's death by G. Abrahams in "On Zangwill," *Jewish Chronicle,* supplement, August 1926, p. 1; S. L. Bensusan in "Israel Zangwill," *Quarterly Review* 247 (April 1926): 287; M. J. Landa in "Israel Zangwill," *Contemporary Review* 130 (September 1926): 316; see also Norman Bentwich, "Israel Zangwill," *Contemporary Review* 205 (January 1964): 39.

74. This distinction between Britons and Jews continues to persist today. Unlike American usage, Anglo-Jews still employ the word "English" to refer to non-Jewish Britons. Thus, if one is informed that a Jewish boy has married an "English" girl it signifies that there has been intermarriage. For their part, non-Jewish Britons use the word "Jew" often to refer to someone not assimi-

lated and acculturated into "their" society, as in "Jews who refuse to be English."

75. Zangwill, tellingly, rejects Arnold's generally negative assessment of the contemporary utility of "Hebraism." It is interesting to note that Zangwill does not seem to have been aware that traditional Jewish sources specifically enjoin a seven-category universal ethical code on all peoples; see Maimonides, *Mishneh Torah*, Hilchot Melachim, 9, for a thorough discussion of this code.

6: Literary Lion

1. " 'The Master' and Its Author," *To-day* 2:25 (28 April 1894): 361.

2. Ruth, the daughter of Zangwill's friend Solomon Schechter, in the throes of an adolescent crush, begged her "Literary Lion" to correspond with her, the "Little Nobody." See Ruth Schechter to Israel Zangwill, 11 December 1902; Central Zionist Archives, Jerusalem, file A/120/58/6. No doubt she was reflecting the general family estimation of Zangwill at the time, a view then widely shared by the anglophone Jewish public.

3. Joseph Leftwich, *Israel Zangwill* (New York: Thomas Yoseloff, 1957), p. 53. Harry Schneiderman, in "Israel Zangwill, A Biographical Sketch," *The American Jewish Year Book 5688* (Philadelphia: Jewish Publication Society of America, 1927), 29:138–39, refers to the informal group as "The Nomads" but otherwise confirms Leftwich's account. The formal organization of the Maccabeans is confirmed in the club's membership ledger; see Anglo-Jewish Archive, London, file AJ17/1/18.

4. See Chapter 8. The storms of these years, with their intense debates over Zionism and Territorialism, are well illustrated in an autobiographic sketch by M. H. Spielman, Maccabean president 1904–07; see Anglo-Jewish Archive, AJ17/2. For an interesting parallel in the life of W. E. B. Du Bois, see Chapter 11.

5. For the records of Zangwill's activity in the Author's Club and the Vagabond's Club see the Sladen Collection, Richmond (England) Central Library, 14252/22.

6. Michael Millgate, *Thomas Hardy* (Oxford: Oxford University Press, 1982), pp. 334–35.

7. Ibid., pp. 249, 440. As late as 1920 Zangwill wrote a card to Hardy on which he had composed a birthday poem comparing the British author to the Jewish philosopher Spinoza; see Israel Zangwill file, Schwadron Collection, Manuscript Division, The Jewish National and University Library, Jerusalem.

8. Correspondence between Sladen and Zangwill evidently began in 1893 and continued until at least 1919, consisting primarily of discussions of social visits, club activities, or of Sladen's various "projects"; see Sladen Collection, 14252/16, 22, 27, 32, 38, 66, 73.

9. Douglas Sladen, *Twenty Years of My Life* (London: Constable and Co.,

1915), p. 91. Of course Zangwill was still alive and in contact with Sladen when these lines were written, although he had greatly aged and changed from this more youthful portrait.

10. Ibid.

11. For a detailed record of the relationship between Zangwill and Jerome, see documentation in Central Zionist Archives, A120/58/2.

12. Israel Zangwill, "Incurable," in *Ghetto Tragedies* (London: McClure and Co., 1893), pp. 191–222.

13. The Sabbath law that is allegedly violated in this instance is that which prohibits one from traveling more than 2,000 cubits beyond a town boundary.

14. Zangwill, *Ghetto Tragedies,* pp. 225–36.

15. Israel Zangwill, *They That Walk in Darkness* (London: William Heinemann, 1899).

16. Ibid., p. 53.

17. Ibid., pp. 57–86.

18. Ibid., p. 81.

19. Ibid., p. 85.

20. Ibid., p. 15.

21. Ibid., p. 28.

22. Ibid., p. 143.

23. Ibid., p. 157.

24. Ibid., p. 131, where the narrator meets in Prague a group still devoted to the pseudomessiah Sabbatai Zevi; in *Dreamers of the Ghetto* Zangwill discusses him at length. If there is any Chassidic source at all for this story, it derives from a very distorted interpretation of the enigmatic figure, the Maid of Ludomir. However, the messianic doctrine expressed in the story has no normative Jewish source, and it is significant to note that Zangwill attributes such Christianized notions of the messiah to any group of Jews.

25. Zangwill, *Walk in Darkness,* pp. 111–26. In fact, Zangwill visited his father in Jerusalem on his trip to Palestine in 1897.

26. Israel Zangwill, "Flutter-duck, A Ghetto Grotesque," in *The King of Schnorrers* (London: William Heinemann, 1894), pp. 369–400. The story is illustrated by the author's brother, Mark.

27. Zangwill, "The King of Schnorrers," in ibid., pp. 3–156.

28. I would like to thank Abba Rubin for pointing out to me many of these observations.

29. Israel Zangwill, "Gratitude," *Jewish Chronicle,* 14 March 1890, p. 8. Zangwill was responding to the newspaper's 7 March congratulations to him on his appointment as editor of *Puck.*

30. Israel Zangwill, *Ghetto Comedies* (London: William Heinemann, 1907).

31. Ibid., p. 25. The identification of the Jews with Jesus and his teachings is treated extensively in the discussion of Zangwill's earlier work, *Dreamers of the Ghetto;* see Chapter 7.

32. Zangwill, *Ghetto Comedies,* p. 36. Emphasis in original.

33. See Chapter 7; and see Chapter 11 for a similar evolution by W. E. B. Du Bois.

34. Zangwill, *Ghetto Comedies,* pp. 193–221.

35. Ibid., p. 197.

36. Ibid., pp. 215–16.

37. Ibid., p. 62. In several places Zangwill identifies the Boers with the Jews.

38. For a discussion of Zangwill's marriage and an explanation for the paradoxical advocacy of Jewish assimilationism *and* Jewish nationalism see Chapters 7–9.

39. Zangwill, *Ghetto Comedies,* pp. 89–115.

40. Ibid., pp. 375–424.

41. Ibid., pp. 419–20.

42. Ibid., p. 420.

43. Ibid., p. 422.

44. Ibid.

45. Israel Zangwill, *The Master* (London: William Heinemann, 1895). The first installment appeared in *To-day* in the 6 May 1894 issue and concluded in the 10 November 1894 issue. It was Jerome's policy that works appearing in *To-day* could not be issued as bound publications for at least six months after appearing in his magazine. The American serialization appeared in *Harper's Weekly,* 5 May to 24 November 1894.

46. " 'The Master' and Its Author," p. 361.

47. Zangwill, *Master,* p. 431.

48. Ibid.

49. Ibid., p. 358.

50. Ibid., pp. 454–55.

51. Max Nordau's most explicit treatment is in *Degeneration* (London: William Heinemann, 1895), which appeared in English translation. In his "The Position of Judaism," *North American Review,* April 1895, p. 435, Zangwill identifies himself with Nordau's "rallying cry of sanity in the face of a Europe given over to morbid literary cults . . . ," as expressed in this work. However, sympathetic though Zangwill is to Nordau's aesthetic ideas, he could not accept the doctrines of Caesar Lombroso and Ernst Haeckel as espoused by Nordau, nor his condemnation of Tolstoyan philosophy. See also Harold Fisch, "Israel Zangwill: Prophet of the Ghetto," *Judaism* 13:4 (Fall 1964): 407.

52. For Nordau's view see *Degeneration,* pp. 556–57, where he says, inter alia, "It is the sacred task of all healthy and moral men to take part in the work of protecting and saving those who are not already too deeply diseased." Employing more felicitous language, Zangwill certainly agreed. Of course these concepts of the social functions of art are quite traditional; see, for instance, Ben Jonson's *The Staple of News* (1626).

53. Zangwill, *Master,* p. 322. In "Position of Judaism," p. 438, Zangwill employs exactly these terms in describing contemporary Judaism's universal

mission. For Zangwill's interpretation of the theological implication of this "Trinity" that is "mysteriously one," see the discussion in Chapter 7.

54. See Chapters 9 and 10.

55. Typical of the reviews are *Athenaeum*, 18 May 1895, p. 638; *Bookman* (London) 8, June 1895, pp. 84–85; *Critic*, 6 July 1895, pp. 3–4; *Dial*, 1 July 1895, p. 20; *Spectator*, 13 July 1895, pp. 55–56.

56. Israel Zangwill, *The Mantle of Elijah* (London: William Heinemann, 1900), pp. 325–26.

57. Ibid., pp. 405–06. That these "female-ideals" are, in fact, her *father*'s "mantle" does not occur to Allegra.

58. "The Torch-Bearer, A Drama In Four Acts, by Israel Zangwill," p. 98. Emphasis in original. A typed ms., it evidently was composed after his marriage in 1903, when his feminism had become even more pronounced, but the play still faithfully reflects the central themes of the novel; Central Zionist Archives, A120/40/2. The dramatic version seems never to have been publicly performed.

59. Ibid., p. 2.

60. See, for instance, *Athenaeum*, 17 November 1900, p. 641; *Bookman* (London) 19, December 1900, p. 86; *Dial*, 16 April 1901, p. 269; *Nation*, 28 February 1901, pp. 181–82; *Outlook*, 1 December 1900, p. 574.

61. Israel Zangwill, *Without Prejudice* (London: T. Fisher Unwin, 1896). Many of these essays were reprinted in the American periodical, *Critic*, in Zangwill's regular column, "Men, Women, and Books," 1894–96.

62. See especially reviews in *Critic*, 27 February 1897, pp. 142–43, and *Spectator*, 2 January 1897, pp. 21–22.

63. Zangwill, *Without Prejudice*, pp. 40–41.

64. Ibid., pp. 83–85, 142–43, 171.

65. Ibid., p. 274.

66. Ibid.

67. Israel Zangwill, *The Grey Wig, Stories and Novelettes* (London: William Heinemann, 1903). As if to carry out this desk-clearing operation most thoroughly, in 1903 Zangwill also published a collection of his various poems, many having originally appeared in the *Jewish Standard*, under the title *Blind Children* (London: William Heinemann, 1903). Zangwill's poetry was generally mediocre and not enthusiastically received by the critics or the general public; see, for instance, *Critic*, September 1903, pp. 264–65. For an explanation of the significance for Zangwill of the year 1903, see Chapter 7.

68. *The Big Bow Mystery* (London: Henry and Co., 1892) was originally serialized in the *Star* and attracted scant attention at that time or later; *Merely Mary Ann* (London: Raphael Tuck and Sons, 1893) appeared with illustration by Mark Zangwill and also attracted little notice when first published. *The Serio-Comic Governess* had previously also appeared separately (London: Shurmer Sibthrop, 1902).

69. Schneiderman, "Zangwill," p. 131. For a discussion of the play, *Merely Mary Ann*, see Chapter 9.

70. Zangwill, *Grey Wig*, p. 396.

71. Israel Zangwill, "The Serio-Comic Governess, Comedy In Four Acts," pp. 92, 94; typed ms. in Central Zionist Archives, A120/41/3.

7: The Crisis

1. Israel Zangwill, "The Position of Judaism," *North American Review* 160:461 (April 1895): 425.

2. Ibid.

3. Ibid., pp. 425, 426.

4. For a discussion of the Hegelian origins of this historical positivist approach and a critique of it, see Karl Popper, *The Open Society and Its Enemies* (Princeton: Princeton University Press, 1966), vol. 2.

5. Zangwill, "Position of Judaism," pp. 426–27. For an echo of this view by W. E. B. Du Bois, see Chapter 11.

6. Ibid., pp. 428–29, 432.

7. Claude Montefiore, "Mr. Smith: A Possibility," *Jewish Quarterly Review* 6 (October 1893): 100–10. Among other concerns in this article, Montefiore was extremely anxious to distinguish his own Liberal Judaism from theologically similar positions espoused by Unitarianism; this is also the case in his "Unitarianism and Judaism in Their Relations to Each Other," *Jewish Quarterly Review* 9 (January 1897): 240–53 and "Liberal Judaism in England: its Difficulties and its Duties," *Jewish Quarterly Review* 12 (April 1900): 618–50. For a useful account of the establishment of Liberal Judaism, see Ellen M. Umansky, "The Origins of Liberal Judaism in England: The Contribution of Lilly H. Montagu," *Hebrew Union College Annual* 55 (1984): 309–22.

8. Letter from I. Zangwill to the editor, *Christian Commonwealth*, 8 December 1908; Central Zionist Archives, Jerusalem, file A120/73.

9. Zangwill, "Position of Judaism," p. 429.

10. Ibid., pp. 435–36.

11. Ibid., pp. 437–38. For Du Bois's views on these concepts see Chapter 11.

12. Ibid., p. 439.

13. Ibid., p. 432.

14. Ibid.

15. Ibid., p. 439.

16. Israel Zangwill, *Dreamers of the Ghetto* (New York: Harper and Brothers, 1898), preface.

17. M. J. Landa, *The Jew in Drama* (London: P. S. King and Sons, 1926), p. 272.

18. Israel Zangwill, "To the American Jew," *Jewish Chronicle*, 18 March 1898, p. 15, as "reprinted from the Appendix to the Jewish Publication Society Special Edition of 'Dreamers of the Ghetto.' " Comments Heinrich Graetz (in *History of the Jews* [Philadelphia: Jewish Publication Society of America, 1895],

5:125), on the contrastive pair: "Without dreaming of it, Spinoza possessed in the East an ally, diametrically his opposite, who worked hard for the destruction of Judaism. . . . Sabbatai Zevi was at once Spinoza's opposite and ally."

19. See Zangwill, *Dreamers,* preface; compare to Solomon Schechter, *Studies in Judiasm* (London: Adams and Charles Black, 1896), chap. 1, and "Dr. Graetz on 'Jewish Sects,' " *Jewish Chronicle,* 17 March 1899, p. 26.

20. There is also a chapter devoted to Theodore Herzl, but for Zangwill he was not a historical character but a contemporary. For Zangwill's treatment of Herzl in *Dreamers of the Ghetto* see discussion on Zionism later in this chapter.

21. Zangwill, "To the American Jew," p. 14. It is interesting that Zangwill completely ignores Maimonides although he also combined the universal and the particular; however, not being a heretic, he would hardly have contributed to Zangwill's argument.

22. Zangwill, *Dreamers,* pp. 201, 205.

23. Ibid., p. 332.

24. Ibid., p. 334.

25. Ibid., pp. 264, 267, 273.

26. Ibid., pp. 281, 283.

27. Ibid., p. 285. This was the contemporary historical assessment; see reference in n. 19 above. However, this view is no longer considered tenable by most historians; see, for instance, Moshe Idel, *Kabbalah: New Perspectives* (New Haven: Yale University Press, 1988). But Zangwill's treatment of Israel Baal Shem Tov as a heretic was largely his own idiosyncratic interpretation.

28. A typed ms., with handwritten corrections, of the drama "The Deliverer of Israel" has been preserved among Zangwill's papers; see Central Zionist Archives, A120/3412. The play seems never to have been publicly produced.

29. Zangwill, *Dreamers,* pp. 120–21.

30. Ibid., p. 177.

31. Ibid., p. 219. Here Zangwill quotes approvingly from the closing lines of the *Ethics:* "We see, then, what is the strength of the wise man, and by how much he surpasses the ignorant who is driven forward by lust alone." This is, in fact, the primary point of this vignette.

32. "The Rencontre," identical to "Moses and Jesus," first appeared in "Morour and Charouseth," *Jewish Standard,* 25 December 1889, p. 5.

33. Zangwill, *Dreamers,* p. 20.

34. Ibid., p. 28.

35. Ibid., pp. 39, 60–61.

36. Ibid., p. 459.

37. Ibid., p. 478.

38. Ibid., pp. 491–92.

39. Ibid., pp. 503–04.

40. Ibid., pp. 505–06. Elizabeth Salter, in an analysis of *Piers Plowman,* refers to this tension between the spiritual ideal and the mundane actual in William Langland's poem as "the quality of disturbance," which characterized his entire era; see Elizabeth Salter, *Fourteenth Century English Poetry* (Oxford: Clarendon Press, 1983), p. 102.

41. Zangwill, *Dreamers,* p. 507.

42. Ibid., p. 510. Zangwill's pessimism contrasts markedly with the optimism of Nordau, as represented in Nordau's *The Interpretation of History* (London: Rebman, 1910), where faith in materialist biological reductionism is untroubled by metaphysical doubt. Considering where such biologisms were to lead in Germany, this absence of doubt serves as a chilling portent.

43. Zangwill, *Dreamers,* p. 511.

44. Ibid., p. 521.

45. Ibid. This assessment of religion echoes the argument expounded in "Position of Judaism"; see quotation cited in n. 11 above.

46. Zangwill, *Dreamers,* p. 522.

47. Israel Zangwill to Salvena Grant, 5 May 1897, from Constantinople; Schwadron Collection, Manuscript Division, The Jewish National and University Library, Jerusalem.

48. See, for instance, *Bookman* (London) 14 April 1898, pp. 7–8; *Critic,* 30 April 1898, p. 299; and *Dial,* 1 August 1898, pp. 78–79.

49. *Jewish Chronicle,* 25 March 1898, p. 25.

50. See, for instance, Elsie Bonita Adams, *Israel Zangwill* (New York: Twayne Publishers, 1971); Maurice Wohlgelernter, *Israel Zangwill* (New York: Columbia University Press, 1964); and Linda G. Zatlin, *The Nineteenth-Century Anglo-Jewish Novel* (Boston: Twayne Publishers, 1981), pp. 114–21.

51. Solomon Schechter to Israel Zangwill, 18 March 1898; Central Zionist Archives, A120/58/6. G. Abrahams, in "On Zangwill," *Jewish Chronicle,* supplement, August 1926, p. 1, also notices that "to Zangwill the suicide in Chad Gadya was the logical end of him who saw the light in the Cathedral" in the opening chapter and remarks that Zangwill leaned toward Christianity (evidently meaning that he believed in Jesus); however, he dismisses *Dreamers of the Ghetto* as an insignificant work, believing Zangwill's reputation rested primarily on *Children of the Ghetto,* which is undoubtedly correct although a non sequitor with regard to the religious questions the later book poses.

52. See Chapter 10. This source confirms that the romantic episode in "The Jewish Trinity" is autobiographical (see Chapter 6).

53. Joseph Leftwich, *Israel Zangwill* (New York: Thomas Yoseloff, 1957), p. 98.

54. Mathilde Schechter to Israel Zangwill, 17 July 1898; Central Zionist Archives, A120/58/6.

55. Mathilde Schechter to Israel Zangwill, 17 August 1898; Central Zionist Archives, A120/58/6. Emphasis in original.

56. Leftwich, *Zangwill,* p. 98. Among Zangwill's papers are several sets of

correspondence that suggest possible romantic attachments, but the evidence is very sketchy and possibly deliberately incomplete. See especially Central Zionist Archives, A120/78/2.

57. Evelyn Sharp, *Hertha Ayrton* (London: Edward Arnold and Co., 1926), pp. 114–16.

58. Edith Ayrton's birth date received in personal communication from her son, Oliver Zangwill.

59. Sharp, *Hertha Ayrton,* p. 36. But see also the discussion in William Baker, *George Eliot and Judaism* (Sulzburg: Institut für Englische Sprache und Literatur, 1975).

60. Sharp, *Hertha Ayrton,* pp. 152–53. Emphasis in original. The account of Hertha Ayrton's biography is based on Sharp and on file 5, the Joseph Moss Family Genealogy, in the Albert Montefiore Hyamson Papers, Anglo-Jewish Archive, London.

61. The *Times* (London), 27 November 1903, p. 9.

62. On Zangwill's dispute with Gaster over Zionist policy, see Chapter 8.

63. See Central Zionist Archives, A120/78/2. It was to A. Chaplin and his wife that Zangwill dedicated his last published novel, *Jinny the Carrier* (London: William Heinemann, 1919); see Chapter 9.

64. Israel Zangwill, "Singer vs. Schechter," *Jewish Chronicle,* 26 October 1900, p. 7. See Chapter 11 for similar depictions of "double consciousness" by W. E. B. Du Bois.

65. Ibid.

66. Weizmann to Ussishkin, 16 December 1903, in *The Letters and Papers of Chaim Weizmann,* ed. M. W. Weisgal (London: Oxford University Press, 1972), vol. 3, ser. A, p. 165.

67. Ibid., Weizmann to Vera Khatzman, 9 July 1904, p. 274, and Weizmann to Ussishkin, 14 July 1904, p. 281. Like Zangwill, Nordau had also intermarried but before his involvement in the Zionist movement.

68. Leopold Kompert, *Scenes from the Ghetto: Studies of Jewish Life* (London: Remington and Co., 1882), pp. 195–96.

69. Moses Hess, "Rome and Jerusalem," in *The Zionist Idea,* ed. Arthur Hertzberg (New York: Harper and Row, 1959), p. 133. Like Zangwill in "Position of Judaism," Hess is concerned with a Jewish universalist mission that will serve to justify continued Jewish ethnic survival.

70. Hess, "Rome and Jerusalem," p. 138.

71. Leo Pinsker, "Auto-Emancipation," in Hertzberg, *Zionist Idea,* pp. 191–92, 193. Emphasis in original. Hertzberg, pp. 180–81, notes that Pinsker took an even more forthright stand on these issues after he became the leader of Chovevei Zion in 1884.

72. Moshe Leib Lilienblum, "The Future of Our People," in Hertzberg, *Zionist Idea,* pp. 176–77.

73. Theodore Herzl, "The Jewish State," in Hertzberg, *Zionist Idea,* pp. 217, 222; this pamphlet originally appeared in 1896.

74. Ibid., p. 221. Emphasis added.

75. Ibid., p. 222. Leo Pinsker in "Auto-Emancipation" had also been willing to entertain alternative sites but later accepted only the Land of Israel as desirable; ibid., pp. 180, 197.

76. Ibid., p. 203. See also Michael Heymann, ed., *The Uganda Controversy* (Jerusalem: Institute for Zionist Research at Tel-Aviv University, 1970), 1:16; Heymann makes it clear that the Russian Jews never accepted a limitation to Herzl's "political" Zionism and an abandonment of "practical" ventures. For a thorough study of the conflicting forces operating during the formation of the nationalist movement, see David Vital, *The Origins of Zionism* (Oxford: Oxford University Press, 1975).

77. Zangwill, *Dreamers*, pp. 441–52.

78. Ibid., p. 445.

79. See Chapter 4 for Zangwill's preoccupation with the persecution of Russian Jewry while he was serving as editor of *Ariel*.

80. *The Complete Diaries of Theodore Herzl*, ed. Raphael Patai and trans. Harry Zohn (New York: Herzl Press/Thomas Yoseloff, 1960), 1:272–73, entry for 17 November 1895.

81. Ibid., pp. 276–77, entry for 21 November 1895.

82. Israel Zangwill, "Passover Ramblings—Without Prejudice," *Jewish Chronicle*, 15 April 1896, p. 16. Numbering added to sentences for expository clarity.

83. Zangwill, *Dreamers*, pp. 430–40.

84. Ibid., pp. 432, 433.

85. Ibid.

86. Ibid., pp. 439–40.

87. Zangwill, "To the American Jew," p. 15.

88. Ibid. Note again the Hegelian assumption here that races "deserve" to survive or disappear depending upon their spiritual contribution to world history.

89. Israel Zangwill, "Zionism," *Contemporary Review* 76 (October 1899): 500–11.

90. Ibid., p. 503.

91. That just such a vibrant religious regeneration had been in process from several decades in Central and Eastern Europe escaped Zangwill's Westerner's insular attention completely.

92. Zangwill, "Zionism," p. 509. Emphasis added.

93. Ibid., p. 507. In a letter to the editor of the *Jewish Chronicle*, 14 April 1898, p. 8, Zangwill expresses the same sentiment that "I hope he [Herzl] has retained the option of making his State outside Palestine, if necessary."

94. Zangwill, "Zionism," pp. 506, 511.

95. Israel Zangwill, "The Return to Palestine," *New Liberal Review* 2:11 (December 1901): 615–34.

96. Ibid., p. 627.

97. Ibid.

98. Ibid., pp. 627, 628, 631.

99. Ibid., p. 627.

100. Zangwill's remark of 1900 is reported in "The Fourth Zionist Congress," *Jewish Chronicle*, supplement, 17 August 1900, p. iv; the list of official English delegates to the Fifth Zionist Congress is reported in "The Zionist Movement," *Jewish Chronicle*, 13 December 1901, p. 25.

101. Zangwill, "Return to Palestine," p. 634.

8: Jewish Nationalist

1. See Chapter 9 for a discussion of Zangwill's universalist program and politics.

2. See Chapter 10 for a discussion of Zangwill's postwar career.

3. "The Maccabean Club," *Jewish Chronicle*, 14 June 1901, pp. 11,12.

4. "The Zionist Movement," *Jewish Chronicle*, 13 December 1901, p. 25.

5. "The Fifth Zionist Congress, A Summary," *Jewish Chronicle*, 10 January 1902, p. 20.

6. Israel Zangwill, "The Return to Palestine," *New Liberal Review* 2:11 (December 1901): 627.

7. Ibid., p. 628.

8. Ibid., p. 634.

9. For a recent scholarly assessment of Zangwill's nationalism see David Vital, "Zangwill and Modern Jewish Nationalism," *Modern Judaism* 4:3 (October 1984): 243–53.

10. Zangwill appears unaware that this was exactly the intention of the emancipators, as discussed in Chapter 2.

11. Zangwill, "Return to Palestine," pp. 625, 627.

12. See Chapter 7 for a further characterization of the views of West and East European Jewish nationalists.

13. George Eliot, *Daniel Deronda* (Harmondsworth: Penguin Books, 1967), p. 592. The parallel of Zangwill's views and Eliot's Mordecai is obvious despite Zangwill's denial in "Zion, Whence Cometh My Help," *World's Work* 2:9 (August 1903): 312.

14. Zangwill, "Return to Palestine," pp. 625, 632.

15. Ibid., pp. 622, 624–25.

16. Zangwill, "Zion," p. 312.

17. In addition to "The Return to Palestine" and "Zion, Whence Cometh My Help," see also "Mr. Lucien Wolf on 'The Zionist Peril,' " *Jewish Quarterly Review* 17 (April 1905): 397–425.

18. Although there is no documentary evidence, no doubt a strong contributing element in the conflict between the two men was Zangwill's 1903 non-Jewish marriage. However, the ideological component was both genuine and potent.

19. "The Fifth Zionist Congress," *Jewish Chronicle*, 3 January 1902, pp. 30–

31. Baron Maurice de Hirsch (1831–1896) had originated the ICA in 1891 to resettle persecuted Russian Jews in "colonies" in North and South America.

20. "The Zionist Movement," *Jewish Chronicle,* 7 February 1902, pp. 20–24. Correspondence between Zangwill and Gaster appears to cease at this point and is only briefly resumed in 1914 when Zangwill solicited Gaster's knowledge of Romania for purposes of British war propaganda; Zangwill to Gaster, 23 September and 16 October 1914; Israel Zangwill File, Anglo-Jewish Archive, London.

21. Israel Zangwill, letter to the editor, "The Hirsch Millions," the *Times* (London), 4 February 1902, p. 10.

22. See, for instance, letters from Israel Zangwill to the editor, subtitled "The Hirsch Millions," the *Times* (London), 14 July 1902, p. 14; 23 March 1903, p. 10; 4 April 1903, p. 9; 16 April 1903, p. 8; "The Jewish Colonization Association Bill," 2 July 1903, p. 10. Lucien Wolf, letter to the editor, subtitled "The Hirsch Millions," the *Times* (London), 30 March 1903, p. 12; 11 April 1903, p. 8.

23. "Zionist Demonstration at the Shoreditch Town Hall," *Jewish Chronicle,* 22 May 1903, p. 24.

24. The WZO majority agreed with the ICA's champions in their assessment of the ethnic traditional heritage but disagreed over the future and legitimacy of the Diaspora, as will become evident in the discussion of Territorialism later in this chapter.

25. See Chapter 2 for discussion of this distinction. In *Zionism: Its History and Its Aims* (London: English Zionist Federation, 1905), Max Nordau, like Zangwill, adopted the predominant Western Jewish interpretation of the nationalist cause, writing (p. 18): "Zionists are firmly convinced that the anxieties of the assimilated Jews are without foundation. The reunion of the Jewish people in Palestine will not have the consequence the latter fear. Once there is a Jewish country, the Jews will have the choice of emigrating thither or of remaining in their present home."

26. For details of Zangwill's speech see "The Sixth Zionist Congress at Basle," *Jewish Chronicle,* supplement, 28 August 1903, pp. v–vii.

27. Although popularly known as the "Uganda scheme" the East African Protectorate, including the region involved, is in contemporary Kenya.

28. Description as given in PRO file "Africa (East) Jewish Settlement 1903," F02/783/111–23.

29. "Draft of letter to [Herzl's official British negotiator, Leopold] Greenberg, 14 August, 1903," PRO file F02/783/34–38. The offer was officially made to the Jewish Colonial Trust and included a detailed draft charter for the self-governing settlement; see "Jewish Colonization Scheme. Terms and Conditions," PRO file F02/783/11–26. For thorough discussions of the East Africa negotiations and of the spectrum of Zionist responses to them, see especially Michael Heymann, ed., *The Uganda Controversy,* 2 vols. (Jerusalem: Institute for Zionist Research at Tel-Aviv University, 1970, 1977); Oskar K. Rabinowicz, *Herzl, Architect of the Balfour Declaration* (New York: Herzl Press, 1958); idem,

"New Light on the East Africa Scheme," in the *Rebirth of Israel*, ed. Israel Cohen (London: Edward Goldston and Sons, 1952), pp. 77–97; and Robert G. Weisbord, "Israel Zangwill's Jewish Territorial Organization and the East Africa Zion," *Jewish Social Studies* 30:2 (April 1968): 89–108.

30. Rabinowicz, *Herzl*, pp. 5–9. These negotiations had begun in October 1902, but the Egyptian government rejected the idea. Oskar K. Rabinowicz, in *Fifty Years of Zionism* (London: Robert Anscombe and Co., 1952), pp. 49–50, and Weisbord, "Zangwill's Jewish Territorial Association," pp. 89–90, insist that Herzl viewed El Arish, a region near Palestine, merely as a temporary humanitarian expedient, not as a permanent alternative to Jewish possession of Palestine. This view seems confirmed in the draft of a letter on the El Arish negotiations Herzl sent to Zangwill on 24 October 1902 to translate into English for Lord Landsdowne, in *The Complete Diaries of Theodore Herzl*, ed. Raphael Patai and trans. Harry Zohn (New York: Herzl Press/Thomas Yoseloff, 1960), 4:1364–67.

31. In January 1902 a royal commission was established to investigate immigrant legislation, and the Aliens Act received final Parliamentary approval 19 July 1905; see discussion in Geoffrey Alderman, *The Jewish Community in British Politics* (Oxford: Clarendon Press, 1983), pp. 86–107, and John A. Garrard, *The English and Immigration 1880–1910* (London: Oxford University Press, 1971), pp. 38–47. Joseph Chamberlain (1836–1914) was, of course, famous for his very vigorous and controversial imperial policy in Africa; see, for instance, Michael L. G. Balfour, *Britain and Joseph Chamberlain* (London: Allen and Unwin, 1985), and Richard Jay, *Joseph Chamberlain, A Political Study* (Oxford: Clarendon Press, 1981).

32. Joseph Chamberlain, "Tariff Reform and Unemployment," 15 December 1904, in *Mr. Chamberlain's Speeches*, ed. Charles W. Boyd (London: Constable and Co., 1914), 2:263, 264–65. The "late Dr. Herzl" had died on 3 July 1904.

33. Rabinowicz, *Fifty Years*, p. 52, and Weisbord, "Zangwill's Jewish Territorial Association," p. 90, agree that Herzl was primarily concerned with obtaining official British recognition of the WZO as a political representative of world Jewry. That Herzl indeed viewed the East Africa offer primarily as a diplomatic bargaining chip is suggested in his diary entry of 13 May 1903; see Patai, *Diaries of Herzl*, 4:1487.

34. Inspired by Menachem Mendel Ussishkin (1863–1941), many East European Zionists were former Chovevei Zion adherents, still deeply influenced by a "practical Zionism" reflecting its Russian Populist romantic heritage; see David Vital, *Zionism: The Formative Years* (Oxford: Oxford University Press, 1982), chap. 12; Heymann, *Uganda Controversy*, 1:16; 2:6; Rabinowicz, *Herzl*, p. 13.

35. Lucien Wolf, letter to the editor, subtitled "Lord Landsdowne and the Zionists," the *Times* (London), 28 August 1903, p. 5.

36. Heymann, *Uganda Controversy*, 2:43.

37. In September 1903 a settlers' committee in Nairobi communicated its

opposition to the Foreign Office, which officially administered the protectorate at this time, and similar hostility was expressed by the bishop of Mombasa and the protectorate's governor; see PRO files F02/785/51, 60–63, 127.

38. Marginal note by Landsdowne; Memorandum, Hurst to Landsdowne, 16 December 1903; PRO file F02/785/172–173.

39. Heymann, *Uganda Controversy*, 2:8.

40. Weizmann to Ussishkin and others, 20 October 1903, in *The Letters and Papers of Chaim Weizmann*, ed. M. W. Weisgal (London: Oxford University Press, 1972), vol. 3, ser. A, pp. 62–63. In this letter, Weizmann displays impressive insight into Zangwill's psychology but misjudges the results: "as a man of conscience and intellect he [Zangwill] is beginning to feel inner contradictions and will now impose some reserve on himself [as a politician and fighter for Africa]."

41. Israel Zangwill, "The Sixth Zionist Congress," in *Speeches, Articles, and Letters of Israel Zangwill*, ed. Maurice Simon (London: Soncino Press, 1937), p. 182. The contents of the speech are also summarized in "The Recent Zionist Congress," *Jewish Chronicle*, 11 September 1903, pp. 10–13.

42. Simon, *Speeches, Articles, and Letters*, p. 185. Emphasis in original.

43. Ibid., pp. 193, 195.

44. Zangwill's criticism of his British opponents is a principal feature of the *Jewish Chronicle* report of the speech. For Wolf's opposition to the East Africa scheme, see n. 35 above; on Gaster's opposition see Heymann, *Uganda Controversy*, 2:125–26.

45. Israel Zangwill, *The East Africa Question; Zionism And England's Offer* (New York: Maccabaean Publishing Co., 1904), p. 5.

46. Ibid., p. 6.

47. Ibid., pp. 6–7.

48. Ibid., pp. 8, 13–14.

49. Ibid., p. 18.

50. Ibid., p. 31. Zangwill evidently became aware of the presence of Arab inhabitants of Palestine during his 1897 visit there as a member of the "Maccabean pilgrimage," and it was this awareness, among other factors, that contributed to his original skepticism about the feasibility of Zionism, as, for example, in Israel Zangwill, "Zionism," *Contemporary Review* 76 (October 1899): 507 (see discussion in Chapter 7). For discussion of other early Zionists' views, see Yosef Gorny, *Zionism and the Arabs 1882–1948: A Study in Ideology* (Oxford: Clarendon Press, 1987), pp. 20–39, 40–77.

51. Zangwill, *East Africa Question*, p. 34. This phrase exactly echoes Zangwill's 1899 observation, "The case against Palestine is indeed so black that one is tempted to say that Zionism would be practical but for Zion" (see Zangwill, "Zionism," p. 507).

52. Zangwill, *East Africa Question*, p. 55. However, by 1905 Zangwill perceived that although the Arab inhabitants of Palestine represented a difficulty for the establishment of a Jewish state there, there was at least a theoretical alternative to that of the Jews choosing to settle elsewhere. During the First

World War, Zangwill became a champion of this Zionist alternative to his Territorialist solution; see the section, "Militant Zionism," later in this chapter.

53. Various speeches and debates are recorded in several venues across Britain in the pages of the *Times* (London) and the *Jewish Chronicle.* Among Zangwill's debate opponents were Lucien Wolf, Moses Gaster, and fellow Maccabean and Zionist, Herbert Bentwich (1856–1932).

54. Zangwill's Congress speech is reported in detail in "The Seventh Zionist Congress," *Jewish Chronicle,* 4 August 1905, pp. 19–21. In his address Zangwill claimed to be carrying on Herzl's vision and bitterly attacked his opponents, particularly Ussishkin's "Zionists of Zion" and the ICA.

55. Greenberg to Lyttleton [Principal Secretary of State for the Colonial Department], 8 August 1905; PRO file "East Africa Protectorate, 1905," CO533/10/89; see also CO879/87/147. Between 1903 and 1905 responsibility for the protectorate had been shifted from the Foreign Office to the Colonial Office.

56. Israel Zangwill to Lucien Wolf, 23 August 1905; Central Zionist Archives, Jerusalem, file A77/9/5.

57. PRO FO2/948/290–93.

58. PRO FO2/948/294–95.

59. Israel Zangwill, letter to the editor, subtitled "The Jewish Territorial Organization," 22 August 1905, the *Times* (London), p. 6. The letter already reflects a curious but persistent elitist bias of the ITO (and many other groups) evident in all its endeavors; Zangwill wrote: "[The ITO's] object is . . . to obtain a measure of self-government with which to attract a superior class of emigrants, so as to build up a modern settlement of the best kind." As Zangwill would learn to his discomfiture, the Foreign Office also had an elitist bias when negotiating with Jewish nationalist organizations, being interested only in "influential people"; see Eric Barrington to Lucien Wolf, 14 September 1905, PRO file FO2/948/299–300. That Zangwill viewed the relationship of the ITO to the WZO as noncompetitive is reflected in his correspondence from this period, as for example as 6 November 1905 letter to Gustav Cohen suggesting individuals might acquire membership in both movements in order to achieve their separate goals; Schwadron Collection, Manuscript Division, The Jewish National and University Library, Jerusalem. However the WZO leadership viewed the matter quite differently, as is evident from Greenberg's immediate and explicit repudiation of Zangwill's Territorialist efforts; see L. J. Greenberg to Alfred Lyttleton, 8 August 1905, PRO file CO533/10/89.

60. Zangwill first officially notified the Colonial Office concerning the formation and purpose of the ITO and requested an appointment to discuss arrangements with the British government, 8 September 1905; PRO file CO879/87/173. Lyttleton, in reply, expressed the view that "it was unlikely that the I.T.O. secession movement would assume important dimensions" and that therefore a meeting with Zangwill could serve no productive purpose; PRO file CO879/87/179. Preceding Lyttleton's draft letter to Zangwill, on the same sheet of paper, is a copy of Greenberg's 8 August negative

assessment of Zangwill's project and also his 24 August request that "you explain to Mr. Zangwill that his proposal cannot be entertained"; draft, Alfred Lyttleton to Israel Zangwill, 12 September 1905; PRO file CO533/10/87–88.

61. Zangwill argued that he had the support of influential and philanthropic individuals and groups committed to implementing the East Africa scheme through the ITO; among those mentioned were Arthur Cohen, Philip S. Hartog, A. M. L. Langdon, R. M. Sebag-Montefiore, Sir Isidore Spielman, and Maj.-Gen. Sir Alfred Turner in Britain and Daniel Gugenheim, A. S. Solomons, Oscar S. Straus, Cyrus Sulzberger, and Mayer Sulzberger in the United States (all of whom would later serve, among others, as members of the International Council of the ITO); PRO file CO533/10/545–47 (30 November 1905), but see also CO533/10/533, 537, 540, 541, 542 and CO879/87/247.

62. PRO file CO533/10/538.

63. PRO file CO533/10/535–36.

64. Israel Zangwill, "Letters and the ITO," *Fortnightly Review*, n.s., 79 (April 1906): 633.

65. Earl of Elgin to Israel Zangwill, 8 May 1906; PRO file CO533/24/153–54, based on draft in CO533/24/13.

66. Israel Zangwill for the ITO to the Undersecretary of State for the Colonies, 28 May 1906; PRO file CO533/24/187–88. See also correspondence in Robert G. Weisbord, "Israel Zangwill's Jewish Territorial Organization and the East Africa Zion," *Jewish Social Studies* 30:2 (April 1968): 89–108.

67. Wolf's doubts are recorded by his ITO secretary, Ruth Phillips, in her diary already on 22 February 1906; see Anglo-Jewish Archive, London, file AJ9.

68. Israel Zangwill, "A Land of Refuge," speech delivered at the Manchester Hippodrome, 8 December 1907, in Simon, *Speeches, Articles, and Letters*, p. 234. Between 1906 and 1909 the *Times* (London) carried many reports of Zangwill's speeches on the Territorialist message before ITO and other audiences.

69. Israel Zangwill, "Territorialism As Practical Politics," speech delivered to the Union of Jewish Literary Societies, March 1913, in Simon, *Speeches, Articles, and Letters*, p. 313.

70. Ibid.

71. Israel Zangwill, "Advice to the Ottoman Jews," *Jewish Review* 1:5 (January 1911): 395.

72. Zangwill, "Territorialism As Practical," pp. 312, 318. See Chapter 11 for discussion of W. E. B. Du Bois's parallel adoption of a nationalist program.

73. M. H. Spielman's Maccabean memoirs, 1904–07, Maccabean Papers, Anglo-Jewish Archive, AJ17/2; Spielman, an ITO officer, was president of the Maccabeans during this period. See also diary of Ruth Phillips, entry for 30 January 1906; Anglo-Jewish Archive, AJ9. On the conflict within Anglo-Jewry in general, see Stuart A. Cohen, *English Zionists and British Jews* (Princeton: Princeton University Press, 1982), chap. 3.

74. The *Jewish Chronicle*'s hostility to the East Africa scheme is clear from

its critical editorial remarks in "The Zionist Movement," 18 November 1904. The paper was briefly controlled by ITO sponsors under the editorship of Lucien Wolf, but in 1907 it was acquired by the WZO's Leopold Greenberg, who dominated it and later also the *Jewish World* until his death in 1925; *The Jewish Chronicle 1841–1941* (London: Jewish Chronicle, 1949), pp. 124–31, 157–60.

75. "Cyrenaica," in Simon, *Speeches, Articles, and Letters,* pp. 292–308. Cyrenaica now is in eastern Libya.

76. Stuart A. Cohen, "Israel Zangwill's Project for Jewish Colonization in Mesopotamia: Its Context and Character," *Middle Eastern Studies* 16:3 (October 1980): 200–208. Cohen remarks that the notion, dropped in 1910, was again briefly revived in 1912 but was met with the same discouraging local conditions.

77. J. W. Gregory, *Report on the work of the Commission sent out by the Jewish Territorial Organization under the auspices of the Portuguese Government to examine the territory proposed for the purpose of a Jewish settlement in Angola* (London: ITO Office, 1913). See also PRO file FO/179/532/47, 54, 109.

78. Israel Zangwill to Mayer Sulzberger, 18 January 1912; quoted in Isaac M. Fein, "Israel Zangwill and American Jewry: A Documentary Study," *Jewish Historical Quarterly* 60:1 (September 1970): 23. Zangwill did not, in fact, resign as president of the ITO until June 1925, when his health was already failing; Israel Zangwill to Edward Good, 15 June 1925, Central Zionist Archives, file K11/88/4. The ITO as an organization, although not Territorialism as an idea, was officially dissolved the same year.

79. Jacob Schiff to Israel Zangwill, 24 August 1906, cited in Fein, "Zangwill and American Jewry," p. 28.

80. Lucien Wolf to Israel Zangwill, 24 and 25 September 1906; Central Zionist Archives, file A77/4. In the first letter Wolf explains "that Schiff's scheme offers an opportunity of our [ITO] making a big splash." Characteristically, Zangwill's immediate and primary concern was alleviating the dangers to Russian Jews.

81. Israel Zangwill to Oscar Straus, 25 September 1906; cited in Fein, "Zangwill and American Jewry," p. 29.

82. The negotiations between Schiff and Zangwill are discussed in Fein, "Zangwill and American Jewry," pp. 29–32. Gary Dean Best, "Jacob H. Schiff's Galveston Movement: An Experiment in Immigration Deflection, 1907–1914," *American Jewish Archives* 30:1 (April 1978): 43–79, is also a very important source; see also Zosa Szajkowski, "The Impact of the Russian Revolution of 1905 on American Jewish Life," *YIVO Annual of Jewish Social Science* 17 (1978): 54–118. The Industrial Removal Organization was founded in 1901 with financing provided by the Baron de Hirsch Fund to assist immigrants to settle successfully in American Jewish communities away from the already congested East Coast; for an interesting study of the IRO and the Galveston Plan, see John Livingston, "The Industrial Removal Office, the Galveston Project, and the Denver Jewish Community," *American Jewish History* 68:4 (June 1979): 434–58.

83. Zangwill, "Land of Refuge," pp. 253, 259.

84. Best, "Schiff's Galveston Movement," pp. 75–76.

85. Ibid., pp. 76–79. Schiff privately blamed Zangwill and the ITO as major contributors to the failure of the Galveston project to achieve his expectations for it; obviously outbreak of war in Europe in August 1914 and changing American attitudes toward immigration also were significant factors.

86. Ottoman hostility to the "dream" of Russian-Jewish settlement in Palestine is the subject of Zangwill's vignette "The Palestine Pilgrim," in *Dreamers of the Ghetto* (New York: Harper and Brothers, 1898), pp. 441–52; see discussion in Chapter 7.

87. Zangwill referred to the problem of the current inhabitants of Palestine in his advocacy of the East African scheme at least as early as 1904; see the discussion earlier in this chapter and reference in n. 50. In his address, "The Jewish Race," on the first day of the 1911 Universal Races Congress in London, Zangwill observed: "the [Jewish] attempt to acquire Palestine would have the opposition of Turkey and of the six hundred thousand Arabs in possession"; in Simon, *Speeches, Articles, and Letters*, p. 94. W. E. B. Du Bois also attended the Congress and delivered his address during this same session.

88. Zangwill, "The East Africa Offer," in Simon, *Speeches, Articles, and Letters*, p. 210.

89. For Zangwill's views on war and pacifism, see Chapter 9.

90. See PRO file WO32/11348, 11350, 11352, 11353.

91. "Mr. Zangwill on Jewish Hopes," the *Times* (London), 13 March 1916, p. 5.

92. Vladimir Jabotinsky to Israel Zangwill, 27 January 1918; Central Zionist Archives, file A120/60/7w. Between 1915 and 1917, of course, Jabotinsky did win widespread Anglo-Jewish and Zionist support for the Jewish Legion; see PRO file WO32/11353.

93. Israel Zangwill, "The Balfour Declaration," in Simon, *Speeches, Articles, and Letters*, pp. 331, 334.

94. Arthur Balfour to Lord Rothschild, 2 November 1917, as reproduced in *Encyclopaedia Judaica* (Jerusalem, 1972), 4:131.

95. "Imperial and Foreign News Items," the *Times* (London), 14 November 1917, p. 5.

96. Israel Zangwill, "Before The Peace Conference," February 1919, in Simon, *Speeches, Articles, and Letters*, p. 340.

97. Ibid., p. 341.

98. Israel Zangwill, letter to the editor, subtitled "Jews and Bolshevism," the *Times* (London), 16 January 1920, p. 8.

9: The Melting Pot

1. Benedict de Spinoza, *The Chief Works, Theologico-Political Treatise*, trans. R. H. M. Elwes (London: George Bell and Sons, 1883), 1:46. For an insightful

study of Spinoza, see H. A. Wolfson, *The Philosophy of Spinoza* (Cambridge: Harvard University Press, 1934).

2. Spinoza, *Treatise,* 1:49.

3. Ibid., p. 55.

4. Ibid., p. 64; see also p. 19. For Spinoza, Old Testament revelation arose from "imagination," the inferior and faulty source of knowledge according to his classification (in *Ethics,* prop. 40, schol. 2), while Jesus' genuine prophecies arose without imagination but corresponded to the highest source of knowledge, intuitive knowledge.

5. Spinoza, *Treatise,* 1:186.

6. Ibid., pp. 186–87.

7. See discussion in Chapter 4.

8. Israel Zangwill, "Two Opposing Forces at Work on the Jew," *Menorah* 35:5 (November 1903): 274, 275, 277. In this essay, Zangwill, the newly converted Zionist, suggested that the Jewish mission could be achieved if there were to be a "third national period."

9. Israel Zangwill to Theodore Roosevelt, 25 August 1908, inviting the President to the premiere; see Central Zionist Archives, Jerusalem, file A120/71. In fact, Zangwill had intended to call the play *The Crucible,* but "my manager . . . has a little doubt as to whether the public would understand this word. I mean by it America"; Israel Zangwill to Mary Berenson, 15 July 1908; Central Zionist Archives, file A120/72.

10. For a survey of critical and popular reactions to the play, see Maurice Wohlgelernter, *Israel Zangwill* (New York: Columbia University Press, 1964), pp. 176–78. The primary complaints were those typical of Zangwill's writing: that the plot is too loosely constructed, that it attempts to cover too many subjects in too constricted a medium, that it is extremely wordy and lacks any dramatic momentum. However, not all the critics objected on purely literary grounds; for instance, Clayton Hamilton, in the *Forum* 42 (November 1909): 434, complained that "this extraordinary idea of the function of America emanates, of course, from an author who is himself foreign in nationality and alien in race; it is a view of an outsider looking at us from afar. If this be a sound statement of how God is at present making the American, then God must have altered His plan of operation within very recent years."

11. Israel Zangwill, *The Melting Pot* (London: William Heinemann, 1914), pp. 33, 34.

12. Ibid., pp. 86–87.

13. Ibid., p. 95.

14. Ibid., p. 124.

15. Ibid., pp. 146, 147. Emphasis in original.

16. Ibid., p. 179.

17. Ibid., p. 185. Emphasis in original.

18. The most thorough study of this aspect of the play is Neil Larry Shumsky, "Zangwill's *The Melting Pot:* Ethnic Tensions on Stage," *American Quarterly* 27:1 (March 1975): 29–41. See also Philip Gleason, "The Melting Pot:

Symbol of Fusion or Confusion," *American Quarterly* 16:1 (Spring 1964): 20–46; Joseph Leftwich, *Israel Zangwill* (New York: Thomas Yoseloff, 1957), pp. 252–58; and M. J. Landa, *The Jew in Drama* (London: P. S. King and Sons, 1926), pp. 228–30.

19. Zangwill would, however, have denied that there were any aesthetic contradictions in the play. These he would have defended on the basis of his rather idiosyncratic theory of drama; *The Melting Pot*'s aesthetic inconsistencies, for Zangwill, indicate not faults in psychological characterizations but rather abstract philosophic realities lying behind the play's surface appearances. See discussion later in this chapter.

20. "Mr. Zangwill on America," 27 October 1908, the *Times* (London), p. 5.

21. Israel Zangwill to Joseph Jacobs, 22 September 1909; Central Zionist Archives, file A120/73. Emphasis added.

22. Zangwill, *The Melting Pot*, "Afterword" (written in January 1914), pp. 204–05. That Zangwill considered the "melting pot" eventually to affect American race relations he likewise makes explicit here, although he was not entirely free of prejudice himself: "Even the negrophobia is not likely to remain eternally at its present barbarous pitch. . . . Even upon the negro the 'Melting Pot' of America will not fail to act in a measure as it has acted on the Red Indian, who has found it almost as facile to mate with his white neighbours as with his black."

23. "Mr. Zangwill on America," p. 5.

24. Israel Zangwill to Stephen S. Wise, 26 October 1909; Central Zionist Archives, file A243/91. Emphasis in original. Even many years later Zangwill continued to maintain this view; for instance in 1924, in answer to a query concerning "the paradox that you [Israel Zangwill] have married out of the faith" despite "your obvious disbelief in intermarriage," Zangwill indignantly replied: "I do not see the paradox to which you refer since my wife . . . has the same Jewish ideals as those which you credit me. . . . Judaism is spiritual and you appear to make it racial"; *The Sentinel*, Chicago, 15 February 1924.

25. Zangwill, *The Melting Pot*, p. 207.

26. Ibid., p. 209.

27. Ibid.

28. Ibid., p. 208.

29. Ibid., p. 215.

30. Ibid., pp. 211–13.

31. "Mr. Zangwill on the Drama," 10 October 1904, the *Times* (London), p. 4.

32. Israel Zangwill, "Speech at the Cheshire Cheese to the Poetry Society," 14 March 1913; Central Zionist Archives, A120/34/6.

33. Ibid.

34. Zangwill also wrote dramas dealing with religious issues; see the section "The Next Religion" later in this chapter.

35. Israel Zangwill, *Merely Mary Ann, A Comedy in Four Acts* (London:

Samuel French, 1921). The play is based on a story published in London in 1893 and reprinted in the 1903 collection *The Grey Wig;* see Chapter 6. It is interesting to note that while the original story concludes with Mary Ann and her beloved, Lancelot, a musician, parting in disillusionment, for the stage adaptation, Zangwill added a fourth act, set six years after the conclusion of act 3, in which the couple is fantastically reconciled by imitating the illusions that created their earlier happiness. An identical structure, which was popular with audiences if not with critics, was later, of course, employed by Zangwill in *The Melting Pot.*

36. Prior to this play, *The Great Demonstration* (1892), *Six Persons* (1893), *Threepenny Bits* (1895), and *Children of the Ghetto* (1899) had appeared. *The Serio-Comic Governess* (1904) has already been discussed in Chapter 6.

37. Israel Zangwill, "The Revolted Daughter, A Play In Three Acts," act 1, pp. 5–6; ms., Central Zionist Archives, A120/40/1.

38. Ibid., act 2, pp. 73–74.

39. Ibid., act 3, p. 79.

40. Ibid., p. 102.

41. Ibid., p. 104.

42. "The Revolted Daughter," *Athenaeum,* 30 March 1901, pp. 411–12.

43. Mss. of these plays are located in Central Zionist Archives, files A120/40,41; *Too Much Money* was published in London by William Heinemann in 1924. The satirical drama *Jinny the Carrier* served as the basis for Zangwill's last published novel, *Jinny the Carrier* (London: William Heinemann, 1919), a dense, overwritten, post–First World War novel hearkening back to the halcyon days of a romanticized rural Victorian England; like the play the novel, too, was critically and financially unsuccessful.

44. Israel Zangwill, *The War God* (London: William Heinemann, 1911), act 1, pp. 12–13, 38.

45. Ibid., act 4, pp. 131, 152.

46. Israel Zangwill, "The War Devil. A Prevision," reprinted from the *Daily Chronicle,* 21 April 1913, in the collection of essays *The War for the World* (London: William Heinemann, 1916), pp. 65–66.

47. Ibid., p. 66.

48. Zangwill, *War God,* act 1, pp. 38, 39.

49. Ibid., pp. 39, 40.

50. F. G. Bettany, "The War God," *Bookman* (London) 41, February 1912, p. 267.

51. Ibid. On the other hand, an enthusiastic Stephen S. Wise wrote to Zangwill, " 'The War God' is tremendous. . . . 'The War God' is a great peace document, and, better still, it is a first-rate work of art"; Stephen S. Wise to Israel Zangwill, 12 June 1912, Central Zionist Archives, file A243/91.

52. J. P. Wearing, *The London Stage, 1910–1919* (Metuchen, N.J.: Scarecrow Press, 1982), no. 11.312.

53. See Chapter 4 for discussion of the essay and Chapter 5 for discussion of the novel.

54. Israel Zangwill, "Of Beauty, Faith, and Death," in *Italian Fantasies* (London: William Heinemann, 1910), pp. 9–10, 12.

55. Zangwill, "Risorgimento: With Some Remarks on San Marino and the Millennium," in *Italian Fantasies*, pp. 368–69. That the president of the ITO could denounce particularist "nationalism" is not surprising when it is recalled that Territorialism, unlike Zionism, sought only to found a "land of refuge" for oppressed Jews (not all Jews), and a haven for their still unacculturated traditional Judaic heritage.

56. Israel Zangwill, *The Principle of Nationalities* (London: Watts and Co., 1917), p. 89. Emphasis in original. This is a reprint of Zangwill's Conway Memorial Lecture, which he delivered on 8 March 1917, at the South Place Institute.

57. Israel Zangwill, *Chosen Peoples* (London: George Allen and Unwin, 1918), pp. 25–26, 32, 37, 69–70. This is a reprint—with foreword by the future British High Commissioner of the Palestine mandate, Herbert Samuel, and afterword by Israel Abrahams, Solomon Schechter's successor at Cambridge—of the first Arthur Davis Memorial Lecture, delivered to the Jewish Historical Society at University College, London, "on Easter-Passover 1918/5678."

58. Israel Zangwill, "The Voice of Jerusalem," in the collection of essays, *The Voice of Jerusalem* (London: William Heinemann, 1920), pp. 6–130. Included in this collection are also various prayers in English that Zangwill had originally translated from the Hebrew for inclusion in the bilingual *Singer Siddur*, the *siddur* (i.e., prayer book) commonly used in United Synagogue congregations.

59. Zangwill, "Voice of Jerusalem," pp. 8–9.

60. Ibid., pp. 30, 41–42.

61. Ibid., pp. 30, 45. While the first half of this essay expounds Hebraic assimilationist views, the entire second half is devoted to a bitter denunciation of the WZO for failing, in Zangwill's view, to take advantage of the wartime collapse of Ottoman power in order to secure Palestine as an exclusively Jewish homeland; see discussion in Chapter 10.

62. Israel Zangwill, *The Next Religion* (London: William Heinemann, 1912). Elsie Bonita Adams, in *Israel Zangwill* (New York: Twayne Publishers, 1971), pp. 120–21, interprets the play as Zangwill's response to G. B. Shaw's *Major Barbara*.

63. Zangwill, *The Next Religion*, act 3, pp. 185, 188, 193. Emphasis in original.

64. Ibid., pp. 165–66. Emphasis in original.

65. The Lord Chamberlain also banned performance of Zangwill's *The Melting Pot* a few months after its British premiere in 1914 in response to complaints lodged against it by Britain's new wartime ally, Russia.

66. Israel Zangwill, *Plaster Saints, A High Comedy in Three Movements* (London: William Heinemann, 1914), second movement, pp. 143, 144; third movement, p. 197.

67. Ibid., third movement, pp. 208, 210.

68. Wearing, *London Stage,* no. 14.129. Typical critical comments noted that *Plaster Saints* was "eminently characteristic of him [Zangwill] as a dramatist. Great and manifold as are his abilities as a writer for the theatre, he will never achieve permanent distinction in this direction until he has learned that the invention of special and extravagant instances to demonstrate the truth of a particular and favorite thesis is not apt to result in dramatic veracity and cogency"; *Nation,* 24 June 1915, pp. 717–18.

69. Zangwill, "Voice of Jerusalem," pp. 106, 116, 122.

10: Satan Mekatrig

1. Israel Zangwill, "Satan Mekatrig: A Romance of the London Ghetto," in *The Jewish Calendar, Manual, and Diary, 5650* (London, 1889), p. 52. See Chapter 4 for a discussion of this story.

2. For W. E. B. Du Bois's reaction to the Paris Peace Conference see Chapter 11.

3. Israel Zangwill, *Hands Off Russia* (London: Workers Socialist Federation, 1919), pp. 6–7. In a "Liberty Demonstration" address in May 1919, at Kingsway Hall, Zangwill voiced similar views on Bolshevism; see speech ms. in Central Zionist Archives, Jerusalem, file A120/34/1.

4. Israel Zangwill, "The World and the Jews," *English Review* 30 (January 1920): 66–67. However, Zangwill would not condone just *any* attempt to employ violence "to precipitate the millennium"; it had to be the "right" sort of millennium. Thus, reacting strongly against the violence of Italian fascism in the draft article "The Fascismo Folly," Zangwill argued that Mussolini's actions were despicable just because they arose from following the same "jingoist" principles of the Versailles settlement. Perceptively he observes here, "Unquestionably democracy has not come out well in the tragic years since 1914, but the fault is less with the mob—subject to abnormally tragic provocation—than with its leaders"; see Central Zionist Archives, file A120/34/6.

5. Israel Zangwill, *The Cockpit, A Romantic Drama in Three Acts* (London: William Heinemann, 1921), act 1, p. 34. The inspiration for "Valdania" and "Bosnovina" appears to be the continuing popularity of Anthony Hope Hawkins's 1894 novel about "Ruritania," *The Prisoner of Zenda.*

6. Zangwill, *The Cockpit,* p. 6.

7. Ibid., p. 54.

8. Ibid., act 2, p. 98.

9. Ibid., act 3, p. 216.

10. Ibid., p. 258.

11. See, for example, E. Graham Sutton's review of the play in *Bookman* 61 (February 1922): 246. Sutton's review is particularly stinging in its unfavorable comparison of Zangwill to G. B. Shaw.

12. Israel Zangwill, *The Forcing House, or The Cockpit Continued. A Tragedy in Four Acts* (London: William Heinemann, 1922), act 3, p. 198.

13. Ibid., p. xiv.

14. Israel Zangwill, letter to the editor, subtitled "Bolshevism and Christianity," *Outlook*, 28 April 1923, p. 355.

15. See Chapter 8 for a discussion of the general unity of reaction among Jewish nationalists.

16. Israel Zangwill to Chaim Weizmann, 15 December 1918; Central Zionist Archives, file Z4/69.

17. Ibid. Weizmann and the WZO leadership rejected both of Zangwill's proposals, i.e., nationalization of land and Arab emigration.

18. For a useful discussion of British views, see Bernard Wasserstein, *The British in Palestine* (London: Royal Historical Society, 1978), pp. 34–57, 73–88.

19. Israel Zangwill, "The Voice of Jerusalem," in *The Voice of Jerusalem* (London: William Heinemann, 1920), pp. 90, 98, 106.

20. Israel Zangwill, letter to the editor, subtitled "Peace in Palestine," 17 May 1921, the *Times* (London), p. 4. During Arab mob violence against Jews in Jerusalem in 1920, Vladimir Jabotinsky had advocated organizing Jewish self-defense and was arrested and sentenced by British military authorities for attempting to do so at this time; see Wasserstein, *British in Palestine*, pp. 63–65, and Joseph B. Schechtman, *Rebel and Statesman, The Early Years* (New York: Thomas Yoseloff, 1956), pp. 322–38.

21. Israel Zangwill, "Preface," in Samuel Roth's *Now and Forever, A Conversation with Mr. Israel Zangwill on the Jews and the Future* (New York: Robert M. McBride and Co., 1925), pp. 17–19; Zangwill's preface is dated 1921, the same year the interview was given.

22. Israel Zangwill, letter to the editor, subtitled, "Zionists' Territorial Needs," 8 May 1922, the *Times* (London), p. 8. In this letter, Zangwill particularly attacks those who advocated establishing Palestine as a "spiritual centre" for the Jewish people, noting that such a center already exists: the Bible; what is needed, he argued, is "not a centre, but a circumscribed circumference, such as every other people enjoys . . . ; not a spiritual sophistication, but a solid surveyable territory."

23. The tour, Zangwill's first to America since 1908, lasted from 6 October 1923 until 6 February 1924, when he sailed to France for a stay to assist in the French production of the stage version of *The King of Schnorrers*. Edith Zangwill joined her husband in the United States only for a few weeks in November, after he had decided to extend his original stay of six weeks.

24. Stephen S. Wise, a distinguished American Reform rabbi, was a major force behind the organization and activities of the pro-Zionist American Jewish Congress (AJC); see Stanley Feldstein, *The Land That I Show You* (Garden City: Anchor Press/Doubleday, 1978), pp. 212–14. In 1923 Wise was officially serving as AJC vice-president and chaired the Carnegie Hall meeting to which he introduced Zangwill.

25. The title of the lecture is taken from Isaiah 21:11. The answer, given

in verse 12, reads: "The morning cometh, and also the night: if ye will inquire, inquire ye: return, come."

26. Zangwill's remarks and the audience reaction are reported in "Mr. Zangwill on Zionism," 16 October 1923, the *Times* (London), p. 11.

27. Israel Zangwill, *Watchman, What of the Night?* (New York: American Jewish Congress, 1923), p. 8. The AJC published Zangwill's speech; the copy used here was presented by the author to the British Library and contains his own handwritten emendations.

28. Ibid., p. 5.

29. Ibid., p. 8.

30. Ibid., p. 20.

31. Ibid., p. 37.

32. Ibid., p. 23.

33. Ibid., p. 41.

34. Ibid., p. 42.

35. Ibid., p. 16.

36. Ibid., pp. 31, 33–34.

37. Ibid., pp. 35, 36. Zangwill reiterated this view in his article "Is Political Zionism Dead? Yes," *Nation,* 12 March 1924, pp. 276–78. Chaim Weizmann replied with "Zionism—Alive and Triumphant," in the same issue, pp. 279–80.

38. Zangwill, *Watchman,* p. 40.

39. However, not only did Stephen S. Wise arrange for the American Jewish Congress to publish "Watchman, What of the Night?" within weeks of its delivery, but in private correspondence he assured Zangwill that "despite the differences in viewpoint you did great service to the Jewish cause by reason of the statesmanlike content of your address and the position of the man who uttered it"; Stephen S. Wise to Israel Zangwill, 25 October 1923, Central Zionist Archives, file A243/91. Although Zangwill gladly cooperated with Wise in the publication of the speech, he remained unmollified concerning the rabbi's public remarks even several months later; see Israel Zangwill to Stephen S. Wise, 26 January 1924, Central Zionist Archives, file A243/91. Nonetheless, the two remained friends until Zangwill's death.

40. See reports in the *New York Times,* 16 October, p. 1; 26 October, p. 36; 27 October, p. 26; 29 October, p. 1; 30 October, p. 18; and 16 December 1923, p. 22. See also Joseph Leftwich, *Israel Zangwill* (New York: Thomas Yoseloff, 1957), pp. 113–14, 123, 131; Leftwich, Zangwill's friend, recounts details of the "flood of abuse that poured out on Zangwill" he himself witnessed in 1923.

41. Israel Zangwill to Stephen S. Wise, 26 January 1924, Central Zionist Archives, file A243/91.

42. "Mr. Zangwill Castigates Americans," *Jewish Chronicle,* 16 November 1923, pp. 17–18. Zangwill's speech at the Brooklyn Academy of Music occurred on 3 November and his Town Hall speech five days later.

43. Ibid.

44. Ibid.

45. Ibid.

46. Harry Schneiderman, "Israel Zangwill, A Biographical Sketch," *The American Jewish Year Book 5688* (Philadelphia: Jewish Publication Society of America, 1927), 29:134. It is interesting to note that Zangwill's friend Stephen S. Wise had earned his Ph.D. at Columbia University in 1902 for his editing and English translation of ibn Gabirol's ethical tract, *Tikkun Middot haNefesh*, published as *The Improvement of the Moral Qualities* (New York: Columbia University Press/Macmillan Co., 1901).

47. Israel Zangwill, "Ibn Gabirol: Poetry and Philosophy," reprinted from *Menorah Journal* 8 (December 1922): 338–46, in *The Menorah Treasury*, ed. Leo W. Schwarz (Philadelphia: Jewish Publication Society of America, 1964), pp. 116, 117.

48. Israel Zangwill, "On Translating Gabirol," in *Selected Religious Poems of Solomon ibn Gabirol* (Philadelphia: Jewish Publication Society of America, 1923), pp. xlvii, liii–liv.

49. Israel Zangwill to Edmond Flag, 28 April 1923; Central Zionist Archives, file K11/67.

50. Israel Zangwill to Stephen S. Wise, 9 March 1923; Central Zionist Archives, file A243/91. Zangwill needed someone fluent in Polish in order to have access to the important study of the Frankist movement by Alexander Kraushar, *Frank i frankisci polscy* (Krakov: Ski gi. u G. Gebethnera i spolki, 1895).

51. Israel Zangwill to Stephen S. Wise, 31 May 1923; Central Zionist Archives, file A243/91. For Zangwill's motive for later agreeing to the American tour, see discussion later in this chapter.

52. Zangwill specifically related his new novel to the earlier work, explaining to an interviewer that at the time he was then working "on a long novel along the lines of 'Dreamers of the Ghetto' "; "Zangwill Arrives to Talk to Jews," *New York Times*, 7 October 1923, p. 9.

53. Israel Zangwill, "The Baron of Offenbach," p. 2; typed draft, Add MS 41485, Manuscripts Division, the British Library; a carbon of this ms. can be found in Central Zionist Archives, file A120/41/6.

54. Ibid., p. 10. Zangwill's historical account of the Frankist movement is augmented here with details from Gershom Scholem, "Jacob Frank and the Frankists," *Encyclopaedia Judaica* (Jerusalem, 1972) 7:55–72. See also the important original Frankist source material (in Hebrew and Polish, with English introduction) in *Ha'Kronika—Te'udah leToldot Ya'akov Frank u'Tenulato*, ed. and trans. Hillel Levine (Jerusalem: Israel Academy of Sciences and Humanities, 1984).

55. Zangwill, "Baron of Offenbach," p. 28.

56. Ibid., pp. 47–48.

57. Ibid., especially sec. 9, set in Spitalfields.

58. Ibid., p. 105.
59. Ibid., p. 109.
60. Ibid., pp. 110–14.
61. Ibid., pp. 121–23.
62. Ibid., p. 124.
63. Ibid., p. 131.
64. Ibid., pp. 132–33.
65. Israel Zangwill to Stephen S. Wise, 31 May 1923; in Central Zionist Archives, file A243/91.
66. Israel Zangwill, "My Religion," in a collection of similarly titled essays by various authors, *My Religion* (London: Hutchinson and Co., n.d.), p. 57.
67. "Zangwill Makes 'Final Reply,' " *New York Times*, 25 November 1923, sec. II, p. 7.
68. "Zangwill in Farewell," *New York Times*, 20 December 1923, p. 12. By "the Jewish question," Zangwill meant the issue of a homeland and ethnic assimilation, not Jewish philosophy, and, in fact, while preparing to board his ship, he chatted with reporters about his views on Judaism, Christianity, and Jesus; see "Liner and Lighter Just Miss Colliding," *New York Times*, 7 February 1924, p. 10.
69. On Zangwill's envy of Noel Coward, see Leftwich, *Zangwill*, p. 259, and Louis Golding, "Zangwill the Man," *Fortnightly Review*, n.s., 21 (April 1927): 523.
70. "Zangwill Arrives to Talk to Jews," *New York Times*, 7 October 1923, p. 9.
71. Israel Zangwill, *We Moderns, A Post-War Comedy in Three Movements (Allegro, Andante, Adagio)* (London: William Heinemann, 1926). Explaining the play's tone in the afterword to the play (p. 219), Zangwill specifically vilified Sigmund Freud because "he ruined a good case by obscene over-statement." For a discussion of "Under Sentence of Marriage," see Chapter 4.
72. Zangwill, *We Moderns*, p. 219. However, the modernist attitudes are much more satirized than are the Victorian, an imbalance noted by many critics.
73. "New Shows in the Provinces," *New York Times*, 30 December 1923, Sec. VII, p. 2, quoting a *Washington Post* review.
74. David Carb, "To See or Not to See," *Bookman* 59:3 (May 1924): 320. Carb further remarks: "Helen Hayes, in this hodgepodge, is fresh and exquisite." The film adaptation of the play received no more favorable critical treatment than had the stage version; the *New York Times* reviewer, in his column "The Screen," 8 December 1925, p. 28, referred to it as "this cumbersome story." Other Zangwill stories that were adapted for English-language motion pictures include *Children of the Ghetto* (1915), *Nurse Marjorie* (1920), *The Bachelors' Club* (1921), *Merely Mary Ann* (1931), and three versions of *The Big Bow Mystery: The Perfect Crime* (1928), *The Crime Doctor* (1934), and *The Verdict* (1946); see J. R. Nash and S. R. Ross, *The Motion Picture Guide*

(Chicago: Cinebooks, 1985–87), and *Variety Films Reviewed, 1907–1980* (New York: Garland Publishing, 1983).

75. John Corbin, "The Play," *New York Times*, 12 March 1924, p. 17.

76. Israel Zangwill, "The Murder of 'We Moderns,' " *Nation*, 7 May 1924, p. 535. This article, dated 10 April, East Preston, is Zangwill's response to this journal's 26 March review of *We Moderns* (pp. 330–331) by Ludwig Lewisohn. Zangwill here specifically mentions that he had feared just this sort of reprisal for his outspokenness while completing the play during his lecture tour; this apprehension might help account for his sudden strategic retreat into "an Ivory Tower of Silence" in November 1923, a month before the play was to open in Washington. On the other hand, his December "vow" of never again speaking on the "Jewish question" is certainly the product of much more complex motivations.

77. Zangwill, "The Murder," p. 535.

78. Ibid.

79. Ibid. The critic most harshly excoriated by Zangwill in this article is John Corbin.

80. Except for chronology, this account of Zangwill's association with Atkins in the British production of *We Moderns* follows Leftwich, *Zangwill*, p. 116.

81. Review of "We Moderns," *Outlook*, 18 July 1925, p. 41.

82. Review of "We Moderns," *Spectator*, 18 July 1925, pp. 100–101, and the *Times* (London), 8 July 1925, p. 13. The *Times* did note, however, that "it seemed 'all werry capital' to the representatives of the Chosen People who were in great force at the New Theatre last night, and who applauded the play with remarkable unanimity."

83. *Spectator* review, 18 July 1925, p. 41.

84. Leftwich, *Zangwill*, pp. 118–19.

85. Ibid., pp. 120–22.

86. Israel Zangwill to Edward Good, 4 December 1924; Central Zionist Archives, file K11/88/4.

87. Israel Zangwill to Edward Good, 15 June 1925; Central Zionist Archives, file K11/88/4.

88. Israel Zangwill to Leopold Greenberg, 28 June 1925; Central Zionist Archives, file A120/85/2.

89. Israel Zangwill to Miss Bacon, 22 April 1926; Central Zionist Archives, file A120/85/2. In an attempt to recoup the financial losses incurred by *We Moderns*, Zangwill arranged for the staging of his earlier satires *Merely Mary Ann* and *Too Much Money*, but this ploy only generated further production and financial complications for him.

90. Edith Zangwill to Stephen S. Wise, 9 July 1926; Central Zionist Archives, file A120/6/1. Mrs. Edith Ayrton Zangwill's fictionalized account of her husband's collapse appeared in her novel, *The House* (London: John Murray, 1928).

91. "Funeral, Mr. Israel Zangwill," the *Times* (London), 6 August 1926, p. 15. The text of Wise's eulogy is reprinted in "Hundreds Mourn at Zangwill's Bier," *New York Times*, 6 August 1926, p. 15.

11: Epilogue: A Midrash

1. From "Zayn a Yid" ["To be a Jew"], by Aaron Zeitlin, in *Gezamlte Lider* (New York: Farlag Matones, 1947), 1:47–48. Translation here by J. H. U. For a complete English translation by Robert Friend, see *The Penguin Book of Modern Yiddish Verse*, ed. I. Howe, R. R. Wisse, and K. Shmeruk (New York: Viking Penguin, 1987), p. 538.

2. Jacob Glatstein, "Shabbos," in *Di Freid Fun Yidishen Wort* (New York: Der Kval, I. London, 1961), pp. 61–62. Translation here by J. H. U.

3. From Jacob Glatstein, "A Gute Nakht Velt," in *Foon Mein Gantzer Mea* (New York: Jacob Gladstone, 1956), p. 245. Translation here by J. H. U. For an English translation of the complete poem see *The Selected Poems of Jacob Glatstein*, ed. and trans. Ruth Whitman (New York: October House, 1972), pp. 59–60.

4. From Jacob Glatstein, "Onhoib," in *Foon Mein Gantzer Mea*, pp. 91–93. Translation here by J. H. U. For an English translation of the complete poem see Howe, Wisse, and Shmeruk, *Modern Yiddish Verse*, pp. 458–62.

5. For an interesting psychological discussion of the phenomenon, see Sander L. Gilman, *Difference and Pathology: Stereotypes of Sexuality, Race and Madness* (Ithaca: Cornell University Press, 1985).

6. For details see W. E. B. Du Bois's autobiographical *Dusk of Dawn* (New York: Harcourt, Brace and Co., 1940), chap. 5. For thorough scholarly studies of Du Bois, see Joseph P. DeMarco, *The Social Thought of W. E. B. Du Bois* (Lanham, Md.: University Press of America, 1983), Jack B. Moore, *W. E. B. Du Bois* (Boston: Twayne Publishers, 1981), and Arnold Rampersad, *The Art and Imagination of W. E. B. Du Bois* (Cambridge: Harvard University Press, 1976).

7. Du Bois was awarded his A.B. from Fisk in 1888 and his B.A. in philosophy, cum laude, from Harvard in 1890, his M.A. in history from Harvard in 1891, and, in 1895, was the first black to receive a Ph.D. from Harvard; see chronology, *W. E. B. Du Bois: Writings*, ed. Nathan Huggins (New York: Library of America, 1986), pp. 1283–86.

8. Du Bois, *Dusk*, chap. 5.

9. On Du Bois's early concern for the preservation of black culture, see his 1890 Harvard commencement address, "Jefferson Davis as a Representative of Civilization," in Huggins, *Du Bois Writings*, pp. 811–14, and his 1897 essay, "The Conservation of Races," in ibid., pp. 815–26. As Zangwill toured the Jewish holy land, so Du Bois toured the rural black South, and his description of its human beauty and its deterioration appear in "Of the Meaning

of Progress," in W. E. B. Du Bois, *The Souls of Black Folk* (Chicago: A. C. McClurg, 1903), pp. 60–74.

10. Du Bois, "Conservation," p. 820.

11. W. E. B. Du Bois, "Criteria of Negro Art," (1926) in Huggins, *Du Bois Writings,* pp. 995, 1000.

12. Du Bois, "Conservation," pp. 821, 822.

13. Du Bois, *Souls of Black Folk,* pp. 2–3. Note the plural "Souls" in the work's title, emphasizing Du Bois's preoccupation with this theme of "double consciousness."

14. Cited in *W. E. B. Du Bois: A Reader,* ed. Meyer Weinberg (New York: Harper and Row, 1970), p. 373.

15. Du Bois, *Dusk,* chap. 7.

16. Shelby Steele, "On Being Black and Middle Class," *Commentary* 85:1 (January 1988): 45.

17. Nor is the experience limited to those living in the West. Israel Zangwill's contemporary, Lu Xun (1881–1936), a major founder of modern Chinese literature, also experienced the anguish of twinned identities and the concomitant qualities of social and psychological alienations; for studies of Lu Xun, see Leo Ou-fan Lee, *Voices from the Iron House: A Study of Lu Xun* (Bloomington: Indiana University Press, 1987), and V. I. Semanov, *Lu Hsun and His Predecessors,* trans. and ed. Charles J. Alber (White Plains: M. E. Sharpe, 1980).

18. The following discussion of the traditional philosophy of the human personality and its transformation by contemporary thought is principally derived from discussions by Schneur Zalman of Liadi (1745–1813), *Likutei Amarim,* bilingual ed. (Brooklyn: Kehot Publication Society, 1973), pt. 1; Joseph B. Soloveitchik (1903–), "The Lonely Man of Faith," *Tradition* 7:2 (Summer 1965): 5–67; and idem, *The Halakhic Mind: An Essay on Jewish Tradition and Modern Thought* (New York: Seth Press/Free Press, 1986). Although Schneur Zalman expresses the *Chabad* Chassidic view and Soloveitchik the opposing *Mitnagdic* view of Volozhin and Brisk (Brest-Litovsk), both draw upon the common traditional Rabbinic analysis of the human personality expressed by the medieval commentator Rashi on Genesis 2:7, which he derived from the ancient *midrashic* commentary, Genesis Rabbah 14:5; see also Maimonides (1135–1204), *Mishneh Torah,* Hilchot Yesodei HaTorah, 4:8; in *The Guide of the Perplexed,* trans. Shlomo Pines (Chicago: University of Chicago Press, 1963), 1:1, 2, 51, Maimonides expresses the traditional Rabbinic views in Greek philosophic terminology. Jacques Maritain (1882–1973) explicates the parallel Thomist analysis (*Summa Theologica,* pt. 1, questions 78–79) in his 1925 essay, *Trois reformateurs,* published in English as *Three Reformers: Luther-Descartes-Rousseau* (London: Sheed and Ward, 1928; reprinted, Westport, Conn.: Greenwood Press, 1970), pp. 19–26 and n. 29, p. 195; a similar exposition is provided by C. S. Lewis, *The Discarded Image* (Cambridge: Cambridge University Press, 1964), pp. 152–65. Alasdair MacIntyre, in *After Virtue,* 2d ed. (Notre Dame: University of Notre Dame Press, 1984), provides an excellent historical-philosophic analysis of the tradition. It is interesting that

the Chinese duality of *yin* and *yang*, particularly as developed in neo-Confucian thought, also reflects a similar analysis. Joseph Campbell, *The Masks of God: Creative Mythology* (New York: Viking Press, 1968), chap. 6, also discusses the phenomenon in a wide variety of cultural contexts although from exactly the perspective emphatically repudiated by all the other authors mentioned here.

19. Schneur Zalman, *Likutei Amarim*, pt. 1, chaps. 9–15, 20.

20. For discussions of this period in the history of science, see A. Rupert Hall, *The Revolution in Science 1500–1750* (New York: Longman, 1983), chaps. 3–7; Jerome J. Langford, *Galileo, Science and the Church*, rev. ed. (Ann Arbor: University of Michigan Press, 1966); Pietro Redondi, *Galileo: Heretic*, trans. Raymond Rosenthal (Princeton: Princeton University Press, 1987); and Stephen Toulmin and June Goodfield, *The Fabric of the Heavens* (New York: Harper and Row, 1961), pp. 169–227.

21. The following discussion of the Cartesian compromise follows Maritain, *Three Reformers*, pp. 57–88, and Stephen Toulmin and June Goodfield, *The Architecture of Matter* (Chicago: University of Chicago Press, 1962), pp. 165–69. As the discussion makes clear, Descartes intended not a pragmatic compromise but an ontology.

22. For a discussion of the psychological processes involved in the projection of internal psychic conflict externally, see Gilman, *Difference and Pathology*, pp. 16–29.

23. Rashi on Ecclesiastes 9:16, based on the *Babylonian Talmud, Nedarim* 32b; see also Rabbi Nachman of Breslov in *Likutey Moharan*, lesson 1, bilingual ed. (Jerusalem: Breslov Research Institute, 1986), 1:4–7. The *Maharal* (acronym for Moreinu HaRav Jacob Loew of Prague [1525–1609]) in his Biblical commentary, *Gur Aryeh* on Genesis 9:23, employs the terms used here in our explanation for his parallel allegorical interpretation of the three sons of Noah and, similarly, the three sons of Adam.

Israel Zangwill's Works

A Selected Bibliography

Short Stories and Novels

"Professor Grimmer," *Society* 5:133–35 (14–30, November 1881)

The Premier and the Painter (London: Spencer Blackett, 1888), with Louis Cowen, under the pseudonym, "J. Freeman Bell"

"Under Sentence of Marriage," *The Jewish Calendar, Manual, and Diary, 5649* (London, 1888), pp. 54–79, with Louis Cowen, under the pseudonym "J. Freeman Bell"

"Satan Mekatrig: A Romance of the London Ghetto," *The Jewish Calendar, Manual, and Diary, 5650* (London, 1889), pp. 52–76, under the pseudonym "Baroness von S."; reprinted in *Ghetto Tragedies*

"Diary of a Meshumad," *The Jewish Calendar, Manual, and Diary, 5651* (London, 1890), pp. 54–76, under the pseudonym "Baroness von S."; reprinted in *Ghetto Tragedies*

The Bachelors' Club (London: Henry and Co., 1891); reprinted in *The Celibates' Club*

The Big Bow Mystery (London: Henry and Co., 1892); reprinted in *The Grey Wig*

Children of the Ghetto (Philadelphia: Jewish Publication Society of America, 1892)

The Old Maids' Club (New York: Tait, Sons, and Co., 1892); reprinted in *The Celibates' Club*

Ghetto Tragedies (London: McClure and Co., 1893); reprinted in *They That Walk in Darkness*

Merely Mary Ann (London: Raphael Tuck and Sons, 1893); reprinted in *The Grey Wig*

"The Abolition of Money," *Idler*, August 1894, pp. 592–601; reprinted in *Without Prejudice*

The King of Schnorrers; Grotesques and Fantasies (London: William Heinemann, 1894)

"The Choice of Parents," *Chapman's Magazine*, Christmas no., 1895, pp. 339–50; reprinted in *Without Prejudice*

The Master (London: William Heinemann, 1895)

The Celibates' Club (London: William Heinemann, 1898)

Dreamers of the Ghetto (New York: Harper and Brothers, 1898)
They That Walk in Darkness (London: William Heinemann, 1899); reprinted as *Ghetto Tragedies* in 1907
The Mantle of Elijah (London: William Heinemann, 1900)
The Serio-Comic Governess (London: Shurmer Sibthrop, 1902); reprinted in *The Grey Wig*
The Grey Wig, Stories and Novelettes (London: William Heinemann, 1903)
Ghetto Comedies (London: William Heinemann, 1907)
Jinny the Carrier (London: William Heinemann, 1919)

Plays

The Great Demonstration (London: Capper and Newton, 1892), with Louis Cowen
Six Persons (London: Samuel French, 1898)
The War God (London: William Heinemann, 1911)
The Next Religion (London: William Heinemann, 1912)
The Melting Pot (London: William Heinemann, 1914)
Plaster Saints, A High Comedy in Three Movements (London: William Heinemann, 1914)
The Cockpit, A Romantic Drama in Three Acts (London: William Heinemann, 1921)
Merely Mary Ann, A Comedy in Four Acts (London: Samuel French, 1921)
The Forcing House, or The Cockpit Continued. A Tragedy in Four Acts (London: William Heinemann, 1922)
Too Much Money, A Farcical Comedy in Three Acts (London: William Heinemann, 1924)
We Moderns, A Post-War Comedy in Three Movements (Allegro, Andante, Adagio) (London: William Heinemann, 1924)

Essays

"Morour and Charouseth," *Jewish Standard*, 1888–91, regular column under the pseudonym "Marshallik"
"English Judaism, A Criticism and a Classification," *Jewish Quarterly Review* 1 (July 1889): 376–407
"Ariel's Album," *Ariel, or The London Puck*, 1890–91, irregular editor's column
"Ariel's Arm Chair," *Ariel, or The London Puck*, 1890–91, regular editor's column
"The Growth of Respectability," *Jewish Chronicle*, Jubilee supplement, 13 November 1891, pp. 19–20
"Hebrew, Jew, Israelite," *Jewish Chronicle*, 18 November 1892, pp. 6–8
"My First Book—The Premier and the Painter," *Idler*, February 1893, pp. 629–

41; reprinted in *My First Book*, ed. Jerome K. Jerome (London: Chatto and Windus, 1894), pp. 164–66
"Men, Women and Books," *Critic*, 1894–96, regular column
"Without Prejudice," *Pall Mall Magazine*, 1894–96, monthly column
"The Abolition of Christmas," *Idler*, January 1895, pp. 638–40, under the pseudonym "J. Freeman Bell"
"Is A Corrupt Government Better Than An Honest One?" *Idler*, 1895, pp. 270–71
"The Position of Judaism," *North American Review* 160:461 (April 1895): 425–39
"Who Should Be Poet Laureate," *Idler*, 1895, pp. 408–09
"Passover Ramblings—Without Prejudice," *Jewish Chronicle*, 15 April 1896, p. 16
Without Prejudice (London: T. Fisher Unwin, 1896)
"The Mission of Judaism," *Jewish Quarterly Review* 9 (January 1897): 221–23
"To the American Jew," *Jewish Chronicle*, 18 March 1898, pp. 14–16
"On American Judaism," *Menorah* 25:5 (November 1898): 284–91
"Zionism," *Contemporary Review* 76 (October 1899): 500–511.
"The Return to Palestine," *New Liberal Review* 2:11 (December 1901): 615–34
"Why Jews Succeed," *New Liberal Review* 3:16 (May 1902): 471–81
"Zion, Whence Cometh My Help," *World's Work* 2:9 (August 1903): 311–13
"Two Opposing Forces at Work on the Jew," *Menorah* 35:5 (November 1903): 272–77
The East Africa Question; Zionism And England's Offer (New York: Maccabaean Publishing Co., 1904)
"The Future of Vaudeville in America," *Cosmopolitan* 38 (April 1905): 639–46
"Mr. Lucian Wolf on 'The Zionist Peril,'" *Jewish Quarterly Review* 17 (April 1905): 397–425
"Tenting in Palestine," *Fortnightly Review*, n.s., 78 (November 1905): 886–93
"Letters and the ITO," *Fortnightly Review*, n.s., 79 (April 1906): 633–47
A Land of Refuge (London: Jewish Territorial Organization, 1907)
One And One Are Two (London: Women's Social and Political Union, 1907)
Talked Out! (London: Women's Social and Political Union, 1907)
Be Fruitful and Multiply (London: Jewish Territorial Organization, 1909)
The Lords and the Ladies (London: Women's Freedom League, 1909)
Old Fogeys and Old Bogeys (London: Woman's Press, 1909)
The Sword and the Spirit (London: Women's Social and Political Union, 1910)
Italian Fantasies (London: William Heinemann, 1910)
"Zionism and Territorialism," *Fortnightly Review*, n.s., 86 (April 1910): 645–55
"Advice to the Ottoman Jews," *Jewish Review* 1:5 (January 1911): 391–402
"On First Reading Dickens," *Bookman* (London) 41 (February 1912): 252
The Problem of the Jewish Race (New York: Judaean Publishing Co., 1912)
The War and the Women (New York: Metropolitan Magazine, 1915); reprinted in *The War for the World*

The War for the World (London: William Heinemann, 1916)
"The Fate of Palestine," *Menorah Journal* 3 (February 1917): 197–201
The Principle of Nationalities (London: Watts and Co., 1917)
Chosen Peoples (London: George Allen and Unwin, 1918)
"The Dilemmas of the Diaspora," *Menorah Journal* 4 (February 1918): 12–16
"Law and History," *Transactions, The Jewish Historical Society* 9 (1918–20): 15–19
"Are the Jews a Nationality?" *Voices* 2:4 (October 1919): 148–52
Hands Off Russia (London: Workers Socialist Federation, 1919)
"The World and the Jews," *English Review* 30 (January 1920): 64–67
"The People of the Abyss," *Menorah Journal* 6 (June 1920): 175–80
The Voice of Jerusalem (London: William Heinemann, 1920)
"Zionism To-day," *Yale Review* 10:2 (January 1921): 246–57
"From Uganda to Palestine," *Menorah Journal* 7 (December 1921): 251–58
"Ibn Gabirol: Poetry and Philosophy," reprinted from *Menorah Journal* 8:6 (December 1922): 338–46, in *Menorah Treasury*, ed. Leo W. Schwarz (Philadelphia: Jewish Publications Society of America, 1964), pp. 111–20
"On Translating Gabirol," in *Selected Religious Poems of Solomon ibn Gabirol* (Philadelphia: Jewish Publication Society of America, 1923), pp. xiii–lix
Watchman, What of the Night? (New York: American Jewish Congress, 1923)
"Is Political Zionism Dead? Yes," *Nation*, 12 March 1924, pp. 276–78
"My Religion," in *My Religion* (London: Hutchinson and Co., [1925])
"When I Am Dead," *Outlook*, 11 August 1926, pp. 502–03
Speeches, Articles, and Letters of Israel Zangwill, ed. Maurice Simon (London: Soncino Press, 1937)

Poetry

"The London Hospital," *Jewish Standard*, 15 June 1888, p. 4
"The Great Conversion," *Jewish Standard*, 23 October 1888, p. 9
"Love and Death," *Jewish Standard*, 14 June 1889, p. 11
"A Song of Life," *Jewish Standard*, 20 September 1889, p. 9
"The Jews in England 1290–1890," *Jewish Standard*, 1 November 1889, p. 10
"The Foolish Flock," *Jewish Standard*, 15 November 1889, p. 11
"A Silly Syllabus," *Jewish Standard*, 6 December 1889, p. 10
"The Death of Eleazar," *Jewish Standard*, 20 December 1889, p. 10
"The Rencontre," *Jewish Standard*, 25 December 1889, p. 5
"Poor Purim," *Jewish Standard*, 7 March 1890, p. 9
"A Passover Sermon," *Jewish Standard*, 10 April 1890, p. 10
"A Vision of the Future," *Jewish Standard*, 6 June 1890, p. 10
"Reflections in a Street in Jerusalem," *Jewish Standard*, 8 May 1891, p. 9
"To the Blessed Christ," *Bookman* (London) 13 (November 1897): 30; reprinted in *Blind Children*
"Love's Labour Lost," *Bookman* (New York) 6:5 (January 1898): 406

"To a Dear Inconstant," *Current Literature* 27 (January 1900): 32
"At the Zoo," *Lippincott's Magazine* 68 (September 1901): 374
Blind Children (London: William Heinemann, 1903)
"Lament," *Jewish Chronicle*, 17 May 1912, p. 19 (reprinted from the *Daily News and Leader*, 12 May 1912); reprinted in *The War for the World* (1916)
"At the Congress," *The War for the World*, pp. 283–84
"Bazalel," *The War for the World*, p. 286
"Oliver Singing," *The War for the World*, p. 348
"On the Coast," *The War for the World*, p. 95
"Theodore Herzl," *The War for the World*, p. 317
"The Old Clo' Man," *The Voice of Jerusalem* (1920), pp. 275–76
"Our Cry," *The Voice of Jerusalem*, pp. 294–96
"The Pillar of Fire," *The Voice of Jerusalem*, p. 351

Bibliographical Essay

This study examines the life and works of Israel Zangwill within their contemporary sociopolitical and cultural contexts. In particular, it explores Zangwill's endeavor to define and perpetuate Jewish identity and values within post-Enlightenment Western societies. Because of the breadth of these concerns, the literature of widely diverse fields is useful to comprehend the historical, political, and philosophical issues involved.

A History of the Jewish People, ed. H. H. Ben-Sasson (Cambridge: Harvard University Press, 1976), provides a useful scholarly survey of Jewish history. Calvin Goldscheider and Alan S. Zuckerman in *The Transformation of the Jews* (Chicago: University of Chicago Press, 1984) and Goldscheider in *Jewish Continuity and Change* (Bloomington: Indiana University Press, 1986) examine the extensive effects of the post-Enlightenment emancipation upon Western Jewry. Jacob Katz's *From Prejudice to Destruction* (Cambridge: Harvard University Press, 1980) discusses the implicitly conditional nature of Enlightenment emancipation and the subsequent anti-Jewish sentiments exhibited by many emancipators when these conditions were not actualized by their Jewish neighbors. Leon Poliakov's *The History of Anti-Semitism*, trans. Miriam Kochan (London: Routledge and Kegan Paul, 1975), 4 vols., provides a scholarly study of the various historical manifestations of anti-Semitism, while Sander L. Gilman in *Difference and Pathology: Stereotypes of Sexuality, Race and Madness* (Ithaca: Cornell University Press, 1985) and in *Jewish Self-Hatred: Anti-Semitism and the Hidden Language of the Jews* (Baltimore: Johns Hopkins University Press, 1986) presents extensive theoretical analyses of the victims' psychological responses to such prejudice; without the theoretical paraphernalia, Harold Fisch's discussion of literature in *The Dual Image* (London: World Jewish Library, 1971) explores similar responses. From a very different perspective, Simon Kuznets's "Immigration of Russian Jews to the United States: Background and Structure," *Perspectives in American History* 9 (1975): 35–124, explores East European Jewry's responses to economic and social change and prejudice.

A History of the Jews in England by Cecil Roth (Oxford: Clarendon Press, 1941) provides a useful introductory survey of the history of British Jewry. Post-Restoration Anglo-Jewish history has been extensively documented. In *The Jews of Georgian England 1714–1830* (Philadelphia: Jewish Publication Society of America, 1979), Todd M. Endelman examines the presuppositions conditioning the toleration offered Britain's Jewish populace by Liberalism as well as those advanced by others to justify continuing opposition to granting such toleration. Michail C. N. Salbstein's *The Emancipation of the Jews in Britain* (Rutherford, N.J.: Fairleigh Dickinson University Press, 1982) continues the historical narration through the final achievement of full civil and political equality in the nineteenth century. The mirror-image of this equality, British anti-Semitism, is delineated in Colin Holmes's *Anti-Semitism in British Society, 1876–1939* (New York: Holmes and Meier, 1979). Various aspects of Anglo-Jewry's own history are thoroughly explored in V. D. Lipman, *Social History of the Jews in England 1850–1950* (London: Watts and Co., 1954), Harold Pollins, *Economic History of the Jews in England* (East Brunswick, N.J.: Associated University Presses, 1982), and Geoffrey Alderman, *The Jewish Community in British Politics* (Oxford: Clarendon Press, 1983). The British response to the nineteenth century's great westward migration of East European Jewry has also been carefully studied. Beatrice (Webb) Potter provides a fascinating, but not unbiased, contemporary account of London's Jewish immigrants in "The Jewish Community," in *Life and Labour of the People of London*, ed. Charles Booth (London: Macmillan and Co., 1889), 1st ser., 3:166–92; scholarly accounts of Jewish immigration during this period include Lloyd P. Gartner's *The Jewish Immigrant in England, 1870–1914* (London: George Allen and Unwin, 1960) and John A. Garrard's *The English and Immigration 1880–1910* (London: Oxford University Press, 1971).

A History of Jewish Literature by Meyer Waxman (New York: Thomas Yoseloff, 1960), 5 vols., rev. ed., provides a comprehensive historical survey, the third and fourth volumes pertaining to the emergence of the secular fiction discussed in this study of Zangwill's career. Abba Rubin, *Images in Transition* (Westport, Conn.: Greenwood Press, 1984), surveys the treatment of Jews in English literature through the eighteenth century, and Anne A. Naman, *The Jew in the Victorian Novel* (New York: AMS Press, 1980), continues the discussion through the nineteenth century. *The Nineteenth-Century Anglo-Jewish Novel* by Linda G. Zatlin (Boston: Twayne Publishers, 1981) provides a comprehensive survey of Jewish authors and their works during the same period.

The history of Zionism is exhaustively examined by David Vital in his three studies, *The Origins of Zionism, Zionism: The Formative Years,* and *Zionism: The Critical Phase* (Oxford: Oxford University Press, 1975, 1982, 1987); for a sympathetic general account, *The Siege* by Conor Cruise O'Brien (New York: Simon and Schuster, 1986) is useful. Anglo-Jewry's response to Zionism is discussed by Stuart A. Cohen in *English Zionists and British Jews* (Princeton: Princeton University Press, 1982). Britain's Palestinian policies are analyzed in Bernard Wasserstein's *The British in Palestine* (London: Royal Historical Society, 1978); and Yosef Gorny, in *Zionism and the Arabs 1882–1948: A Study in Ideology* (Oxford: Clarendon Press, 1987), analyzes a spectrum of Jewish attitudes toward Palestinian issues. The history of the "Uganda Scheme" is comprehensively presented in *The Uganda Controversy*, ed. Michael Heymann (Jerusalem:

Institute for Zionist Research at Tel-Aviv University, 1970, 1977), 2 vols. Zangwill's activities on behalf of the scheme are discussed in Robert G. Weisbord's "Israel Zangwill's Jewish Territorial Organization and the East Africa Zion," *Jewish Social Studies* 30:2 (April 1968): 89–108 and his ITO activities on behalf of the Galveston Plan are discussed in Gary Dean Best's "Jacob H. Schiff's Galveston Movement: An Experiment in Immigrant Deflection, 1907–1914," *American Jewish Archives* 30:1 (April 1978): 43–79.

Israel Zangwill's life and works are the subject of few book-length studies. Joseph Leftwich's *Israel Zangwill* (New York: Thomas Yoseloff, 1957) is a useful but uncritical memoir by a friend. Maurice Wohlgelernter's scholarly *Israel Zangwill* (New York: Columbia University Press, 1964), although intended as a comprehensive biography, concentrates primarily on literature, as does Elsie Bonita Adams's *Israel Zangwill* (New York: Twayne Publishers, 1971). Insightful literary interpretations are also offered in Harold Fisch, "Israel Zangwill: Prophet of the Ghetto," *Judaism* 13:4 (Fall 1964): 407–21; Bernard Winehouse, "Israel Zangwill's *Children of the Ghetto:* A Literary History of the First Anglo-Jewish Best-Seller," *English Literature in Transition* 16:2 (1973): 93–117; Philip Gleason, "The Melting Pot: Symbol of Fusion or Confusion," *American Quarterly* 16:1 (Spring 1964): 20–46; Neil Larry Shumsky, "Zangwill's *The Melting Pot:* Ethnic Tensions on Stage," *American Quarterly* 27:1 (March 1975): 29–41, and Meri-Jane Rochelson, "Language, Gender, and Ethnic Anxiety in Zangwill's *Children of the Ghetto,*" *English Literature in Transition* 31:4 (1988): 399–412. Zangwill's prewar political interaction with American Jews is the subject of Isaac M. Fein's "Israel Zangwill and American Jewry: A Documentary Study," *Jewish Historical Quarterly* 60:1 (September 1970): 12–36.

Philosophic inquiries offering insights toward resolving the issues raised by the confluence of Jewish identity with modernity that so predominated Zangwill's writings and actions include the pioneering essays of Jacques Maritain, *Three Reformers: Luther-Descartes-Rousseau* (London: Sheed and Ward, 1928; reprinted, Westport, Conn.: Greenwood Press, 1970), originally published in French in 1925; Leo Strauss, *Philosophy and Law,* trans. Fred Baumann (Philadelphia: Jewish Publication Society, 1987), originally published in German in 1935; and Joseph B. Soloveitchik, *The Halakhic Mind: An Essay on Jewish Tradition and Modern Thought* (New York: Seth Press/Free Press, 1986), originally written in 1944. Alasdair MacIntyre has contributed significantly to the analysis and understanding of the issues in *After Virtue,* 2d ed. (Notre Dame: University of Notre Dame Press, 1984), and *Whose Justice? Which Rationality?* (Notre Dame: University of Notre Dame Press, 1988). Very useful, also, is *Political Order* (Baton Rouge: Louisiana State University Press, 1987) by David J. Levy. From a very different perspective are the perceptive contributions to the colloquy offered by Hillel Goldberg in *Between Berlin and Slobodka* (Hoboken: Ktav Publishing, 1989), Jonathan Sacks in *Traditional Alternatives* (London: Jews' College Publications, 1989), and Adin Steinsaltz in *The Strife of the Spirit* (Northvale, N.J.: Jason Aronson, 1988), the work of a scholar imbued with the teachings of the Talmud and of Chassidism.

Index